PROCESS PHILOSOPHY:

Basic Writings

**Edited by
Jack R. Sibley
Pete A. Y. Gunter**

University Press
of America™

Copyright © 1978 by

University Press of America™
division of
R.F. Publishing, Inc.
4710 Auth Place, S.E., Washington, D.C. 20023

ISBN: 0-8191-0531-7

Library of Congress Catalog Card Number: 78-57668

PROCESS PHILOSOPHY

"This is the doctrine that
the creative advance of this world
is the becoming, the perishing,
and the objective immortalities
of those things which jointly constitute
<u>stubborn</u> <u>fact</u>."

Alfred North Whitehead

ACKNOWLEDGEMENTS

The "Preface" was written specifically for this volume by Dr. Charles Hartshorne, the Dean of American Philosophers in the area of process philosophy.

"An Introduction to Metaphysics" by Henri Bergson: from An Introduction to Metaphysics (New York: Liberal Arts Press, 1955), pp. 21-32, 36-40, 41-42, 48-56, 59-62. Used by the permission of the Bobbs-Merrill Publishing Company.

"Symbolic Rererence" by Alfred North Whitehead: from Process and Reality (New York: Macmillan, 1929), pp. 101, 103, 105, 112, 125, 184, 188-192, 255-268, 274-279 and 441. Used by permission of the Macmillan Publishing Company.

"Toward a Widening of the Notion of Causality" by Milic Capek: from Diogenes, 28 (1959), 63-90. Used by the permission of Diogene: Revue internationale des sciences humaines and Professor Capek.

"Perception and Cognition" by Henry Nelson Wieman: from the Journal of Philosophy, XL, 3 (1943), 73-77. Used by the permission of the Journal of Philosophy and Mrs. Henry Nelson Wieman.

"The Dilemma of Determinism" by William James: from the Unitarian Review (1884).

"The Ideal Genesis of Matter and the Meaning of Evolution" by Henri Bergson: from Creative Evolution (New York: Henry Holt, 1913), pp. 247-271.

"Vitalism" by C. Lloyd Morgan: from the Monist, IX (1899), 179-196.

"Present Prospects for Metaphysics" by Charles Hartshorne: from Creative Synthesis and Philosophic Method (London: SCM Press LTD, 1970), pp. 43-56. Used by the permission of the Monist, 47 (1963), 188-210, Open Court, and Charles Hartshorne.

"The Holistic Universe" by Jan Smuts: from Holism and Evolution (New York: Macmillan, 1926), pp. 319-345. Used by the permission of the Macmillan Publishing Company.

"The Analysis of Experience" by Alfred North Whitehead: from the Adventures of Ideas (New York: Macmillan, 1933), pp. 225-235, 258-282. Used by permission of the Macmillan Publishing Company.

"A World of Organisms" by Charles Hartshorne: from The Logic of Perfection and Other Essays in Neoclassical Metaphysics (La Salle, Illinois: Open Court, 1962), pp. 191-215. Used by permission of the Open Court Publishing Company and Charles Hartshorne.

"The Second Scientific Revolution" by Milic Capek: from Diogenes, 63 (1968), 114-133. Used by the permission of Diogene: Revue internationale des sciences humaines and Milic Capek.

"Meland's Alternative in Ethics: An Aesthetic Approach" by John B. Spencer: also in Process Studies, VI, 3 (1976), 165-180. Used by permission of Process Studies and John Spencer.

"Moral Obligation in Process Philosophy" by Daniel Day Williams: from the Journal of Philosophy, LVI, 6 (1959), 263-270. Used by permission of the Journal of Philosophy.

"Creative Good" by Henry Nelson Wieman: from The Source of Human Good (Chicago: University of Chicago Press, 1946), pp. 54-70. Used by permission of Southern Illinois University Press and Mrs. Henry Nelson Wieman.

"Beyond Enlightened Self-Interest: A Metaphysics of Ethics" by Charles Hartshorne: from Ethics, LXXXIV, 3 (1974), 201-216. Used by permission of the University of Chicago Press and Charles Hartshorne.

"Two Paths to the Good Life" by Bernard E. Meland: from the Personalist, XXIII, 1 (1942), 53-61. Used by permission of the Personalist and Bernard E. Meland.

"Towards Clarity in Aesthetics" by John B. Cobb: from
Philosophy and Phenomenological Research, XVIII, 2
(1957), 169-189. Used by permission of Philosophy and
Phenomenological Research and John Cobb.

"Art as ·Experience" by John Dewey: from Art as Experience (New York: Minton, Balch, 1934), pp. 3-19, 22-25,
35-38. Used by permission of Minton and Balch Publishing Company.

"The Romantic Reaction" by Alfred North Whitehead:
from Science and the Modern World (New York: Macmillan, 1925), pp. 75-94. Used by permission of Macmillan
Publishing Company.

"The Future of Process Philosophy" by Bernard M. Loomer
was written specifically for this volume.

To

Norma,
Jackie
and
Jim

Elizabeth
and
Sheila

A NOTE OF APPRECIATION

Our gratitude for the opportunity
to do this particular work extends
to many, many people; friends, former
teachers, fellow faculty members, and
students. For helpful suggestions
and criticisms we are most grateful
to Charles Hartshorne, Bernard Loomer,
Bernard Meland, Milic Capek, and Mrs.
Henry Nelson Wieman. For the typing
and proofreading of the manuscript we
are very appreciative of the capable
assistance of Katie Napier and Dora
Vela. A special thanks also goes to
William W. Wan of the Texas Woman's
University Library Systems for his
very patient and competent assistance
in all matters pertaining to library
research and the procurement of the
necessary information and materials.

The Editors.

TABLE OF CONTENTS

xiii

P R E F A C E

"Some things are hastening to be,
others to be no more,
while of those
that haste into being
some part is already extinct."

Marcus Aurelius

Charles Hartshorne

PREFACE

I wish first to express gratitude to the two editors for including three essays of mine, two of which have hitherto appeared only in periodicals, and with all three of which I find myself, upon rereading them, reasonably content. I also appreciate the inclusion of my favorite James essay, The Dilemma of Determinism.

As the reader will see, my philosophy is considerably different from that of at least some of the writers (including perhaps the editors) of this volume. It is perhaps least different from that of Whitehead, and perhaps most different from that of Dewey and Mead.

Process philosophers agree in treating being as an abstraction from becoming, rather than becoming as an inferior form or mere appearance of being. They agree in rejecting such radical pluralisms as the philosophies of Ockam, Hume, or Russell; and such radical monisms as Advaita Vedantism, or the views of Parmenides, Spinoza, or Bradley. They regard classical or LaPlacean determinism as absurdly trivializing becoming by denying its creativity, that is, its essential function of adding to the definiteness of the world, bit by bit. They regard unqualified monism as also trivializing becoming by denying its production of genuinely new, additional actualities.

On two other issues philosophies that may reasonably be termed "process philosophies" have not agreed: the issue of psychicalism vs. a psycho-physical dualism, and that of theism vs. agnosticism or atheism. Smuts, Mead, and Dewey are non-theistic dualists, as I define these terms. They imply that there is some positive concrete content for the idea of matter even when every possible form of experiencing, however other than human, however simple or primitive, is abstracted from. If there is no such positive content, then dualism can be avoided by non-psychicalists only by what amounts to sheer agnosticism as to what "matter without mind" positively connotes. And, with Peirce, Bergson, Montague, Whitehead, and many kinds

1

of idealists, I deny that there is such positive content for "mindless matter."

As Descartes, with all his errors, does help us to see, concrete actuality is most unambiguously and clearly given to us in our own experiencing. We can generalize this basic sample of reality so that adult human experiencing appears as an extremely special case, and even animal experiencing as a decidedly special case. But to generalize simply beyond experiencing as such is, I believe, to substitute empty verbiage for positive ideas. Even physicists are really conceiving nature by analogy with patterns in their own minds, very abstract and hence mathematically expressible patterns. What makes nature concrete and no mere set of abstractions, the terms "matter," "action," "energy," or "process" do not tell us. On this point two of the essays by Whitehead and the admirable essay by Capek are relevant.

The theistic issue is too marginal for this book to deal with here. I remark, however, that theistic process philosophers have in general been psychicalists and psychicalist process philosophers theists. If we cannot generalize simply beyond experience as such, then to conceive the cosmic reality may well mean to conceive a cosmic form of experiencing. I remark also that process theology, implying some form of process philosophy, is both pre- and post-Darwinian, since the theologians had it in the seventeenth century. Hegel, Schelling, and Marx can in a very broad sense be called process philosophers, though in my opinion not very good ones. Nonevolutionary philosophies are not wrong solely or essentially because of empirical facts, such as those to which Darwin appealed. It never was good philosophizing, I maintain, to affirm the eternity of species, any more than it was good empirical science. Absolute fixity of species is not conceivably observable. Even on Aristotelian grounds it cannot be justified. According to Aristotle, the eternal and the unconditionally necessary are the same; hence if species are eternal they are necessary. But how could a particular finite number of species, or a particular set of animal shapes, be necessary, that is, without conceivable alternatives? If species are necessary, the only explanation of their contingent reality is an account of how they came to be under the operation of causes or forces the operation of which is still discoverable in nature. In my view Darwin rescued science, theology, and metaphysics from errors that, ideally, should never have been made.

What is missing in this book seems to me a clear account of the exact way in which extremes of monism and pluralism are avoided by process philosophy. I hold with Whitehead that the only way to do this is to make explicit what the singular <u>units</u> in the real and growing multiplicity of nature <u>are</u>, and what their <u>relations of dependence and independence</u> are. Bergson talks about unity and multiplicity and urges the impossibility of applying these concepts to becoming. However, his discussion, like so many philosophical discussions, fails to argue from an exhaustive division of possible doctrines. He asks, are the successive states (mutually) distinct and outside one another, or are they (mutually) interpenetrating? He thus invites us to choose between two symmetrical forms of dependence or independence. He never clearly states the idea that (definitely plural) successive states are in one temporal direction dependent and in the other temporal direction independent. They must, as Bergson and Whitehead agree, intuit, "house," "prehend," and thus depend on, their predecessors, but never their successors. First we have x, then y prehending x, then z prehending y, and so on. Thus there is <u>plurality in time</u> not merely in space. What else is the meaning of creation?

The <u>mutual</u> independence of unit events in space is the <u>fact that</u> all prehension is of predecessors, and either of successors or of contemporaries. Spatial plurality is derivative from temporal. Space is the order of <u>mutual</u> independence or dependence. Event sequences, (<u>which</u> Whitehead calls "societies") if close enough spatially or enduring enough temporally, interact, but event or actualities, taken singly, have only either mutual independence (space) or one-way dependence (time). In either case there is genuine plurality. It is true that Whitehead sometimes writes as though actualities, that is, unit events, were mutually implicative. But when he is being most careful, as when he is explicating key technical terms like prehension, past, contemporary, future, or creativity, he clearly implies one-way dependences. (Only in <u>Process and Reality</u>, or in <u>Adventures of Ideas</u>, Parts III and IV, can one learn what Whitehead's metaphysics amount to.)

3

There is a limited agreement between Whitehead and Bergson with respect to unity and multiplicity, in the following sense: in the becoming of a single actual entity there is no definite plurality of successive or simultaneous states. Abstractly one can speak of genetic or coordinate phases of such a becoming, yet it is really a single concrete act of self-creation. Such singular acts or actualities, however, succeed one another in a definite plurality, finite in number in a finite time. That we cannot <u>distinctly</u> introspect (retrospect) this plurality is simply one of the ways, there are others, in which our self-knowledge, even the most direct and intuitive, is human, not divine, imperfect not perfect. Whitehead deliberately rejects (using a form of Zeno argument) the idea that continuity in the strict sense applies to actual becoming. He holds that it is possibility that is continuous, not actuality. Here he breaks not only with Bergson but with Peirce and many others. Bergson's cinema analogy can be turned against the Bergsonian doctrine. A finite succession of "shots" is the reality, the continuity of action is the appearance (for our feeble intuition) of that reality. Mathematics takes space and time as continuous because mathematics deals with possibilities, with concepts, not with actuality as such.

Bergson's rejection of logic as relevant to metaphysics definitely repelled Russell, Peirce, and Whitehead, three great logicians. It also repelled me, a student of these logicians, and of C. I. Lewis and H. M. Sheffer. Whitehead has, I think, shown how creative becoming can be given a logical structure.

For Whitehead, or me, prehension, or intuiting of reality, is not something peculiar either to perception or memory, but is their common element. To remember is to prehend one's own previous experiencings, to perceive is also to prehend past events (most directly some of those in one's own body), but events not belonging to one's own stream of awareness, though nevertheless, according to psychicalism, experiences on some level.

It is also important that, for Whitehead (or for Peirce) even the most direct intuition is lacking in anything like full distinctness as to details. Bergson's use of the word "absolute" to describe a human mode of knowing (his "intuition") is suspect. What we intuit is in a sense absolute, that is, independent of our intuiting it, but our intuition of it is relative,

partial. This is why concepts must be used if we are
to get much help from our awareness of self-creativity.
Bergson uses concepts, but the wrong ones, such as
mutual interdependence, "interpenetration," thus ruling
out by neglect one-way dependence, with independence in
the other temporal direction. Yet he was wonderfully
right in declaring that all experiencing is creative,
that becoming is "reality itself," and that the past is
not simply dropped out but is retained in the depths of
awareness. Yet it is the, for our introspection, indistinct depths that do this retaining.

Bergson's complaint that it is only retrospectively that there seems to be a plurality of states is,
from the Whiteheadian point of view, merely his failure
to realize that no unit-actuality prehends itself.
(Nor does it prehend its contemporaries.) It prehends
only its predecessors. Introspection just is (one form
of) retrospection. (Here Whitehead agrees with Ryle, I
am happy to say.) But retrospection never gives full
distinctness. So we must make a conceptual decision as
to its deliverances. There is no absolute security in
knowing, unless for God.

I am persuaded, with the editors, that the only
comprehensive world view appropriate to our culture
(psychicalistic) is process philosophy in some form.
I also agree with them that all the process systems
"have loose ends." But for chronological reasons, if
for no others, this observation has a somewhat different significance in the various cases. The other
authors have read Bergson and James and have done what
they could to remedy their defects. Whitehead not only
read Bergson, but also Alexander, James, and Dewey, all
of whom had read Bergson. I do not think that Bergson,
and certainly not James, had to a comparable extent
read these others. Thus I incline to think that the
value for the future of Bergson's or James's ideas consists primarily, though not solely, in what they had in
common with ideas of some of their great contemporaries
or successors. I exempt a few of James's essays and
one book of Bergson's from this judgment. This book,
the product of Bergson's full maturity and wisdom, is
The Two Sources of Morality and Religion, still in some
ways the best book ever written on the philosophical
anthropology of ethics and religion. It depends, I
think, less for its value upon the state of knowledge
at the time than do Bergson's other works, except perhaps for that other late work Creative Mind. I also
think, with Paul Valérie, that Bergson (like James)

5

should be rated one of the great and noble minds in all history. He taught and inspired an entire generation of thinkers. And as Gunter and Capek have shown, he anticipated the discoveries of physics in the century to a greater extent than other philosophers, with the exception of Peirce, can be shown to have done.

To illustrate how the earlier process thinkers have been to some extent superseded, consider James's essay on consciousness. Whitehead read this essay and decided that it did not solve the problem of dualism. It is too abstract and at times ambiguous for that. The entities of which James says that, combined in one way, they constitute mind, and combined in another way they constitute matter, are called bits of pure experience. This sounds like psychicalist theory of reality. Yet James, though interested in what was then called "panpsychism," could never make up his mind to accept that doctrine. But did he have a clear alternative to it and also to dualism? What is the principle of unity, hence of any multiplicity that is involved if not the unity of a single instance of experiencing. And what is the principle of relatedness or dependence that makes a cause world out of the bits of pure experience if not the dependence of subject upon objects. If this is not dualism, then the objects must themselves be subjects. Otherwise to call them bits of experience merely means that they can be experienced by subjects, and what materialist or dualist wants to deny that?

That James's essay is ambiguous can be seen from the fact that it was influential in Russell's decision to return to a radical pluralism like Hume's atomism of distinguishable and separable impressions. Russell, like R. B. Perry and the New Realists, took James as enabling us to dispense with the subject-object relation. The price is that the causal connectedness of the world becomes, as Russell virtually admits, pure magic or mystery. This is far from process philosophy. Indeed it is a form of pluralistic absolutism: each entity is wholly independent, and thus in the clearest meaning of the word "absolute." This is not what James wants to hold. He believed in a mixture of internal and external relations. So did Whitehead, though un-luckily he did not say so in so many words. The inter-nal relatedness is prehension, the external relatedness is either being prehended (in the one-way case) or ab-sence of prehension either way (in the symmetrical case). But this solution requires psychicalism.

6

James's essay also seems to me to show insufficient awareness of the indistinctness of direct intuition. The subjects which have become objects for other subjects are too vaguely intuited for their individual subjectivities to be readily detected.

Wieman's insights into the creative aspects of human interaction are justly famous. His abstractions are a bit difficult sometimes to grasp. And it seems arbitrary to limit "the work of man" to those cases in which the precise outcome of individuals' efforts is known beforehand or deliberately aimed at by the individuals themselves. For a process philosopher, of course, this cannot ever, strictly speaking, be the case. Perhaps Wieman's positive insights and my neoclassicism are less completely incompatible than we have both inclined to suppose.

It is appropriate that a section on aesthetics is included. As Meland so well indicates, Whitehead's philosophy makes harmony and adventure, that is, in a broad sense beauty, the aim of all nature and of deity. No previous great system maker had done this so explicitly and in such detail. Dewey's thought, without going so far, points in the same direction.

It is also appropriate that four theologians are included--Williams, Wieman, Meland, and Cobb. For it can scarcely be denied that process philosophy has acquired its largest following among those theologically inclined. Not only Protestants, but Catholics and Jews, have been concerning themselves with this topic. Williams' The Spirit and Forms of Love is one of the happiest expressions of this concern. But there are many others.

The twentieth century does have a metaphysics, and it is genuinely new. Until critics stop trying to dispose of metaphysics by refuting its pre-process philosophy versions, or such nontypical and nebulous forms of process philosophy as that of Heidegger, the case for or against metaphysics will not be properly evaluated.

Charles Hartshorne

INTRODUCTION

"The passage of time
is
the journey of the world towards
the gathering of new ideas
into actual fact."

Alfred North Whitehead

Jack R. Sibley
Pete A. Y. Gunter

INTRODUCTION

Twentieth century philosophy exhibits remarkable
diversity. Absolute idealism, marxism, pragmatism,
positivism, existentialism, linguistic analysis, phe-
nomenology: each has spawned its quota of books,
articles, learned journals, each has drawn on a broad
background of special knowledge and an arsenal of analytical and rhetorical tools. Each has captured the
attention of a segment of the broad reading public--or,
more often, of those small coteries of academic specialists who make up professional philosophy. Yet for
all their wealth of intellectual background and virtu-
oso displays of dialectical skill, the philosophies
mentioned above suffer from a remarkable partiality.

Twentieth century philosophy has sometimes been
described as the Age of Analysis; but in terms of the
concerns which have absorbed the interests of many of
its philosophers, it might equally well be called the
Age of One-Sidedness. Examples of such one-sidedness
are not hard to find. Existentialists have focused on
subjectivity to the exclusion of natural science, mi-
nutely analyzing forlornness, despair, "dreadful freedom"; logical positivists have sought, by contrast, to
limit philosophical inquiry to the purely objective
methods and concepts of the sciences, particularly
physics, and have expressed disinterest in "subjectivity." Neither has considered the concerns of the
other to be worthy of serious consideration. Pragmatists, to take another example, have sought to confine
truth to the sphere of the "practical"; phenomenologists, in reply, have sought methodically to eliminate
pragmatic considerations from philosophy in order to
concentrate on "pure," unprejudiced data. Meanwhile,
the ordinary man, whose interests include the subjective, the objective, the useful, the useless, and much
else besides, can rarely find the many-sidedness of
his world depicted by philosophers. For that he has
had to turn elsewhere--wherever that might be.

If the concerns of recent philosophers have been,
arguably, one-sided, their views of reality have
clearly suffered from the fragmentation of knowledge.
Traditionally, philosophers have sought to give synop-
tic views of knowledge and of the world. The knowledge

11

explosion and the specialization of the sciences have
rendered the pursuit of knowledge-as-a-whole extremely
difficult, if not impossible, with the result that philosophers have avoided the task of providing either
overviews of knowledge or overall views of the world.
Often they have insisted that such views are a priori
impossible (as if such a priori skepticism did not itself rest on some universal and presumably certain view
of things). The universal mind of a Leibniz, an Aristotle or a Hegel, attempting to complete the knowledge
of their time in an all-encompassing Weltanschauung,
scarcely finds a counterpart among the philosophers of
this century, who have often sought, like the sciences,
to achieve precision by narrowing their scope. Overviews, systematic coherence, world-views have been left
to someone else--or to no one.

The process philosophers, with their evolutionary,
expansive vision, stand resolutely outside of the tendency of recent philosophy towards narrowed scope and
one-sided interests. From Henri Bergson through Alfred
North Whitehead to Charles Hartshorne, they have sought
to give full accounts of human experience and to embrace the knowledge of their times in a systematic
viewpoint. In this they cannot be said to have entirely succeeded, for the "systems" of each admittedly
contain loose ends and require correction. That this
is true, however, is no embarrassment. For these
thinkers have been the first to insist that knowledge
is as much a perpetual quest as a set of received conclusions, more a matter of evolving insights than of
fixed certainties. Rather than expect their views,
however plausible or however tenaciously defended, to
stand forever unchallenged, they have viewed wholeness
and completeness as ideals: as culminations of a knowing process which, while it does describe reality, demands to be improved upon. Process philosophy quarrels
with its past in order to be able to inherit a future.

In one sense such a philosophy, with its systematic bent, recalls the classical metaphysical systems
of the past. In another it is quite "new." That is,
it is scarcely thinkable apart from modern evolutionary
theory, with its stress on continual transformation.
As a precursor of all philosophies of process stands
Charles Darwin, whose Origin of Species proved that
man, like other living creatures, has developed over
countless aeons from far more primitive ancestors and
that life itself has emerged from the broad background
of nonliving nature. Now, over a century since the

publication of Darwin's classic, we have become accustomed to the idea of evolution. But we should not forget that this idea explosively transformed man's view of himself and his world. From Aristotle to Descarte to Kant men had assumed that the basic characteristics of species remain constant through time; suddenly that static view was overturned.

Gladly accepting the dynamic, developmental import of evolutionary theory, philosophers of process have made it the fundamental feature (the "root metaphor") of both their metaphysics and their theories of knowledge. But they have lodged criticisms of varying severity against what they have considered to be Darwinism's more negative (and static) aspects: namely, the thesis that the generating mechanism of evolution is simply "chance" and that the emergence of the remarkably diverse tapestry of life forms is a purely mechanical affair. The meaning of biological evolution is, they have argued, not randomness but creativity: creativity, and in some sense, purpose. Whether expressed in terms of the vitalism of a Bergson, with its _élan_ _vital_ and unpredictability, or in terms of the more cautious "organismic" views of a Lloyd Morgan, philosophers of process have insisted that the fundamental fact with which biology and philosophy must deal is not the accidental interaction of particles in space but the emergence of novel forms in time.

This basic evolutionary, or better yet, emergent, metaphor is applied by process philosophers consistently to the theory of knowledge to which their most distinctive contribution is their realization that we must revise, if not totally reject, tenaciously held conceptions of what knowledge is. Classical Greek and Medieval philosophers had proposed that reality is not process but form, and that, therefore, the theory of knowledge must explain how it is possible for the mind to transcend the flux of appearance to grasp the timeless forms which give the world its structure. For all its departures from the ancients, modern science began by merely displacing this assumption without revising it. That is, science has viewed its task as one of piercing the qualitative and misleading veil of ordinary perception to discover the remarkable precise (and, of course, unchanging) mathematical laws which determine the world's undeviating course. Whatever concepts they may have used, whether materialist or idealist, to explain the extraordinary success of mathematical physics, modern philosophers and scientists had described the knowing process as a journey from the temporal to the timeless.

Yet if the fundamental fact which philosophers must explain is what Alfred North Whitehead has termed the "creative advance of nature," then the traditional assumptions of epistemology must be reversed. We should not neglect the changing in order to pursue the timeless. The aim of knowledge should be rather to transcend "timeless" conceptions in order more fully to conceive a thoroughly dynamic reality. The point is to catch the bird (or the evolutionary advance, or the permutations of energy) in flight: the living bird, not the one embalmed in a misleading theory.

The question remains, however: how is it possible to "catch the bird in flight," that is, to think process? In varying ways the philosophers whose works are published in this book have founded their epistemologies on a basic awareness or experience. Thus Henri Bergson criticizes "analysis," whose conceptual schemes are static and fragmentary, in favor of "intuition," through which we participate in the duration of ourselves and other things. Similarly, Whitehead contrasts "presentational immediacy," with its vivid but superficial picture of a seemingly solid world, with our insistent, powerful, but vague experience in the mode of "causal efficacy." It is through the experience of "causal efficacy" that we confront, almost viscerally, a real world of things that affect us and which we affect. The ordinary man, therefore, is right to think that we live in a world of actual things that can help or harm us. He errs, however, if he allows abstract, essentially spectator-oriented concepts and modes of perception to miscast our world in essentially static terms.

This tendency to misconstrue our experience has been subjected by process philosophers to extensive analysis. It has been described by Bergson as the "spatialisation of time," and by Whitehead, in more general terms, as leading to "the fallacy of misplaced concreteness," that is, the error of confusing our abstract conceptual frameworks with the concrete, dynamic world we actually experience. Clearly we cannot do without abstractions, but taken together our abstractions cannot create a real world. What is necessary is to reformulate our abstractions to bring them nearer to reality. Such a revolution in our ways of viewing the world would of course have repercussions for far

14

more than our theory of knowledge. It would (as we have already seen) transform our metaphysics. And it would reshape our ethics, aesthetics, and our philosophy of science as well.

Since the eighteenth century the growing success of the natural sciences has been accompanied by the growing popularity of a mechanical and materialistic world-view, on whose terms nothing exists except inert material particles, space, and motion. In this billiard-ball universe all events are predetermined; moreover, this predetermination would seem to involve no overriding purpose, since the mass particles of which the universe is made are driven not by any final aim or goal but by the impulsions transmitted by other particles. Originally this atomistic-mechanical model found its basic applications in physics, more especially in (celestial and terrestrial) mechanics. It was inevitable, however, that it should be applied to biology, physiology, medicine, psychology: to the whole gamut of natural relations. The Darwinian theory of evolution was, as originally formulated at least, thoroughly impregnated with this model, as, for example is much of contemporary biochemistry. On the basis of it every scientific advance was interpreted as one more nail driven into the coffin of presumably outdated non-materialist, non-mechanistic conceptions.

Unfortunately for the clarity and consistency of this sweeping vision, twentieth century physics was to be strikingly different from that of the eighteenth and nineteenth centuries. Relativity theory, for example, was to warp space and time in patterns Sir Isaac Newton could not have imagined, uniting mass and energy while transforming gravitation into the behavior of a time-space field with variable curvature. Quantum theories were to transform the once solid, impenetrable mass particle into a burst of energy occurring with dizzying rapidity, and to picture the "particle" (if that is possible) as having in some contexts the characteristics of a particle and in others the characteristics of a wave: without being "really" either. To add to the perplexity, quantum physics was forced finally to renounce deterministic predictions and to defend indeterminism within the very physical bastion where it had once reigned supreme. The revolution in twentieth century physics, which began around the turn of the century and which is by no means complete today, did away with empty space, inert particles and simple place-to-place concept of motion which had seemed to so many to

15

be the final word in matters scientific. Exactly what
was to replace the old view, however? To those process
philosophers who concerned themselves directly with the
interpretation of the sciences, the answer seemed clear.
What physics is attempting to deal with, they held, is
process, i.e., the thoroughly dynamic activity of "matter," which can no longer be represented by inert, impenetrable particles or simple impact. The persistence
of material entities (electrons, atoms, molecules) is
on this view more like the continuity of a melody than
it is like the passive persistence of a billiard ball.

     In large part then, process philosophy of science
has been devoted to combatting static and mechanical
interpretations in their place. We have already cited
one example of this confrontation: that is, the process critique or critiques of neo-Darwinism, combined
with various non-mechanistic models which process philosophers proposed to account for evolutionary progress.
Similar examples of critique-and-conjecture methods
could be cited from the literature of process philosophy for many other sciences: physiology, neurophysi-
ology, psychology, sociology, cosmology, to name a few.
Process philosophers could argue that, far from proposing anti-scientific conceptions, their viewpoint
best harmonizes with the spirit and the letter of recent scientific progress. This is a very important
consideration to be kept in mind as one evaluates the
strength and relevance of process thought.

     This philosophy of science, with its critique of
mechanism and its emphasis on the dynamic, ongoing aspects of nature, is closely related by process philosophers to their views of man as an ethical being. Proponents of scientific determinism from Thomas Hobbes to
B. F. Skinner have insisted that man is a passive creature, driven by material causes of which he is scarcely
aware. It ought to be possible to predict human behavior, therefore, simply by spelling out causes external
to the individual, environmental causes which drive him
to do what he does. Yet how strangely different the
actual experience of a living, choosing, surprising
human being is from this presumably scientific picture.
In "real-life situations" we often choose the stimuli
to which we wish to respond, while our responses issue
from our entire development as human beings. To view
ourselves as if we were inert particles bombarded by
external forces is not only to conceive ourselves on
the analogy of an outmoded physics, but to do violence
to our most common awareness of ourselves. We add to

our past, and do not simply bear the burden of its effects.

If this conception of freedom is true, then our feeling of responsibility for our acts is not based on an illusion. We are responsible to a significant degree not only for our acts but for salient aspects of our own characters. We create ourselves, out of the materials which circumstances place in our paths. What is true of human beings taken singly is also taken by most process philosophers to be true of human beings en masse: that is, as involved in history, in broad social and political change. The course of history can easily be made to appear as the functioning of blind forces whose results are inevitable. But in fact history consists of the interactions of men whose choices involve a measure of contingency. The outcomes of historical processes are not yet established and what we do can conceivably make a difference. Hence it makes sense to feel a sense of responsibility for what things become.

This linking of freedom and responsibility is not new. There is a tradition in ethics stemming from Immanuel Kant (1724-1804) which has argued that the experience of responsibility is indissolubly connected with the idea of freedom. Indeed, for this Kantian tradition it is questionable whether an act not accompanied by a sense of duty can be morally good. Similarly, there has been a strong tendency to connect this linkage of duty and freedom with notions of punishment. Man has a sense of duty, it has been argued, and is therefore freely responsible for what he does; and if so, then he can rightly be punished for doing wrong. It is important to see that process philosophers, while insisting on the interrelations between freedom and responsibility, precisely invert the Kantian (or "deontological") conception, insisting that our awareness of our own freedom is precisely what gives rise to our sense of responsibility and that our freedom enters into many aspects of human activity besides the purely moral. They have thereby immeasurably broadened the field of ethics while rescuing it from the accusation of being too closely tied to retributive notions of punishment. In the end, process ethics is based not on duty but on love, not upon moral precepts but upon creativity. Its locus is future-oriented possibility, not past-derived obligation.

17

Closely allied with this future-oriented conception of freedom is the emergent, developmental thrust of process ethics, which has presupposed a "self-realizationist" theory according to which the goal of life is the realization of human potential. (The subverting of this potential is, by contrast, considered to be the supreme evil.) Self-realizationist ethics have been criticized for leading to a sterile and possibly arrogant self-centeredness, which dries up the springs of creativity by isolating the individual from the world. But process philosophers have, almost to a man, never tired of protesting against conceiving the human self as an isolated atom. They insist that individuals cannot realize themselves in isolation but, rather, depend on a broad complex of social relations which reach out without limit, ultimately to the whole of humanity and beyond, to the whole of nature. Each of us must realize ourselves in humanity; and humanity must realize itself through us.

It might be thought that the self-realizationist component of process ethics is based on a complacent optimism about the prospects for human life. To say this is to overlook the existential aspects of self-realization. Personality is not a hereditary possession; it is an achievement, the result of persistent effort. As cases of regression and psychological disintegration too clearly show, this effort may meet with disaster. This side of tragedy, moreover, for most of us this achievement is incomplete or faltering. Even so, in spite of the possibility of defeat and banal resignation, man can, to transpose the words of a famous novelist, endure, and not merely endure, but also prevail. The developmental vector is a key to both the understanding and the valuing of man.

From what has been said so far it should already be possible for the reader to surmise something of the process view of art. While philosophers of process have contributed surprisingly little in the field of aesthetics, their writings leave no doubt of the direction in which a process aesthetic must go. In his own way the artist, like the philosopher, attempts to sound the depths of process, participating in the richness of experience and making that richness evident to a forgetful world. In the novels of a Marcel Proust or a William Faulkner, in the music of a Claude Debussy, we are drawn beneath the customary appearances of things and the conventional masks of the self to experience our world anew. Thus process aesthetics, while it may

18

concede (or even insist on) the "artificiality" of the art work itself, views the Beautiful as being closely allied with the True. Through the medium of highly selective focus and highly developed techniques the artist returns us to nature, dissolving what is constraining, artificial, abstract or overly partial in our view of things. The harmonies he finds, even in the midst of discord, are valid insights into reality. Hence, though his creations may be forged in the profoundest or fiercest emotional heat, it does not follow that artistic judgments are "nothing but" expressions of emotion and hence "merely" subjective. The old maxim "There is no disputing about tastes" (De gustabus non disputandem est.) is not true, or at best is a half-truth. We do dispute about tastes; we do evaluate art. If process philosophers are correct, our evaluations occur not in a void, but in a plenum, i.e., in the fullness of an experienced world.

A world in which men have their share of creative freedom, in which life is characterized by directed development, and values, both moral and aesthetic, are a real component of things, seems to many thinkers to point towards an ultimate Being which subsumes all reality in a final embrace. Such a being is in philosophical and religious tradition termed "God," and the effort to know about and talk about God is termed theology. Process philosophers have with only a few exceptions posited the existence of God and have introduced novel theological conceptions to account for such an actual phenomenon as a concrete participant in our universe. Though this book of readings contains no section on process theology, the theologies of the process philosophers are too integral a part of their thought to be negelected here. (For a more extensive treatment of the basic issues of process theology see Ewert H. Cousins, Process Theology, Newman Press, 1971.)

Several strands of thought characterize process theology, throughout the now almost century-long period of its development. Most striking of all perhaps is the tendency of process philosophers to extend to the Deity the properties of process. By and large theologians (influenced by traditional Biblical interpretation, and perhaps more strongly by Greek metaphysics) had viewed God as timeless, unmoving, immune to the corruptions of change. How God, so conceived, could act or love, or care about His creation is something of a mystery. Most of those in the Judeo-Christian

19

tradition, moreover, have conceived of their Deity precisely as involved in the world and as caring about it. From Charles Sanders Peirce to Charles Hartshorne, therefore, process philosophers have sought to include in God some aspect of temporality, thereby allowing God and World to share characteristics in common.

In bringing God nearer to nature they have, almost inadvertently, undermined theology's traditional downgrading of the natural order and paved the way for a new ecological awareness. From the viewpoint of process theology, the romantic poets were not mistaken when they saw God in nature, though they were mistaken if they simply identified God and nature, in a sort of nebulous pantheism. The most recent attempt to do justice to the closeness of God and World is Charles Hartshorne's panentheism, for which nature is in God, participating in God's being, while God nonetheless remains distinguishable from the world, however much He may be enriched by the world's unfolding pageant.

The two assumptions just mentioned (that God may be said in some sense to change, and that God and the World are not entirely separated), are closely related to two other conclusions: namely, that religious truth is not simply and totally rooted in the past, and that narrow, literal interpretations cannot hope to portray basic religious insights. Traditionally, organized religions (and certainly those in the Judeo-Christian tradition) have tended to construe religious verities as being once-and-for-all affairs, given by a divinely inspired leader at the beginning of things and not to be diluted or otherwise subsequently changed. But if so, of what use is the rest of human history, with its continual groping for insight and its steadily unrolling scroll of new knowledge? With almost one voice philosophers of process have protested that the present and the future may contain their own revelations, and that our traditional religious texts cry out to be supplemented by broader and conceivably more profound theological intuitions.

Philosophers of process have not all viewed the growth of religious insight in the same way. For example, Samuel Alexander proposed that God be viewed as both the next level in human evolution and the cosmic thrust or push that will lead to this spiritual quantum jump. He thus entirely reversed the traditional conception of the locus of religious truth, placing the final "revelation" in the future almost to the exclusion

20

of the past. Alfred North Whitehead, by contrast, attempted to counter views like Alexander's by contrasting God's primordial nature (external, changeless,
aloof) with his consequent nature, which he viewed as
changing, growing, enriched by the triumphs and trage-
dies of history.

Such a theology is almost by definition "liberal,"
since it demands of the believer an openness to new insights and a capacity to transcend prior convictions--
and since its conception of God would seem to impute
such a process to the Deity himself. The urge to define truth literally, in some purely complete and formal codex, is as old as the laws of the Medes and the
Persians, which, tradition consoles us, never changed.
It is as alive among positivists as among contemporary
Biblical fundamentalists, but it receives its most
telling rebuke in the writings of philosophers of process. Those who seek some simple unity in things might
do well to tolerate diversity instead. As William
James so amply portrayed in The Varieties of Religious
Experience (1906), the extraordinary diversity of religious attitudes and practices ought to make us pause
before we begin by ruling out possibilities.

A word needs to be said concerning the choice of
philosophers presented in this text. We have attempted
to select both traditional and contemporary readings
which display the basic claims of process philosophy.
Many of the traditional selections are historically
important, representing significant turning points in
the history of philosophy--of process philosophy and
of a still broader philosophical community. It has not
been possible to include all such papers, any more than
it has been possible to include every historically significant process philosopher. (Those familiar with the
process tradition will note the absence in these pages
of Charles Sanders Peirce [1839-1914], Pierre Teilhard
de Chardin [1881-1958], Pierre Lecomte du Noüy [1883-
1947], John Elof Boodin [1869-1950] and any number of
contemporary authors whose works might profitably have
been presented.) For these omissions apologies are
offered. Though a book of greater length is not feasible, hopefully this volume will encourage further ex-
plorations. For those so interested a brief bibliog-
raphy of process philosophy is appended to each of the
personages and areas.

The introductions to each of the readings in this
text have been kept intentionally brief. The purpose

has been to present only the leading themes of each selection and a brief description of its author. This
initial focus should provide for most students a sufficient entrance to the readings. The editors are convinced, in any case, that the philosophers presented in
the following selections are their own best expositors.

Finally, our use of the term process may require
explanation. Though the phrase 'process philosophy' is
associated with the work of Alfred North Whitehead
(1861-1947) and his successors, we intend to portray
the entire spectrum of thought which might be termed
process philosophy. There is historical justification
for this choice. Whitehead was a serious disciple of
those who were (like C. Lloyd Morgan, William James,
Samuel Alexander, and Henri Bergson) his own precursors,
while Whitehead's disciples in turn have reacted to interests and challenges which Whitehead did not directly
confront. By now the process tradition is an amalgam
of the insights of a great variety of philosophers.
But even if this historical overview might be disputed,
there is the simple matter of practicality. No phrase
currently in use more accurately and intelligibly conveys the basic tendencies of the thinkers presented
here than does the phrase process philosophy. We
therefore feel justified in using it in this broadest
sense.

The Editors

E P I S T E M O L O G Y

"Your acquaintance with reality
 grows literally
 by buds or drops of perception."

William James

Henri Bergson
Alfred North Whitehead
Milic Capek
Henry Nelson Wieman

1. AN INTRODUCTION TO METAPHYSICS

Henri Bergson

Henri Bergson (1859-1941) was educated at the
École Normale Supérieure and the Sorbonne in
Paris where he was a student of the famous
Emile Boutroux (1845-1921). Bergson later
taught philosophy at the Lycée Henri IV, the
Ecole Normale Superieure, and the Collège de
France in Paris from 1900 until the time of
his retirement in 1921. He was one of the
most noted philosophers of France.

In the article which follows* Henri Bergson teaches
us that there are two profoundly different ways of
knowing. The first, termed "analysis," uses static,
general and discrete concepts. The second, termed "intuition," brings us in contact with the dynamic continuity of things. Analysis, he holds, leads to a
strangely abstract conception of the world. It is a
conception which sacrifices intrinsic relationships in
favor of "external" relations. A philosophy based
solely on "analysis," therefore, leads inevitably to
relativism and skepticism. Intuition, by contrast, allows us to participate in, and become immediately aware
of, a world of ongoing processes. For Bergson intuition is not merely "subjective," for it focuses on all
sorts of phenomena, not merely our own psychologies.
The paradigm case of intuitive knowing, however, is for
him our acquaintance with ourselves. By the use of
sharply contrasting images such as the unrolling coil,
the spectrum, and the lengthening line, for example, he
attempts to bring us to a more profound awareness of
ourselves as ceaselessly changing, multiple-single
beings. This heightened awareness enables us to overcome artificially clearcut pictures of ourselves (a

---

*This presentation is made up of chosen selections
from An Introduction to Metaphysics (New York: Liberal
Arts Press, 1955), pp. 21-32, 36-40, 41-42, 48-56, 59-
62. Trans. T. E. Hulme. Used by permission of the
Liberal Arts Press.

very common picture in turn-of-the-century psychology)
as made up of so many clearcut states, images, pleasures, pains controlled by quasi-mechanical laws. It
must not be thought that intuition, though it transcends symbolism, is a one-way flight into the ineffable. Bergson makes clear his belief that intuition
has been at the source of really important scientific
advances. And since such advances involve newly transformed symbol-systems (especially those of mathematics)
intuition is at the source of reformed, more "supple"
symbolism. Intuition ought to be as fruitful for the
sciences as for philosophy. As an example, Bergson
cites the creation of the infinitesimal calculus, with
its exploitation, for the first time in the history of
human thought, of the dual notions of acceleration and
"continuous" change.[#]

[#]This particular work is an excellent propaedutic
to the general philosophical perspective of Bergson.

A comparison of the definitions of metaphysics and
the various concepts of the absolute leads to the discovery that philosophers, in spite of their apparent
divergencies, agree in distinguishing two profoundly
different ways of knowing a thing. The first implies
that we move round the object; the second, that we
enter into it. The first depends on the point of view
at which we are placed and on the symbols by which we
express ourselves. The second neither depends on a
point of view nor relies on any symbol. The first kind
of knowledge may be said to stop at the relative; the
second, in those cases where it is possible, to attain
to the absolute.

Consider, for example, the movement of an object
in space. My perception of the motion will vary with
the point of view, moving or stationary, from which I
observe it. My expression of it will vary with the
systems of axes, or the points of reference, to which
I relate it; that is, with the symbols by which I
translate it. For this double reason I call such motion relative: in the one case, as in the other, I am
placed outside the object itself. But when I speak of
an absolute movement, I am attributing to the moving
object an interior and, so to speak, states of mind; I
also imply that I am in sympathy with those states, and
that I insert myself in them by an effort of imagination. Then, according as the object is moving or stationary, according as it adopts one movement or another,
what I experience will vary. And what I experience
will depend neither on the point of view I may take up
in regard to the object, since I am inside the object
itself, nor on the symbols by which I may translate the
motion, since I have rejected all translations in order
to possess the original. In short, I shall no longer
grasp the movement from without, remaining where I am,
but from where it is, from within, as it is in itself.
I shall possess an absolute.

Consider, again, a character whose adventures are
related to me in a novel. The author may multiply the
traits of his hero's character, may make him speak and
act as much as he pleases, but all this can never be
equivalent to the simple and indivisible feeling which
I should experience if I were able for an instant to
identify myself with the person of the hero himself.
Out of that indivisible feeling, as from a spring, all

29

51629

the words, gestures, and actions of the man would appear to me to flow naturally. They would no longer be
accidents which, added to the idea I had already formed
of the character, continually enriched that idea, without ever completing it. The character would be given
to me all at once, in its entirety, and the thousand
incidents which manifest it, instead of adding themselves to the idea and so enriching it, would seem to
me, on the contrary, to detach themselves from it,
without, however, exhausting it or impoverishing its
essence. All the things I am told about the man provide me with so many points of view from which I can
observe him. All the traits which describe him, and
which can make him known to me only by so many comparisons with persons or things I know already, are signs
by which he is expressed more or less symbolically.
Symbols and points of view, therefore, place me outside
him; they give me only what he has in common with others, and not what belongs to him and to him alone. But
that which is properly himself, that which constitutes
his essence, cannot be perceived from without, being
internal by definition, nor be expressed by symbols,
being incommensurable with everything else. Description, history, and analysis leave me here in the relative. Coincidence with the person himself would alone
give me the absolute.

It is in this sense, and in this sense only, that
absolute is synonymous with perfection. Were all the
photographs of a town, taken from all possible points
of view, to go on indefinitely completing one another,
they would never be equivalent to the solid town in
which we walk about. Were all the translations of a
poem into all possible languages to add together their
various shades of meaning and, correcting each other by
a kind of mutual retouching, to give a more and more
faithful image of the poem they translate, they would
yet never succeed in rendering the inner meaning of the
original. A representation taken from a certain point
of view, a translation made with certain symbols, will
always remain imperfect in comparison with the object
of which a view has been taken, or which the symbols
seek to express. But the absolute, which is the object
and not its representation, the original and not its
translation, is perfect, by being perfectly what it is.

It is doubtless for this reason that the absolute
has often been identified with the infinite. Suppose
that I wished to communicate to someone who did not
know Greek the extraordinarily simple impression that

a passage in Homer makes upon me; I should first give a translation of the lines, I should then comment on my translation, and then develop the commentary; in this way, by piling up explanation on explanation, I might approach nearer and nearer to what I wanted to express; but I should never quite reach it. When you raise your arm, you accomplish a movement of which you have, from within, a simple perception; but for me, watching it from the outside, your arm passes through one point, then through another, and between these two there will be still other points; so that, if I began to count, the operation would go on forever. Viewed from the inside, then, an absolute is a simple thing; but looked at from the outside, that is to say, relatively to other things, it becomes, in relation to these signs which express it, the gold coin for which we never seem able to finish giving small change. Now, that which lends itself at the same time both to an indivisible apprehension and to an inexhaustible enumeration is, by the very definition of the word, an infinite.

It follows from this that an absolute could only be given in an intuition, whilst everything else falls within the province of analysis. By intuition is meant the kind of intellectual sympathy by which one places oneself within an object in order to coincide with what is unique in it and consequently inexpressible. Analysis, on the contrary, is the operation which reduces the object to elements already known, that is, to elements common both to it and other objects. To analyze, therefore, is to express a thing as a function of something other than itself. All analysis is thus a translation, a development into symbols, a representation taken from successive points of view from which we note as many resemblances as possible between the new object which we are studying and others which we believe we know already. In its eternally unsatisfied desire to embrace the object around which it is compelled to turn, analysis multiplies without end the number of its points of view in order to complete its always incomplete representation, and ceaselessly varies its symbols that it may perfect the always imperfect translation. It goes on, therefore, to infinity. But intuition, if intuition is possible, is a simple act.

Now it is easy to see that the ordinary function of positive science is analysis. Positive science works, then, above all, with symbols. Even the most concrete of the natural sciences, those concerned with life, confine themselves to the visible form of living

31

beings, their organs and anatomical elements. They make comparisons between these forms, they reduce the more complex to the more simple; in short, they study the workings of life in what is, so to speak, only its visual symbol. If there exists any means of possessing a reality absolutely instead of knowing it relatively, of placing oneself within it instead of looking at it from outside points of view, of having the intuition instead of making the analysis: in short, of seizing it without any expression, translation, or symbolic representation--metaphysics is that means. <u>Metaphysics, then, is the science which claims to dispense with symbols.</u>

* * *

There is one reality, at least, which we all seize from within, by intuition and not by simple analysis. It is our own personality in its flowing through time--our self which endures. We may sympathize intellectually with nothing else, but we certainly sympathize with our own selves.

When I direct my attention inward to contemplate my own self (supposed for the moment to be inactive), I perceive at first, as a crust solidified on the surface, all the perceptions which come to it from the material world. These perceptions are clear, distinct, juxtaposed or juxtaposable one with another; they tend to group themselves into objects. Next, I notice the memories which more or less adhere to these perceptions and which serve to interpret them. These memories have been detached, as it were, from the depth of my personality, drawn to the surface by the perceptions which resemble them; they rest on the surface of my mind without being absolutely myself. Lastly, I feel the stir of tendencies and motor habits--a crowd of virtual actions, more or less firmly bound to these perceptions and memories. All these clearly defined elements appear more distinct from me, the more distinct they are from each other. Radiating, as they do, from within outwards, they form, collectively, the surface of a sphere which tends to grow larger and lose itself in the exterior world. But if I draw myself in from the periphery towards the center, if I search in the depth of my being that which is most uniformly, most constantly, and most enduringly myself, I find an altogether different thing.

There is, beneath these sharply cut crystals and this frozen surface, a continuous flux which is not comparable to any flux I have ever seen. There is a succession of states, each of which announces that which follows and contains that which precedes it. They can, properly speaking, only be said to form multiple states when I have already passed them and turn back to observe their track. Whilst I was experiencing them they were so solidly organized, so profoundly animated with a common life, that I could not have said where any one of them finished or where another commenced. In reality no one of them begins or ends, but all extend into each other.

This inner life may be compared to the unrolling of a coil, for there is no living being who does not feel himself coming gradually to the end of his role; and to live is to grow old. But it may just as well be compared to a continual rolling up, like that of a thread on a ball, for our past follows us, it swells incessantly with the present that it picks up on its way; and consciousness means memory.

But actually it is neither an unrolling nor a rolling up, for these two similes evoke the idea of lines and surfaces whose parts are homogeneous and superposable on one another. Now, there are no two identical moments in the life of the same conscious being. Take the simplest sensation, suppose it constant, absorb in it the entire personality: the consciousness which will accompany this sensation cannot remain identical with itself for two consecutive moments, because the second moment always contains, over and above the first, the memory that the first has bequeathed to it. A consciousness which could experience two identical moments would be a consciousness without memory. It would die and be born again continually. In what other way could one represent unconsciousness?

It would be better, then, to use as a comparison the myriad-tinted spectrum, with its insensible gradations leading from one shade to another. A current of feeling which passed along the spectrum, assuming in turn the tint of each of its shades, would experience a series of gradual changes, each of which would announce the one to follow and would sum up those which preceded it. Yet even here the successive shades of the spectrum always remain external one to another. They are juxtaposed; they occupy space. But pure duration, on

33

the contrary, excludes all idea of juxtaposition, reciprocal externality, and extension.

Let us, then, rather, imagine an infinitely small
elastic body, contracted, if it were possible, to a
mathematical point. Let this be drawn out gradually
in such a manner that from the point comes a constantly
lengthening line. Let us fix our attention not on the
line as a line, but on the action by which it is traced.
Let us bear in mind that this action, in spite of its
duration, is indivisible if accomplished without stopping, that if a stopping-point is inserted, we have two
actions instead of one, that each of these separate actions is then the indivisible operation of which we
speak, and that it is not the moving action itself
which is divisible, but, rather, the stationary line it
leaves behind it as its track in space. Finally, let
us free ourselves from the space which underlies the
movement in order to consider only the movement itself,
the act of tension or extension; in short, pure mobility. We shall have this time a more faithful image of
the development of our self in duration.

However, even this image is incomplete, and, indeed, every comparison will be insufficient, because
the unrolling of our duration resembles in some of its
aspects the unity of an advancing movement and in others the multiplicity of expanding states; and, clearly,
no metaphor can express one of these two aspects without sacrificing the other. If I use the comparison of
the spectrum with its thousand shades, I have before me
a thing already made, whilst duration is continually in
the making. If I think of an elastic which is being
stretched, or of a spring which is extended or relaxed,
I forget the richness of color, characteristic of duration that is lived, to see only the simple movement by
which consciousness passes from one shade to another.
The inner life is all this at once: variety of qualities, continuity of progress, and unity of direction.
It cannot be represented by images.

But it is even less possible to represent it by
concepts, that is by abstract, general, or simple ideas.
It is true that no image can reproduce exactly the original feeling I have of the flow of my own conscious
life. But it is not even necessary that I should attempt to render it. If a man is incapable of getting
for himself the intuition of the constitutive duration
of his own being, nothing will ever give it to him,
concepts no more than images. Here the single aim of

34

the philosopher should be to promote a certain effort,
which in most men is usually fettered by habits of mind
more useful to life. Now the image has at least this
advantage, that it keeps us in the concrete. No image
can replace the intuition of duration, but many diverse
images, borrowed from very different orders of things,
may, by the convergence of their action, direct consciousness to the precise point where there is a certain intuition to be seized. By choosing images as
dissimilar as possible, we shall prevent any one of
them from usurping the place of the intuition it is intended to call up, since it would then be driven away
at once by its rivals. By providing that, in spite of
their differences of aspect, they all require from the
mind the same kind of attention, and in some sort the
same degree of tension, we shall gradually accustom
consciousness to a particular and clearly defined dis-
position--that precisely which it must adopt in order
to appear to itself as it really is, without any veil.
But, then, consciousness must at least consent to make
the effort. For it will have been shown nothing: It
will simply have been placed in the attitude it must
take up in order to make the desired effort, and so
come by itself to the intuition. Concepts, on the con-
trary--especially if they are simple--have the disad-
vantage of being in reality symbols substituted for the
object they symbolize, and demand no effort on our part.
Examined closely, each of them, it would be seen, retains only that part of the object which is common to
it and to others, and expresses, still more than the
image does, a comparison between the object and others
which resemble it. But as the comparison has made manifest a resemblance, as the resemblance is a property
of the object, and as a property has every appearance
of being a part of the object which possesses it, we
easily persuade ourselves that by setting concept beside concept we are reconstructing the whole of the object with its parts, thus obtaining, so to speak, its
intellectual equivalent. In this way we believe that
we can form a faithful representation of duration by
setting in line the concepts of unity, multiplicity,
continuity, finite or infinite divisibility, etc.
There precisely is the illusion. There also is the
danger. Just in so far as abstract ideas can render
service to analysis, that is, to the scientific study
of the object in its relations to other objects, so far
are they incapable of replacing intuition, that is, the
metaphysical investigation of what is essential and
unique in the object. For, on the one hand, these concepts, laid side by side never actually give us more

35

than an artificial reconstruction of the object, of
which they can only symbolize certain general and, in a
way, impersonal aspects; it is therefore useless to believe that with them we can seize a reality of which
they present to us the shadow alone. And, on the other
hand, besides the illusion there is also a very serious
danger. For the concept generalizes at the same time
as it abstracts. The concept can only symbolize a particular property by making it common to an infinity of
things. It therefore always more or less deforms the
property by the extension it gives to it. Replaced in
the metaphysical object to which it belongs, a property
coincides with the object, or at least molds itself on
it, and adopts the same outline. Extracted from the
metaphysical object, and presented in a concept, it
grows indefinitely larger, and goes beyond the object
itself, since henceforth it has to contain it, along
with a number of other objects. Thus the different
concepts that we form of the properties of a thing inscribe round it so many circles, each much too large
and none of them fitting it exactly. And yet, in the
thing itself the properties coincided with the thing,
and coincided consequently with one another. So that
if we are bent on reconstructing the object with concepts, some artifice must be sought whereby this coincidence of the object and its properties can be brought
about. For example, we may choose one of the concepts
and try, starting from it, to get round to the others.
But we shall then soon discover that according as we
start from one concept or another, the meeting and combination of the concepts will take place in an altogether different way. According as we start, for example, from unity or from multiplicity, we shall have
to conceive differently the multiple unity of duration.
Everything will depend on the weight we attribute to
this or that concept, and this weight will always be
arbitrary, since the concept extracted from the object
has no weight, being only the shadow of a body. In
this way, as many different systems will spring up as
there are external points of view from which the reality can be examined, or larger circles in which it can
be enclosed. Simple concepts have, then, not only the
inconvenience of dividing the concrete unity of the object into so many symbolical expressions; they also
divide philosophy into distinct schools, each of which
takes its seat, chooses its counters, and carries on
with the others a game that will never end. Either
metaphysics is only this play of ideas, or else, if it
is a serious occupation of the mind, if it is a science
and not simply an exercise, it must transcend concepts

36

in order to reach intuition. Certainly, concepts are necessary to it, for all the other sciences work as a rule with concepts, and metaphysics cannot dispense with the other sciences. But it is only truly itself when it goes beyond the concept, or at least when it frees itself from rigid and ready-made concepts in order to create a kind very different from those which we habitually use; I mean supple, mobile, and almost fluid representations, always ready to mold themselves on the fleeting forms of intuition. We shall return later to this important point. Let it suffice us for the moment to have shown that our duration can be presented to us directly in an intuition, that it can be suggested to us indirectly by images, but that it can never--if we confine the word concept to its proper meaning--be enclosed in a conceptual representation.

Let us try for an instant to consider our duration as a multiplicity. It will then be necessary to add that the terms of this multiplicity, instead of being distinct, as they are in any other multiplicity, encroach on one another; and that while we can no doubt, by an effort of imagination, solidify duration once it has elapsed, divide it into juxtaposed portions and count all these portions, yet this operation is accomplished on the frozen memory of the duration, on the stationary trace which the mobility of duration leaves behind it, and not on the duration itself. We must admit, therefore, that if there is a multiplicity here, it bears no resemblance to any other multiplicity we know. Shall we say, then, that duration has unity? Doubtless, a continuity of elements which prolong themselves into one another participates in unity as much as in multiplicity; but this moving, changing, colored, living unity has hardly anything in common with the abstract, motionless, and empty unity which the concept of pure unity circumscribes. Shall we conclude from this that duration must be defined as unity and multiplicity at the same time? But singularly enough, however much I manipulate the two concepts, portion them out, combine them differently, practice on them the most subtle operations of mental chemistry, I never obtain anything which resembles the simple intuition that I have of duration; while, on the contrary, when I replace myself in duration by an effort of intuition, I immediately perceive how it is unity, multiplicity, and many other things besides. These different concepts, then, were only so many standpoints from which we could consider duration. Neither separated nor reunited have they made us penetrate into it.

We do penetrate into it, however, and that can only be by an effort of intuition. In this sense, an inner, absolute knowledge of the duration of the self by the self is possible. But if metaphysics here demands and can obtain an intuition, science has none the less need of an analysis. Now it is a confusion between the function of analysis and that of intuition which gives birth to the discussions between the schools and the conflicts between systems.

Psychology, in fact, proceeds like all the other sciences by analysis. It resolves the self, which has been given to it at first in a simple intuition, into sensations, feelings, ideas, etc., which it studies separately. It substitutes, then, for the self a series of elements which form the facts of psychology. But are these elements really parts? That is the whole question, and it is because it has been evaded that the problem of human personality has so often been stated in insoluble terms.

It is incontestable that every psychical state, simply because it belongs to a person, reflects the whole of a personality. Every feeling, however simple it may be, contains virtually within it the whole past and present of the being experiencing it, and, consequently, can only be separated and constituted into a "state" by an effort of abstraction or of analysis. But it is no less incontestable that without this effort of abstraction or analysis there would be no possible development of the science of psychology. What, then, exactly, is the operation by which a psychologist detaches a mental state in order to erect it into a more or less independent entity? He begins by neglecting that special coloring of the personality which cannot be expressed in known and common terms. Then he endeavors to isolate, in the person already thus simplified, some aspect which lends itself to an interesting inquiry. If he is considering inclination, for example, he will neglect the inexpressible shade which colors it, and which makes the inclination mine and not yours; he will fix his attention on the movement by which our personality leans toward a certain object: he will isolate this attitude, and it is this special aspect of the personality, this snapshot of the mobility of the inner life, this "diagram" of concrete inclination, that he will erect into an independent fact.

. . .

But a true empiricism is that which proposes to get as
near to the original itself as possible, to search
deeply into its life, and so, by a kind of intellectual
auscultation, to feel the throbbing of its soul; and
this true empiricism is the true metaphysics. It is
true that the task is an extremely difficult one, for
none of the ready-made conceptions which thought employs in its daily operations can be of any use. Nothing is more easy than to say that the ego is multiplicity, or that it is unity, or that it is the synthesis
of both. Unity and multiplicity are here representations that we have no need to cut out on the model of
the object; they are found ready-made, and have only to
be chosen from a heap. They are stock-size clothes
which do just as well for Peter as for Paul, for they
set off the form of neither. But an empiricism worthy
of the name, an empiricism which works only to measure,
is obliged for each new object that it studies to make
an absolutely fresh effort. It cuts out for the object
a concept which is appropriate to that object alone, a
concept which can as yet hardly be called a concept,
since it applies to this one thing. It does not proceed by combining current ideas like unity and multiplicity; but it leads us, on the contrary, to a simple,
unique representation, which, however once formed, enables us to understand easily how it is that we can
place it in the frames unity, multiplicity, etc., all
much larger than itself. In short, philosophy thus defined does not consist in the choice of certain concepts, and in taking sides with a school, but in the
search for a unique intuition from which we can descend
with equal ease to different concepts, because we are
placed above the divisions of the schools.

That personality has unity cannot be denied; but
such an affirmation teaches one nothing about the extraordinary nature of the particular unity presented by
personality. That our self is multiple I also agree,
but then it must be understood that it is a multiplicity which has nothing in common with any other multiplicity. What is really important for philosophy is to
know exactly what unity, what multiplicity, and what
reality superior both to abstract unity and multiplicity the multiple unity of the self actually is. Now
philosophy will know this only when it recovers possession of the simple intuition of the self by the self.
Then, according to the direction it chooses for its
descent from this summit, it will arrive at unity or
multiplicity, or at any one of the concepts by which
we try to define the moving life of the self. But no

mingling of these concepts would give anything which at all resembles the self that endures.

If we are shown a solid cone, we see without any difficulty how it narrows towards the summit and tends to be lost in a mathematical point, and also how it enlarges in the direction of the base into an indefinitely increasing circle. But neither the point nor the circle, nor the juxtaposition of the two on a plane, would give us the least idea of a cone. The same thing holds true of the unity and multiplicity of mental life, and of the zero and the infinite towards which empiricism and rationalism conduct personality.

Concepts, as we shall show elsewhere, generally go together in couples and represent two contraries. There is hardly any concrete reality which cannot be observed from two opposing standpoints, which cannot consequently be subsumed under two antagonistic concepts. Hence a thesis and an antithesis which we endeavor in vain to reconcile logically, for the very simple reason that it is impossible, with concepts and observations taken from outside points of view, to make a thing. But from the object, seized by intuition, we pass easily in many cases to the two contrary concepts; and as in that way thesis and antithesis can be seen to spring from reality, we grasp at the same time how it is that the two are opposed and how they are reconciled.

It is true that to accomplish this, it is necessary to proceed by a reversal of the usual work of the intellect. Thinking usually consists in passing from concepts to things, and not from things to concepts. To know a reality, in the usual sense of the word "know" is to take ready-made concepts, to portion them out and to mix them together until a practical equivalent of the reality is obtained. But it must be remembered that the normal work of the intellect is far from being disinterested. We do not aim generally at knowledge for the sake of knowledge, but in order to take sides, to draw profit--in short, to satisfy an interest. We inquire up to what point the object we seek to know is this or that, to what known class it belongs, and what kind of action, bearing, or attitude it should suggest to us. These different possible actions and attitudes are so many conceptual directions of our thought, determined once for all; it remains only to follow them: in that precisely consists the application of concepts to things. To try to fit a concept on an object is simply to ask what we can do with the object, and what it can do for us. To label an object with a certain concept is to mark in precise terms the kind of action or attitude the object should suggest to us. All knowledge, properly so called, is then oriented in a certain direction, or taken from a certain point of view. It is true that our interest is often complex. This is why it happens that our knowledge of the same object may face several successive directions and may be taken from various points of view. It is this which constitutes, in the usual meaning of the terms, a "broad" and "comprehensive" knowledge of the object; the object is then brought not under one single concept, but under several in which it is supposed to "participate." How does it participate in all these concepts at the same time? This is a question which does not concern our practical action and about which we need not trouble. It is, therefore, natural and legitimate in daily life to proceed by the juxtaposition and portioning out of concepts; no philosophical difficulty will arise from this procedure, since by a tacit agreement we shall abstain from philosophizing. But to carry this modus operandi into philosophy, to pass here also from concepts to the thing, to use in order to obtain a disinterested knowledge of an object (that this time we desire to grasp as it is in itself) a manner of knowing inspired by a determinate interest, consisting by definition in an externally taken view of the object, is to go against the end that we have chosen, to condemn philosophy to an eternal skirmishing between the schools and to install contradiction in the very heart of the object and of the method. Either there is no philosophy possible, and all knowledge of things is a practical knowledge aimed at the profit to be drawn from them, or else philosophy consists in placing oneself within the object itself by an effort of intuition.

. . .

. . .intuition places itself in mobility, or, what comes to the same thing, in duration. There lies the very distinct line of demarcation between intuition and analysis. The real, the experienced, and the concrete are recognized by the fact that they are variability itself; the element by the fact that it is invariable. And the element is invariable by definition, being a diagram, a simplified reconstruction, often a mere symbol, in any case a motionless view of the moving reality.

But the error consists in believing that we can reconstruct the real with these diagrams. As we have already said and may as well repeat here--from intuition one can pass to analysis, but not from analysis to intuition.

Out of variability we can make as many variations, qualities, and modifications as we please, since these are so many static views, taken by analysis, of the mobility given to intuition. But these modifications, put end to end, will produce nothing which resembles variability, since they are not parts of it, but elements, which is quite a different thing.

. . .

It is quite otherwise if we place ourselves from the first, by an effort of intuition, in the concrete flow of duration. Certainly, we shall then find no logical reason for positing multiple and diverse durations. Strictly, there might well be no other duration than our own, as, for example, there might be no other color in the world but orange. But just as a consciousness based on color, which sympathized internally with orange instead of perceiving it externally, would feel itself held between red and yellow, would even perhaps suspect beyond this last color a complete spectrum into which the continuity from red to yellow might expand naturally, so the intuition of our duration, far from leaving us suspended in the void as pure analysis would do, brings us into contact with a whole continuity of durations which we must try to follow, whether downwards or upwards; in both cases we can extend ourselves indefinitely by an increasingly violent effort, in both cases we transcend ourselves. In the first we advance towards a more and more attenuated duration, the pulsations of which, being more rapid than ours, and dividing our simple sensation, dilute its quality into quantity; at the limit would be pure homogeneity, that pure repetition by which we define materiality. Advancing in the other direction, we approach a duration which strains, contracts, and intensifies itself more and more; at the limit would be eternity. No longer conceptual eternity, which is an eternity of death, but an eternity of life. A living and therefore still moving eternity in which our own particular duration would be included as the vibrations are in light; an eternity which would be the concentration of all duration, as materiality is its dispersion. Between these two

42

extreme limits intuition moves, and this movement is
the very essence of metaphysics.

* * *

There can be no question of following here the
various states of this movement. But having presented
a general view of the method and made a first application of it, it may not be amiss to formulate, as precisely as we can, the principles on which it rests.
Most of the following propositions have already received in this essay some degree of proof. We hope to
demonstrate them more completely when we come to deal
with other problems.

I. There is a reality that is external and yet
given immediately to the mind. Common sense is right
on this point, as against the idealism and realism of
the philosophers.

II. This reality is mobility. Not things made,
but things in the making, not self-maintaining states,
but only changing states, exist. Rest is never more
than apparent, or, rather, relative. The consciousness
we have of our own self in its continual flux introduces us to the interior of a reality, on the model of
which we must represent other realities. All reality,
therefore, is tendency, if we agree to mean by tendency
an incipient change of direction.

III. Our mind, which seeks for solid points of
support, has for its main function in the ordinary
course of life that of representing states and things.
It takes, at long intervals, almost instantaneous views
of the undivided mobility of the real. It thus obtains
sensations and ideas. In this way it substitutes for
the continuous the discontinuous, for motion stability,
for tendency in process of change, fixed points marking
a direction of change and tendency. This substitution
is necessary to common sense, to language, to practical
life, and even, in a certain sense, which we shall endeavor to determine, to positive science. Our intellect, when it follows its natural bent, proceeds, on
the one hand, by solid perceptions, and, on the other,
by stable conceptions.

. . .

IV. The inherent difficulties of metaphysics,
the antinomies which it gives rise to, and the

43

contradictions into which it falls, the division into antagonistic schools, and the irreducible opposition between systems are largely the result of our applying, to the disinterested knowledge of the real, processes which we generally employ for practical ends. They arise from the fact that we place ourselves in the immobile in order to lie in wait for the moving thing as it passes, instead of replacing ourselves in the moving thing itself, in order to traverse with it the immobile positions. They arise from our professing to reconstruct reality--which is tendency and consequently mobility--with percepts and concepts whose function it is to make it stationary. With stoppages, however numerous they may be, we shall never make mobility; whereas, if mobility is given, we can, by means of diminution, obtain from it by thought as many stoppages as we desire.

. . .

V.   In this it was bound to fail. It is on this impotence and on this impotence only that the skeptical, idealist, critical doctrines really dwell: in fact, all doctrines that deny to our intelligence the power of attaining the absolute. But because we fail to reconstruct the living reality with stiff and ready-made concepts, it does not follow that we cannot grasp it in some other way. The demonstrations which have been given of the relativity of our knowledge are therefore tainted with an original vice; they imply, like the dogmatism they attack, that all knowledge must necessarily start from concepts with fixed outlines, in order to clasp with them the reality which flows.

VI.   But the truth is that our intelligence can follow the opposite method. It can place itself within the mobile reality, and adopt its ceaselessly changing direction; in short, can grasp it by means of that intellectual sympathy which we call intuition. This is extremely difficult. The mind has to do violence to itself, has to reverse the direction of the operation by which it habitually thinks, has perpetually to revise, or rather to recast, all its categories. But in this way it will attain to fluid concepts, capable of following reality in all its sinuosities and of adopting the very movement of the inward life of things. Only thus will a progressive philosophy be built up, freed from the disputes which arise between the various schools, and able to solve its problems naturally, because it will be released from the artificial expression

44

in terms of which such problems are posited. To philosophize, therefore, is to invert the habitual direction of the work of thought.

VII. This inversion has never been practiced in a methodical manner; but a profoundly considered history of human thought would show that we owe to it all that is greatest in the sciences, as well as all that is permanent in metaphysics. The most powerful of the methods of investigation at the disposal of the human mind, the infinitesimal calculus, originated from this very inversion. Modern mathematics is precisely an effort to substitute the being made for the ready-made, to follow the generation of magnitudes, to grasp motion no longer from without and in its displayed result, but from within and in its tendency to change; in short, to adopt the mobile continuity of the outlines of things. It is true that it is confined to the outline, being only the science of magnitudes. It is true also that it has only been able to achieve its marvelous applications by the invention of certain symbols, and that if the intuition of which we have just spoken lies at the origin of invention, it is the symbol alone which is concerned in the application. But metaphysics, which aims at no application, can and usually must abstain from converting intuition into symbols.

. . .

Having then discounted beforehand what is too modest, and at the same time too ambitious, in the following formula, we may say that the object of metaphysics is to perform qualitative differentiations and integrations.

VIII. The reason why this object has been lost sight of, and why science itself has been mistaken in the origin of the processes it employs, is that intuition, once attained, must find a mode of expression and of application which conforms to the habits of our thought, and one which furnishes us, in the shape of well-defined concepts, with the solid points of support which we so greatly need.

. . .

From the overlooking of this intuition proceeds all that has been said by philosophers and by men of science themselves about the "relativity" of scientific knowledge. What is relative is the symbolic

45

knowledge by pre-existing concepts, which proceeds
from the fixed to the moving, and not the intuitive
knowledge which installs itself in that which is moving and adopts the very life of things. This intuition attains the absolute.

Science and metaphysics therefore come together
in intuition. A truly intuitive philosophy would realize the much-desired union of science and metaphysics.

. . .

IX. That there are not two different ways of
knowing things fundamentally, that the various sciences have their root in metaphysics, is what the ancient philosophers generally thought. Their error did
not lie there. It consisted in their being always dominated by the belief, so natural to the human mind,
that a variation can only be the expression and development of what is invariable.

. . .

Modern science dates from the day when mobility
was set up as an independent reality. It dates from
the day when Galileo, setting a ball rolling down an
inclined plane, firmly resolved to study this movement
from top to bottom for itself, in itself, instead of
seeking its principle in the concepts of high and low,
two immobilities by which Aristotle believed he could
adequately explain the mobility. And this is not an
isolated fact in the history of science. Several of
the great discoveries, of those at least which have
transformed the positive sciences or which have created new ones, have been so many soundings in the
depths of pure duration. The more living the reality
touched, the deeper was the sounding.

. . .

How could the masters of modern philosophy, who
have been renovators of science as well as of metaphysics, have had no sense of the moving continuity of
reality? How could they have abstained from placing
themselves in what we call concrete duration? They
have done so to a greater extent than they were aware;
above all, much more than they said. If we endeavor
to link together, by a continuous connection, the intuitions about which systems have become organized, we
find, together with other convergent and divergent

46

lines, one very determinate direction of thought and of feeling. What is this latent thought? How shall we express the feeling? To borrow once more the language of the Platonists, we will say--depriving the words of their psychological sense, and giving the name of Idea to a certain settling down into easy intelligibility, and that of Soul to a certain longing after the restlessness of life--that an invisible current causes modern philosophy to place the Soul above the Idea. It thus tends, like modern science, and even more so than modern science, to advance in an opposite direction to ancient thought.

. . .

Modern science is neither one nor simple. It rests, I freely admit, on ideas which in the end we find clear; but these ideas have gradually become clear through the use made of them; they owe most of their clearness to the light which the facts, and the applications to which they led, have by reflection shed on them--the clearness of a concept being scarcely anything more at bottom than the certainty, at last obtained, of manipulating the concept profitably. At its origin, more than one of these concepts must have appeared obscure, not easily reconcilable with the concepts already admitted into science, and indeed very near the borderline of absurdity. This means that science does not proceed by an orderly dovetailing together of concepts predestined to fit each other exactly. True and fruitful ideas are so many close contacts with currents of reality, which do not necessarily converge on the same point.

. . .

In conclusion, we may remark that there is nothing mysterious in this faculty. Every one of us has had occasion to exercise it to a certain extent. Any one of us, for instance, who has attempted literary composition, knows that when the subject has been studied at length, the materials all collected, and the notes all made, something more is needed in order to set about the work of composition itself, and that is an often very painful effort to place ourselves directly at the heart of the subject, and to seek as deeply as possible an impulse, after which we need only let ourselves go. This impulse, once received, starts the mind on a path where it rediscovers all the information it had collected, and a thousand other details besides; it

47

develops and analyzes itself into terms which could be enumerated indefinitely. The farther we go, the more terms we discover; we shall never say all that could be said, and yet, if we turn back suddenly upon the impulse that we feel behind us, and try to seize it, it is gone; for it was not a thing, but the direction of a movement, and though indefinitely extensible, it is infinitely simple. Metaphysical intuition seems to be something of the same kind. What corresponds here to the documents and notes of literary composition is the sum of observations and experience gathered together by positive science. For we do not obtain an intuition from reality--that is, an intellectual sympathy with the most intimate part of it--unless we have won its confidence by a long fellowship with its superficial manifestations. And it is not merely a question of assimilating the most conspicuous facts; so immense a mass of facts must be accumulated and fused together, that in this fusion all the preconceived and premature ideas which observers may unwittingly have put into their observations will be certain to neutralize each other. In this way only can the bare materiality of the known facts be exposed to view. Even in the simple and privileged case which we have used as an example, even for the direct contact of the self with the self, the final effort of distinct intuition would be impossible to anyone who had not combined and compared with each other a very large number of psychological analyses. The masters of modern philosophy were men who had assimilated all the scientific knowledge of their time, and the partial eclipse of metaphysics for the last half-century has evidently no other cause than the extraordinary difficulty which the philosopher finds today in getting into touch with positive science, which has become far too specialized. But metaphysical intuition, although it can be obtained only through material knowledge, is quite other than the mere summary or synthesis of that knowledge. It is distinct from these, we repeat, as the motor impulse is distinct from the path traversed by the moving body, as the tension of the spring is distinct from the visible movements of the pendulum. In this sense metaphysics has nothing in common with a generalization of facts, and nevertheless it might be defined as integral experience.

SUGGESTED READINGS

Henri Bergson

Bergson, Henri. Time and Free Will: An Essay on the Immediate Data of Consciousness (New York: Macmillan, 1910). F. L. Pogson (Auth. Trans.).

_____. Creative Evolution (London: Macmillan, 1964). Arthur Mitchell (Auth. Trans.).

_____. Duration and Simultaneity (Indianapolis: Bobbs-Merrill, 1964). Leon Jacobson (Trans.).

_____. The Creative Mind (New York: Philosophical Library, 1946). Mabelle Andison (Trans.).

* * *

_____. "Intellectual Effort," in Mind-Energy: Lectures and Essays (New York: Henry Holt, 1920), pp. 186-230. H. Wildon Carr (Trans.).

_____. "A Propos de L'Evolution de l'intelligence géometrique: Repense à un article d'E. Borel," Revue de Métaphysique et de Morale, XVI, 1 (Janvier 1908), 28-33.

_____. "Introductions I and II," in The Creative Mind (New York: Philosophical Library, 1946), pp. 9-106. Mabelle Andison (Trans.).

* * *

Gunter, Pete A. Y. "Bergsonian Method and the Evolution of Science," in Bergson and the Evolution of Science (Knoxville: University of Tennessee Press, 1969), pp. 23-42. Pete A. Y. Gunter (Ed., Trans., Intro.).

James, William. "The Philosophy of Bergson," in
A Pluralistic Universe (New York: Longmans,
Green, 1919), pp. 223-272.

Merleau-Ponty, Maurice. "Bergson," in In Praise
of Philosophy (Evanston, Ill.: Northwestern
University Press, 1963), pp. 9-33.

* * *

Capek, Milic. Bergson and Modern Physics (New
York: Humanities Press; Dordrecht, Holland:
Reidel, 1971).

Carr, H. W. The Philosophy of Change: A Study of
the Fundamental Principles of the Philosophy of
Bergson (London: Macmillan, 1914).

Gunn, J. A. Bergson and His Philosophy (London:
Methven, 1920).

Stephen, Karin. The Misuse of Mind: A Study of
Bergson's Attack on Intellectualism (London:
Kegan Paul, 1922).

2. SYMBOLIC REFERENCE

Alfred North Whitehead

Alfred North Whitehead (1861-1947) did not
take his position at Harvard University until
he was sixty-three years of age, but it was
during this time that he was most creative
and prolific with respect to his philosophy
of organism. He readily professes his relationship to the thought of Alexander, Bergson,
James, Leibniz, and Morgan, but he is without
a doubt one of the most formidable and popular of those within the movement toward a new
realism.

Whitehead's epistemology is very closely related
to and dependent upon both his metaphysics and conception of nature, or natural philosophy. In them he
wrestles basically with the problem of dualism, especially as he sees this expressed in Newtonian physics.
In contrast to what had been presented formerly as the
disconnectedness of things (specifically in nature),
he proposes we consider their interconnectedness or relatedness which he has called the doctrine of 'significance.' Since the relatedness which is the subject of
natural knowledge cannot possibly be understood without
reference to "the general characteristics of perception," the study of relatedness leads directly to an
examination of perception. Perhaps the most explicit
expressions of his epistemology (and metaphysics) are
contained in Process and Reality and the Adventures of
Ideas.* In those works he acknowledges that language
and mathematical symbols are important with respect to

---

*The selections appearing here are taken from
Process and Reality (New York: Macmillan, 1929), pp.
101, 103, 105, 112, 125, 184, 185, 188-192, 255-268,
and 274-279. Selections from Adventures of Ideas also
appear in this volume. On this subject Whitehead also
refers the reader to his Barbour-Page lectures, Symbolism, Its Meaning and Importance, delivered at the University of Virginia, April, 1927, Macmillan.

human understanding and communication, but insists
there is a much more fundamental type of 'symbolism'
which has tended to be neglected; namely, the combination of sense perception and symbolism referred to by
Whitehead as 'direct recognition' and 'symbolic reference.'   Direct recognition is divided into two closely
connected but distinctive modes of direct perception:
presentational immediacy and causal efficacy.   The
basic theme of his epistemology, therefore, is that
human symbolism has its origin in the interplay between
these two distinct modes of direct perception.   Symbolic reference represents the synthetic activity
through which the two modes are fused into one perception, and the result of the process is "what the actual
world is for us, as that datum in our experience pro-
ductive of feelings, emotions, satisfactions, actions,
and finally as the topic for conscious recognition when
our mentality intervenes with its conceptual analysis."#

#Symbolism: (New York: Capricorn, 1959), p. 18.
"In short," says Whitehead, "truth and error dwell in
the world by reason of synthesis: every actual thing
is synthetic: and symbolic reference is one primitive
form of synthetic activity whereby what is actual
arises from its given phases."   Ibid., p. 21.

Perception in its primary form is consciousness of
the causal efficacy of the external world by reason of
which the percipient is a concrescence from a definitely constituted datum. The vector character of the
datum is this causal efficacy. Thus perception, in
this primary sense, is perception of the settled world
in the past as constituted by its feeling-tones, and
as efficacious by reason of those feeling-tones. Perception, in this sense of the term, will be called
'perception in the mode of causal efficacity.'

* * *

It is evident that 'perception in the mode of
causal efficacy' is not that sort of perception which
has received chief attention in the philosophical tradition. Philosophers have disdained the information
about the universe obtained through their visceral
feelings, and have concentrated on visual feelings.

What we ordinarily term our visual perceptions
are the result of the later stages in the concrescence
of the percipient occasion. When we register in consciousness our visual perception of a grey stone, something more than bare sight is meant. The 'stone' has
a reference to its past, when it could be used as mis-
sile if small enough, or as a seat if large enough. A
'stone' has certainly a history, and probably a future.
It is one of the elements in the actual world which has
got to be referred to as an actual reason and not as an
abstract potentiality. But we all know that the mere
sight involved, in the perception of the grey stone, is
the sight of a grey shape contemporaneous with the percipient, and with certain spatial relations to the percipient, more or less vaguely defined. Thus the mere
sight is confined to the illustration of the geometrical perspective relatedness, of a certain contemporary
spatial region, to the percipient, the illustration
being effected by the mediation of 'grey.' The sensum
'grey' rescues that region from its vague confusion
with other regions.

Perception which merely, by means of a sensum,
rescues from vagueness a contemporary spatial region,
in respect to its spatial shape and its spatial perspective from the percipient, will be called 'perception in the mode of presentational immediacy.'

The definition, which has just been given, extends
beyond the particular case of sight. The unravelling
of the complex interplay between the two modes of per-
ception--causal efficacy and presentational immediacy
is one main problem of the theory of perception.[1] The
ordinary philosophical discussion of perception is almost wholly concerned with this interplay, and ignores
the two pure modes which are essential for its proper
explanation. The interplay between the two modes will
be termed 'symbolic reference.'

* * *

The organic doctrine is closer to Descartes than
to Newton. Also it is close to Spinoza; but Spinoza
bases his philosophy upon the monistic substance, of
which the actual occasions are inferior modes. The
philosophy of organism inverts this point of view.

As to the direct knowledge of the actual world as
a datum for the immediacy of feeling, we first refer to
Descartes in <u>Meditation I</u>, "These hands and this body
are <u>mine</u>"; also to Hume in his many assertions of the
type, we see <u>with our eyes</u>. Such statements witness to
direct knowledge of the antecedent functioning of the
body in sense-perception. Both agree--though Hume more
explicitly--that sense-perception of the contemporary
world is accompanied by perception of the 'withness' of
the body; and thus confined perception to presentational immediacy.

* * *

This account of 'presentational immediacy' presupposes two metaphysical assumptions:

(i) That the actual world, in so far as it is a
community of entities which are settled, actual, and
already become, conditions and limits the potentiality
for creativeness beyond itself. This 'given' world provides determinate data in the form of those objectifications of themselves which the characters of its actual
entities can provide. This is a limitation laid upon
the general potentiality provided by eternal objects,
considered merely in respect to the generality of their
natures. Thus, relatively to any actual entity, there
is a 'given' world of settled actual entities and a
'real' potentiality, which is the datum for creativeness beyond that standpoint. This datum, which is the
primary phase in the process constituting an actual

54

entity, is nothing else than the actual world itself in its character of a possibility for the process of being felt. This exemplifies the metaphysical principle that every 'being' is a potential for a 'becoming.' The actual world is the 'objective content' of each new creation.

(ii) The second metaphysical assumption is that the real potentialities relative to all standpoints are coordinated as diverse determinations of one extensive continuum. This extensive continuum is one relational complex in which all potential objectifications find their niche. It underlies the whole world, past, present, and future. Considered in its full generality, apart from the additional conditions proper only to the cosmic epoch of electrons, protons, molecules, and star-systems, the properties of this continuum are very few and do not include the relationships of metrical geometry. An extensive continuum is a complex of entities united by the various allied relationships of whole to part, and of overlapping so as to possess common parts, and of contact, and of other relationships derived from these primary relationships. The notion of a 'continuum' involves both the property of indefinite divisibility and the property of unbounded extension. There are always entities beyond entities, because nonentity is no boundary. This extensive continuum expresses the solidarity of all possible standpoints throughout the whole process of the world. It is not a fact prior to the world; it is the first determination of order--that is, of real potentiality--arising out of the general character of the world. In its full generality beyond the present epoch, it does not involve shapes, dimensions, or measurability; these are additional determinations of real potentiality arising from our cosmic epoch.

This extensive continuum is 'real,' because it expresses a fact derived from the actual world and concerning the contemporary actual world. All actual entities are related according to the determinations of this continuum; and all possible actual entities in the future must exemplify these determinations in their relations with the already actual world. The extensive continuum is that general relational element in experience whereby the actual entities experienced, and that unit experience itself, are united in the solidarity of one common world.

Extension, apart from its spatialization and temporalization, is that general scheme of relationships providing the capacity that many objects can be welded into the real unity of one experience. Thus, an act of experience has an objective scheme of extensive order by reason of the double fact that its own perspective standpoint has extensive content, and that the other actual entities are objectified with the retention of their extensive relationships.

* * *

These extensive relations do not make determinate what is transmitted; but they do determine conditions to which all transmission must conform. They represent the systematic scheme which is involved in the real potentiality from which every actual occasion arises. This scheme is also involved in the attained fact which every actual occasion is. The 'extensive' scheme is nothing else than the generic morphology of the internal relations which bind the actual occasions into a nexus, and which bind the prehensions of any one actual occasion into a unity.

* * *

Presentational immediacy illustrates the contemporary world in respect to its potentiality for extensive subdivision into atomic actualities and in respect to the scheme of perspective relationships which thereby eventuates. But it gives no information as to the actual atomization of this contemporary 'real potentiality.' By its limitations it exemplifies the doctrine, already stated above, that the contemporary world happens independently of the actual occasion with which it is contemporary. This is in fact the definition of contemporaneousness (cf. Part II, Ch. II, Sect. I); namely, that actual occasions, A and B, are mutually contemporary, when A does not contribute to the datum for B, and B does not contribute to the datum for A, except that both A and B are atomic regions in the potential scheme of spatio-temporal extensiveness which is a datum for both A and B.

Hume's polemic respecting causation is, in fact, one prolonged, convincing argument that pure presentational immediacy does not disclose any causal influence, either whereby one actual entity is constitutive of the percipient actual entity, or whereby one perceived actual entity is constitutive of another perceived actual entity. The conclusion is that, in so far as concerns their disclosure by presentational immediacy, actual

56

entities in the contemporary universe are causally independent of each other.

The two pure modes of perception in this way disclose a variety of loci defined by reference to the
percipient occasion M. For example, there are the actual occasions of the settled world which provide the
datum for M; these lie in M's causal past. Again,
there are the potential occasions for which M decides
its own potentialities of contribution to their data;
these lie in M's causal future. There are also those
actual occasions which lie neither in M's causal past,
nor in M's causal future. Such actual occasions are
called M's 'contemporaries.' These three loci are defined solely by reference to the pure mode of causal
efficacy.

We now turn to the pure mode of presentational immediacy. One great difference from the previous ways
of obtaining loci at once comes into view. In considering the causal mode, the past and the future were defined positively, and the contemporaries of M were defined negatively as lying neither in M's past nor in
M's future. In dealing with presentational immediacy
the opposite way must be taken. For presentational immediacy gives positive information only about the immediate present as defined by itself. Presentational immediacy illustrates, by means of sensa, potential subdivisions within a cross-section of the world, which is
in this way objectified for M. This cross-section is
M's immediate present. What is in this way illustrated
is the potentiality for subdivision into actual atomic
occasions; we can also recognize potentialities for
subdivision of regions whose subdivisions remain unil-
lustrated potentiality, a perception outrunning the
real illustration of division by contrasted sensa.
Such limitations constitute the minima sensibilia.

Hume's polemic respecting causation constitutes a
proof that M's 'immediate present' lies within the locus of M's contemporaries. The presentation to M of
this locus, forming its immediate present, contributes
to M's datum two facts about the universe: one fact is
that there is a 'unison of becoming,' constituting a
positive relation of all the occasions in this community to any one of them. The members of this community
share in a common immediacy; they are in 'unison' as to
their becoming: that is to say, any pair of occasions
in the locus are contemporaries. The other fact is the
subjective illustration of the potential extensive

subdivision with complete vagueness respecting the actual atomization. For example, the stone, which in the immediate present is a group of many actual occasions, is illustrated as one grey spatial region. But, to go back to the former fact, the many actual entities of the present stone and the percipient are connected together in the 'unison of immediate becoming.' This community of concrescent occasions, forming M's immediate present, thus establishes a principle of common relatedness, a principle realized as an element in M's datum. This is the principle of mutual relatedness in the 'unison of becoming.' But this mutual relatedness is independent of the illustration by those sensa, through which presentational immediacy for M is effected. Also the illustration by these sensa has unequal relevance for M, throughout the locus. In its spatially remote parts it becomes vaguer and vaguer, fainter and fainter; and yet the principle of 'unison of becoming' still holds, in despite of the fading importance of the sensa. We thus find that the locus-- namely, M's immediate present--is determined by the condition of 'mutual unison' independently of variations of relevant importance in M's illustrative sensa, and extends to their utmost bounds of faintness, and is equally determinate beyond such bounds. We thus gain the conception of a locus in which any two atomic actualities are in 'concrescent unison,' and which is particularized by the fact that M belongs to it, and so do all actual occasions belonging to extensive regions which lie in M's immediate present as illustrated by importantly relevant sensa. This complete region is the prolongation of M's immediate present beyond M's direct perception, the prolongation being effected by the principle of 'concrescent unison.'

A complete region, satisfying the principle of 'concrescent unison,' will be called a 'duration.' A duration is a cross-section of the universe; it is the immediate present condition of the world at some epoch, according to the old 'classical' theory of time--a theory never doubted until within the last few years. It will have been seen that the philosophy of organism accepts and defines this notion. Some measure of acceptance is imposed upon metaphysics. If the notion be wholly rejected no appeal to universal obviousness of conviction can have any weight; since there can be no stronger instance of this force of obviousness.

The 'classical' theory of time tacitly assumed that a duration included the directly perceived immediate present of each one of its members. The converse proposition certainly follows from the account given above, that the immediate present of each actual occasion lies in a duration. An actual occasion will be said[2] to be 'congredient with' or 'stationary in' the duration including its directly perceived immediate present. The actual occasion is included in its own immediate present; so that each actual occasion through its percipience in the pure mode of presentational immediacy--if such percipience has important relevance--defines one duration in which it is included. The percipient occasion is 'stationary' in this duration.

But the classical theory also assumed the converse of this statement. It assumed that any actual occasion only lies in one duration; so that if N lies in the duration including M's immediate present, then M lies in the duration including N's immediate present. The philosophy of organism, in agreement with recent physics, rejects this conversion; though it holds that such rejection is based on scientific examination of our cosmic epoch, and not on any more general metaphysical principle. According to the philosophy of organism, in the present cosmic epoch only one duration includes all M's immediate present; this one duration will be called M's 'presented duration.' But M itself lies in many durations; each duration including M also includes some portions of M's presented duration. In the case of human perception practically all the important portions are thus included; also in human experience the relationship to such durations is what we express by the notion of 'movement.'

To sum up this discussion. In respect to any one actual occasion M there are three distinct nexus of occasions to be considered:

(i) The nexus of M's contemporaries, defined by the characteristic that M and any one of its contemporaries happen in causal independence of each other.

(ii) Durations including M, any such duration is defined by the characteristic that any two of its members are contemporaries. (It follows that any member of such a duration is contemporary with M, and thence that such durations are all included in the locus (i). The characteristic property of a duration is termed 'unison of becoming.')

(iii) M's presented locus, which is the contemporary nexus perceived in the mode of presentational immediacy, with its regions defined by sensa. It is assumed, on the basis of direct intuition, that M's presented locus is closely related to some one duration
including M. It is also assumed, as the outcome of
modern physical theory, that there is more than one duration including M. The single duration which is so
related to M's presented locus is termed 'M's presented
duration.'

* * *

The pure mode of presentational immediacy gives no
information as to the past or the future. It merely
presents an illustrated portion of the presented duration. It thereby defines a cross-section of the universe: but does not in itself define on which side
lies the past, and on which side the future. In order
to solve such questions we now come to the interplay
between the two pure modes. This mixed mode of perception is here named 'symbolic reference.' The failure
to lay due emphasis on symbolic reference is one of the
reasons for metaphysical difficulties; it has reduced
the notion of 'meaning' to a mystery.

The first principle, explanatory of symbolic reference, is that for such reference a 'common ground' is
required. By this necessity for a 'common ground' it
is meant that there must be components in experience
which are directly recognized as identical in each of
the pure perceptive modes. In the transition to a
higher phase of experience, there is a concrescence in
which prehensions in the two modes are brought into a
unity of feeling: this concrescent unity arises from a
congruity of their subjective forms in virtue of the
identity relation between the two prehensions, owing to
some components in common. Thus the symbolic reference
belongs to one of the later originative phases of experience. These later phases are distinguished by their
new element of originative freedom. Accordingly, while
the two pure perceptive modes are incapable of error,
symbolic reference introduces this possiblity. When
human experience is in question, 'perception' almost
always means 'perception in the mixed mode of symbolic
reference.' Thus, in general, human perception is subject to error, because, in respect to those components
most clearly in consciousness, it is interpretative.
In fact, error is the mark of the higher organisms, and
is the schoolmaster by whose agency there is upward

evolution. For example, the evolutionary use of intelligence is that it enables the individual to profit by error without being slaughtered by it. But at present, we are not considering conceptual or intellectual functioning.

One main element of common ground, shared between the two pure modes, is the presented locus. This locus enters subordinately into the perceptive mode of causal efficacy, vaguely exemplifying its participation in the general scheme of extensive interconnection, involved in the real potentiality. It is not disclosed by that perceptive mode in any other way; at least it is not directly disclosed. The further disclosure must be indirect, since contemporary events are exactly those which are neither causing, nor caused by, the percipient actual occasion. Now, although the various causal pasts (i.e., 'actual worlds') of the contemporary actual occasions are not wholly identical with the causal past of the percipient actual occasion, yet, so far as important relevance is concerned, these causal pasts are practically identical. Thus there is, in the mode of causal efficacy, a direct perception of those antecedent actual occasions which are causally efficacious both for the percipient and for the relevant events in the presented locus. The percipient therefore, under the limitation of its own perspective, prehends the causal influences to which the presented locus in its important regions is subjected. This amounts to an indirect perception of this locus, a perception in which the direct components belong to the pure mode of causal efficacy. If we now turn to the perceptive mode of presentational immediacy, the regions, perceived by direct and indirect knowledge respectively, are inverted in comparison with the other mode. The presented locus is directly illustrated by the sensa; while the causal past, the causal future, and the other contemporary events, are only indirectly perceived by means of their extensive relations to the presented locus. It must be remembered that the presented locus has its fourth dimension of temporal thickness 'spatialized' as the specious present of the percipient. Thus the presented locus, with the animal body of the percipient as the region from which perspectives are focussed, is the regional origin by reference to which in this perceptive mode the complete scheme of extensive regions is rendered determinate. The respective roles of the two perceptive modes in experience are aptly exemplified by the fact that all scientific observations, such as measurements, determinations of relative spatial position, determinations of sense-data such as colours, sounds, tastes, smells, temperature feelings, touch feelings, etc., are made in the perceptive mode of presentational immediacy; and that great care is exerted to keep this mode pure, that is to say, devoid of symbolic reference to causal efficacy. In this way accuracy is secured, in the sense that the direct observation is purged of all interpretation. On the other hand all scientific theory is stated in terms referring exclusively to the scheme of relatedness, which, so far as it is observed, involves the percepta in the pure mode of causal efficacy. It thus stands out at once, that what we want to know about, from the point of view either of curiosity or of technology, chiefly resides in those aspects of the world disclosed in causal efficacy: but that what we can distinctly register is chiefly to be found among the percepta in the mode of presentational immediacy.

The presented locus is a common ground for the symbolic reference, because it is directly and distinctly perceived in presentational immediacy, and is indistinctly and indirectly perceived in causal efficacy. In the latter mode, the indistinctness is such that the detailed geometrical relationships are, for the most part, incurably vague. Particular regions are, in this perceptive mode, in general not distinguishable. In this respect, causal efficacy stands in contrast to presentational immediacy with its direct illustration of certain distinct regions.

But there are exceptions to this geometrical indistinctness of causal efficacy. In the first place, the separation of the potential extensive scheme into past and future lies with the mode of causal efficacy and not with that of presentational immediacy. The mathematical measurements, derivable from the latter, are indifferent to this distinction; whereas the physical theory, expressed in terms of the former, is wholly concerned with it. In the next place, the animal body of the percipient is a region for which causal efficacy acquires some accuracy in its distinction of regions--not all the distinctness of the other mode, but sufficient to allow of important identifications. For example, we see with our eyes, we taste with our palates, we touch with our hands, etc.: here the causal efficacy defines regions which are identified with themselves as perceived with greater distinctness by the other mode. To take one example, the slight eye-strain in the act of sight is an instance of regional

definition by presentational immediacy. But in itself
it is no more to be correlated with projected sight
than is a contemporary stomach-ache, or a throb in the
foot. The obvious correlation of the eye-strain with
sight arises from the perception, in the other mode,
of the eye as efficacious in sight. This correlation
takes place in virtue of the identity of the two regions, the region of the eye-strain, and the region of
eye-efficacy. But the eye-strain is so immeasurably
the superior in its power of regional definition that,
as usual, we depend upon it for explicit geometrical
correlations with other parts of the body. In this
way, the animal body is the great central ground underlying all symbolic reference. In respect to bodily
perceptions the two modes achieve the maximum of symbolic reference, and pool their feelings referent to
identical regions. Every statement about the geometrical relationships of physical bodies in the world is
ultimately referable to certain definite human bodies
as origins of reference. A traveller, who has lost his
way, should not ask, Where am I? What he really wants
to know is, Where are the other places? He has got his
own body, but he has lost them.

The second 'ground' for symbolic reference is the
connection between the two modes effected by the identity of an eternal object ingredient in both of them.
It will be remembered that the former 'ground' was the
identity of the extensive region throughout such stages
of direct perception and synthesis, when there was a
diversity of eternal objects, for example, eye-region,
visual sensa, eye-strain. But now we pass to a diversity of regions combined with an identity of the eternal object, for example, visual sensa given by efficacity of eye-region, and the region of the stone perceived in the mode of presentational immediacy under
the illustration of the same visual sense. In this
connection the 'make-believe' character of modern empiricism is well shown by putting into juxtaposition
two widely separated passages[3] from Hume's Treatise:
"Impressions may be divided into two kinds, those of
sensation, and those of reflection. The first kind
arises in the soul originally, from unknown causes."
And "If it be perceived by the eyes, it must be a colour; . . ."

The earlier passage is Hume's make-believe, when
he is thinking of his philosophical principles. He
then refers the visual sensations 'in the soul' to 'unknown causes.' But in the second passage, the heat of

argument elicits his real conviction--everybody's real
conviction--that visual sensations arise 'by the eyes.'
The causes are not a bit 'unknown,' and among them
there is usually to be found the efficacity of the
eyes. If Hume had stopped to investigate the alternative causes for the occurrence of visual sensations--
for example, eye-sight, or excessive consumption of
alcohol--he might have hesitated in his profession of
ignorance. If the causes be indeed unknown, it is absurd to bother about eye-sight and intoxication. The
reason for the existence of oculists and prohibition-
ists is that various causes are known.

We can now complete our account of presentational
immediacy. In this perceptive mode the sensa are
'given' for the percipient, but this donation is not
to be ascribed to the spatial object which is thereby
presented, the stone, for example. Now it is a primary
doctrine that what is 'given' is given by reason of objectifications of actual entities from the settled
past. We therefore seek for the actual occasions to
whose objectifications this donation is to be ascribed.
In this procedure we are only agreeing with the spirit
of Descartes' fifty-second principle (Part I): "For
this reason, when we perceive any attribute, we therefore conclude that some existing thing or substance to
which it may be attributed, is necessarily present."
Common sense, physical theory, and physiological theory, combine to point out a historic route of inheritance, from actual occasion to succeeding actual occasion, first physically in the external environment,
then physiologically--through the eyes in the case of
visual data--up the nerves, into the brain. The dona-
tion--taking sight as an example--is not confined to
definite sensa, such as shades of colour: it also includes geometrical relationships to the general environment. In this chain of inheritances, the eye is
picked out to rise into perceptive prominence, because
another historic route of physiological inheritance
starts from it, whereby a later occasion (almost identical with the earlier) is illustrated by the sensum
'eye-strain' in the mode of presentational immediacy;
but this eye-strain is another allied story. In the
visual datum for the percipient there are first these
components of colour-sensa combined with geometrical
relationships to the external world of the settled
past: secondly, there are also in the datum the general geometrical relationships forming the completion
of this potential scheme into the contemporary world,
and into the future. The responsive phase absorbs

these data as material for a subjective unity of feeling: the supplemental stage heightens the relevance of the colour-sensa, and supplements the geometrical relationships of the past by picking out the contemporary region of the stone to be the contemporary representative of the efficacious historic routes. There then results in the mode of presentational immediacy, the perception of the region illustrated by the sensum termed 'grey.' The term 'stone' is primarily applied to a certain historic route in the past, which is an efficacious element in this train of circumstance. It is only properly applied to the contemporary region illustrated by 'grey' on the assumption that this contemporary region is the prolongation, of that historic route, into the presented locus. This assumption may, or may not, be true. Further, the illustration of the contemporary region of 'grey' may be due to quite other efficacious historic routes--for example, to lighting effects arranged by theatrical producers--and in such a case, the term 'stone' may suggest an even more violent error than in the former example. What is directly perceived, certainly and without shadow of doubt, is a grey region of the presented locus. Any further interpretation, instinctive or by intellectual judgment, must be put down to symbolic reference.

This account makes it plain that the perceptive mode of presentational immediacy arises in the later, originative, integrative phases of the process of concrescence. The perceptive mode of causal efficacy is to be traced to the constitution of the datum by reason of which there is a concrete percipient entity. Thus we must assign the mode of causal efficacy to the fundamental constitution of an occasion so that in germ this mode belongs even to organisms of the lowest grade; while the mode of presentational immediacy requires the more sophistical activity of the later stages of process, so as to belong only to organisms of a relatively high grade. So far as we can judge, such high-grade organisms are relatively few, in comparison with the whole number of organisms in our immediate environment. Presentational immediacy is an outgrowth from the complex datum implanted by causal efficacy. But, by the originative power of the supplemental phase, what was vague, ill defined, and hardly relevant in causal efficacy, becomes distinct, well defined, and importantly relevant in presentational immediacy. In the responsive phase, the grey-colour, and the geometrical relations between the efficacious, bodily routes and the contemporary occasions, were

65

subjective sensation associated with barely relevant
geometrical relations: they represented the vivid sen-
sational qualities in the enjoyment of which the percipient subject barely distinguished vague indirect relationships to the external world. The supplemental
phase lifts the presented duration into vivid distinctness, so that the vague efficacity of the indistinct
external world in the immediate past is precipitated
upon the representative regions in the contemporary
present. In the usual language, the sensations are
projected. This phraseology is unfortunate; for there
never were sensations apart from these geometrical relations. Presentational immediacy is the enhancement
of the importance of relationships which were already
in the datum, vaguely and with slight relevance. This
fact, that 'presentational immediacy' deals with the
same datum as does 'causal efficacy,' gives the ultimate reason why there is a common 'ground' for 'symbolic reference.' The two modes express the same datum
under different proportions of relevance. The two genetic processes involving presentational immediacy must
be carefully distinguished. There is first the complex
genetic process in which presentational immediacy originates. This process extends downwards even to occasions which belong to the historic routes of certain
types of inorganic enduring objects, namely, to those
enduring objects whose aggregates form the subject-
matter of the science of Newtonian Dynamics. Secondly,
prehensions in the mode of presentational immediacy are
involved as components in integration with other prehensions which are usually, though not always in other
modes. These integrations often involve various types
of 'symbolic reference.' This symbolic reference is
the interpretive element in human experience. Language
almost exclusively refers to presentational immediacy
as interpreted by symbolic reference. For example, we
say that 'we see the stone' where stone is an interpretation of stone-image: also we say that 'we see the
stone-image with our eyes'; this is an interpretation
arising from the complex integration of (i) the causal
efficacy of the antecedent eye in the vision, (ii) the
presentational immediacy of the stone-image, (iii) the
presentational immediacy of the eye-strain. When we
say that 'we see the stone with our eyes,' the interpretations of these two examples are combined.

The discussion of the problem, constituted by the
connection between causation and perception, has been
conducted by the various schools of thought derived
from Hume and Kant under the misapprehension generated

by an inversion of the true constitution of experience. The inversion was explicit in the writings of Hume and of Kant: for both of them presentational immediacy was the primary fact of perception, and any apprehension of causation was, somehow or other, to be elicited from this primary fact. This view of the relation between causation and perception, as items in experience, was not original to these great philosophers. It is to be found presupposed in Locke and Descartes; and they derived it from mediaeval predecessors. But the modern critical movement in philosophy arose when Hume and Kant emphasized the fundamental, inescapable, importance which this doctrine possesses for any philosophy admitting its truth. The philosophy of organism does not admit its truth, and thus rejects the touchstone which is the neolithic weapon of 'critical' philosophy. It must be remembered that clearness in consciousness is no evidence for primitiveness in the genetic process: the opposite doctrine is more nearly true.

Owing to its long dominance, it has been usual to assume as an obvious fact the primacy of presentational immediacy. We open our eyes and our other sense-organs; we then survey the contemporary world decorated with sights, and sounds, and tastes; and then, by the sole aid of this information about the contemporary world, thus decorated, we draw what conclusions we can as to the actual world. No philosopher really holds that this is the sole source of information: Hume and his followers appeal vaguely to 'memory' and to 'practice,' in order to supplement their direct information; and Kant wrote other 'Critiques' in order to supplement his Critique of Pure Reason. But the general procedure of modern philosophical 'criticism' is to tie down opponents strictly to the front door of presentational immediacy as the sole source of information, while one's own philosophy makes its escape by a back door veiled under the ordinary usages of language.

If this 'Humian' doctrine be true, certain conclusions as to 'behavior' ought to follow--conclusions which, in the most striking way, are not verified. It is almost indecent to draw the attention of philosophers to the minor transactions of daily life, away from the classic sources of philosophic knowledge; but, after all, it is the empiricists who began this appeal to Caesar.

According to Hume, our behaviour presupposing causation is due to the repetition of associated

presentational experiences. Thus the vivid presentment
of the antecedent percepts should vividly generate the
behaviour, in action or thought, towards the associated
consequent. The clear, distinct, overwhelming perception of the one is the overwhelming reason for the subjective transition to the other. For behaviour, inter-
pretable as implying causation, is on this theory the
subjective response to presentational immediacy. According to Hume this subjective response is the beginning and the end of all that there is to be said about
causation. In Hume's theory the response is response
to presentational immediacy, and to nothing else. Also
the situation elicited in response is nothing but an
immediate presentation, or the memory of one. Let us
apply this explanation to reflex action: In the dark,
the electric light is suddenly turned on and the man's
eyes blink. There is a simple physiological explanation of this trifling incident.

But this physiological explanation is couched
wholly in terms of causal efficacy: it is the conjec-
tural record of the travel of a spasm of excitement
along nerves to some nodal centre, and of the return
spasm of contraction back to the eyelids. The correct
technical phraseology would not alter the fact that the
explanation does not involve any appeal to presentational immediacy either for actual occasions resident
in the nerves, or for the man. At the most there is a
tacit supposition as to what a physiologist, who in
fact was not there, might have seen if he had been
there, and if he could have vivisected the man without
affecting these occurrences, and if he could have observed with a microscope which also in fact was absent.
Thus the physiological explanation remains, from the
point of view of Hume's philosophy, a tissue of irrele-
vancies. It presupposes a side of the universe about
which, on Hume's theory, we must remain in blank ignorance.

Let us now dismiss physiology and turn to the private experience of the blinking man. The sequence of
percepts, in the mode of presentational immediacy, are
flash of light, feeling of eye-closure, instant of
darkness. The three are practically simultaneous;
though the flash maintains its priority over the other
two, and these two latter percepts are indistinguishable as to priority. According to the philosophy of
organism, the man also experiences another percept in
the mode of causal efficacy. He feels that the experiences of the _eye_ in the matter of the flash are causal

of the blink. The man himself will have no doubt of
it. In fact, it is the feeling of causality which enables the man to distinguish the priority of the flash;
and the inversion of the argument, whereby the temporal
sequence 'flash to blink' is made the premise for the
'causality' belief, has its origin in pure theory. The
man will explain his experience by saying, 'The flash
made me blink'; and if his statement be doubted, he
will reply, 'I know it, because I felt it.'

    The philosophy of organism accepts the man's
statement, that the flash made him blink. But Hume
intervenes with another explanation. He first points
out that in the mode of presentational immediacy there
is no percept of the flash making the man blink. In
this mode there are merely the two percepts--the flash
and the blink--combining the two latter of the three
percepts under the one term 'blink.' Hume refuses to
admit the man's protestation, that the compulsion to
blink is just what he did feel. The refusal is based
on the dogma, that all percepts are in the mode of
presentational immediacy--a dogma not to be upset by a
mere appeal to direct experience. Besides Hume has
another interpretation of the man's experience: what
the man really felt was his habit of blinking after
flashes. The word 'association' explains it all, according to Hume. But how can a 'habit' be felt, when
a 'cause' cannot be felt? Is there any presentational
immediacy in the feeling of a 'habit'? Hume by a
sleight of hand confuses a 'habit of feeling blinks
after flashes' with a 'feeling of the habit of feeling
blinks after flashes.'

    We have here a perfect example of the practice of
applying the test of presentational immediacy to procure the critical rejection of some doctrines, and of
allowing other doctrines to slip out by a back door,
so as to evade the test. The notion of causation arose
because mankind lives amid experiences in the mode of
causal efficacity.

    We will keep to the appeal to ordinary experience,
and consider another situation, which Hume's philosophy
is ill equipped to explain. The 'causal feeling' according to that doctrine arises from the long association of well-marked presentations of sensa, one prece-
dent to the other. It would seem therefore that inhi-
bitions of sensa, given in presentational immediacy,
should be accompanied by a corresponding absence of
'causal feeling'; for the explanation of how there is

69

'causal feeling' presupposes the well-marked familiar
sensa, in presentational immediacy. Unfortunately the
contrary is the case. An inhibition of familiar sensa
is very apt to leave us a prey to vague terrors respecting a circumambient world of causal operations.
In the dark there are vague presences, doubtfully
feared; in the silence, the irresistible causal efficacy of nature presses itself upon us; in the vagueness
of the low hum of insects in an August woodland, the
inflow into ourselves of feelings from enveloping nature overwhelms us; in the dim consciousness of half-
sleep, the presentations of sense fade away, and we are
left with the vague feeling of influences from vague
things around us. It is quite untrue that the feelings
of various types of influences are dependent upon the
familiarity of well-marked sensa in immediate presentment. Every way of omitting the sensa still leaves us
a prey to vague feelings of influence. Such feelings,
divorced from immediate sensa, are pleasant, or un-
pleasant, according to mood; but they are always vague
as to spatial and temporal definition, though their explicit dominance in experience may be heightened in the
absence of sensa.

Further, our experience of our various bodily
parts are primarily perceptions of them as reasons for
'projected' sense: the hand is the reason for the projected touch-sensum, the eye is the reason for the projected sight-sensum. Our bodily experience is primarily an experience of the dependence of presentational
immediacy upon causal efficacy. Hume's doctrine inverts this relationship by making causal efficacy, as
an experience, dependent upon presentational immediacy.
This doctrine, whatever be its merits, is not based
upon any appeal to experience.

Bodily experiences, in the mode of causal efficacy, are distinguished by their comparative accuracy
of spatial definition. The causal influences from the
body have lost the extreme vagueness of those which inflow from the external world. But, even for the body,
causal efficacy is dogged with vagueness compared to
presentational immediacy. These conclusions are con-
firmed if we descend to the scale of organic being. It
does not seem to be the sense of causal awareness that
the lower living things lack, so much as variety of
sense-presentation, and then vivid distinctness of
presentational immediacy. But animals, and even vegetables, in low forms of organism exhibit modes of behaviour directed towards self-preservation. There is

every indication of a vague feeling of causal relationship with the external world, of some intensity, vaguely
defined as to quality, and with some vague definition
as to locality. A jellyfish advances and withdraws,
and in so doing exhibits some perception of causal relationship with the world beyond itself; a plant grows
downwards to the damp earth, and upwards towards the
light. There is thus some direct reason for attributing dim, slow feelings of causal nexus, although we
have no reason for any ascription of the definite percepts in the mode of presentational immediacy.

* * *

Symbolic reference between the two perceptive
modes affords the main example of the principles which
govern all symbolism. The requisites for symbolism are
that there be two species of percepta; and that a perceptum of one species has some 'ground' in common with
a perceptum of another species, so that a correlation
between the pair of percepta is established. The feelings, and emotions, and general characteristics associated with the members of one species are in some ways
markedly diverse from those associated with the other
species. Then there is 'symbolic reference' between
the two species when the perception of a member of one
species evokes its correlate in the other species, and
precipitates upon this correlate the fusion of feelings,
emotions, and derivate actions, which belong to either
of the pair of correlates, and which are also enhanced
by this correlation. The species from which the symbolic reference starts is called the 'species of symbols,' and the species which it ends is called the
'species of meanings.' In this way there can be symbolic reference between two species in the same perceptive mode: but the chief example of symbolism, upon
which is based a great portion of the lives of all high-
grade animals, is that between the two perceptive modes.

Symbolism can be justified, or unjustified. The
test of justification must always be pragmatic. In so
far symbolism has led to a route of inheritance, along
the percipient occasions forming the percipient 'person,' which constitutes a fortunate evolution, the symbolism is justified; and, in so far as the symbolism
has led to an unfortunate evolution, it is unjustified.
In a slightly narrower sense the symbolism can be right
or wrong; and rightness or wrongness is also tested
pragmatically. Along the 'historic route' there is the
inheritance of feelings derived from symbolic reference:

71

now, if feelings respecting some definite element in experience be due to two sources, one source being this inheritance, and the other source being direct perception in one of the pure modes, then, if the feelings from the two sources enhance each other by synthesis, the symbolic reference is right; but, if they are at variance so as to depress each other, the symbolic reference is wrong. The rightness, or wrongness, of symbolism is an instance of the symbolism being fortunate or unfortunate; but mere 'rectitude,' in the sense defined above, does not cover all that can be included in the more general concept of 'fortune.' So much of human experience is bound up with symbolic reference, that it is hardly an exaggeration to say that the very meaning of truth is pragmatic. But though this statement is hardly an exaggeration, still it is an exaggeration, for the pragmatic test can never work, unless on some occasion--in the future, or in the present--there is a definite determination of what is true on that occasion. Otherwise the poor pragmatist remains an intellectual Hamlet, perpetually adjourning decision of judgment to some later date. According to the doctrines here stated, the day of judgment arrives when the 'meaning' is sufficiently distinct and relevant, as a perceptum in its proper pure mode, to afford comparison with the precipitate of feeling derived from symbolic reference. There is no inherent distinction between the sort of percept which are symbols, and the sort of percepta which are meanings. When two species are correlated by a 'ground' of relatedness, it depends upon the experiential process, constituting the percipient subject, as to which species is the group of symbols, and which is the group of meanings. Also it equally depends upon the percipient as to whether there is any symbolic reference at all.

Language is the example of symbolism which most naturally presents itself for consideration of the uses of symbolism. Its somewhat artificial character makes the various constitutive elements in symbolism to be the more evident. For the sake of simplicity, only spoken language will be considered here.

A single word is not one definite sound. Every instance of its utterance differs in some respect from every other instance: the pitch of the voice, the intonation, the accent, the quality of sound, the rhythmic relations of the component sounds, the intensity of sound, all vary. Thus a word is a species of sounds, with specific identity and individual differences.

72

When we recognize the species, we have heard the word. But what we have heard is merely the sound--euphonious or harsh, concordant with or discordant with other accompanying sounds. The word is heard in the pure perceptive mode of immediacy, and primarily elicits merely the contrasts and identities with other percepta in that mode. So far there is no symbolic interplay.

If the meaning of the word be an event, then either that event is directly known, as a remembered perceptum in an earlier occasion of the percipient's life, or that event is only vaguely known by its dated spatio-temporal nexus with events which are directly known. Anyhow there is a chain of symbolic references (inherited along the historic route of the percipient's life, and reinforced by the production of novel and symbolic references at various occasions along that route) whereby in the datum for the percipient occasion there is a faintly relevant nexus between the word in that occasion of utterance and the event. The sound of the word in presentational immediacy, by symbolic references elicits this nexus into important relevance, and thence precipitates feelings, and thoughts, upon the enhanced objectification of the event. Such enhanced relevance of the event may be unfortunate, or even unjustified; but it is the function of words to produce it. The discussion of mentality is reserved for Part III: it is a mistake to think of words as primarily the vehicle of thoughts.

Language also illustrates the doctrine that, in regard to a couple of properly correlated species of things, it depends upon the constitution of the percipient subject to assign which species is acting as 'symbol' and which as 'meaning.' The word 'forest' may suggest of memories of forests; but equally the sight of a forest, or memories of forests, may suggest the word 'forest.' Sometimes we are bothered because the immediate experience has not elicited the word we want. In such a case the word with the right sort of correlation with the experience has failed to become importantly in the constitution of our experience.

But we do not usually think of the things as symbolizing the words correlated to them. This failure to invert our ideas arises from the most useful aspect of symbolism. In general the symbols are more handy elements in our experience than are the meanings. We can say the word 'forest' whenever we like; but only under certain conditions can we directly experience an existent forest. To procure such an experience usually involves a problem of transportation only possible on our holidays. Also it is not so easy even to remember forest scenes with any vividness; and we usually find that the immediate experience of the word 'forest' helps to elicit such recollections. In such ways language is handy as an instrument of communication along the successive occasions of the historic route forming the life of one individual. By an extension of these same principles of behaviour, it communicates from the occasions of one individual to the succeeding occasions of another individual. The same means which are handy for procuring the immediate presentation of a word to oneself are equally effective for presenting it to another person. Thus we may have a two-way system of symbolic reference involving two persons, A and B. The forest, recollected by A, symbolizes the word 'forest' for A; then A, for his own sake and for B's sake, pronounces the word 'forest'; then by the efficacy of the environment and of B's bodily parts, and by the supplemental enhancement due to B's experiential process, the word 'forest' is perceived by B in the mode of immediacy; and, finally by symbolic reference, B recollects vaguely various forest scenes. In this use of language for communication between two persons, there is in principle nothing which differs from its use by one person for communication along the route of his own actual occasions.

This discussion shows that one essential purpose of symbols arises from their handiness. For this reason the Egyptian papyrus made ink-written language a more useful symbolism than the Babylonian language impressed on brick. It is easier to smell incense than to produce certain religious emotions; so, if the two can be correlated, incense is a suitable symbol for such emotions. Indeed, for many purposes, certain aesthetic experiences which are easy to produce make better symbols than do words, written or spoken. Quarrels over symbolism constitute one of the many causes of religious discord. One difficulty in symbolism is that the unhandy meanings are often vague. For instance, this is the case with the percepta in the mode of efficacy which are symbolized by percepta in the mode of immediacy: also, as another instance, the incense is definite, but the religious emotions are apt to be indefinite. The result is that the meanings are often shifting and indeterminate. This happens even in the case of words: other people misunderstand their import. Also, in the case of incense the exact religious

74

emotions finally reached are very uncertain: perhaps we would prefer that some of them were never elicited.

Symbolism is essential for the higher grades of life; and the errors of symbolism can never be wholly avoided.

FOOTNOTES

[1]Cf. my Barbour-Page lectures, <u>Symbolism, Its</u> <u>Meaning and Importance</u>, delivered at the University of Virginia, April, 1927. Macmillan. Another discussion of this question is there undertaken, with other illustrations. Cf. also Professor Norman Kemp Smith's <u>Prolegomena to an Idealist Theory of Knowledge</u>, Macmillan, 1924.

[2]Cf. my <u>Principles of Natural Knowledge</u>, Ch. XI, and my <u>Concept of Nature</u>, Ch. V.

[3]Cf. Book I, Part I, Sects. II and VI (italics mine).

SUGGESTED READINGS

Alfred North Whitehead

Whitehead, A. N. The Organization of Thought (London: Williams and Norgate, 1917).

_____. Symbolism, Its Meaning and Effect (New York: Macmillan, 1927).

_____. Process and Reality (New York: Macmillan, 1929), pp. 3-54.

_____. The Function of Reason (Princeton: Princeton University Press, 1929).

_____. Modes of Thought (New York: Macmillan, 1938).

* * *

Cory, D. "Whitehead on Perception," The Journal of Philosophy, 30 (1933), 29-43.

Kultgen, J. H. "Whitehead's Epistemology 1915-1917," Journal of the History of Philosophy, 4 (1966), 43-61.

Ritchie, A. D. "Whitehead's Defense of Speculative Reason," The Philosophy of Alfred North Whitehead (Evanston: Northwestern University Press, 1941), pp. 329-349. P. A. Schilpp (Ed.).

* * *

Blyth, J. W. Whitehead's Theory of Knowledge (New York: Brown University Press, 1941).

Emmet, D. M. The Nature of Metaphysical Thinking (London: Macmillan, 1945).

Hill, T. E. Contemporary Theories of Knowledge (New York: Ronald Press, 1961), pp. 265-290.

Langer, S. K. Mind: An Essay on Human Feeling
(Baltimore: John Hopkins University Press,
1973.

Murphy, A. The Uses of Reason (New York: Macmillan, 1944).

Schmidt, P. F. Perception and Cosmology in Whitehead's Philosophy (New Brunswick: Rutgers University Press, 1967).

3.   TOWARD A WIDENING OF THE NOTION OF CAUSALITY

Milic Capek

Professor Milic Capek has concerned himself
throughout his career with the interpretation
of science. This concern is evident in the
titles of his two major works The Philosophical Impact of Contemporary Physics (1961)
and Bergson and Modern Physics (1971). In
both books and in numerous articles he has
argued forcefully for the view that twentieth
century physics involves a profound transformation of our habitual ways of viewing nature.

In this article,* Capek begins with Democritus
and traces the career of the doctrine of strict determinism briefly through the centuries, pointing out not
only that basic features of the concept of strict determinism remain virtually unchanged in such modern
thinkers as Laplace, Du Bois-Reymond, and Anatole
France, but that these features permeated the Medieval
mind, which tended strongly toward theological determinism. The difficulties of theological determinism
were inadvertently made clear by early modern panthe-
ists like Giordano Bruno and Spinoza, who identified
God with nature, thereby fusing theological and scientific determinisms. These thinkers saw clearly that
if the future of God (i.e., for them, of Nature) is
strictly predetermined, the future preexists and is simultaneous with the present. But in that case succession is a mere appearance. Time is unreal. This remarkably non-intuitive conception, though warmly embraced by Spinoza and certain philosophical idealists,
has seemed particularly unsatisfying to the scientifically minded, who can scarcely hold that time, motion,
succession are unreal. Many scientists and philosophers, hence, have held both that succession is real

*This article is from the journal Diogenes, 28
(1959), 63-90. Used by the permission of Diogène:
Revue internationale des sciences humaines and Professor Capek.

and that events are strictly determined. Capek argues, however, that succession and strict determinism are logically incompatible. Strict determinists, he says, must hold that the connections between successive events are necessary connections. But to say this is to say that future events can be deduced from past events; and logical relations of implication (which are involved in all deduction) are non-temporal. What we deduce to (the conclusion) is simultaneous with what we deduce from (the premise or premises). Inference merely discovers the preexisting conclusion, as Columbus discovered a preexistent America. Many have feared that to admit a degree of indetermination in events and thereby deny strict determinism is to open the door to intellectual chaos, destroying the concept of cause and effect on which knowledge is based. In fact, to admit limited indeterminism is simply to admit a broadened notion of causality, thereby making causality more comprehensible while at the same time clearing it of paradoxical consequences.

Toward a Widening of the Notion of Causality

If we wish to speak of the widening of the idea of causality, we must first specify the exact meaning of this concept, the modification of which is now being considered by many contemporary philosophers and scientists. In order to shed light on the classical concept of causality, it is almost impossible to avoid approaching it from the genetic point of view. Without a historical perspective we have only a very limited understanding of the content of the classical concepts by which this philosophic as well as scientific tradition has been constituted. By showing the deep and tenacious roots of our belief in rigorous determinism, we shall better understand certain types of resistance which today are opposed to any attempt at making determinism more flexible.

It is no exaggeration to say that the belief in strict determinism is almost as old as Western thought itself. Without discussing the mythical belief in an impersonal "destiny" to which even the gods were submitted, we find the first precise formulation of determinism in Democritus, when he writes: "All things are determined by necessity, things that have been, things which are, and things which are going to happen." Twenty-two centuries after Democritus, Laplace expressed the same conviction, based on a conception of the universe which does not differ essentially from that of Greek atomism:

> Given for one instant an intelligence which could comprehend all the forces by which nature is animated and the respective situation of the beings who compose it--an intelligence sufficiently vast to submit these data to analysis--it would embrace in the same formula the movements of the greatest bodies of the universe and those of the lightest atom; for it, nothing would be uncertain and the future, as the past, would be present to its eyes.[1]

It is true that there is a very important difference between the determinism of Democritus and that of Laplace. The latter possessed a conceptual apparatus far more complex and flexible than the former. This is only natural; in the interval of time which separated Greek determinism from modern determinism, there

occurred two events, which were, moreover, very closely
associated with each other: the discovery of infinitesimal calculus and the founding of classical mechanics. The laws of mechanics, especially the law of inertia and of the conservation of the quantity of motion
and of energy, were only guessed at by the Greek atomists, and their precise formulation had to await the
cosmological revolution of Copernicus and Giordano
Bruno. It is still true, however, that Democritus insisted just as vigorously as did Laplace and the modern
determinists on the absence of contingency in nature.
It is also true that in other respects Democritus anticipated certain aspects of Newtonian physics, for example, the infinity and the homogeneity of space, as
well as the qualitative unity of matter, its permanence,
and its atomic structure. Thus we see the justification of the Meyerson thesis, according to which, philosophically speaking, the difference between Greek
atomism and classical physics is one of degree and not
of nature, which means that, given the close connection
between the corpuscular models of nature and absolute
determinism, the distinction between the "necessity"
(ἀνάγκn) of Democritus and the "necessity" of Laplace
is also a difference of degree.

Laplace's formula, so frequently quoted, has been
expressed many times in more concrete and more colorful
language, pointing out clearly that not only inorganic
nature but also the most concrete details--and, in appearance, the most contingent details--of human history
are only parts of the same network of universal necessity by which all effects are joined to their causes.
According to Du Bois-Reymond, Laplacian intelligence
would be capable of deducing the most insignificant details as well as the most important events of human
history from its huge system of differential equations.
It matters little if the events to be deduced belong to
the past or to the future. However, it would be a serious mistake to think that rigorous determinism had
never been associated with any philosophic system other
than the mechanistic and materialistic ones. The doctrine of absolute necessity, which implies the integral
predetermination of the future, represents a tendency
which is present in idealism as well as in naturalism,
at least in their classical forms.

A brief survey of the history of philosophy will
show that this conclusion is not so paradoxical as it
may seem. Rigorous determinism has appeared three
times in the history of Western thought: in ancient

82

Greece, in the Middle Ages, and in the science of Galileo and Newton. As we have already stated, it appeared for the first time in the system of Leucippus and of Democritus. By placing the name of Democritus beside that of Laplace, we have already indicated that the modern form of determinism differs only in degree from its classical form. The global vision of reality is, on all essential points, the same in Greek atomism as in Newtonian physics: the universe is composed of little grains of homogenous matter which move according to strict laws. All diversity of nature is due to differences in configuration and in motion. Any qualitative transformation is only an appearance produced by the changes in position of particles which always remain the same. Any contingency and any novelty are merely illusions due to our ignorance. Thus it is scarcely an exaggeration to say that the first and the third forms of determinism differ only in details which, however important they may be for the historian of the sciences, are of secondary importance from the philosophical point of view.

In the period which separated Greek atomism and Newtonian mechanics, there appeared a second form of determinism which seemed to be completely different. This was the theological determinism, which found its most striking expression in the doctrine of predestination. This form of determinism has certainly been no less rigid than the naturalistic determinism of the Greek and of the modern period. All the concessions--verbal ones, moreover--which have been made by theologians to the notion of human freedom were inspired by motives which were completely foreign to the doctrine itself. Human freedom, in the systems of Augustine, of Thomas, and of the Protestant reformers, is as incompatible with the doctrine of absolute predeterminism as the clinamen of Lucretius was with his mechanistic system. The modern doctrine of absolute necessity is, according to Professor Charles Hartshorne, the result of the "secret alliance" between naturalistic determinism and theological determinism.[2] An assertion of this kind is less surprising when we take into account the common historical origin of these two determinisms. We intend to show that this common source is the philosophy of Parmenides of Elea, whose decisive influence on the development of Western thought is probably without parallel.

The Eleatic origin of Greek atomism is generally recognized. It is known that Leucippus and Democritus,

according to Windelband's picturesque expression,
"broke Parmenides' sphere into little pieces" which
move through empty space according to strict laws.
Parmenides' principle of the permanence of Being became
the principle of the conservation of matter of the atomists, who, on this point also, anticipated another
discovery of modern science. It is true that there are
important differences between Democritus and Parmenides. The latter is a monist, while the former was a
pluralist. Parmenides denied all change; Democritus
admitted at least the reality of change of position.
But, despite these differences, there is a profound
kinship. Democritus' atom is as permanent, that is, as
uncreatable and indestructible, as Parmenidean Being.
The quantity of matter which it contains always remains
the same. Its essential quality, that is, its pleni-
tude, remains as absolute and as immutable as the same
quality in the Eleatic Being. If the atomists admitted
change, they admitted it in its most innocuous form,
that is, in the form of change of place, which affects
neither the total quantity nor the quality of Being.
The change admitted by the atomists is change in the
spatial relations of atoms, that is, change which is
only half-real. For the void of the atomists, although
different from the pure non-Being of Parmenides, does
not have the same degree of reality as matter itself.
Consequently, the changing of relations in the void is
doubly removed from the primordial reality of the substantial plenum. Since the time of Democritus, change,
as well as multiplicity, is admitted by philosophers;
no one, not even Spinoza or Bradley, returned to static
monism, as radical and as arrogant as that of the Ele-
atics. However, the influence of the latter was strong
enough to induce most philosophers to regard change and
plurality as semireal, that is, as not possessing the
same dignity as the underlying Being which remains one
and immutable. As Émile Meyerson has shown in his
classical works, static monism has remained an ideal
model which, although never attained, has inspired
philosophic systems as well as scientific explanations.

The continuity of theological determinism with Eleatic philosophy is probably less known and less evident, but it remains no less real. Space does not per-
mit us to give a detailed historical analysis; we shall
merely sketch the essential points. What is certain is
that the fusion of the idea of Good with that of One,
proposed for the first time by Euclid of Megara, and
later accepted by Plato and Plotinus, had a profound
influence on the formation of Christian theology. In

spite of all the differences between Neo-Platonism and the philosophy of Aristotle, the medieval idea of God has the same Eleatic traits. That is why all the eminent Christian philosophers, such as Augustine, Johannes Scotus Erigena, Anselm, and Thomas, identify God with Being, which is One, indivisible, and absolutely immutable--for no change, however insignificant it may be, is compatible with the supreme perfection and incorruptibility of the divine Being. We must not forget that all change, all development, all succession, were regarded by the Christian theologians--as they were, moreover, by the Jewish and Moslem theologians--in a completely Platonistic and Eleatic way, as a corruption unworthy of the absolute perfection of the supreme Being.

The transition from theological determinism to modern naturalistic determinism was not a sudden one. The most important transitional phases were the pantheism of Bruno and, a century later, that of Spinoza. In medieval theology pantheism was only virtual, although several eminent thinkers were coming close to it; but, as long as the duality of the world and of God remained preserved by the very structure of the Aristotelian world, that is, by the duality of the celestial world and the sublunar world, lurking pantheism could not become explicit. But when Giordano Bruno swept away the last sphere of the fixed stars, which was still retained by Copernicus, and when he thus proclaimed the unity of nature in the infinity of cosmic space, the way was open to the explicit and heretical pantheism which could replace the Deus et Natura of the Scholastics with the Deus sive Natura of Spinoza. We know the profound upheaval which this passage from medieval theism to modern pantheism produced in the sixteenth and seventeenth centuries. But we must not forget that the revolutionary character of modern pantheism was only apparent, because it was virtually present in the thought of theologians before the Renaissance. That explains why the God of Bruno and of Spinoza possessed the same Eleatic traits as the God of medieval theology and of Neo-Platonistic philosophy. Let us remember this conclusion, which is of capital importance: the causal order of classical knowledge is a metaphysical entity which is outside of time and which thus implies a radical denial of succession.

* * * * *

Thus, if we accept strict determinism in all its consequences, we are faced with this question: Why do we have the appearance, or, if one prefers, the illu- sion, of time? What is the true place of succession in a strictly determined world? We have already empha- sized the fact that no one after Parmenides had had the audacity to deny the reality of time and of change in such a complete and radical manner as the School of Elea had done. A rather curious compromise was gener- ally preferred: becoming, instead of being completely denied, was banished only from the metaphysical realm of the true Being to be lodged modestly in the region of phenomena. In other terms, ultimate reality was placed outside of time while the true Being was almost always regarded as static and immutable. It was only its phenomenal aspect--a surface aspect--which was con- sidered as unrolling in time. It matters little if this true Being was the Sphere of Parmenides, the Mat- ter of Democritus, the Ens realissimum of the medieval Scholastics, the Substance of Spinoza, the Ding an sich of Kant, the Unknowable of Spencer, the Absolute of Bradley, or the impersonal order of nature symbolized by the Universal Intelligence of Laplace--the conclu- sion always remained the same: time, change, succes- sion, becoming, do not belong to "reality in itself" but to the semireal region of phenomena. Thus the dy- namic aspect of reality was merely reduced in rank, or weakened, instead of being simply eliminated.

Although various explanations of the relation of the temporal and the eternal have been attempted, those who have done it have most often been satisfied with mere words. It has been compared to the relationship of the Perfect to the Imperfect, of the Original to its Copy; Aristotle would quickly have emphasized that such metaphors have no explanatory value and that the theory of the two regions of reality creates metaphysical dif- ficulties instead of solving them. However, this judg- ment did not stop Aristotle from remaining more Pla- tonic than he wished to, and, consequently, it did not stop philosophers from continuing to split reality in a more or less Platonic manner into two domains without explaining their relationship and, above all, without explaining the superfluity of the temporal.

A reconciliation of non-temporal reality with its successive and changing appearance is purely verbal [as is expressed, for example, in Spinoza's word "quatenus"][3] but at least these philosophic prestidigitations, by their very vanity, reveal the impossibility of eliminating succession and change. The temporal character of experience is too authentic and too obstinate to be ignored, and the fact that even static monism in its most varied forms at least recognizes its "phenominal," that is, its semireal, character without simply denying it, is very significant. It was only natural that scientists and even philosophers inspired by science, and who, for that reason, were less obsessed with subtle metaphysical problems, did not hesitate to admit the reality of time, frankly and without reservations. However, they also believed, as late as the beginning of this century--and there are many who still believe it even today--that the authentically temporal character of the world is compatible with the most rigorous determinism. Is this true? Are temporality and determinism of the Laplacian type truly compatible? We are now facing the basic question of this article. Upon our answer will depend our attitude toward the general question of determinism and indeterminism.

At first glance, the question so stated seems strange and almost devoid of meaning because the answer given to it by common sense is completely clear and negative: there is no incompatibility between succession and strict determinism. From the days of the mythical belief in Destiny to the Newtonian concept of strict causality this answer has not varied. This is only natural. Nothing seems more familiar than the notion of the temporal process the phases of which, although strictly determined, are nevertheless successive. All classical scientific thought, not only in the physical sciences, but also in the biological and social sciences, is based on, or appears to be based on, the idea of the necessary connection of successive events. The association between the idea of succession and that of causality is so close and so familiar that, before the French contingentists and especially before Bergson, no one questioned their compatibility. Kant, followed on this point by many others, instead of questioning the compatibility of causal necessity and temporal succession, insisted on their inseparability; for him, the only way of saving freedom was to put it outside of time. Even after Bergson people continued to believe the same thing and were surprised if the question was raised. This is, moreover, only natural. Even among physicists today the question of the strict

determinism of phenomena is still being debated. Before discussing briefly the changes which have taken
place in contemporary physics, we must first expose a
serious difficulty which arises for all who claim that
the necessary determination of events is compatible
with their successive character.

What, then, is the precise meaning of the concept
of necessary connection between two successive events?
There is agreement on this point: if we affirm that
event b follows necessarily after event a, we are af-
firming that all the particular traits of the former
can be deduced from the latter; supposing our knowledge
of a certain event to be complete, there would be no
uncertainty even about the most individual and apparently most contingent details of any future event whatsoever. According to the determinists, there is in
principle no difference between the causal determination of physical events and the necessity of historical
events--there are only differences of complexity. It
is only their complexity which makes the prediction of
events in society so difficult. However, "social physics" does not differ essentially from physics conceived
in its original sense. In the one as in the other, the
present state implies, without any ambiguity, all future states.

However, by this very assertion, a determinist encounters a difficulty which, in my opinion, is insurmountable. It is known that any logical implication is
ex definitione non-temporal. It is a commonplace in
elementary courses of logic to distinguish logical implication, which is outside of time, from the psychological process of inference by which we deduce a conclusion from premises. Although, psychologically
speaking, the conclusion is preceded by the premises,
that is, preceded in the temporal sense, it nevertheless remains true that, logically speaking, there is no
succession, no unrolling, in the temporal sense of the
word. And let no one be deceived by the ambiguity of
the word "flow"; there is no logical flow in the temporal sense of the word. If we say that the conclusion
"flows" from the premises, we are using this word only
in the metaphorical sense. A logical antecedent is not
a temporal antecedent; a logical sequence has nothing
in common with temporal succession. The premises are
not, in the temporal sense, before the conclusion, and,
in the same way, the conclusion does not follow the
premises in time. It is more exact to say that the
conclusion pre-exists in the premises or that it is

contained in them logically. We discover it after the
premises in the actual process of human thought, but we
do not create it by that process itself. The simultaneity of the conclusion with the premises can be illustrated in a convincing way by analyzing a form of classical syllogism: All men are mortal; Socrates is a
man; consequently, Socrates is mortal. Or, in symbols:
All M are P; all S are M; consequently, all S are P.
It is obvious that the expression "consequently" has no
temporal meaning. One is easily persuaded of this if
he draws the famous Euler's circles, which symbolize
the classes, or the logical extensions in question.
Not only is class M contained in class P at the same
time that class S is contained in class M but it is
easy to see that class S is contained at the same time
in class P. In other words, the conclusion and the
premises are simultaneous. The very possibility of
symbolizing logical relationships of inclusion by spatial diagrams whose parts are, by their very nature,
juxtaposed, therefore simultaneous, is the reason for
this. For there is not a trace of succession in the
relationship of inclusion, that is, in the relationship
of container and contents. Unquestionably, every conclusion coexists in the logical sense with its premises, although it is thought and pronounced after the
premises.

We must not confine our attention to one particular example of the traditional syllogism, for the pre-
existence of the conclusion is postulated in every
valid reasoning. That is why we say that we discover
the truth, instead of saying that we create it. Just
as in the classical syllogism the inclusion of class S
in class P coexists with the two inclusions symbolizing
the two premises, so in the solving of a mathematical
equation, for example, the "unknown" quantity is determined in advance without any ambiguity; thus it is unknown only to us, and we discover it in the same way
that Columbus discovered America. We say that the solution is simply waiting for our discovery, that it
exists, so to speak, before our discovery, just as the
American continent existed before the voyage of Columbus. In the same way, if the future is determined in
all its details and without any ambiguity, have we not
the right to conclude with Laplace that it is already
present and that it is merely waiting to be unveiled to
our limited consciousness?

But, if that is true, the same question we have
already asked arises again: Where does the illusion

89

of succession come from? The incompatibility of causal necessity with the fact of succession was fully emphasized by several French thinkers of the second half of the nineteenth century, such as Jules Lequier, Charles Renouvier, Émile Boutroux, Joseph Delboeuf, and, finally, Henri Bergson. Outside France, it was principally Charles S. Peirce and William James--the latter influenced, at least partially, first by Renouvier and later by Bergson--who insisted on the reality of objective contingency as an essential element of temporal reality. But the intellectual climate of that time was not very favorable to the ideas of this kind. The principle of causality appeared as a simple consequence of the law of conservation of energy (Spencer's law of persistence of force), which in its turn expressed in a new and much more precise way the ancient principle of the indestructibility of substance. This law was considered a sacred dogma, not only by virtue of the empirical evidence in its favor, but also because it was looked upon as a prolongation, and even as a culmination, of the tendencies which had dominated philosophic thought since its beginnings. It is only quite recently that, under the pressure of the new physical discoveries, we have begun to treat the concept of objective contingency with more tolerance. Nevertheless, in Boutroux's time, and even in Bergson's, necessitarian dogmatism, to use Peirce's expression, continuously strengthened by the triumphs of scientific prediction and by the constantly repeated successes of mathematical deduction in the physical sciences, so fascinated minds that almost no one paid any attention to Bergson when he showed that absolute necessity and real succession cannot be reconciled. In his Creative Evolution, in a passage which has become classical, Bergson pointed out that the equations of mechanics are concerned only with the extremities of temporal intervals while the intervals themselves are ignored. Even when we talk about them, we scarcely attach any importance to them:

> Common sense, which is occupied with detached objects, and also science, which considers isolated systems, are concerned only with the ends of the intervals and not with the intervals themselves. Therefore the flow of time might assume an infinite rapidity, the entire past, present, and future of material objects or of isolated systems might be spread out all at once in space without there being anything to change either in the

90

formulae of the scientist or even in the language of common sense. The number t would always stand for the same thing; it would still count the same number of correspondences between the states of the objects or systems and the points of the line, ready drawn, which would be then the "course of time."[4]

Several pages farther on, after having quoted the famous passage from Laplace, Bergson adds:

In such a doctrine, time is still spoken of: one pronounces the word, but one does not think of the thing. For time is here deprived of efficacy, and if it _does_ nothing, it _is_ nothing.[5]

Bergson was probably not entirely right when he affirmed that a determinist pronounces the word "time" without thinking of real succession. The state of mind of an average determinist is certainly more complex, and it was more accurately analyzed by Bergson in his first book, where he showed that belief in the necessary connection of events consists in the association of two irreconcilable ideas: that of logical necessity which requires the preformation and even the pre-existence of the future, which ceases to be future by the very reason of its pre-existence, and the idea of the temporal process of which the phases are authentically successive.[6] These two ideas are combined in such a close association that they are almost inseparable, and their incompatibility, their very distinction, is, as it were, submerged by the deceptive feeling of familiarity which is only an effect of habit, of prolonged automatization. After Bergson, philosophers should have shown more mistrust in respect to such deceptive feelings of familiarity.

More frequently, the incompatibility between real succession and deductive necessity was only vaguely felt, but this vague feeling at least found its expression in certain particularities of language, invented to hide the incompatibility. The difference between cause and effect is too real to be entirely ignored. There is nothing surprising in the fact that the feeling of this difference is not entirely absent, even in the most uncompromising determinist mind. However as the determinist insists on the absolute equivalence of cause and effect, unwittingly he faces a dilemma of

91

which he is only half-aware. According to what we have
said, it is obviously necessary to choose one of two
assertions: either real succession with the element of
real contingency or complete determinism with the total
absence of succession. Since most frequently the deterministic scientist does not see this dilemma clearly, he tries to retain causal necessity alongside temporal succession, but, as these two ideas are incompatible, he succeeds only in veiling with ingenious verbal
formulas the conflict which goes on in the depths of
his thinking. What is more, this conflict, as we have
already said, suppressed by his conscious thought, man-
ifests itself indirectly by certain particularities of
his language. William James showed this in a very
clear and precise way in his posthumous book:

> Nemo dat quod non habet is the real
> principle from which the causal philosophy
> flows; and the proposition causa aequat ef-
> fectum practically sums up the whole of it.
> . . . But if the maxim holds firm that quid-
> quid est in effectu debet esseprius aliquo
> modo in causa, it follows that the next mo-
> ment can contain nothing genuinely original,
> and that the novelty that appears to leak
> into our lives so unremittingly, must be an
> illusion, ascribable to the shallowness of
> the perceptual point of view. Scholasticism
> always respected common sense, and in this
> case escaped the frank denial of all genuine
> novelty by the vague qualification "aliquo
> modo." This allowed the effect also to dif-
> fer, aliquo modo, from its cause. But con-
> ceptual necessities have ruled the situation
> and have ended, as usual, by driving nature
> and perception to the wall. A cause and its
> effect are two numerically discrete concepts,
> and yet in some inscrutable way the former
> must "produce" the latter. How can it in-
> telligibly do so, save by already hiding the
> latter in itself?[7]

And in a footnote on the next page James adds:

> The cause becomes a reason, the effect
> a consequence; and since logical consequence
> follows only from the same to the same, the
> older vaguer causation-philosophy develops
> into the sharp rationalistic dogma that cause
> and effect are two names for one persistent

being, and that if the successive moments
of the universe be causally connected, no
genuine novelty leaks in.

There is no need to emphasize how that which James
calls "the sharp rationalistic dogma" agreed with the
energetist conception of reality, in which the cause
and its effect were only two energy equivalents, the
apparent succession of which masked their underlying
identity. Thus, as in the monistic idealisms, ultimate
and authentic reality is conceived of as permanent and
as always identical with itself, whereas succession belongs only to its phenomenal manifestations. To avoid
conflict with our immediate consciousness, which remains irremediably temporal, both physical determinism
and idealistic determinism invent ingenious formulas.
Instead of denying the reality of time outright, one
says that time is only "phenomenal"; instead of saying
that the effect is entirely identical with its cause,
one says that it is "virtually," or aliquo modo, present. Through these verbal concessions, it is possible
to avoid the truthless conclusion of Parmenides, which
by eliminating succession entirely at the same time
eliminates even the superficial difference between
cause and effect. Let us say it again: if modern determinism, in its scientific as well as in its idealistic form, hesitates to follow the Eleatic School all
the way, it is because the incompatibility of rigorous
determinism with the reality of time is at least vaguely sensed.

* * * * *

If we admit that absolute necessity is incompatible with the reality of succession, a single conclusion
forces itself upon us. We must abandon the classical
concept, that is, the Laplacian or Spinozist concept of
causality. Such a conclusion frightens many serious
thinkers. They are frightened because they believe
that, with the denial of classical determinism, the intelligible character of the world is forever destroyed.
For them the denial of classical causality is equivalent to a "capitualation," even to a "suicide," of reason. Similar apprehensions were expressed when non-
Euclidean geometry supplanted the classical geometry of
Euclid. Naturally, if one looks upon Euclidean geometry as the only possible geometry, such fears would be
justified. In that case, and only in that case, the

denial of the fifth postulate of Euclid would result in the ruin of all geometric thought. In an analogous way, if Laplacian causality is the only form of rational coherence which the universe may assume, there would be a reason for fearing that, in eliminating it, we might destroy all possibility of rational explanation. The arguments of Herbert Spencer, John Fiske, Hippolyte Taine, and all the other determinists of the last century against free will were inspired by this facile confusion of the two terms "rational" and "determinist." As William James remarked in 1884 in his essay "The Dilemma of Determinism":

> Nevertheless, many persons talk as if the minutest dose of disconnectedness of one part with another, the smallest modicum of independence, the faintest tremor of ambiguity about the future, for example, would ruin everything, and turn this goodly universe into a sort of insane sand-heap or nulliverse, no universe at all.[8]

In other words, it is believed that, without strict causality, the world is only the domain of the most capricious chance. It is feared that the rational universe may crumble into a shapeless mass of disjoined and capricious facts.

Let us say immediately that such fears are hardly justified because they are based on the gratuitous supposition that the indetermination now being envisaged is a complete and, so to speak, absolute indetermination. Now this is not at all the case. Absolute determinism is a very rare phenomenon, even with philosophers. It can be found in Epicurus and in Lucretius and, in the modern era, in Renouvier, at least in a certain phase of his philosophy when he was defending the notion of "absolute beginning." But, if we read carefully the works of those who defend the indetermination of the universe in the name of the reality of time, we see that their indeterminism is far from being absolute. The temporalistic philosophers, or, as they are called in English-speaking countries, the "process-philosophers," insist vigorously on the continuity of the past with the present, on the cohesion of the successive phases of becoming. Reread the passages of William James on the stream of consciousness or on the continuity of the perceptual flux; reread Bergson, especially that passage, so infrequently quoted, in Matter and Memory, where he affirms that creation is never creatio ex nihilo because each present moment is colored by its past; reread Whitehead when he speaks of "causal efficacy" in nature.[9] What, then, is the difference which separates them from the classical determinists? There is only one: when they speak of connection, of continuity, of cohesion of cause and of effect, they affirm that this connection, this continuity, this cohesion, is temporal in the true sense of the word, and as such it cannot be the equivalent of static connection, of logical implication; consequently, that it must contain an element of irreducible novelty, an authentic differentiation between cause and effect, a differentiation which has in it nothing irrational and nothing miraculous because it expresses the distance between the present and the anterior moment. Briefly, if we venture to use a formula which is perhaps too condensed, we can say that for a modern contingentist time truly flows and that the partial indetermination of each temporal moment is only a manifestation of this real flow, whereas, for the classical determinists, time flows, according to Bergson's expression, only because reality demands this sacrifice, "taking advantage of an inadvertence in their logic."[10] We can also say that, for modern contingentism, the future remains future, that is, virtual by its own nature, whereas for Spinoza, Laplace, and the others, the future is only a hidden present.

In recognizing the virtual character of the future, modern contingentism admits the category of possibility which, according to classical determinism, possesses no objective character, being only a manifestation of our ignorance. For Spinoza, for Hegel, and for Laplace, the real and the necessary are two synonymous expressions--for that which is not real is impossible. Consequently, there is no middle ground between the necessary and the impossible. That is why the future, being necessary, must be, for a consistent determinist, as actual as the present and as completed as the past. The unlikely and even absurd character of such a consequence has already been fully exposed by Émile Boutroux:

> It is to be admitted that all possibles are, in their essence, eternally actual; that the present is made up of the past and is big with the future, instead of being contingent, already exists in the mind of the one supreme purpose or understanding; and that the distinction between being and the possible is

but an illusion caused by the interposition of time between our point of view and things in themselves?

This doctrine is not only unwarranted and impossible of proof, it is also unintelligible. To say that each thing is actually all it is capable of being is to say that it unites and reconciles, within itself, contraries, which, from the knowledge we have of them, can exist only by replacing one another. But how can we conceive of these essences as formed of elements that are mutually exclusive?[11]

The fear that the elimination of rigorous causality may destroy all intelligibility of the universe is, let us say again, childish. On the contrary, it is contingentism which makes causality--or rather let us say causation (reserving the term "causality" for Laplacian causality)--more intelligible. We have seen that rigorous determinism virtually destroys the temporal character of reality as well as all the difference between cause and effect. But have we not then the right to wonder, along with Boutroux: "Would this also be a consequent, an effect, a change, if it differed from its antecedent neither in quantity nor in quality?"[12] By re-establishing the temporal character of causation, we escape the bizarre paradoxes of necessitarian determinism of which the determinists themselves were often unaware. But in thus restoring the real difference between cause and effect, we are conceding the reality of contingency, or at least of the element of contingency; for the difference between the successive phases of becoming is only another name for the element of contingency, of unpredictability, of radical novelty, which is the very essence of temporal causation.

Let us stress the fact that it is this notion of widened causation which contemporary physicists--or at least most contemporary physicists--are tending to adopt under the impact of recent discoveries. The concept of objective possibility, which was always looked upon as legitimate by the contingentists, comes into the field of science in the form of the concept of object probability. For the classical physicists the concept of probability was only a useful conceptual tool which could be used when the physical events were too complex to be analyzed in detail. However, nothing

objective corresponded to this conceptual fiction despite its practical utility. Such an attitude was entirely logical. If there are no real possibilities,
there are no real probabilities, either; for, as the
German physicist, Weizsäcker, quite recently observed,
the concept of probability is only the quantitative
form of the concept of possibility.

In the light of quantum physics we can today answer the objection which Ralph Barton Perry raised
against the Bergsonian affirmation of the incompatibility between rigorous necessity and the reality of
time.[13] It will be remembered that, according to Professor Perry, the simple fact of mechanical motion establishes irrefutably the compatibility of time with
rigorous necessity: a material particle, whose trajectory is entirely determined by the laws of mechanics,
nevertheless moves, that is, it occupies diverse positions in space in successive moments. But this example
is obviously borrowed from macroscopic (that is, from
classical) physics. Its plausibility and its apparent
clarity are completely deceptive in the light of recent
physics. The predictability of the positions of any
given macrophysical particle--and we observe only macrophysical particles--is only approximate and, as such,
remains entirely compatible with the fundamental contingency of underlying microphysical events. The predicted trajectory of a particle, which, in our macrophysical perspective, appears as a precise geometric
curve with no transverse thickness, is, in reality, a
thin tube, a bundle of possible routes, which, although
very thin, still has transversed dimensions corresponding to the quantic indeterminations of the future positions.[14] Thus even in the example considered by Professor Perry, the so-called route of the future is far
from being "the only possible route," because it is
composed in reality of the entire field of the possibilities, which, although very close to each other,
still remain distinct. In other words, it is only by
virtue of our macroscopic myopia that the field of the
diverse possibilities seems to shrink so that it appears finally as a precise infinitely thin line of "the
only possible route." There is no need to emphasize
that such expressions as "the only possible future
route" and "the necessary route of the future" are completely equivalent; classical determinism, by eliminating all the future possibilities save one, in fact
eliminated the category of possibility, which was thus
reduced to a human and temporary ignorance. In the
light of recent physics such an elimination of the

concept of possibility is no longer legitimate, although we understand how the character of the macroscopic world, as well as the limitations of our perception, made it inevitable before the time of quantum physics. Nor is there any need to emphasize that the concept of a solid and permanent particle is no longer adequate on the microphysical scale, since solidity itself is only an illusion--a necessary illusion, it is true--of our gross perception. The microscopic reality seems to be composed of <u>events</u> rather than of <u>things</u>. We may wonder to what extent the Eleatic and atomistic habits of our thinking have been determined by this "logic of solids," which, according to Bergson and Bachelard, is a subconscious foundation of the classical intelligence and which is virtually outlined in the very structure of our macroscopic perception. This is the question which the modern followers of Parmenides and Democritus do not ask themselves.

Not only quantum physics but also relativistic physics confirm the temporal, therefore contingentist, conception of reality. Such an affirmation may appear surprising because it is opposed to the rather widespread presumption according to which the fusion of time with space in the theory of relativity operates in favor of space and that the spacetime of Minkowski is a static entity in which the alleged successive phases of cosmic history coexist in their eternal juxtaposition. We do not have space here for a detailed critical analysis of this singular misunderstanding, to which Minkowski himself contributed. Let us merely remember the numerous criticisms made of this erroneous interpretation, from Langevin to Eddington and to Meyerson. Quite justifiably, we can affirm that the fusion of space with time operates, contrary to the easy popular notions, in favor of time and that, instead of the spatialization of time we have rather a temporalization, or at least a dynamization, of space.[15] Let us simply recall the fundamental principle of relativistic dynamics according to which there is an upper limit to the transmission of any causal action: this is the speed of the electromagnetic waves. This is, as Paul Langevin said, the speed limit of causality. Thus there are no instantaneous transmissions in nature; there are only successive connections. In other terms, the theory of relativity has boldly stressed the idea that <u>the effect is never contemporaneous with its cause</u> and that causation is always irremediably, and by its very nature, successive. We have already seen that the reality of contingency inevitably follows from the

successive character of causation. One may raise an
objection by pointing out that contingency is not at
all introduced into the theory of relativity. But that
is due to the macrophysical character of the theory--
the microphysical indetermination is, so to speak,
masked by the laws of the big numbers on the macrophysical scale, and that is why it has been discovered only
on the microphysical scale. But we must not be deceived here: the dynamic and unfinished character of
physical reality is as present on the macrophysical
scale as it is in the microcosm.

If real novelties exist even in the physical world,
there is nothing surprising about finding them in the
area of life and of consciousness. Moreover, almost
all the objections which have been raised against indetermination on the biological and psychological scale
have been inspired by dogmatic belief in physical determinism. It is obvious that the widening of the notion of causality creates a novel situation for the
problem of freedom. All the contingentists were aware
of it, although they have confused microphysical indeterminism with the freedom of living beings. But the
discussion of the very complex problem of relationships
between contingency and freedom would lie outside the
scope of this article.

FOOTNOTES

[1]Pierre Simon, Marquis de Laplace, A Philosophical Essay on Probabilities, trans. F. W. Truscott and F. L. Emory (New York: John Wiley and Sons, 1902), p. 4.

[2]Charles Hartshorne, "Contingency and the New Era in Metaphysics," Journal of Philosophy, XXIX (1932), 429.

[3]William James, A Pluralistic Universe (New York: Longmans, Green, 1909), p. 47.

[4]Creative Evolution, authorized trans. Arthur Mitchell (New York: Henry Holt, 1913), p. 9.

[5]Ibid., pp. 38-39.

[6]Time and Free Will, an Essay on the Immediate Data of Consciousness, authorized trans. (of Essai sur les données immédiates de la conscience) R. L. Pogson (New York: Macmillan, 1913), pp. 212-218.

[7]William James, Some Problems of Philosophy: A Beginning of an Introduction to Philosophy (New York: Longmans, Green, 1931), pp. 192-193 and n., p. 194.

[8]William James, "The Dilemma of Determinism," The Will to Believe, pp. 154-155.

[9]A. N. Whitehead, Process and Reality (Cambridge: Cambridge University Press, 1929), passim.

[10]H. Bergson, The Creative Mind, trans. (of La Pensée et le mouvant) Mabelle Andison (New York: Philosophical Library, 1946), p. 220.

[11]É. Boutroux, The Contingency of the Laws of Nature, trans. F. Rothwell (Chicago: Open Court, 1920), pp. 21-22.

[12]Ibid., p. 29.

[13]Cf. R. B. Perry, Present Philosophical Tendencies (New York: Longmans, Green, 1916), pp. 251-252.

[14]See my articles: "The Doctrine of Necessity Re-examined," Review of Metaphysics, V, 5 (1951), 40-55; "Relativity and the Status of Space," Ibid., IX, 2 (1955); and "La Théorie bergsonienne de la matière et la physique moderne," Review Philosophique, LXXVII (1953).

[15]Louis de Broglie, "L'Espace et le temps dans la physique quantique," Revue de métaphysique et de morale, LIV (1949), 119-120.

SUGGESTED READINGS

Milic Capek

Capek, Milic. The Philosophical Impact of Contemporary Physics (New York: D. Van Nostrand,
1961).

_____. Bergson and Modern Physics: A Re-
interpretation and Re-evaluation (Dordrecht-
Holland: D. Reidel Publishing Company, 1971).

* * *

_____. "The Doctrine of Necessity Re-
examined," Review of Metaphysics, V, (1951),
18-27.

* * *

Bohr, Niels. "Causality and Complementarity," in
Essays 1958-1962 on Atomic Physics and Human
Knowledge (New York: Vintage, 1966), pp. 1-7.

Broglie, Louis de. "The Concepts of Contemporary
Physics and Bergson's Idea on Time and Motion,"
in Bergson and the Evolution of Physics. Ed.
P. A. Y. Gunter (Knoxville: The University of
Tennessee Press, 1969), pp. 45-62.

Hanson, Norwood Russell. "The Copenhagen Inter-
pretation," in Arthur Coleman Danto and Sidney
Morgenbesser. Philosophy of Science (New York:
Meridan Books, 1960), pp. 450-470.

Wartofsky, Marx W. "Uncertainty, Indeterminacy,
and Complementarity," in Conceptual Foundations
of Scientific Thought (New York: Macmillan,
1968), pp. 337-343.

* * *

Brillouin, Leon. Scientific Uncertainty, and Information (New York: Academic Press, 1964).

Hanson, Norwood Russell. The Concept of the Posi-
    tron (Cambridge: At the University Press,
    1963).

Heisenberg. Physics and Philosophy: The Revolu-
    tion in Modern Science (New York: Harper and
    Brothers, 1958).

Lindeman, F. A. The Physical Significance of
    Quantum Theory (Oxford: Clarendon Press,
    1932).

4.   PERCEPTION AND COGNITION

Henry Nelson Wieman

Henry Nelson Wieman's intellectual biography
has been one stimulated by such teachers and
philosophers as: Ernest McAffee, Silas Evans,
Rudolf Eucken, Wilhelm Windelband, Ernst
Troeltsch, William Ernest Hocking, Henri
Bergson, Ralph Barton Perry, Josiah Royce,
John Dewey, Alfred North Whitehead, George
Herbert Mead, Charles Morris, Paul Tillich,
and Karl Barth.*

Henry Nelson Wieman was very early a student and
interpreter of process philosophy, and found the notion
of the immediacies of experience in keeping with his
method of empiricism which involved the combination of
observation and reason. As an heir of James and Whitehead, Wieman sought to express an epistemology in keeping with the element of creative activity and purposive
growth empirically and valuationally at work within the
world. In the exceptionally well written essay which
follows,# Dr. Wieman presents a theory of the generic
nature of perception. As a description of man's most
elemental feeling capacity it relates directly to experience as the foundation of the philosophy of organism,
and besides being a brilliant introduction to process
epistemology in general also serves as an excellent
propaedeutic to his later article on Creative Good.
According to Wieman, perception is to be understood as
the apprehension of something as a single unitary whole
with its parts so ordered that they are distinguishable
and vivify one another, and yet all together compose an

---

*Cf. Wieman's personal "Intellectual Autobiogra-
phy" in The Empirical Theology of Henry Nelson Wieman
(New York: Macmillan Press, 1963), pp. 3-18. Robert
W. Bretall (Ed.).

#This article is from The Journal of Philosophy,
XL, 3 (February 1943), 73-77. Used by permission.

indivisible being.+ The emphasis is thus placed upon perception in its deepest sense as an end in itself and not a means to any ulterior end. What we ordinarily perceive, he insists, is infinitesimally small in comparison to the density and fullness of being which is there to be perceived when proper selection is made and all the powers of perception are aroused. The powers of perception include, in addition to sensation and sensitivity, all the resources of imagination, of intellectual interpretation and comprehension, evaluative judgement, aspiration, hope and fear, together with the total system of habits and impulses built up through a lifetime of struggle with the difficulties and triumphs of human existence. All these resources of the individual are exercised when perception reaches its maximum compass, clarity and truth. The whole of one's life, in a sense, can be poured into the act of perception! To perceive anything in the full depth of its being is then to perceive its relation to what Wieman calls man's ultimate commitment to the Creative Good.°

+Cf. The Empirical Theology of Henry Nelson Wieman (New York: Macmillan, 1963), pp. 241ff. Robert W. Bretall (Ed.).

°See specifically "Intrinsic, Instrumental, and Creative Value," The Journal of Philosophy, XLII (March 1945), 180-185; and "Experience, Mind, and Concept," The Journal of Philosophy, XXI (October 1924), 651-672.

Perception and Cognition

Recent discussion of perception and how it participates in cognition has led to the interpretation here presented.[1] For sake of brevity I shall not discuss in detail the points raised by these writers but shall state the outcome of my analysis of the issues they raise, and the tentative conclusions reached by debating with them. My attempt is to carry a little farther the work done by Lewis, Dewey, Pepper, Hahn, and others. Perhaps I do not carry their work any farther, but in any case I am working on the problem in somewhat the same way that they have done.

I can get most directly at the heart of what I want to say by beginning with the difference between true and false perception. When I perceive what looks like a ghost, or when one pencil becomes two with a shift of my eyeglasses, or my double appears behind the mirror, I am not having false perceptions. Such perceptions exemplify the way my psychophysical organism must react under the conditions there present. If it did not react regularly in this way under such conditions I could never achieve true perception. True perception is achieved by discovering the conditions under which certain kinds of perceptual events occur and thereby being able to infer that certain past perceptual events and future possibilities are related to the present one according to a certain structure of interrelatedness. If I perceive a tree or table truly it is because I know that my present perceptual event is related to past perceptual events and possibilities in a certain definite way. This I could never know if my mind and body did not react according to certain regularities and these regularities are exemplified just as faithfully when I see mirages and pink rats and ghosts as when I see sugar on the table and grass in the lawn.

If this view of the matter be correct, a perceptual event taken by itself alone is never either true or false. Only propositions about how it is related to other perceptual events can be true or false. The perceptual event itself is a psycho-physical event. If I affirm that the perception happened when it did not, or that it did not when it did, that affirmed proposition is false. But the event itself simply happened. It could not be true or false. Only propositions about it can be.

Suppose in the twilight the event happens called "seeing a man" but further inquiry reveals only a bush. Or suppose "seeing water" happens when investigation discovers a mirage. The perceptual events are neither true nor false. However, if I affirm the proposition, "That is a man" or, "That is water," I imply that further approach will elicit characteristically human responses from the "man," and quenching of thirst from the "water." Such an affirmed proposition is false, although the perceptual event was not.

From all this we gather that truth and error pertain to perception only when the perception includes the affirmation or denial of a proposition with its implications and inferences, and that the truth or error applies to this proposition and not to anything else entering into the perceptual event. Therefore the question about any object is never correctly expressed by asking: Is it perceived object or inferred object? Correctly put the question is thus: Is it both perceived and inferred or is it inferred without being perceived? When we perceive anything at all in such a way as to involve truth and error, it is by perceptual inference and never by perception apart from inference.

We can now state the difference between perceived object and inferred. A perceived object is a structure of inter-related events, some of which must be perceptual events. An object not perceived but inferred only is also a structure of inter-related events, but none of the events which enter into the structure of inferred object is a perceptual event, unless one wishes to say that the linguistic events used in thinking about it are a part of its structure.

A perceptual event as here understood is never "in the mind" only. It is a happening that is physical since it includes light rays, sound waves, molecular and molar masses. It is physiological since living tissue, nervous and muscular reactions are involved. It is psychological and social since signs and referents are included. If it is cognitive in the sense here defended, linguistic signs must be operative in the perceptual event, for without these no proposition can be affirmed or denied. The perceptual event is very complex. It includes everything which, if changed, would make a difference to the perceptual experience. This obviously makes it inclusive of vastly more than enters conscious awareness at the moment, although it does not include anything beyond what is necessary to

108

such conscious awareness. Simple experiment easily demonstrates that much going on in the world at the time makes no difference to the perceptual experience and so has no part in the perceptual event.

The perceptual event in all its complexity is never cognized by the perceiver. As we have already seen, it may not be cognized at all, but even when it is, only a part of the structure of its complexity is known by the perceiver at the time of the perception. How much he knows depends on how much information relevant to the perception is at his command when the perceptual event occurs. A perceived object is always more than the present perceptual event. It is this event plus many others all joined together in such a way as to make up a structure of relations. This structure pervading the interrelated events is the perceived object.

This analysis of perception escapes the difficulties involved in narrowing perception down to sense data such as H. H. Price and many others have done. It follows C. I. Lewis in distinguishing between "the given" and the concept but it represents the given as a massive happening which can be investigated progressively by common sense and science, rather than being those minutia to which Lewis seems to reduce the data for all cognition. On the other hand this understanding of perception does not identify true perception with "successful working" as the pragmatists have been inclined to do. While Dewey has not done this to the degree that some would accuse him, the present writer feels that he has not made sufficiently plain the difference between true perception and the psycho-biological fulfilment of anticipated consequences. When Blanshard, Hahn, and others try to correct this defect in Dewey's analyses of perception by speaking of propositions that are "implicit" in the perception, one wonders what is meant by implicit. It seems to me more accurate to cut clean on this point and simply say that the linguistic signs being used in the perceptual event (if there be such) which specify some relation between the perceptual event and others, are what is true or false. If the perception does not carry such signs, then the perception is a happening, peculiar in carrying in it psychic anticipations, fears, and aversions, which may be consummated or not. But in no case is such a complex mind-body event true or false without the linguistic signs specifying a structure of relations between the present event and others that have occurred in the past, along with possibilities that might be actualized

109

in the future if certain further conditions are provided.

Perhaps no perceptual event occurs in human experience without linguistic signs. One might almost set-
tle this by definition, asserting that the perception
would not be human if it lacked such signs. But that
does not at all mean that the linguistic signs present
in the perceptual event are being used to specify the
structure of relations pertaining to the present occurrence. One may be applying his linguistic signs to
metaphysical speculation while the current perceptual
event with its biological behavior and anticipatory
feelings is guided by non-linguistic signs which are
not cognitive because they are not propositional.

The scope and complexity of awareness, called immediacy, which enters into the perceptual event is determined first of all by the sensitivity of the organism and its conditioning by past events that have happened to it. The reach and richness of immediacy that
can be achieved without linguistic signs, however,
would seem to be very limited. Only when the perspective of another can become my own, being added to the
perspective I had and through this addition transforming both, can immediacy be progressively magnified.[2]
Thus immediacy has no fixed and final limits. It can
be transformed and enriched indefinitely. The event of
cognizing in one perception a vast complex structure of
inter-relatedness between the present perceptual event
and others is a part of the present immediacy. Of
course this structure of inter-relatedness holds whether I know it or not and is what it is, regardless of my
ideas about it. If this were not true, error would be
impossible. Therefore this structure is not itself a
part of the immediacy. But the cognitive event of being aware of it is. The emergence of the idea of it in
the present perceptual event belongs to the immediacy
of the present moment. Thus immediacy can be indefinitely magnified in richness of content.

The immediacy of the perceptual event can be magnified in two dimensions, by increasing the complexity of
nuance in discriminated feelings and by increasing the
complexity of structure by which the inter-relatedness
of events and possibilities are cognized. Art special-
izes in the one and science in the other. However, it
is the give and take of everyday interchange between
individuals whereby they acquire the perspectives of
one another that is the chief source of this enrichment

and growth of appreciative consciousness. Art and science impoverish rather than magnify the scope and content of the appreciative mind except as they serve to provide materials, techniques, and structures for this interchange in daily converse, and especially for this interchange in time of crisis when the thought and feeling of the persons involved reach a peak.

It would seem that the human mind is created and magnified by this interchange of perspectives. When I get several perspectives from others, meaning their thought and feeling about this and that, these several perspectives do not remain with me as a miscellany gathered by way of communication. They are transformed. Either they merge into a single perspective or are organized into two or more conflicting ways of thinking and feeling. In any case, they become my own mind and personality, not so much thought about as being the materials and equipment by which I apprehend the impact of circumstances in the future.

If value be considered the capacity to appreciate and appraise the good as well as the evil, if evil be considered the limiting or impoverishing of the scope and content of what the mind can appreciate and appraise, if good be the increase of this scope and content, truth, beauty, and virtue being forms and dimensions of this increase, then the root source of value peculiar to the human level of existence is this interchange of perspectives by which the immediacy of the perceptual event is magnified.

If religion in any worthy form that it may assume is man's endeavor to put himself under the sovereign control of the root source of creativity which generates all value, then a worthy religion would be one that sought by whatsoever effective methods to bring self and others to serve above all else this interchange of perspectives. The more free and full, more honest and deep, this interchange can be, the greater the value to be found in human living. In this way the immediacy of the perceptual event can be magnified for each individual to the limit of his physiological and mental capacity. Religion would not be the achievement of this interchange of perspectives between individuals and groups. The interchange would be the work of all the arts and sciences. Religion would be the use of all those devices by which men might be led to recognize the supreme importance of this interchange, free, full, honest, and deep, and allow themselves to be

111

transformed by it in any way that it might require.
But the construction of instrumentalities, conditions,
and materials by which the interchange is accomplished
is the work of industry and politics, education, science, and art.

We may seem to have gotten rather far afield from
the problem of perception and cognition, but I do not
think that we have. The relevance of these technical
problems of philosophical research to the urgent, practical issues of our time and all time should, I think,
be kept before us. Otherwise philosophy is a luxury
which this age can not afford.

[1]Aesthetic Quality, by S. C. Pepper; World Hypotheses, by S. C. Pepper; Nature of Thought, by Brand Blanshard; A Contextualistic Theory of Perception, by L. E. Hahn. Other works not quite so recent have been very potent in shaping the view here presented, whether by agreement or disagreement: Mind and the World Order, by C. I. Lewis; Logic, the Theory of Inquiry, by John Dewey; Mind, Self and Society, by G. H. Mead; Perception, by H. H. Price.

[2]See Mind, Self and Society, by G. H. Mead.

SUGGESTED READINGS

Henry Nelson Wieman

Wieman, Henry N. The Directive of History (Boston: Beacon Press, 1949).

_____. Religious Inquiry: Some Explanations (Boston: Beacon Press, 1968).

* * *

_____. "The Nature of Mentality," The Psychological Review, XXVI (May 1919), 230-246.

_____. "Knowledge of Other Minds," The Journal of Philosophy, XIX (October 1922), 605-611.

_____. "Experience, Mind, and Concept," The Journal of Philosophy, XXI (October 1924), 561-572.

_____. "How Do We Know?" Christian Century, XLVIII (May 1931), 713-715.

_____. "The Responsibility of Philosophical Inquiry," The Journal of Philosophy, XXXVIII (July 1941), 365-374.

_____. "The Problem of Religious Inquiry," Zygon: Journal of Religion and Science, I, 4 (December 1966), 373-400.

* * *

Bretall, Robert W., (Ed.). The Empirical Theology of Henry Nelson Wieman (New York: Macmillan, 1963; Carbondale: Southern Illinois University Press, 1970).

Hartshorne, Charles, and Reese, William L. Philosophers Speak of God (Chicago: The University of Chicago Press, 1953), pp. 395-408.

114

Meland, Bernard E. "Nature and the Human Problem," in Reawakening of the Christian Faith
(New York: Macmillan Press, 1949), pp. 1-61.

M E T A P H Y S I C S

"Diversicosity
is the germ
of all things."

Charles S. Peirce

William James
Henri Bergson
C. Lloyd Morgan
Charles Hartshorne

5. THE DILEMMA OF DETERMINISM

William James

William James (1842-1910), one of the most influential of all American philosophers, gained
a broad education in the fields of art, science,
anatomy, physiology and psychology before turning to philosophy under the influence of such
men as Gottfried W. Leibniz (1646-1716), David
Hume (1711-1776), Charles Renouvier (1818-1903),
Charles Saunders Peirce (1839-1914), and Ralph
Waldo Emerson (1803-1882).

In this very popular and influential essay,* William James makes some very illuminating suppositions
about the concept of determinism and its philosophical
implications. Few would doubt that this essay delivered a devastating blow to the notion of determinism
which had for so long suppressed the human spirit, and
in turn served as a challenge for men to experience the
world as novel, open-ended and venturesome. Always intent upon portraying conscience as a real combatant in
the arena of life, James was deeply concerned with the
implications of fate and free will in reference to the
living of life. Such is demanded, he says, by our desire for rationality. This is all very much in keeping
with and perhaps something of a fulfillment of his definition of the philosophical problem; namely, that we
seek to distinguish between the empirical order of
things and their rational order of comparison, and as
far as possible, to translate the former into the latter.# In endeavoring to answer this problem James

---

*Taken from the Unitarian Review (September 1884).
A number of footnotes have been omitted.

#Cf. The Principles of Psychology (New York:
Henry Holt, 1890), II, pp. 676, 677. In reading James
with respect to this particular problem one should keep
in mind his great appreciation for Charles Renouvier's
defense of free will and Charles Peirce's defense of
novelty. Both men played an important part in the

119

argues that possibilities seem to be the more common
characteristics of our world "as things that may, but
need not, be." He seeks to make this point by various
illustrations pertaining to "chance" choices or events
as being a definite part of the world in which we live.
The implication which follows from this then is "that
no part of the world, however big, can claim to control
absolutely the destinies of the whole." And once we
are aware of the theoretical difference between a (pluralistic) world with chances in it and a (monistic)
world of determinism, we are asked to draw our own conclusions as to their various implications with respect
to a world which either has a place for chance and regret or where what ought to be would be impossible--
thus posing what is here called "the dilemma of determinism."

---

formulation of his thought, especially in reference to
empiricism and free will. Cf. John Passmore, A Hundred
Years of Philosophy (Baltimore: Penguin, 1968), pp.
100ff.

The Dilemma of Determinism

A common opinion prevails that the juice has ages ago been pressed out of the free-will controversy, and that no new champion can do more than warm up stale arguments which everyone has heard. This is a radical mistake. I know of no subject less worn out, or in which inventive genius has a better chance of breaking open new ground--not, perhaps, of forcing a conclusion or of coercing assent, but of deepening our sense of what the ideas of fate and of free will imply. At our very side almost, in the past few years, we have seen falling in rapid succession from the press works that present the alternative in entirely novel lights. Not to speak of the English disciples of Hegel, such as Green and Bradley; not to speak of Hinton and Hodgson, nor of Hazard here--we see in the writings of Renouvier, Fouillée, and Delboeuf how completely changed and refreshed is the form of all the old disputes. I cannot pretend to vie in originality with any of the masters I have named, and my ambition limits itself to just one little point. If I can make two of the necessarily implied corollaries of determinism clearer to you than they have been made before, I shall have made it possible for you to decide for or against that doctrine with a better understanding of what you are about. And if you prefer not to decide at all, but to remain doubters, you will at least see more plainly what the subject of your hesitation is. I thus disclaim openly on the threshold all pretension to prove to you that the freedom of the will is true. The most I hope is to induce some of you to follow my own example in assuming it true, and acting as if it were true. If it be true, it seems to me that this is involved in the strict logic of the case. Its truth ought not to be forced willy-nilly down our indifferent throats. It ought to be freely espoused by men who can equally well turn their backs upon it. In other words, our first act of freedom, if we are free, ought in all inward propriety to be to affirm that we are free. This should exclude, it seems to me, from the free-will side of the question all hope of a coercive demonstration--a demonstration which I, for one, am perfectly contented to go without.

With thus much understood at the outset, we can advance. But not without one more point understood as well. The arguments I am about to urge all proceed on two suppositions: first, when we make theories about the world and discuss them with one another, we do so in order to attain a conception of things which shall give us subjective satisfaction; and, second, if there be two conceptions, and the one seems to us, on the whole, more rational than the other, we are entitled to suppose that the more rational one is the truer of the two. I hope that you are all willing to make these suppositions with me; for I am afraid that if there be any of you here who are not, they will find little edification in the rest of what I have to say. I cannot stop to argue the point; but I myself believe that all the magnificent achievements of mathematical and physical science--our doctrines of evolution, of uniformity of law, and the rest--proceed from our indomitable desire to cast the world into a more rational shape in our minds than the shape into which it is thrown there by the crude order of our experience. The world has shown itself, to a great extent, plastic to this demand of ours for rationality. How much farther it will show itself plastic no one can say. Our only means of finding out is to try; and I, for one, feel as free to try conceptions of moral as of mechanical or of logical rationality. If a certain formula for expressing the nature of the world violates my moral demand, I shall feel as free to throw it overboard, or at least to doubt it, as if it disappointed my demand for uniformity of sequence, for example; the one demand being, so far as I can see, quite as subjective and emotional as the other is. The principle of causality, for example-- what is it but a postulate, an empty name covering simply a demand that the sequence of events shall some day manifest a deeper kind of belonging of one thing with another than the mere arbitrary juxtaposition which now phenomenally appears? It is as much an altar to an unknown god as the one that Saint Paul found at Athens. All our scientific and philosophic ideals are altars to unknown gods. Uniformity is as much so as is free will. If this be admitted, we can debate on even terms. But if anyone pretends that while freedom and variety are, in the first instance, subjective demands, necessity and uniformity are something altogether different, I do not see how we can debate at all.

To begin, then, I must suppose you acquainted with all the usual arguments on the subject. I cannot stop to take up the old proofs from causation, from statistics, from the certainty with which we can foretell one another's conduct, from the fixity of character, and all the rest. But there are two words which usually encumber these classical arguments, and which we must immediately dispose of if we are to make any progress.

One is the eulogistic word freedom, and the other is the opprobrious word chance. The word "chance" I wish to keep, but I wish to get rid of the word "freedom." Its eulogistic associations have so far overshadowed all the rest of its meaning that both parties claim the sole right to use it, and determinists today insist that they alone are freedom's champions. Old-fashioned determinism was what we may call hard determinism. It did not shrink from such words as fatality, bondage of the will, necessitation, and the like. Nowadays, we have a soft determinism which abhors harsh words, and, repudiating fatality, necessity, and even predetermination, says that its real name is freedom; for freedom is only necessity understood, and bondage to the highest is identical with true freedom. Even a writer as little used to making capital out of soft words as Mr. Hodgson hesitates not to call himself a "free-will determinist."

Now, all this is a quagmire of evasion under which the real issue of fact has been entirely smothered. Freedom in all these senses presents simply no problem at all. No matter what the soft determinist means by it--whether he means the acting without external constraint; whether he means the acting rightly, or whether he means the acquiescing in the law of the whole-- who cannot answer him that sometimes we are free and sometimes we are not? But there is a problem, an issue of fact and not of words, an issue of the most momentous importance, which is often decided without discussion in one sentence--nay, in one clause of a sentence --by those very writers who spin out whole chapters in their efforts to show what "true" freedom is; and that is the question of determinism, about which we are to talk tonight.

Fortunately, no ambiguities hang about this word or about its opposite, indeterminism. Both designate an outward way in which things may happen, and their cold and mathematical sound has no sentimental associations that can bribe our partiality either way in advance. Now, evidence of an external kind to decide between determinism and indeterminism is, as I intimated a while back, strictly impossible to find. Let us look at the difference between them and see for ourselves. What does determinism profess?

It professes that those parts of the universe already laid down absolutely appoint and decree what the other parts shall be. The future has no ambiguous possibilities hidden in its womb; the part we call the present is compatible with only one totality. Any other future complement than the one fixed from eternity is impossible. The whole is in each and every part, and welds it with the rest into an absolute unity, an iron block, in which there can be no equivocation or shadow of turning.

> With earth's first clay they did the last man
>   knead,
> And there of the last harvest sowed the seed.
> And the first morning of creation wrote
> What the last dawn of reckoning shall read.

Indeterminism, on the contrary, says that the parts have a certain amount of loose play on one another, so that the laying down of one of them does not necessarily determine what the others shall be. It admits that possibilities may be in excess of actualities, and that things not yet revealed to our knowledge may really in themselves be ambiguous. Of two alternative futures which we conceive, both may now be really possible; and the one becomes impossible only at the very moment when the other excludes it by becoming real itself. Indeterminism thus denies the world to be one unbending unit of fact. It says there is a certain ultimate pluralism in it; and, so saying, it corroborates our ordinary unsophisticated view of things. To that view, actualities seem to float in a wider sea of possibilities from out of which they are chosen; and, somewhere, indeterminism says, such possibilities exist, and form a part of truth.

Determinism, on the contrary, says they exist nowhere, and that necessity on the one hand and impossibility on the other are the sole categories of the real. Possibilities that fail to get realized are, for determinism, pure illusions: they never were possibilities at all. There is nothing inchoate, it says, about this universe of ours, all that was or is or shall be actual in it having been from eternity virtually there. The cloud of alternatives our minds escort this mass of actuality withal is a cloud of sheer deceptions, to which "impossibilities" is the only name that rightfully belongs.

The issue, it will be seen, is a perfectly sharp one, which no eulogistic terminology can smear over or wipe out. The truth must lie with one side or the other, and its lying with one side makes the other false.

The question relates solely to the existence of possibilities, in the strict sense of the term, as things that may, but need not, be. Both sides admit that a volition, for instance, has occurred. The indeterminists say another volition might have occurred in its place: the determinists swear that nothing could possibly have occurred in its place. Now, can science be called in to tell us which of these two point-blank contradicters of each other is right? Science professes to draw no conclusions but such as are based on matters of fact, things that have actually happened; but how can any amount of assurance that something actually happened give us the least grain of information as to whether another thing might or might not have happened in its place? Only facts can be proved by other facts. With things that are possibilities and not facts, facts have no concern. If we have no other evidence than the evidence of existing facts, the possibility-question must remain a mystery never to be cleared up.

And the truth is that facts practically have hardly anything to do with making us either determinists or indeterminists. Sure enough, we make a flourish of quoting facts this way or that; and if we are determinists, we talk about the infallibility with which we can predict one another's conduct; while if we are indeterminists, we lay great stress on the fact that it is just because we cannot foretell one another's conduct, either in war or statecraft or in any of the great and small intrigues and businesses of men, that life is so intensely anxious and hazardous a game. But who does not see the wretched insufficiency of this so-called objective testimony on both sides? What fills up the gaps in our minds is something not objective, not external. What divides us into possibility men and anti-possibility men is different faiths or postulates-- postulates of rationality. To this man the world seems more rational with possibilities in it--to that man more rational with possibilities excluded; and talk as we will about having to yield to evidence, what makes us monists or pluralists, determinists or indeterminists, is at bottom always some sentiment like this.

The stronghold of the deterministic sentiment is the antipathy to the idea of chance. As soon as we begin to talk indeterminism to our friends, we find a number of them shaking their heads. This notion of alternative possibilities, they say, this admission that any one of several things may come to pass, is, after

125

all, only a roundabout name for chance; and chance is something the notion of which no sane mind can for an instant tolerate in the world. What is it, they ask, but barefaced crazy unreason, the negation of intelligibility and law? And if the slightest particle of it exists anywhere, what is to prevent the whole fabric from falling together, the stars from going out, and chaos from recommencing her topsy-turvy reign?

Remarks of this sort about chance will put an end to discussion as quickly as anything one can find. I have already told you that "chance" was a word I wished to keep and use. Let us then examine exactly what it means, and see whether it ought to be such a terrible bugbear to us. I fancy that squeezing the thistle boldly will rob it of its sting.

The sting of the word "chance" seems to lie in the assumption that it means something positive, and that if anything happens by chance, it must needs be something of an intrinsically irrational and preposterous sort. Now, chance means nothing of the kind. It is a purely negative and relative term,[1] giving us no information about that of which it is predicated, except that it happens to be disconnected with something else --not controlled, secured, or necessitated by other things in advance of its own actual presence. As this point is the most subtile one of the whole lecture, and at the same time the point on which all the rest hinges, I beg you to pay particular attention to it. What I say is that it tells us nothing about what a thing may be in itself to call it "chance." It may be a bad thing, it may be a good thing. It may be lucidity, transparency, fitness incarnate, matching the whole system of other things, when it has once befallen, in an unimaginably perfect way. All you mean by calling it "chance" is that this is not guaranteed, that it may also fall out otherwise. For the system of other things has no positive hold on the chance-thing. Its origin is in a certain fashion negative: it escapes, and says, Hands off! coming, when it comes, as a free gift, or not at all.

This negativeness, however, and this opacity of the chance-thing when thus considered ab extra, or from the point of view of previous things or distant things, do not preclude its having any amount of positiveness and luminosity from within, and at its own place and moment. All that its chance-character asserts about it is that there is something in it really of its own,

126

something that is not the unconditional property of the whole. If the whole wants this property, the whole must wait till it can get it, if it be a matter of chance. That the universe may actually be a sort of joint-stock society of this sort, in which the sharers have both limited liabilities and limited powers, is of course a simple and conceivable notion.

Nevertheless, many persons talk as if the minutest dose of disconnectedness of one part with another, the smallest modicum of independence, the faintest tremor of ambiguity about the future, for example, would ruin everything, and turn this goodly universe into a sort of insane sand-heap or nulliverse--no universe at all. Since future human volitions are as a matter of fact the only ambiguous things we are tempted to believe in, let us stop for a moment to make ourselves sure whether their independent and accidental character need be fraught with such direful consequences to the universe as these.

What is meant by saying that my choice of which way to walk home after the lecture is ambiguous and matter of chance as far as the present moment is concerned? It means that both Divinity Avenue and Oxford Street are called; but that only one, and that one either one, shall be chosen. Now, I ask you seriously to suppose that this ambiguity of my choice is real; and then to make the impossible hypothesis that the choice is made twice over, and each time falls on a different street. In other words, imagine that I first walk through Divinity Avenue, and then imagine that the powers governing the universe annihilate ten minutes of time with all that it contained, and set me back at the door of this hall just as I was before the choice was made. Imagine then that, everything else being the same, I now make a different choice and traverse Oxford Street. You, as passive spectators, look on and see the two alternative universes--one of them with me walking through Divinity Avenue in it, the other with the same me walking through Oxford Street. Now, if you are determinists you believe one of these universes to have been from eternity impossible: you believe it to have been impossible because of the intrinsic irrationality or accidentality somewhere involved in it. But looking outwardly at these universes, can you say which is the impossible and accidental one, and which the rational and necessary one? I doubt if the most ironclad determinist among you could have the slightest glimmer of light on this point. In other words, either

127

universe _after the fact_ and once there would, to our
means of _observation_ and understanding, appear just as
rational as the other. There would be absolutely no
criterion by which we might judge one necessary and the
other matter of chance. Suppose now we relieve the
gods of their hypothetical task and assume my choice,
once made, to be made forever. I go through Divinity
Avenue for good and all. If, as good determinists, you
now begin to affirm, what all good determinists punctu-
ally do affirm, that in the nature of things I _couldn't_
have gone through Oxford Street--had I done so _it would_
have been chance, irrationality, insanity, a horrid gap
in nature--I simply call your attention to this, that
your affirmation is what the Germans call a _Machtspruch,_
a mere conception fulminated as a dogma and based on no
insight into details. Before my choice, either street
seemed as natural to you as to me. Had I happened to
take Oxford Street, Divinity Avenue would have figured
in your philosophy as the gap in nature; and you would
have so proclaimed it with the best deterministic conscience in the world.

But what a hollow outcry, then, is this against a
chance which, if it were presented to us, we could by
no character whatever distinguish from a rational necessity! I have taken the most trivial of examples,
but no possible example could lead to any different result. For what are the alternatives which, in point of
fact, offer themselves to human volition? What are
those futures that now seem matters of chance? Are
they not one and all like the Divinity Avenue and Oxford Street of our example? Are they not all of them
kinds of things already here and based in the existing
frame of nature? Is anyone ever tempted to produce an
absolute accident, something utterly irrelevant to the
rest of the world? Do not all the motives that assail
us, all the futures that offer themselves to our choice,
spring equally from the soil of the past; and would not
either one of them, whether realized through chance or
through necessity, the moment it was realized, seem to
us to fit that past, and in the completest and most
continuous manner to interdigitate with the phenomena
already there?[2]

The more one thinks of the matter, the more one
wonders that so empty and gratuitous a hubbub as this
outcry against chance should have found so great an
echo in the hearts of men. It is a word which tells
us absolutely nothing about what chances, or about the
modus operandi of the chancing; and the use of it as a

war cry shows only a temper of intellectual absolutism, a demand that the world shall be a solid block, subject to one control--which temper, which demand, the world may not be found to gratify at all. In every outwardly verifiable and practical respect, a world in which the alternatives that now actually distract your choice were decided by pure chance would be by me absolutely undistinguished from the world in which I now live. I am, therefore, entirely willing to call it, so far as your choices go, a world of chance for me. To yourselves, it is true, those very acts of choice, which to me are so blind, opaque, and external, are the opposites of this, for you are within them and effect them. To you they appear as decisions; and decisions, for him who makes them, are altogether peculiar psychic facts. Self-luminous and self-justifying at the living moment at which they occur, they appeal to no outside moment to put its stamp upon them or make them continuous with the rest of nature. Themselves it is rather who seem to make nature continuous; and in their strange and intense function of granting consent to one possibility and withholding it from another, to transform an equivocal and double future into an unalterable and simple past.

But with the psychology of the matter we have no concern this evening. The quarrel which determinism has with chance fortunately has nothing to do with this or that psychological detail. It is a quarrel altogether metaphysical. Determinism denies the ambiguity of future volitions, because it affirms that nothing future can be ambiguous. But we have said enough to meet the issue. Indeterminate future volitions do mean chance. Let us not fear to shout it from the housetops if need be; for we now know that the idea of chance is, at bottom, exactly the same thing as the idea of gift--the one simply being a disparaging, and the other a eulogistic, name for anything on which we have no effective claim. And whether the world be the better or the worse for having either chances or gifts in it will depend altogether on what these uncertain and unclaimable things turn out to be.

And this at last brings us within sight of our subject. We have seen what determinism means: we have seen that indeterminism is rightly described as meaning chance; and we have seen that chance, the very name of which we are urged to shrink from as from a metaphysical pestilence, means only the negative fact that no part of the world, however big, can claim to control absolutely the destinies of the whole. But although, in discussing the word "chance," I may at moments have seemed to be arguing for its real existence, I have not meant to do so yet. We have not yet ascertained whether this be a world of chance or no; at most, we have agreed that it seems so. And I now repeat what I said at the outset, that, from any strict theoretical point of view, the question is insoluble. To deepen our theoretic sense of the <u>difference</u> between a world with chances in it and a <u>deterministic</u> world is the most I can hope to do; and this I may now at last begin upon, after all our tedious clearing of the way.

I wish first of all to show you just what the notion that this is a deterministic world implies. The implications I call your attention to are all bound up with the fact that it is a world in which we constantly have to make what I shall, with your permission, call judgments of regret. Hardly an hour passes in which we do not wish that something might be otherwise; and happy indeed are those of us whose hearts have never echoed the wish of Omar Khayam--

That we might clasp, ere closed, the book of fate,
    And make the writer on a fairer leaf
Inscribe our names, or quite obliterate.

Ah! Love, could you and I with fate conspire
To mend this sorry scheme of things entire,
    Would we not shatter it to bits, and then
Remold it nearer to the heart's desire?

Now, it is undeniable that most of these regrets are foolish, and quite on a par in point of philosophic value with the criticisms on the universe of that friend of our infancy, the hero of the fable "The Atheist and the Acorn"--

Fool! had that bough a pumpkin bore,
Thy whimsies would have worked no more, etc.

Even from the point of view of our own ends, we should probably make a botch of remodeling the universe. How much more then from the point of view of ends we cannot see! Wise men therefore regret as little as they can. But still some regrets are pretty obstinate and hard to stifle--regrets for acts of wanton cruelty or treachery, for example, whether performed by others or by ourselves. Hardly any one can remain <u>entirely</u> optimistic after reading the confession of the murderer at

130

Brockton the other day: how, to get rid of the wife
whose continued existence bored him, he inveigled her
into a desert spot, shot her four times, and then, as
she lay on the ground and said to him, "You didn't do
it on purpose, did you, dear?" replied, "No, I didn't
do it on purpose," as he raised a rock and smashed her
skull. Such an occurrence, with the mild sentence and
self-satisfaction of the prisoner, is a field for a
crop of regrets, which one need not take up in detail.
We feel that, although a perfect mechanical fit to the
rest of the universe, it is a bad moral fit, and that
something else would really have been better in its
place.

But for the deterministic philosophy the murder,
the sentence, and the prisoner's optimism were all necessary from eternity; and nothing else for a moment had
a ghost of a chance of being put in their place. To
admit such a chance, the determinists tell us, would be
to make a suicide of reason; so we must steel our
hearts against the thought. And here our plot thickens,
for we see the first of those difficult implications of
determinism and monism, which it is my purpose to make
you feel. If this Brockton murder was called for by
the rest of the universe, if it had to come at its pre-
appointed hour, and if nothing else would have been
consistent with the sense of the whole, what are we to
think of the universe? Are we stubbornly to stick to
our judgment of regret, and say, though it couldn't be,
yet it would have been a better universe with something
different from this Brockton murder in it? That, of
course, seems the natural and spontaneous thing for us
to do; and yet it is nothing short of deliberately es-
pousing a kind of pessimism. The judgment of regret
calls the murder bad. Calling a thing bad means, if it
means anything at all, that the thing ought not to be,
that something else ought to be in its stead. Determinism, in denying that anything else can be in its
stead, virtually defines the universe as a place in
which what ought to be is impossible--in other words,
as an organism whose constitution is afflicted with an
incurable taint, an irremediable flaw. The pessimism
of a Schopenhauer says no more than this--that the murder is a symptom; and that it is a vicious symptom because it belongs to a vicious whole, which can express
its nature no otherwise than by bringing forth just
such a symptom as that at this particular spot. Regret
for the murder must transform itself, if we are determinists and wise, into a larger regret. It is absurd
to regret the murder alone. Other things being what

131

they are, it could not be different. What we should
regret is that whole frame of things of which the murder is one member. I see no escape whatever from this
pessimistic conclusion if, being determinists, our
judgment of regret is to be allowed to stand at all.

The only deterministic escape from pessimism is
everywhere to abandon the judgment of regret. That
this can be done, history shows to be not impossible.
The devil, quoad existentiam, may be good. That is,
although he be a principle of evil, yet the universe,
with such a principle in it, may practically be a better universe than it could have been without. On every
hand, in a small way, we find that a certain amount of
evil is a condition by which a higher form of good is
brought. There is nothing to prevent anybody from generalizing this view, and trusting that if we could but
see things in the largest of all ways, even such matters as this Brockton murder would appear to be paid
for by the uses that follow in their train. An optimism quand meme, a systematic and infatuated optimism
like that ridiculed by Voltaire in his Candide, is one
of the possible ideal ways in which a man may train
himself to look on life. Bereft of dogmatic hardness
and lit up with the expression of a tender and pathetic
hope, such an optimism has been the grace of some of
the most religious characters that ever lived.

Throb thine with Nature's throbbing breast,
And all is clear from east to west.

Even cruelty and treachery may be among the absolutely blessed fruits of time, and to quarrel with any
of their details may be blasphemy. The only real blasphemy, in short, may be that pessimistic temper of the
soul which lets it give way to such things as regrets,
remorse, and grief.

Thus, our deterministic pessimism may become a deterministic optimism at the price of extinguishing our
judgments of regret.

But does not this immediately bring us into a curious logical predicament? Our determinism leads us to
call our judgments of regret wrong, because they are
pessimistic in implying that what is impossible yet
ought to be. But how then about the judgments of regret themselves? If they are wrong, other judgments,
judgments of approval presumably, ought to be in their
place. But as they are necessitated, nothing else can

be in their place; and the universe is just what it was before--namely, a place in which what ought to be appears impossible. We have got one foot out of the pessimistic bog, but the other one sinks all the deeper. We have rescued our actions from the bonds of evil, but our judgments are now held fast. When murders and treacheries cease to be sins, regrets are theoretic absurdities and errors. The theoretic and the active life thus play a kind of see-saw with each other on the ground of evil. The rise of either sends the other down. Murder and treachery cannot be good without regret being bad: regret cannot be good without treachery and murder being bad. Both, however, are supposed to have been foredoomed; so something must be fatally unreasonable, absurd, and wrong in the world. It must be a place of which either sin or error forms a necessary part. From this dilemma there seems at first sight no escape. Are we then so soon to fall back into the pessimism from which we thought we had emerged? And is there no possible way by which we may, with good intellectual consciences, call the cruelties and treacheries, the reluctances and the regrets, all good together?

Certainly there is such a way, and you are probably most of you ready to formulate it yourselves. But, before doing so, remark how inevitably the question of determinism and indeterminism slides us into the question of optimism and pessimism, or, as our fathers called it, "the question of evil." The theological form of all these disputes is the simplest and the deepest, the form from which there is the least escape --not because, as some have sarcastically said, remorse and regret are clung to us with a morbid fondness by the theologians as spiritual luxuries, but because they are existing facts of the world, and as such must be taken into account in the deterministic interpretation of all that is fated to be. If they are fated to be error, does not the bat's wing of irrationality still cast its shadow over the world?

The refuge from the quandary lies, as I said, not far off. The necessary acts we erroneously regret may be good, and yet our error in so regretting them may be also good, on one simple condition; and that condition is this: The world must not be regarded as a machine whose final purpose is the making real of any outward good, but rather as a contrivance for deepening the theoretic consciousness of what goodness and evil in their intrinsic natures are. Not the doing either of

good or evil is what nature cares for, but the knowing
of them. Life is one long eating of the fruit of the
tree of knowledge. I am in the habit, in thinking to
myself, of calling this point of view the gnostical
point of view. According to it, the world is neither
an optimism nor a pessimism, but a gnosticism. But as
this term may perhaps lead to some misunderstandings, I
will use it as little as possible here, and speak
rather of subjectivism, and the subjectivistic point of
view.

Subjectivism has three great branches--we may call
them scientificism, sentimentalism, and sensualism, respectively. They all agree essentially about the universe, in deeming that what happens there is subsidiary
to what we think or feel about it. Crime justifies its
criminality by awakening our intelligence of that criminality and eventually our remorses and regrets; and
the error included in remorses and regrets, the error
of supposing that the past could have been different,
justifies itself by its use. Its use is to quicken our
sense of what the irretrievably lost is. When we think
of it as that which might have been ("the saddest words
of tongue or pen"), the quality of its worth speaks to
us with a wilder sweetness; and, conversely, the dis-
satisfaction wherewith we think of what seems to have
driven it from its natural place gives us the severer
pang. Admirable artifice of nature! we might be
tempted to exclaim--deceiving us in order the better to
enlighten us, and leaving nothing undone to accentuate
to our consciousness the yawning distance of those opposite poles of good and evil between which creation
swings.

We have thus clearly revealed to our view what may
be called the dilemma of determinism, so far as determinism pretends to think things out at all. A merely
mechanical determinism, it is true, rather rejoices in
not thinking them out. It is very sure that the universe must satisfy its postulate of a physical continuity and coherence, but it smiles at anyone who comes
forward with a postulate of moral coherence as well. I
may suppose, however, that the number of purely mechanical or hard determinists among you this evening is
small. The determinism to whose seductions you are
most exposed is what I have called soft determinism--
the determinism which allows considerations of good and
bad to mingle with those of cause and effect in deciding what sort of a universe this may rationally be held
to be. The dilemma of this determinism is one whose

left horn is pessimism and whose right horn is subjectivism. In other words, if determinism is to escape
pessimism, it must leave off looking at the goods and
ills of life in a simple objective way, and regard them
as materials, indifferent in themselves, for the production of consciousness, scientific and ethical, in
us.

To escape pessimism is, as we all know, no easy
task. Your own studies have sufficiently shown you the
almost desperate difficulty of making the notion that
there is a single principle of things, and that principle absolute perfection, rhyme together with our daily
vision of the facts of life. If perfection be the
principle, how comes there any imperfection here? If
God be good, how came he to create--or, if he did not
create, how comes he to permit--the devil? The evil
facts must be explained as seeming: the devil must be
whitewashed, the universe must be disinfected, if neither God's goodness nor His unity and power are to remain impugned. And of all the various ways of operating the disinfection, and making bad seem less bad, the
way of subjectivism appears by far the best.[3]

For, after all, is there not something rather absurd in our ordinary notion of external things being
good or bad in themselves? Can murders and treacheries, considered as mere outward happenings, or motions
of matter, be bad without anyone to feel their badness?
And could paradise properly be good in the absence of a
sentient principle by which the goodness was perceived?
Outward goods and evils seem practically indistinguishable except in so far as they result in getting moral
judgments made about them. But then the moral judgments seem the main thing, and the outward facts mere
perishing instruments for their production. This is
subjectivism. Everyone must at some time have wondered
at that strange paradox of our moral nature, that,
though the pursuit of outward good is the breath of its
nostrils, the attainment of outward good would seem to
be its suffocation and death. Why does the painting of
any paradise or utopia, in heaven or on earth, awaken
such yawnings for nirvana and escape? The white-robed
harp-playing heaven of our sabbath-schools, and the
ladylike tea-table elysium represented in Mr. Spencer's
Data of Ethics, as the final consummation of progress,
are exactly on a par in this respect--lubberlands, pure
and simple, one and all. We look upon them from this
delicious mess of insanities and realities, strivings
and deadnesses, hopes and fears, agonies and exultations,

135

which forms our present state, and tedium vitae is the only sentiment they awaken in our breasts. To our crepuscular natures, born for the conflict, the Rembrandtesque moral chiaroscuro, the shifting struggle of the sunbeam in the gloom, such pictures of light upon light are vacuous and expressionless, and neither to be enjoyed nor understood. If this be the whole fruit of the victory, we say; if the generations of mankind suffered and laid down their lives; if prophets confessed and martyrs sang in the fire, and all the sacred tears were shed for no other end than that a race of creatures of such unexampled insipidity should succeed, and protract in saecula saeculorum their contented and inoffensive lives--why, at such a rate, better lose than win the battle, or at all events better ring down the curtain before the last act of the play, so that a business that began so importantly may be saved from so singularly flat a winding-up.

All this is what I should instantly say, were I called on to plead for gnosticism; and its real friends, of whom you will presently perceive I am not one, would say without difficulty a great deal more. Regarded as a stable finality, every outward good becomes a mere weariness to the flesh. It must be menaced, be occasionally lost, for its goodness to be fully felt as such. Nay, more than occasionally lost. No one knows the worth of innocence till he knows it is gone forever, and that money cannot buy it back. Not the saint, but the sinner that repenteth, is he to whom the full length and breadth, and height and depth, of life's meaning is revealed. Not the absence of vice, but vice there, and virtue holding her by the throat, seems the ideal human state. And there seems no reason to suppose it not a permanent human state. There is a deep truth in what the school of Schopenhauer insists on--the illusoriness of the notion of moral progress. The more brutal forms of evil that go are replaced by others more subtle and more poisonous. Our moral horizon moves with us as we move, and never do we draw nearer to the far-off line where the black waves and the azure meet. The final purpose of our creation seems most plausibly to be the greatest possible enrichment of our ethical consciousness, through the intensest play of contrasts and the widest diversity of characters. This of course obliges some of us to be vessels of wrath, while it calls others to be vessels of honor. But the subjectivist point of view reduces all these outward distinctions to a common denominator. The wretch languishing in the felon's cell may be drinking draughts of the wine of truth that will never pass the lips of the so-called favorite of fortune. And the peculiar consciousness of each of them is an indispensable note in the great ethical concert which the centuries as they roll are grinding out of the living heart of man.

So much for subjectivism! If the dilemma of determinism be to choose between it and pessimism, I see little room for hesitation from the strictly theoretical point of view. Subjectivism seems the more rational scheme. And the world may possibly, for aught I know, be nothing else. When the healthy love of life is on one, and all its forms and its appetites seem so unutterably real; when the most brutal and the most spiritual things are lit by the same sun, and each is an integral part of the total richness--why, then it seems a grudging and sickly way of meeting so robust a universe to shrink from any of its facts and wish them not to be. Rather take the strictly dramatic point of view, and treat the whole thing as a great unending romance which the spirit of the universe, striving to realize its own content, is eternally thinking out and representing to itself.

No one, I hope, will accuse me, after I have said all this, of underrating the reasons in favor of subjectivism. And now that I proceed to say why those reasons, strong as they are, fail to convince my own mind, I trust the presumption may be that my objections are stronger still.

I frankly confess that they are of a practical order. If we practically take up subjectivism in a sincere and radical manner and follow its consequences, we meet with some that make us pause. Let a subjectivism begin in never so severe and intellectual a way, it is forced by the law of its nature to develop another side of itself and end with the corruptest curiosity. Once dismiss the notion that certain duties are good in themselves, and that we are here to do them, no matter how we feel about them; once consecrate the opposite notion that our performances and our violations of duty are for a common purpose, the attainment of subjective knowledge and feeling, and that the deepening of these is the chief end of our lives--and at what point on the downward slope are we to stop? In theology, subjectivism develops as its "left wing" antinomianism. In literature, its left wing is romanticism. And in

practical life it is either a nerveless sentimentality
or a sensualism without bounds.

Everywhere it fosters the fatalistic mood of mind.
It makes those who are already too inert more passive
still; it renders wholly reckless those whose energy is
already in excess. All through history we find how
subjectivism, as soon as it has a free career, exhausts
itself in every sort of spiritual, moral, and practical
license. Its optimism turns to an ethical indifference,
which infallibly brings dissolution in its train. It
is perfectly safe to say now that if the Hegelian gnosticism, which has begun to show itself here and in
Great Britain, were to become a popular philosophy, as
it once was in Germany, it would certainly develop its
left wing here as there, and produce a reaction of disgust. Already I have heard a graduate of this very
school express in the pulpit his willingness to sin
like David, if only he might repent like David. You
may tell me he was only sowing his wild, or rather his
tame, oats; and perhaps he was. But the point is that
in the subjectivistic or gnostical philosophy oat-
sowing, wild or tame, becomes a systematic necessity
and the chief function of life. After the pure and
classic truths, the exciting and rancid ones must be
experienced; and if the stupid virtues of the philis-
tine herd do not then come in and save society from the
influence of the children of light, a sort of inward
putrefaction becomes its inevitable doom.

Look at the last runnings of the romantic school,
as we see them in that strange contemporary Parisian
literature, with which we of the less clever countries
are so often driven to rinse out our minds after they
have become clogged with the dullness and heaviness of
our native pursuits. The romantic school began with
the worship of subjective sensibility and the revolt
against legality of which Rousseau was the first great
prophet: and through various fluxes and refluxes,
right wings and left wings, it stands today with two
men of genius, M. Renan and M. Zola, as its principal
exponents--one speaking with its masculine, and the
other with what might be called its feminine, voice.
I prefer not to think now of less noble members of the
school, and the Renan I have in mind is of course the
Renan of latest dates. As I have used the term gnostic,
both he and Zola are gnostics of the most pronounced
sort. Both are athirst for the facts of life, and
both think the facts of human sensibility to be of all
facts the most worthy of attention. Both agree,

moreover, that sensibility seems to be there for no
higher purpose--certainly not, as the Philistines say,
for the sake of bringing mere outward rights to pass
and frustrating outward wrongs. One dwells on the sensibilities for their energy, the other for their sweetness; one speaks with a voice of bronze, the other with
that of an Aeolian harp; one ruggedly ignores the distinction of good and evil, the other plays the coquette
between the craven unmanliness of his Philosophic Dialogues and the butterfly optimism of his Souvenirs de
Jeunesse. But under the pages of both there sounds incessantly the hoarse bass of vanitas vanitatum, omnia
vanitas, which the reader may hear, whenever he will,
between the lines. No writer of this French romantic
school has a word of rescue from the hour of satiety
with the things of life--the hour in which we say, "I
take no pleasure in them"--or from the hour of terror
at the world's vast meaningless grinding, if perchance
such hours should come. For terror and satiety are
facts of sensibility like any others, and at their own
hour they reign in their own right. The heart of the
romantic utterances, whether poetical, critical, or
historical, is this inward remedilessness, what Carlyle
calls this far-off whimpering of wail and woe. And
from this romantic state of mind there is absolutely no
possible theoretic escape. Whether, like Renan, we
look upon life in a more refined way, as a romance of
the spirit; or whether, like the friends of M. Zola, we
pique ourselves on our "scientific" and "analytic"
character, and prefer to be cynical, and call the world
a roman experimental on an infinite scale--in either
case the world appears to us potentially as what the
same Carlyle once called it, a vast, gloomy, solitary
Golgotha and mill of death.

        The only escape is by the practical way. And
since I have mentioned the nowadays much-reviled name
of Carlyle, let me mention it once more, and say it is
the way of his teaching. No matter for Carlyle's life,
no matter for a great deal of his writing. What was
the most important thing he said to us? He said:
"Hang your sensibilities! Stop your snivelling com-
plaints, and your equally snivelling raptures! Leave
off your general emotional tomfoolery, and get to work
like men!" But this means a complete rupture with the
subjectivist philosophy of things. It says conduct,
and not sensibility, is the ultimate fact for our recognition. With the vision of certain works to be done,
of certain outward changes to be wrought or resisted,
it says our intellectual horizon terminates. No matter

how we succeed in doing these outward duties, whether gladly and spontaneously, or heavily and unwillingly, do them we somehow must; for the leaving of them undone is perdition. No matter how we feel; if we are only faithful in the outward act and refuse to do wrong, the world will in so far be safe, and we quit of our debt toward it. Take, then, the yoke upon our shoulders; bend our neck beneath the heavy legality of its weight; regard something else than our feeling as our limit, our master, and our law; be willing to live and die in its service--and, at a stroke, we have passed from the subjective into the objective philosophy of things, much as one awakens from some feverish dream, full of bad lights and noises, to find one's self bathed in the sacred coolness and quiet of the air of the night.

But what is the essence of this philosophy of objective conduct, so old-fashioned and finite, but so chaste and sane and strong, when compared with its romantic rival? It is the recognition of limits, foreign and opaque to our understanding. It is the willingness, after bringing about some external good, to feel at peace; for our responsibility ends with the performance of that duty, and the burden of the rest we may lay on higher powers.[4]

Look to thyself, O Universe,
Thou are better and not worse--

we may say in that philosophy, the moment we have done our stroke of conduct, however small. For in the view of that philosophy the universe belongs to a plurality of semi-independent forces, each one of which may help or hinder, and be helped or hindered by, the operations of the rest.

But this brings us right back, after such a long detour, to the question of indeterminism and to the conclusion of all I came here to say tonight. For the only consistent way of representing a pluralism and a world whose parts may affect one another through their conduct being either good or bad is the indeterministic way. What interest, zest, or excitement can there be in achieving the right way, unless we are enabled to feel that the wrong way is also a possible and a natural way--nay, more, a menacing and an imminent way? And what sense can there be in condemning ourselves for taking the wrong way, unless we need have done nothing of the sort, unless the right way was open to us as well? I cannot understand the willingness to act, no

140

matter how we feel, without the belief that acts are really good and bad. I cannot understand the belief that an act is bad, without regret at its happening. I cannot understand regret without the admission of real, genuine possibilities in the world. Only _then_ is it other than a mockery to feel, after we have failed to do our best, that an irreparable opportunity is gone from the universe, the loss of which it must forever after mourn.

If you insist that this is all superstition, that possibility is in the eye of science and reason impossibility, and that if I act badly 'tis that the universe was foredoomed to suffer this defect, you fall right back into the dilemma, the labyrinth, of pessimism and subjectivism, from out of whose toils we have just found our way.

Now, we are of course free to fall back, if we please. For my own part, though, whatever difficulties may beset the philosophy of objective right and wrong, and the indeterminism it seems to imply, determinism, with its alternative of pessimism or romanticism, contains difficulties that are greater still. But you will remember that I expressly repudiated a while ago the pretension to offer any arguments which could be coercive in a so-called scientific fashion in this matter. And I consequently find myself, at the end of this long talk, obliged to state my conclusions in an altogether personal way. This personal method of appeal seems to be among the very conditions of the problem; and the most anyone can do is to confess as candidly as he can the grounds for the faith that is in him, and leave his example to work on others as it may.

Let me, then, without circumlocution say just this. The world is enigmatical enough in all conscience, whatever theory we may take up toward it. The indeterminism I defend, the free-will theory of popular sense based on the judgment of regret, represents that world as vulnerable, and liable to be injured by certain of its parts if they act wrong. And it represents their acting wrong as a matter of possibility or accident, neither inevitable nor yet to be infallibly warded off. In all this, it is a theory devoid either of transparency or of stability. It gives us a pluralistic, restless universe, in which no single point of view can ever take in the whole scene; and to a mind possessed of the love of unity at any cost, it will, no doubt, remain forever unacceptable. A friend with such

141

a mind once told me that the thought of my universe made him sick, like the sight of the horrible motion of a mass of maggots in their carrion bed.

But while I freely admit that the pluralism and the restlessness are repugnant and irrational in a certain way, I find that every alternative to them is irrational in a deeper way. The indeterminism with its maggots, if you please to speak so about it, offends only the native absolutism of my intellect--an absolutism which, after all, perhaps, deserves to be snubbed and kept in check. But the determinism with its necessary carrion, to continue the figure of speech, and with no possible maggots to eat the latter up, violates my sense of moral reality through and through. When, for example, I imagine such carrion as the Brockton murder, I cannot conceive it as an act by which the universe, as a whole, logically and necessarily expresses its nature without shrinking from complicity with such a whole. And I deliberately refuse to keep on terms of loyalty with the universe by saying blankly that the murder, since it does flow from the nature of the whole, is not carrion. There are some instinctive reactions which I, for one, will not tamper with. The only remaining alternative, the attitude of gnostical romanticism, wrenches my personal instincts in quite as violent a way. It falsifies the simple objectivity of their deliverance. It makes the goose flesh the murder excites in me a sufficient reason for the perpetration of the crime. It transforms life from a tragic reality into an insincere melodramatic exhibition, as foul or as tawdry as anyone's diseased curiosity pleases to carry it out. And with its consecration of the roman naturaliste state of mind, and its enthronement of the baser crew of Parisian littérateurs among the eternally indispensable organs by which the infinite spirit of things attains to that subjective illumination which is the task of its life, it leaves me in presence of a sort of subjective carrion considerably more noisome than the objective carrion I called it in to take away.

No! better a thousand times, than such systematic corruption of our moral sanity, the plainest pessimism, so that it be straightforward; but better far than that the world of chance. Make as great an uproar about chance as you please, I know that chance means pluralism and nothing more. If some of the members of the pluralism are bad, the philosophy of pluralism, whatever broad views it may deny me, permits me, at least, to turn to the other members with a clean breast of

142

affection and an unsophisticated moral sense. And if I still wish to think of the world as a totality, it lets me feel that a world with a chance in it of being altogether good, even if the chance never come to pass, is better than a world with no such chance at all. That "chance" whose very notion I am exhorted and conjured to banish from my view of the future as the suicide of reason concerning it, that "chance" is--what? Just this--the chance that in moral respects the future may be other and better than the past has been. This is the only chance we have any motive for supposing to exist. Shame, rather, on its repudiation and its denial! For its presence is the vital air which lets the world live, the salt which keeps it sweet.

And here I might legitimately stop, having expressed all I care to see admitted by others tonight. But I know that if I do stop here, misapprehensions will remain in the minds of some of you, and keep all I have said from having its effect; so I judge it best to add a few more words.

In the first place, in spite of all my explanations, the word "chance" will still be giving trouble. Though you may yourselves be adverse to the deterministic doctrine, you wish a pleasanter word than "chance" to name the opposite doctrine by; and you very likely consider my preference for such a word a perverse sort of a partiality on my part. It certainly is a bad word to make converts with; and you wish I had not thrust it so butt-foremost at you--you wish to use a milder term.

Well, I admit there may be just a dash of perversity in its choice. The spectacle of the mere word-grabbing game played by the soft determinists has perhaps driven me too violently the other way; and, rather than be found wrangling with them for the good words, I am willing to take the first bad one which comes along, provided it be unequivocal. The question is of things, not of eulogistic names for them; and the best word is the one that enables men to know the quickest whether they disagree or not about the things. But the word "chance," with its singular negativity, is just the word for this purpose. Whoever uses it instead of "freedom," squarely and resolutely gives up all pretense to control the things he says are free. For him, he confesses that they are no better than mere chance would be. It is a word of impotence, and is therefore the only sincere word we can use, if, in granting freedom to certain things, we grant it honestly, and really risk the game. "Who chooses me must give and forfeit all he hath." Any other word permits of quibbling, and lets us, after the fashion of the soft determinists, make a pretense of restoring the caged bird to liberty with one hand, while with the other we anxiously tie a string to its leg to make sure it does not get beyond our sight.

But now you will bring up your final doubt. Does not the admission of such an unguaranteed chance or freedom preclude utterly the notion of a Providence governing the world? Does it not leave the fate of the universe at the mercy of the chance-possibilities, and so far insecure? Does it not, in short, deny the craving of our nature for an ultimate peace behind all tempests, for a blue zenith above all clouds?

To this my answer must be very brief. The belief in free will is not in the least incompatible with the belief in Providence, provided you do not restrict the Providence to fulminating nothing but _fatal_ degrees. If you allow him to provide possibilities as well as actualities to the universe, and to carry on his own thinking in those two categories just as we do ours, chances may be there, uncontrolled even by him, and the course of the universe be really ambiguous; and yet the end of all things may be just what he intended it to be from all eternity.

An analogy will make the meaning of this clear. Suppose two men before a chessboard--the one a novice, the other an expert player of the game. The expert intends to beat. But he cannot foresee exactly what any one actual move of his adversary may be. He knows, however, all the _possible_ moves of the latter; and he knows in advance how to meet each of them by a move of his own which leads in the direction of victory. And the victory infallibly arrives, after no matter how devious a course, in the one predestined form of checkmate to the novice's king.

Let now the novice stand for us finite free agents, and the expert for the infinite mind in which the universe lies. Suppose the latter to be thinking out his universe before he actually creates it. Suppose him to say, I will lead things to a certain end, but I will not _now_[5] decide on all the steps thereto. At various points, ambiguous possibilities shall be left open, _either_ of which, at a given instant, may become actual. But whichever branch of these bifurcations becomes

144

real, I know what I shall do at the <u>next</u> bifurcation to keep things from drifting away from the final result I intend.[6]

The creator's plan of the universe would thus be left blank as to many of its actual details, but all possibilities would be marked down. The realization of some of these would be left absolutely to chance; that is, would only be determined when the moments of realization came. Other possibilities would be <u>contingently</u> determined; that is, their decision would have to wait till it was seen how the matters of absolute chance fell out. But the rest of the plan, including its final upshot, would be rigorously determined once for all. So the creator himself would not need to know all the details of actuality until they came; and at any time his own view of the world would be a view partly of facts and partly of possibilities, exactly as ours is now. Of one thing, however, he might be certain; and that is that his world was safe, and that no matter how much of it might zigzag he could surely bring it home at last.

Now, it is entirely immaterial, in this scheme, whether the creator leave the absolute chance-possibilities to be decided by himself, each when its proper moment arrives, or whether, on the contrary, he alienate this power from himself, and leave the decision out and out to finite creatures such as we men are. The great point is that the possibilities are really <u>here</u>. Whether it be we who solve them, or he working <u>through</u> us, at those soul-trying moments when fate's scales seem to quiver, and good snatches the victory from evil or shrinks nerveless from the fight, is of small account, so long as we admit that the issue is decided nowhere else than <u>here</u> and <u>now</u>. <u>That</u> is what gives the palpitating reality to our moral <u>life</u> and makes it tingle, as Mr. Mallock says, with so strange and elaborate an excitement. This reality, this excitement, are what the determinisms, hard and soft alike, suppress by their denial that <u>anything</u> is decided here and now, and their dogma that all things were foredoomed and settled long ago. If it be so, may you and I then have been foredoomed to the error of continuing to believe in liberty.[7] It is fortunate for the winding up of controversy that in every discussion with determinism this <u>argumentum ad hominem</u> can be its adversary's last word.

FOOTNOTES

[1]Speaking technically, it is a word with a positive denotation, but a connotation that is negative.
Other things must be silent about what it is: it alone
can decide that point at the moment in which it reveals
itself.

[2]A favorite argument against free will is that if
it be true, a man's murderer may as probably be his
best friend as his worst enemy, a mother be as likely
to strangle as to suckle her first-born, and all of us
be as ready to jump from fourth-story windows as to go
out of front doors, etc. Users of this argument should
properly be excluded from debate till they learn what
the real question is. "Free will" does not say that
everything that is physically conceivable is also morally possible. It merely says that of alternatives
that really tempt our will more than one is really possible. Of course, the alternatives that do thus tempt
our will are vastly fewer than the physical possibilities we can coldly fancy. Persons really tempted often
do murder their best friends, mothers do strangle their
first-born, people do jump our of fourth-story windows,
etc.

[3]To a reader who says he is satisfied with a pessimism, and has no objection to thinking the whole bad,
I have no more to say: he makes fewer demands on the
world than I, who, making them, wish to look a little
further before I give up all hope of having them satisfied. If, however, all he means is that the badness of
some parts does not prevent his acceptance of a universe whose other parts give him satisfaction, I welcome him as an ally. He has abandoned the notion of
the Whole, which is the essence of deterministic monism, and views things as a pluralism, just as I do in
this paper.

[4]The burden, for example, of seeing to it that the
end of all our righteousness be some positive universal
gain.

[5]This of course leaves the creative mind subject
to the law of time. And to anyone who insists on the
timelessness of that mind I have no reply to make. A

146

mind to whom all time is simultaneously present must
see all things under the form of actuality, or under
some form to us unknown. If he thinks certain moments
as ambiguous in their content while future, he must simultaneously know how the ambiguity will have been decided when they are past. So that none of his mental
judgements can possibly be called hypothetical, and his
world is one from which chance is excluded. Is not,
however, the timeless mind rather a gratuitous fiction?
And is not the notion of eternity being given at a
stroke to omniscience only just another way of whacking
upon us the block-universe, and of denying that possibilities exist?--just the point to be proved. To say
that time is an illusory appearance is only a roundabout manner of saying there is no real plurality, and
that the frame of things is an absolute unit. Admit
plurality, and time may be its form.

6And this of course means "miraculous" interposition, but not necessarily of the gross sort our fathers
took such delight in representing, and which has so
lost its magic for us. Emerson quotes some Eastern
sage as saying that if evil were really done under the
sun, the sky would incontinently shrivel to a snakeskin
and cast it out in spasms. But, says Emerson, the
spasms of Nature are years and centuries; and it will
tax man's patience to wait so long. We may think of
the reserved possibilities God keeps in his own hand,
under as invisible and molecular and slowly self-
summating a form as we please. We may think of them
as counteracting human agencies which he inspires ad
hoc. In short, signs and wonders and convulsions of
the earth and sky are not the only neutralizers of obstruction to a god's plans of which it is possible to
think.

7As long as languages contain a future perfect
tense, determinists, following the bent of laziness or
passion, the lines of least resistance, can reply in
that tense, saying, "It will have been fated," to the
still small voice which urges an opposite course; and
thus excuse themselves from effort in a quite unanswerable way.

SUGGESTED READINGS

William James

James, William. The Varieties of Religious Experience: A Study in Human Nature (New York:
Longmans, Green, 1902).

_____. A Pluralistic Universe (New York:
Longmans, Green, 1909).

_____. Memories and Studies (New York:
Longmans, Green, 1911).

_____. Essays in Radical Empiricism (New
York: Longmans, Green, 1912).

_____. Collected Essays and Reviews (New
York: Longmans, Green, 1920).

* * *

_____. "The Essence of Humanism," Jour-
nal of Philosophy, Psychology, and Scientific
Methods, II, 5 (March 1905), 113-118.

_____. "Is Radical Empiricism Solipsis-
tic?" Journal of Philosophy, Psychology, and
Scientific Methods, II, 9 (April 1905), 235-
238.

* * *

Boodin, J. E. "Fictions in Science and Philosophy, I," The Journal of Philosophy, XL, 25 (December 1943), 673-682.

_____. "Fictions in Science and Philoso-
phy, II," The Journal of Philosophy, XL, 26
(December 1943), 701-716.

Gotshalk, D. W. "Causality as an Ontological Relation," Monist, XL, 2 (April 1930), 231-255.

_____. "The Nature of Change," Monist,
XL, 3 (July 1930), 363-380.

148

Gotshalk, D. W.   "Change as Substance:," Monist,
    XLI, 2 (April 1931), 292-303.

Flournoy, T.   The Philosophy of William James (New
    York: Henry Holt, 1917).

Moore, E. C. William James (New York: Washington
    Square Press, 1965).

Perry, R. B.   The Thought and Character of William
    James (Boston: Little, Brown, 1935). Vols. I
    and II.

_____ .   In the Spirit of William James (New
    Haven: Yale University Press, 1938).

6. THE IDEAL GENESIS OF MATTER AND
THE MEANING OF EVOLUTION

Henri Bergson

Henri Bergson (1859-1941) is the outstanding
French philosopher of the twentieth century.
He is also one of the important sources of
process philosophy, strongly influencing most,
if not all, of those who succeeded him. His
characteristic blend of literary elegance and
scientific erudition were to win for him a
wide international audience and many honors,
which included the Nobel Prize for Literature
in 1928.

In the following passages Henri Bergson, one of
the great pioneers in process philosophy, develops a
"vitalist" interpretation of biology.* His style of
writing is unique among recent philosophers in its use
of images and metaphors (the steam jet, the moving arm,
the rocket). Such images must not be conceived as mere
literary ornaments however. They are very carefully
chosen to help the reader "think duration"; that is, in
this case, to grasp the dynamic of evolution and of
living things. Evolution is best understood, Bergson
contends, as an interaction between two contrasting
"currents," that of life, which achieves progressively
higher levels of form and of activity, and that of matter, which continually degrades itself in the direction
of total entropy. It is the creative "push" of life
(termed "vital impetus" or "élan vital") which distinguishes living things from non-living things and constitutes life's essence. The human understanding or
"intellect" tends to see the living organism as a simple aggregate of inert physical atoms. The dynamic of

*This selection is from Creative Evolution.
Trans. Arthur Mitchell, (New York: Henry Holt, 1913),
pp. 247-271. This may be said to be Bergson's major
work and most clearly explicates his view of time,
life, and mind which had evolved in previous works.

life, however, transcends its material components. It must be approached through intuition. Bergson insists that life is not to be conceived as sheer random drift, but as a striving after increased freedom. This is evident especially in the evolution of animals, whose nervous systems have gradually achieved both greater precision and flexibility, and hence have made possible a broader range of possible actions. By joining this broad potential for action with an increased capacity to accumulate and expend chemical energy, the conditions for the free act are created. It happens that such conditions have, on this planet, been fully achieved only in man, so that man can in a sense be termed the end or goal of evolution. Thanks to our brains we have escaped the virtual automatism of the other animals, and see before us almost unlimited possibilities. Creative evolution, formerly limited to the creation of new species, now becomes reflective and enters into the broad path of human social evolution.

The Ideal Genesis of Matter and
the Meaning of Evolution

Let us imagine a vessel full of steam at a high
pressure, and here and there in its sides a crack
through which the steam is escaping in a jet. The
steam thrown into the air is nearly all condensed into
little drops which fall back, and this condensation and
this fall represent simply the loss of something, an
interruption, a deficit. But a small part of the jet
of steam subsists, uncondensed, for some seconds; it is
making an effort to raise the drops which are falling;
it succeeds at most in retarding their fall. So, from
an immense reservoir of life, jets must be gushing out
unceasingly, of which each, falling back, is a world.
The evolution of living species within this world represents what subsists of the primitive direction of the
original jet, and of an impulsion which continues it
self in a direction the inverse of materiality. But
let us not carry too far this comparison. It gives us
but a feeble and even deceptive image of reality, for
the crack, the jet of steam, the forming of the drops,
are determined necessarily, whereas the creation of a
world is a free act, and the life within the material
world participates in this liberty. Let us think rather of an action like that of raising the arm; then let
us suppose that the arm, left to itself, falls back,
and yet that there subsists in it, striving to raise it
up again, something of the will that animates it. In
this image of a creative action which unmakes itself we
have already a more exact representation of matter. In
vital activity we see, then, that which subsists of the
direct movement in the inverted movement, a reality
which is making itself in a reality which is unmaking
itself.

Everything is obscure in the idea of creation if
we think of things which are created and a thing which
creates, as we habitually do, as the understanding cannot help doing. We shall show the origin of this illusion in our next chapter. It is natural to our intellect, whose function is essentially practical, made to
present to us things and states rather than changes and
acts. But things and states are only views, taken by
our mind, of becoming. There are no things, there are
only actions. More particularly, if I consider the
world in which we live, I find that the automatic and
strictly determined evolution of this well-knit whole
is action which is unmaking itself, and that the unforeseen forms which life cuts out in it, forms capable

153

of being themselves prolonged into unforeseen movements, represent the action that is making itself. Now, I have every reason to believe that the other worlds are analogous to ours, that things happen there in the same way. And I know they were not all constructed at the same time, since observation shows me, even today, nebulae in course of concentration. Now, if the same kind of action is going on everywhere, whether it is that which is unmaking itself or whether it is that which is striving to remake itself, I simply express this probable similitude when I speak of a centre from which worlds shoot out like rockets in a fire-works display--provided, however, that I do not present this centre as a thing, but as a continuity of shooting out. God thus defined, has nothing of the already made; He is unceasing life, action, freedom. Creation, so conceived, is not a mystery; we experience it in ourselves when we act freely. That new things can join things already existing is absurd, no doubt, since the thing results from a solidification performed by our understanding, and there are never any things other than those that the understanding has thus constituted. To speak of things creating themselves would therefore amount to saying that the understanding presents to itself more than it presents to itself--a self-contradictory affirmation, an empty and vain idea. But that action increases as it goes on, that it creates in the measure of its advance, is what each of us finds when he watches himself act. Things are constituted by the instantaneous cut which the understanding practices, at a given moment, on a flux of this kind, and what is mysterious when we compare the cuts together becomes clear when we relate them to the flux. Indeed, the modalities of creative action, in so far as it is still going on in the organization of living forms, are much simplified when they are taken in this way. Before the complexity of an organism and the practically infinite multitude of interwoven analyses and syntheses it presupposes, our understanding recoils disconcerted. That the simple play of physical and chemical forces, left to themselves, should have worked this marvel, we find hard to believe. And if it is a profound science which is at work, how are we to understand the influence exercised on this matter without form by this form without matter? But the difficulty arises from this, that we represent statically ready-made material particles juxtaposed to one another, and, also statically, an external cause which plasters upon them a skilfully contrived organization. In reality, life is a movement, materiality is the inverse movement, and each of these two

154

movements is simple, the matter which forms a world being an undivided flux, and undivided also the life that
runs through it, cutting out in it living beings all
along its track. Of these two currents the second runs
counter to the first, but the first obtains, all the
same, something from the second. There results between
them a modus vivendi, which is organization. This organization takes, for our senses and for our intellect,
the form of parts entirely external to other parts in
space and in time. Not only do we shut our eyes to the
unity of the impulse which, passing through generations, links individuals with individuals, species with
species, and makes of the whole series of the living
one single immense wave flowing over matter, but each
individual itself seems to us as an aggregate, aggregate of molecules and aggregate of facts. The reason
of this lies in the structure of our intellect, which
is formed to act on matter from without, and which succeeds by making, in the flux of the real, instantaneous
cuts, each of which becomes, in its fixity, endlessly
decomposable. Perceiving, in an organism, only parts
external to parts, the understanding has the choice between two systems of explanation only: either to regard the infinitely complex (and thereby infinitely
well-contrived) organization as a fortuitous concatena-
tion of atoms, or to relate it to the incomprehensible
influence of an external force that has grouped its
elements together. But this complexity is the work of
the understanding; this incomprehensibility is also its
work. Let us try to see, no longer with the eyes of
the intellect alone, which grasps only the already made
and which looks from the outside, but with the spirit,
I mean with that faculty of seeing which is immanent in
the faculty of acting and which springs up, somehow, by
the twisting of the will on itself, when action is
turned into knowledge, like heat, so to say, into light.
To movement, then, everything will be restored, and
into movement everything will be resolved. Where the
understanding, working on the image supposed to be
fixed of the progressing action, shows us parts infinitely manifold and an order infinitely well contrived,
we catch a glimpse of a simple process, an action which
is making itself across an action of the same kind
which is unmaking itself, like the fiery path torn by
the last rocket of a fire-works display through the
black cinders of the spent rockets that are falling
dead.

From this point of view, the general considerations we have presented concerning the evolution of

life will be cleared up and completed. We will distinguish more sharply what is accidental from what is essential in this evolution.

The impetus of life, of which we are speaking,
consists in a need of creation. It cannot create absolutely, because it is confronted with matter, that is
to say with the movement that is the inverse of its
own. But it seizes upon this matter, which is necessity itself, and strives to introduce into it the largest possible amount of indetermination and liberty.
How does it go to work?

An animal high in the scale may be represented in
a general way, we said, as a sensori-motor nervous system imposed on digestive, respiratory, circulatory systems, etc. The function of these latter is to cleanse,
repair and protect the nervous system, to make it as
independent as possible of external circumstances, but,
above all, to furnish it with energy to be expended in
movements. The increasing complexity of the organism
is therefore due theoretically (in spite of innumerable
exceptions due to accidents of evolution) to the necessity of complexity in the nervous system. No doubt,
each complication of any part of the organism involves
many others in addition, because this part itself must
live, and every change in one point of the body rever-
berates, as it were, throughout. The complication may
therefore go on to infinity in all directions; but it
is the complication of the nervous system which conditions the others in right, if not always in fact. Now,
in what does the progress of the nervous system itself
consist? In a simultaneous development of automatic
activity and of voluntary activity, the first furnishing the second with an appropriate instrument. Thus,
in an organism such as ours, a considerable number of
motor mechanisms are set up in the medulla and in the
spinal cord, awaiting only a signal to release the corresponding act: the will is employed, in some cases,
in setting up the mechanism itself, and in the others
in choosing the mechanisms to be released, the manner
of combining them and the moment of releasing them.
The will of an animal is the more effective and the
more intense, the greater the number of the mechanisms
it can choose from, the more complicated the switchboard on which all the motor paths cross, or, in other
words, the more developed its brain. Thus, the progress of the nervous system assures to the act increasing precision, increasing variety, increasing efficiency and independence. The organism behaves more and

156

more like a machine for action, which reconstructs itself entirely for every new act, as if it were made of
india-rubber and could, at any moment, change the shape
of all its parts. But, prior to the nervous system,
prior even to the organism properly so called, already
in the undifferentiated mass of the amoeba, this essential property of animal life is found. The amoeba deforms itself in varying directions; its entire mass
does what the differentiation of parts will localize in
a sensori-motor system in the developed animal. Doing
it only in a rudimentary manner, it is dispensed from
the complexity of the higher organisms; there is no
need here of the auxiliary elements that pass on to motor elements the energy to expend; the animal moves as
a whole, and, as a whole also, procures energy by means
of the organic substances it assimilates. Thus, whether low or high in the animal scale, we always find that
animal life consists (1) in procuring a provision of
energy; (2) in expending it, by means of a matter as
supple as possible, in directions variable and unforeseen.

Now, whence comes the energy? From the ingested
food, for food is a kind of explosive, which needs only
the spark to discharge the energy it stores. Who has
made this explosive? The food may be the flesh of an
animal nourished on animals and so on; but, in the end
it is to the vegetable we always come back. Vegetables
alone gather in the solar energy, and the animals do
but borrow it from them, either directly or by some
passing it on to others. How then has the plant stored
up this energy? Chiefly by the chlorophyllian function, a chemicism sui generis of which we do not possess the key, and which is probably unlike that of our
laboratories. The process consists in using solar energy to fix the carbon of carbonic acid, and thereby to
store this energy as we should store that of a water-
carrier by employing him to fill an elevated reservoir:
the water, once brought up, can set in motion a mill or
a turbine, as we will and when we will. Each atom of
carbon fixed represents something like the elevation of
the weight of water, or like the stretching of an elastic thread uniting the carbon to the oxygen in the carbonic acid. The elastic is relaxed, the weight falls
back again, in short the energy held in reserve is restored, when, by a simple release, the carbon is permitted to rejoin its oxygen.

So that all life, animal and vegetable, seems in
its essence like an effort to accumulate energy and

then to let it flow into flexible channels, changeable
in shape, at the end of which it will accomplish infinitely varied kinds of work. That is what the vital
impetus, passing through matter, would fain do all at
once. It would succeed, no doubt, if its power were
unlimited, or if some reinforcement could come to it
from without. But the impetus is finite, and it has
been given once for all. It cannot overcome all obstacles. The movement it starts is sometimes turned aside,
sometimes divided, always opposed; and the evolution of
the organized world is the unrolling of this conflict.
The first great scission that had to be effected was
that of the two kingdoms, vegetable and animal, which
thus happen to be mutually complementary, without, however, any agreement having been made between them. It
is not for the animal that the plant accumulates energy,
it is for its own consumption; but its expenditure on
itself is less discontinuous, and less concentrated,
and therefore less efficacious, than was required by
the initial impetus of life, essentially directed toward free actions: the same organism could not with
equal force sustain the two functions at once, of gradual storage and sudden use. Of themselves, therefore,
and without any external intervention, simply by the
effect of the duality of the tendency involved in the
original impetus and of the resistance opposed by matter to this impetus, the organisms leaned some in the
first direction, others in the second. To this scission there succeeded many others. Hence the diverging
lines of evolution, at least what is essential in them.
But we must take into account retrogressions, arrests,
accidents of every kind. And we must remember, above
all, that each species behaves as if the general movement of life stopped at it instead of passing through
it. It thinks only of itself, it lives only for itself. Hence the numberless struggles that we behold in
nature. Hence a discord, striking and terrible, but
for which the original principle of life must not be
held responsible.

The part played by contingency in evolution is
therefore great. Contingent, generally, are the forms
adopted, or rather invented. Contingent, relative to
the obstacles encountered in a given place and at a
given moment, is the dissociation of the primordial
tendency into such and such complementary tendencies
which create divergent lines of evolution. Contingent
the arrests and set-backs; contingent, in large measure, the adaptations. Two things only are necessary:
(1) a gradual accumulation of energy; (2) an elastic

canalization of this energy in variable and indeterminable directions, at the end of which are free acts.

This twofold result has been obtained in a particular way on our planet. But it might have been obtained by entirely different means. It was not necessary that life should fix its choice mainly upon the carbon of carbonic acid. What was essential for it was to store solar energy; but, instead of asking the sun to separate, for instance, atoms of oxygen and carbon, it might (theoretically at least, and, apart from practical difficulties possibly insurmountable) have put forth other chemical elements, which would then have had to be associated or dissociated by entirely different physical means. And if the element characteristic of the substances that supply energy to the organism had been other than carbon, the element characteristic of the plastic substances would probably have been other than nitrogen, and the chemistry of living bodies would then have been radically different from what it is. The result would have been living forms without any analogy to those we know, whose anatomy would have been different, whose physiology also would have been different. Alone, the sensori-motor function would have been preserved, if not in its mechanism, at least in its effects. It is therefore probable that life goes on in other planets, in other solar systems also, under forms of which we have no idea, in physical conditions to which it seems to us, from the point of view of our physiology, to be absolutely opposed. If its essential aim is to catch up usable energy in order to expend it in explosive actions, it probably chooses, in each solar system and on each planet, as it does on the earth, the fittest means to get this result in the circumstances with which it is confronted. That is at least what reasoning by analogy leads to, and we use analogy the wrong way when we declare life to be impossible wherever the circumstances with which it is confronted are other than those on the earth. The truth is that life is possible wherever energy descends the incline indicated by Carnot's law and where a cause of inverse direction can retard the descent--that is to say, probably, in all the worlds suspended from all the stars. We go further: it is not even necessary that life should be concentrated and determined in organisms properly so called, that is, in definite bodies presenting to the flow of energy ready-made through elastic canals. It can be conceived (although it can hardly be imagined) that energy might be saved up, and then expended on varying lines running across a matter not yet

159

solidified. Every essential of life would still be there, since there would still be slow accumulation of energy and sudden release. There would hardly be more difference between this vitality, vague and formless, and the definite vitality we know, than there is, in our psychical life, between the state of dream and the state of waking. Such may have been the condition of life in our nebula before the condensation of matter was complete, if it be true that life springs forward at the very moment when, as the effect of an inverse movement, the nebular matter appears.

It is therefore conceivable that life might have assumed a totally different outward appearance and designed forms very different from those we know. With another chemical substratum, in other physical conditions, the impulsion would have remained the same, but it would have split up very differently in course of progress; and the whole would have traveled another road--whether shorter or longer who can tell? In any case, in the entire series of living beings no term would have been what it now is. Now, was it necessary that there should be a series, or terms? Why should not the unique impetus have been impressed on a unique body, which might have gone on evolving?

This question arises, no doubt, from the comparison of life to an impetus. And it must be compared to an impetus, because no image borrowed from the physical world can give more nearly the idea of it. But it is only an image. In reality, life is of the psychological order, and it is of the essence of the psychical to enfold a confused plurality of interpenetrating terms. In space, and in space only, is distinct multiplicity possible: a point is absolutely external to another point. But pure and empty unity, also, is met with only in space; it is that of a mathematical point. Abstract unity and abstract multiplicity are determinations of space or categories of the understanding, whichever we will, spatiality and intellectuality being molded on each other. But what is of psychical nature cannot entirely correspond with space, nor enter perfectly into the categories of the understanding. Is my own person, at a given moment, one or manifold? If I declare it one, inner voices arise and protest--those of the sensations, feelings, ideas, among which my individuality is distributed. But, if I make it distinctly manifold, my consciousness rebels quite as strongly; it affirms that my sensations, my feelings, my thoughts are abstractions which I effect on myself, and that each of my states implies all the others. I am then (we must adopt the language of the understanding, since only the understanding has a language) a unity that is multiple and a multiplicity that is one;[1] but unity and multiplicity are only views of my personality taken by an understanding that directs its categories at me; I enter neither into one nor into the other nor into both at once, although both, united, may give a fair imitation of the mutual interpenetration and continuity that I find at the base of my own self. Such is my inner life, and such also is life in general. While, in its contact with matter, life is comparable to an impulsion or an impetus, regarded in itself it is an immensity of potentiality, a mutual encroachment of thousands and thousands of tendencies which nevertheless are "thousands and thousands" only when once regarded as outside of each other, that is, when spatialized. Contact with matter is what determines this dissociation. Matter divides actually what was but potentially manifold; and, in this sense, individuation is in part the work of matter, in part the result of life's own inclination. Thus, a poetic sentiment, which bursts into distinct verses, lines and words, may be said to have already contained this multiplicity of individuated elements, and yet, in fact, it is the materiality of language that creates it.

But through the words, lines and verses runs the simple inspiration which is the whole poem. So, among the dissociated individuals, one life goes on moving: everywhere the tendency to individualize is opposed and at the same time completed by an antagonistic and complementary tendency to associate, as if the manifold unity of life, drawn in the direction of multiplicity, made so much the more effort to withdraw itself on to itself. A part is no sooner detached than it tends to reunite itself, if not to all the rest, at least to what is nearest to it. Hence, throughout the whole realm of life, a balancing between individuation and association. Individuals join together into a society; but the society, as soon as formed, tends to melt the associated individuals into a new organism, so as to become itself an individual, able in its turn to be part and parcel of a new association. At the lowest degree of the scale of organisms we already find veritable associations, microbial colonies, and in these associations, according to a recent work, a tendency to individuate by the constitution of a nucleus.[2] The same tendency is met with again at a higher stage, in the protophytes, which, once having quitted the parent

161

cell by way of division, remain united to each other by
the gelatinous substance that surrounds them--also in
those protozoa which begin by mingling their pseudopo-
dia and end by welding themselves together. The "colonial" theory of the genesis of higher organisms is well
known. The protozoa, consisting of one single cell,
are supposed to have formed, by assemblage, aggregates
which, relating themselves together in their turn, have
given rise to aggregates of aggregates; so organisms
more and more complicated, and also more and more differentiated, are born of the association of organisms
barely differentiated and elementary.[3] In this extreme
form, the theory is open to grave objections: more and
more the idea seems to be gaining ground, that polyzo-
ism is an exceptional and abnormal fact.[4] But it is
none the less true that things happen as if every higher organism was born of an association of cells that
have subdivided the work between them. Very probably
it is not the cells that have made the individual by
means of association; it is rather the individual that
has made the cells by means of dissociation.[5] But this
itself reveals to us, in the genesis of the individual,
a haunting of the social form, as if the individual
could develop only on the condition that its substance
should be split up into elements having themselves an
appearance of individuality and united among themselves
by an appearance of sociality. There are numerous
cases in which nature seems to hesitate between the two
forms, and to ask herself if she shall make a society
or an individual. The slightest push is enough, then,
to make the balance weigh on one side or the other. If
we take an infusorian sufficiently large, such as the
Stentor, and cut it into two halves each containing a
part of the nucleus, each of the two halves will generate an independent Stentor; but if we divide it incompletely, so that a protoplasmic communication is left
between the two halves, we shall see them execute, each
from its side, corresponding movements: so that in
this case it is enough that a thread should be maintained or cut in order that life should affect the social or the individual form. Thus, in rudimentary organisms consisting of a single cell, we already find
that the apparent individuality of the whole is the
composition of an undefined number of potential individualities potentially associated. But, from top to
bottom of the series of living beings, the same law is
manifested. And it is this that we express when we say
that unity and multiplicity are categories of inert
matter, that the vital impetus is neither pure unity
nor pure multiplicity, and that if the matter to which

it communicates itself compels it to choose one of the two, its choice will never be definitive: it will leap from one to the other indefinitely. The evolution of life in the double direction of individuality and association has therefore nothing accidental about it: it is due to the very nature of life.

Essential also is the progress to reflextion. If our analysis is correct, it is consciousness, or rather supra-consciousness, that is at the origin of life. Consciousness, or supra-consciousness, is the name for the rocket whose extinguished fragments fall back as matter; consciousness, again, is the name for that which subsists of the rocket itself, passing through the fragments and lighting them up into organisms. But this consciousness, which is a need of creation, is made manifest to itself only where creation is possible. It lies dormant when life is condemned to automatism; it wakens as soon as the possibility of a choice is restored. That is why, in organisms unprovided with a nervous system, it varies according to the power of locomotion and of deformation of which the organism disposes. And in animals with a nervous system, it is proportional to the complexity of the switchboard on which the paths called sensory and the paths called motor intersect--that is, of the brain. How must this solidarity between the organism and consciousness be understood?

We will not dwell here on a point that we have dealt with in former works. Let us merely recall that a theory such as that according to which consciousness is attached to certain neurons, and is thrown off from their work like a phosphorescence, may be accepted by the scientist for the detail of analysis; it is a convenient mode of expression. But it is nothing else. In reality, a living being is a centre of action. It represents a certain sum of contingency entering into the world, that is to say, a certain quantity of possible action--a quantity variable with individuals and especially with species. The nervous system of an animal marks out the flexible lines on which its action will run (although the potential energy is accumulated in the muscles rather than in the nervous system itself); its nervous centres indicate, by their development and their configuration, the more or less extended choice it will have among more or less numerous and complicated actions. Now, since the awakening of consciousness in a living creature is the more complete, the greater the latitude of choice allowed to it and the larger the amount of action bestowed upon it, it is clear that the development of consciousness will appear to be dependent on that of the nervous centres. On the other hand, every state of consciousness being, in one aspect of it, a question put to the motor activity and even the beginning of a reply, there is no psychical event that does not imply the entry into play of the cortical mechanisms. Everything seems, therefore, to happen as if consciousness sprang from the brain, and as if the detail of conscious activity were modeled on that of the cerebral activity. In reality, consciousness does not spring from the brain; but brain and consciousness correspond because equally they measure, the one by the complexity of its structure and the other by the intensity of its awareness, the quantity of choice that the living being has at its disposal.

It is precisely because a cerebral state expresses simply what there is of nascent action in the corresponding psychical state, that the psychical state tells us more than the cerebral state. The consciousness of a living being, as we have tried to prove elsewhere, is inseparable from its brain in the sense in which a sharp knife is inseparable from its edge: the brain is the sharp edge by which consciousness cuts into the compact tissue of events, but the brain is no more coextensive with consciousness than the edge is with the knife. Thus, from the fact that two brains, like that of the ape and that of the man, are very much alike, we cannot conclude that the corresponding consciousnesses are comparable or commensurable.

But the two brains may perhaps be less alike than we suppose. How can we help being struck by the fact that, while man is capable of learning any sort of exercise, of constructing any sort of object, in short of acquiring any kind of motor habit whatsoever, the faculty of combining new movements is strictly limited in the best-endowed animal, even in the ape? The cerebral characteristic of man is there. The human brain is made, like every brain, to set up motor mechanisms and to enable us to choose among them, at any instant, the one we shall put in motion by the pull of a trigger. But it differs from other brains in this, that the number of mechanisms it can set up, and consequently the choice that it gives as to which among them shall be released, is unlimited. Now, from the limited to the unlimited there is all the distance between the closed and the open. It is not a difference of degree, but of kind.

164

Radical therefore, also, is the difference between
animal consciousness, even the most intelligent, and
human consciousness. For consciousness corresponds exactly to the living being's power of choice; it is co-
extensive with the fringe of possible action that surrounds the real action: consciousness is synonymous
with invention and with freedom. Now, in the animal,
invention is never anything but a variation on the
theme of routine. Shut up in the habits of the species,
it succeeds, no doubt, in enlarging them by its individual initiative; but it escapes automatism only for an
instant, for just the time to create a new automatism.
The gates of its prison close as soon as they are
opened; by pulling at its chain it succeeds only in
stretching it. With man, consciousness breaks the
chain. In man, and in man alone, it sets itself free.
The whole history of life until man has been that of
the effort of consciousness to raise matter, and of the
more or less complete overwhelming of consciousness by
the matter which has fallen back on it. The enterprise
was paradoxical, if, indeed, we may speak here otherwise than by metaphor of enterprise and of effort. It
was to create with matter, which is necessity itself,
an instrument of freedom, to make a machine which
should triumph over mechanism, and to use the determinism of nature to pass through the meshes of the net
which this very determinism had spread. But, everywhere except in man, consciousness has let itself be
caught in the net whose meshes it tried to pass through:
it has remained the captive of the mechanisms it has
set up. Automatism, which it tries to draw in the direction of freedom, winds about it and drags it down.
It has not the power to escape, because the energy it
has provided for acts is almost all employed in maintaining the infinitely subtle and essentially unstable
equilibrium into which it has brought matter. But man
not only maintains his machine, he succeeds in using it
as he pleases. Doubtless he owes this to the superiority of his brain, which enables him to build an unlimited number of motor mechanisms, to oppose new habits
to the old ones unceasingly, and, by dividing automatism against itself, to rule it. He owes it to his
language, which furnishes consciousness with an immaterial body in which to incarnate itself and thus exempts
it from dwelling exclusively on material bodies, whose
flux would soon drag it along and finally swallow it
up. He owes it to social life, which stores and preserves efforts as language stores thought, fixes thereby a mean level to which individuals must raise themselves at the outset, and by this initial stimulation

165

prevents the average man from slumbering and drives the superior man to mount still higher. But our brain, our society, and our language are only the external and various signs of one and the same internal superiority. They tell, each after its manner, the unique, exceptional success which life has won at a given moment of its evolution. They express the difference of kind, and not only of degree, which separates man from the rest of the animal world. They let us guess that, while at the end of the vast springboard from which life has taken its leap, all the others have stepped down, finding the cord stretched too high, man alone has cleared the obstacle.

It is in this quite special sense that man is the "term" and the "end" of evolution. Life, we have said, transcends finality as it transcends the other categories. It is essentially a current sent through matter, drawing from it what it can. There has not, therefore, properly speaking, been any project or plan. On the other hand, it is abundantly evident that the rest of nature is not for the sake of man: we struggle like the other species, we have struggled against other species. Moreover, if the evolution of life had encountered other accidents in its course, if, thereby, the current of life had been otherwise divided, we should have been, physically and morally, far different from what we are. For these various reasons it would be wrong to regard humanity, such as we have it before our eyes, as pre-figured in the evolutionary movement. It cannot even be said to be the outcome of the whole of evolution, for evolution has been accomplished on several divergent lines, and while the human species is at the end of one of them, other lines have been followed with other species at their end. It is in a quite different sense that we hold humanity to be the ground of evolution.

From our point of view, life appears in its entirety as an immense wave which, starting from a centre, spreads outwards, and which on almost the whole of its circumference is stopped and converted into oscillation: at one single point the obstacle has been forced, the impulsion has passed freely. It is this freedom that the human form registers. Everywhere but in man, consciousness has had to come to a stand; in man alone it has kept on its way. Man, then, continues the vital movement indefinitely, although he does not draw along with him all that life carries in itself. On other lines of evolution there have traveled other tendencies

166

which life implied, and of which, since everything in-
terpenetrates, man has, doubtless, kept something, but
of which he has kept only very little. <u>It is as if a
vague and formless being, whom we may call, as we will,
man or superman, had sought to realize himself, and had
succeeded only by abandoning a part of himself on the
way</u>. The losses are represented by the rest of the animal world, and even by the vegetable world, at least
in what these have that is positive and above the accidents of evolution.

From this point of view, the discordances of which
nature offers us the spectacle are singularly weakened.
The organized world as a whole becomes as the soil on
which was to grow either man himself or a being who
morally must resemble him. The animals, however distant they may be from species, however hostile to it,
have none the less been useful traveling companions, on
whom consciousness has unloaded whatever encumbrances
it was dragging along, and who have enabled it to rise,
in man, to heights from which it sees an unlimited horizon open again before it.

It is true that it has not only abandoned cumbersome baggage on the way; it has also had to give up
valuable goods. Consciousness, in man, is pre-eminently
intellect. It might have been, it ought, so it seems,
to have been also intuition. Intuition and intellect
represent two opposite directions of the work of consciousness: intuition goes in the very direction of
life, intellect goes in the inverse direction, and thus
finds itself naturally in accordance with the movement
of matter. A complete and perfect humanity would be
that in which these two forms of conscious activity
should attain their full development. And, between
this humanity and ours, we may conceive any number of
possible stages, corresponding to all the degrees imaginable of intelligence and of intuition. In this lies
the part of contingency in the mental structure of our
species. A different evolution might have led to a humanity either more intellectual still or more intuitive.
In the humanity of which we are a part, intuition is,
in fact, almost completely sacrificed to intellect. It
seems that to conquer matter, and to reconquer its own
self, consciousness has had to exhaust the best part of
its power. This conquest, in the particular conditions
in which it has been accomplished, has required that
consciousness should adapt itself to the habits of matter and concentrate all its attention on them, in fact
determine itself more especially as intellect.

167

Intuition is there, however, but vague and above all
discontinuous. It is a lamp almost extinguished, which
only glimmers now and then, for a few moments at most.
But it glimmers wherever a vital interest is at stake.
On our personality, on our liberty, on the place we occupy in the whole of nature, on our origin and perhaps
also on our destiny, it throws a light feeble and vac-
illating, but which none the less pierces the darkness
of the night in which the intellect leaves us.

These fleeting intuitions, which light up their
object only at distant intervals, philosophy ought to
seize, first to sustain them, then to expand them and
so unite them together. The more it advances in this
work, the more will it perceive that intuition is mind
itself, and, in a certain sense, life itself: the intellect has been cut out of it by a process resembling
that which has generated matter. Thus is revealed the
unity of the spiritual life. We recognize it only when
we place ourselves in intuition in order to go from intuition to the intellect, for from the intellect we
shall never pass to intuition.

Philosophy introduces us thus into the spiritual
life. And it shows us at the same time the relation of
the life of the spirit to that of the body. The great
error of the doctrines on the spirit has been the idea
that by isolating the spiritual life from all the rest,
by suspending it in space as high as possible above the
earth, they were placing it beyond attack, as if they
were not thereby simply exposing it to be taken as an
effect of mirage! Certainly they are right to listen
to conscience when conscience affirms human freedom;
but the intellect is there, which says that the cause
determines its effect, that like conditions like, that
all is repeated and that all is given. They are right
to believe in the absolute reality of the person and in
his independence toward matter; but science is there,
which shows the interdependence of conscious life and
cerebral activity. They are right to attribute to man
a privileged place in nature, to hold that the distance
is infinite between the animal and man; but the history
of life is there, which makes us witness the genesis of
species by gradual transformation, and seems thus to
reintegrate man in animality. When a strong instinct
assures the probability of personal survival, they are
right not to close their ears to its voice; but if
there exist "souls" capable of an independent life,
whence do they come? When, how and why do they enter
into this body which we see arise, quite naturally,

168

from a mixed cell derived from the bodies of its two
parents? All these questions will remain unanswered, a
philosophy of intuition will be a negation of science,
will be sooner or later swept away by science, if it
does not resolve to see the life of the body just where
it really is, on the road that leads to the life of the
spirit. But it will then no longer have to do with
definite living beings. Life as a whole, from the initial impulsion that thrust it into the world, will appear as a wave which rises, and which is opposed by the
descending movement of matter. On the greater part of
its surface, at different heights, the current is converted by matter into a vortex. At one point alone it
passes freely, dragging with it the obstacle which will
weigh on its progress but will not stop it. At this
point is humanity; it is our privileged situation. On
the other hand, this rising wave is consciousness, and,
like all consciousness, it includes potentialities
without number which interpenetrate and to which consequently neither the category of unity nor that of multiplicity is appropriate, made as they both are for inert matter. The matter that it bears along with it,
and in the interstices of which it inserts itself,
alone can divide it into distinct individualities. On
flows the current, running through human generations,
subdividing itself into individuals. This subdivision
was vaguely indicated in it, but could not have been
made clear without matter. Thus souls are continually
being created, which, nevertheless, in a certain sense
pre-existed. They are nothing else than the little
rills into which the great river of life divides itself, flowing through the body of humanity. The movement of the stream is distinct from the river bed, although it must adopt its winding course. Consciousness
is distinct from the organism it animates, although it
must undergo its vicissitudes. As the possible actions
which a state of consciousness indicates are at every
instant beginning to be carried out in the nervous
centres, the brain underlies at every instant the motor
indications of the state of consciousness; but the in-
terdependency of consciousness and brain is limited to
this; the destiny of consciousness is not bound up on
that account with the destiny of cerebral matter. Finally, consciousness is essentially free; it is freedom
itself; but it cannot pass through matter without settling on it, without adapting itself to it: this adaptation is what we call intellectuality; and the intellect, turning itself back toward active, that is to say
free, consciousness, naturally makes it enter into the
conceptual forms into which it is accustomed to see

matter fit. It will therefore always perceive freedom
in the form of necessity; it will always neglect the
part of novelty or of creation inherent in the free
act; it will always substitute for action itself an imitation artificial, approximative, obtained by com-
pounding the old with the old and the same with the
same. Thus, to the eyes of a philosophy that attempts
to reabsorb intellect in intuition, many difficulties
vanish or become light. But such a doctrine does not
only facilitate speculation; it gives us also more
power to act and to live. For, with it, we feel ourselves no longer isolated in humanity, humanity no
longer seems isolated in the nature that it dominates.
As the smallest grain of dust is bound up with our entire solar system, drawn along with it in that undivided movement of descent which is materiality itself, so
all organized beings, from the humblest to the highest,
from the first origins of life to the time in which we
are, and in all places as in all times, do but evidence
a single impulsion, the inverse of the movement of matter, and in itself indivisible. All the living hold
together, and all yield to the same tremendous push.
The animal takes its stand on the plant, man bestrides
animality, and the whole of humanity, in space and in
time, is one immense army galloping beside and before
and behind each of us in an overwhelming charge able to
beat down every resistance and clear the most formidable obstacles, perhaps even death.

FOOTNOTES

[1]We have dwelt on this point in an article entitled "Introduction à la métaphysique" (Revue de métaphysique et de morale, January, 1903, pp. 1-25).

[2]Cf. a paper written (in Russian) by Serkovski,
and reviewed in the Année biologique, 1898, p. 317.

[3]Ed. Perrier, Les Colonies animales, Paris, 1897
(2nd edition).

[4]Delage, L'Hérédité, 2nd edition, Paris, 1903, p.
97. Cf. by the same author, "La Conception polyzoïque
des êtres" (Revue scientifique, 1896, pp. 641-653).

[5]This is the theory maintained by Kunstler,
Delage, Sedgwick, Labbé, etc. Its development, with
bibliographical references, will be found in the work
of Busquet, Les êtres vivants, Paris, 1899.

SUGGESTED READINGS

Henri Bergson

Bergson, Henri. Matter and Memory (New York: Macmillan, 1911). Nancy Paul and W. Scott Palmer (Trans.).

_____. The Two Sources of Morality and Religion (London: Macmillan, 1935). Ashley Audra and Cloudesly Brereton with W. H. Carter (Trans.).

* * *

_____. "Life and Consciousness," in Mind-Energy: Lectures and Essays (New York: Holt, 1920), pp. 3-36. H. Wildon Carr (Trans.).

_____. "The Philosophy of Claude Bernard," in The Creative Mind (New York: Philosophical Library, 1946), pp. 238-247. Mabelle L. Andison (Trans.).

* * *

Gunter, Pete A. Y. "Bergson's Theory of Matter and Modern Cosmology," Journal of History of Ideas, XXXII, 4 (October-December 1971), 525-542.

_____. "The Heuristic Force of Creative Evolution," Southwestern Journal of Philosophy, I, 3 (1970), 111-118.

Sipfle, David A. "Henri Bergson and the Epochal Theory of Time," in Bergson and the Evolution of Physics (Knoxville: University of Tennessee Press, 1969), pp. 275-294. Pete A. Y. Gunter (Ed.).

* * *

Chevalier, Jacques. Henri Bergson (Freeport, New York: AMS Press, 1969). Lilian A. Clare (Trans.).

Driesch, Hans. The History and Theory of Vitalism
    (New York: Macmillan, 1914). C. K. Ogden
    (Trans.).

Johnstone, James. The Philosophy of Biology (Cam-
    bridge: Cambridge University Press, 1914).

Waddington, C. H. (Ed.). Towards a Theoretical
    Biology Vol. I of Prolegomena (Chicago: Aldine,
    1968).

7.   VITALISM

Conwy Lloyd Morgan

C. Lloyd Morgan (1852-1936) was educated primarily in the Sciences at the London School of
Mines and Royal College of Science. He first
taught at the Diocesan College, South Africa,
before taking a position in the areas of geol-
ogy and zoology at University College in Bristol
where he remained from 1884 until the time of
his retirement in 1919.

C. Lloyd Morgan, who had a background in biology,
zoology, and psychology, was one of the early promoters
of the concept of emergence as a means of interpreting
the universe, and more specifically, as providing a
means of going beyond the biological and evolutionary
conceptions of Darwin and Spencer. His realism and
conceptual imagery contributed, in a degree far greater
than is usually recognized, to the thought of H. Bergson, S. Alexander, and A. N. Whitehead. Morgan laid
the groundwork for this organismic view in his notewor-
thy article which follows* and further explicated the
concept in his more formidable work Emergent Evolution
(1923). Morgan is intent to explicate an "emergent" or
vital force as an entirely novel event within the process of the natural world. It is a new appearance which
can in no way be accounted for by any previous level of
the evolutionary process. In relationship to this dynamic, vitalistic view of emergence, indicative as it
is of a new kind of relatedness which exceeds prediction or explanation on the basis of the lower levels
which preceded it, the imagery of former evolution is
considered to be quite static. Morgan later speaks of
this former conception or production of the evolutionary process as a "resultant,"# by which he means a new

---

*From The Monist, IX (1899), 179-196. Used by
permission.

#C. Lloyd Morgan, Emergent Evolution (London:
Williams and Norgate, 1923), pp. 2ff. For a good

quality, but one that is entirely explicable in terms of its antecedents. Such resultants are not without importance of course because they add an element of continuity in a process that is otherwise quite discontinuous and indeterminate. Consequently, even though there is an actual qualitative change of direction which takes place in the course of events which makes up the emergent process, he believes it is not a discontinuous aperture. Morgan began his studies and drew his first conclusions pertaining to emergence on the basis of an empirical methodology and this is undoubtedly where he made his major contribution as a promoter of emergent thought. In fact, modern biochemistry seems to confirm some of his premonitions concerning the notion of progress in continuity through emergence.

---

introduction to Morgan's definition of evolution and emergence as well as his methodology and how this brings him to construct a metaphysical scheme Cf. Eric E. Rust, <u>Evolutionary Philosophers and Contemporary Theology</u> (Philadelphia: Westminster Press, 1969), pp. 77ff.

Vitalism

There are certain undying questions which periodically recur in varying forms at successive stages in the advance of knowledge. And when these are critically examined they will generally be found to contain a metaphysical or noumenal element. Such a question is that which falls under the head of Vitalism. Is the conception of Vital Force valid, and is it necessary for the comprehension of the phenomena of organic life? This is the question I propose to discuss in the light of principles already considered. It will probably conduce to clearness if the question is distributed thus: Is Vital Force a valid and necessary conception in the sphere of metaphysics? Has it any locus standi in the sphere of science?

A reminder as to the distinction already drawn between science and metaphysics may here be necessary. Both deal with causation; both offer explanations. But whereas the explanations of science refer particular events to the generalisations within which they are comprised (thus the fall of a stone to the earth is referred to the generalised statement of universal gravitation); and whereas they deal with causation in terms of antecedence and sequence, the facts being accepted as data; the explanations of metaphysics offer an answer to the question: Why are the facts such as we find them to be? They deal with causation in terms of noumenal origin or raison d'être. The science of dynamics tells us that, given such and such nature and distribution of the parts of a material system, such and such movements or states of strain do as a matter of fact occur. If we ask why such movements or strains occur under these circumstances, metaphysics replies that Force is the noumenal Cause of motion or of strain. It is true that at the beginning of treatises on the science of dynamics there is usually a reference to Force as the Cause of motion. But this is merely a pious tribute to metaphysics, like grace before meat, and has no influence on either the quality of the dinner or its subsequent digestion. Of such a nature is Vital Force. It is a perfectly legitimate metaphysical conception of the noumenal Cause of certain observed phenomena, and should take its place alongside Gravitative Force, Chemical Force, Crystalline Force and the rest of the stalwart metaphysical grenadiers.

It is in large degree because, when Vitalism is
the topic of discussion, the disputants on each side
fail to distinguish the metaphysical from the scientific elements of the question, that we seem to be as far
from a satisfactory solution of the problem as were our
fathers a generation ago. Only when the distinction is
adequately realised will the combatants be prepared to
confess that the battle is drawn, each side holding un-
conquered an impregnable fortress--the shattering of
certain weak outworks, which should never have been occupied, serving only to show the real strength of the
central position of either contending host.

It is unnecessary to enter at any length into the
past history of the subject. Sufficient unto the generation are the conditions under which its problems
must be discussed. Of old, before the forces of science had girt their strength about them, Vitalism held
the field in easy if somewhat lax possession. Then
came a period of organised attack. Chemistry and molecular physics had formulated and extended their generalisations and began to urge that the problems of
physiology were problems of chemistry and physics--
nothing more. There was no vital remainder. Taking
their stand on the conservation of energy, they con-
tended that the conception of Vital Force involved the
appearance of energy without physical or chemical antecedents. This carried conviction among some of our
leading physiologists. Prof. Burdon Sanderson wrote:
"The proof of the non-existence of a special 'vital
force' lies in the demonstration of the adequacy of the
known sources of energy in the organism to account for
the actual day by day expenditure of heat and work."
But an answer in due course came from the vitalists.
It was pointed out that the application of a force to a
moving body at right angles to its course, alters the
direction of motion without affecting its amount. The
energy remains unchanged. Of such a directive character, it is sometimes urged, may be the application of
vital force without presenting any phenomena contradictory of the generalisation that, in the operations of
nature, energy is nowhere either destroyed or created.

So long as the metaphysical conceptions of Force
are carelessly commingled with the generalisations of
dynamics as a science, this line of argument may appear
to possess a cogency which is in truth fictitious. But
what is the basal law of dynamics? That every movement
of a part in any material system and every state of
strain therein, has, as its antecedent, the assignable

nature and distribution of the constituent parts in
that system. This is a generalised statement of dynamic fact which quietly ignores (though it does not deny)
the existence of Force as the noumenal cause of motion.
Granting therefore that a vital force is conceivable
which alters the direction of motion without producing
any change in the amount of energy, the question still
remains: Is the movement so produced in accordance
with, or is it contradictory to, the basal law of dynamics? For the change of direction of motion is itself a motion, though it be unaccompanied by any increase or diminution of energy. If therefore the motion
in question is the outcome of the nature and distribution of the constituent parts in a material system it
is a natural movement co-ordinate with other physical
movements, and Prof. Burdon Sanderson's contention is
in essence valid, as a protest against supernaturalism,
though it is incompletely stated; if on the other hand
the motion is not such an outcome, then, though the
conservation of energy may still hold its ground, what
I have termed the basal law of dynamics cannot. There
are movements of material particles which are outside
this generalisation. It is questionable, however,
whether there are many vitalists of scientific training
who would care to contend for the truth of this conclusion.

It may be said that I have here quietly ignored
certain essential features in any dynamical configura-
tion--namely, the nature of the forces (gravitative,
crystalline, chemical, electrical, and so forth) at work
within the given system. But from the point of view of
science the attractions or repulsions attributed to
these forces are merely data to be accepted and stated
as simple facts of observation. They are the outcome
of the nature and distribution of the parts of the sys-
tem--including under the head "nature and distribution"
the totality of the antecedent conditions. No doubt
the antecedent conditions are different according as we
place a piece of cork or a piece of sodium on the surface of water. In the one case certain chemical attractions have to be taken into account which in the other
case are absent. These form part of the dynamical data
without which the problem is insoluble. Science accepts these data as facts in the phenomenal chain of
antecedence and sequence. Metaphysics attempts to account for the facts by the conception of Chemical Force.
The chemist, as man of science, says: Give me the
facts of chemical dynamics and I will comprise them
under broad generalisations. The Force, for what it

is worth, may be given to that poor beggar of a metaphysician who sings his doleful ditty in the street.

At the same time it should be noticed that we do
here open up an obviously important issue. No one has
yet been able to show how certain observed modes of attraction can be developed out of others. No one has
been able to suggest how, for example, the specific
mode of attraction we call cohesion can originate from
that which we call gravitation. All that we can say is
that, amid all the varied modes of attraction, the sum
of energy remains constant. A candid and impartial inquiry into the facts enables us to realise that, under
these or those assignable conditions, new modes of attraction supervene--modes which, with our present
knowledge, no one could have foretold, since in science
it must not infrequently suffice to be wise after the
event.

These facts are too often forgotten or overlooked
by those who attempt a merely mechanical interpretation
of phenomena. It appears to be undeniable that when
oxygen and hydrogen combine to form water, or when
aqueous vapor in the atmosphere condenses, under these
conditions to form rain-drops, and under those to form
crystalline snowflakes, new modes of attraction are
manifested for our study and new properties in the
products for our investigation. Metaphysically regarded, these are new manifestations of Force, the underlying Cause of attraction. And if by the doctrine
of Vitalism no more is implied than this--that, when
organic matter first came into being, new modes of attraction and new properties appeared in the field of
phenomena, few biologists, I conceive, would hesitate
to acknowledge themselves Vitalists to the core. Who
is prepared to assert that the molecular changes involved in the attraction and coalescence of the male
and female pronuclei, or the rhythmic pulsation of the
contractile vesicle in amoeba, or the fission of the
lowest protozoan animalcule, is anywhere foreshadowed
in the inorganic sphere? It is questionable whether
the absorption of fluid by any living membrane is a
matter of mere osmosis. And though not a few organic
products have been artifiically manufactured in the
laboratory, we seem as far as ever from simulating the
synthesis of the digestive secretions. If Vitalism
have such facts as these in view it need send forth no
missionaries to convert biologists to the true faith.
And if Vital Force mean the underlying Cause of such
phenomena it may be as freely admitted as Gravitative

Force or that which underlies the observed facts of cohesion.

But the champions of Vitalism mean something more than this--or so it appears from the language they are wont to employ. They make no parade of the mystery of gravitation; they do not plead with us to regard chemical attraction as something outside the recognised order of nature; they do not press upon us the conclusion that when the first doubly-oblique crystal came into being, a directive force was brought into play--a force of precisely the same character as that which enables the sculptor by the exercise of his Will to carve from the shapeless marble a Venus of Milo; they do not write books and magazine articles to convince us that the natural origin of the lightning flash is inconceivable. But of this kind are the attitudes they too often assume when the phenomena of life are in question. The origin of life is a mystery; it marked a new epoch in Creation; its phenomena demand the belief in a quasi-intelligent directive force; its natural genesis is not only unproven but beyond the limits of human conception. Against such a doctrine of Vitalism an energetic protest should be entered, both by science and by a metaphysics which (if such a thing be possible) preserves its sanity.

In his recent presidential address before the chemical section of the British Association on the occasion of its meeting in Bristol (1898), Professor Japp urged the claims of Vitalism from the point of view occupied a generation ago by Pasteur. His presentation of the subject was admirably lucid, and his arguments ably marshalled. It is worth while to examine the position taken up by so well-accredited an advocate.

The salient facts and conclusions are briefly as follows: When polarised light passes through certain substances the plane of polarisation is rotated--in some cases to the right in others to the left. "The effect is as if the ray had been forced through a twisted medium--a medium with a right-handed or a left-handed twist--and had itself received a twist in the process; and the amount of rotation will depend (1) upon the degree of twist in the medium (that is, on the rotatory power of the substance), and (2) upon the thickness of the stratum of the substance through which the ray passes; just as the angle through which a bullet turns, in passing from the breech to the muzzle of a rifle, will depend upon the degree of twist in the rifling and the length of the barrel."

Now these optically active substances, as they are termed, may be divided into two classes. Some, like quartz, produce rotation only in the crystallised state; the dissolved or fused substances are inactive. Others, like sugar, are optically active and produce rotation, not only in the crystallised state but also in the liquid state or in solution. In the former case the molecules of the substance have no twisted structure, but they unite to form crystals having such a structure. As Pasteur expressed it, we may build up a spiral staircase--an asymmetric figure--from symmetric bricks; when the staircase is again resolved into its component bricks, the asymmetry disappears. In the case however of compounds which, like sugar, are optically active in the liquid state, the twisted structure must belong to the molecules themselves. Such molecular asymmetry is, so far as we know, only found in organic substances; and their production is one of the distinguishing characteristics of living matter.

But there are sundry substances, such as racemic acid, which, though they are inactive, owe their inactivity to the equilibrium of opposite rotations. When a solution of one of the salts of this acid is evaporated, beautiful hemihedral crystals, belonging to the rhombic system, are obtained. Such hemihedral crystals are asymmetrical. But Pasteur found that they are not all alike. Half of them are lopsided in one direction; the other half in the other direction. They answer to each other as our right hand answers to the left; each is the mirror image of the other. Such pairs are termed enantiomorphs. Furthermore, if all the right-handed crystals, and all the left-handed ones, be picked out and dissolved to make two solutions, each solution will be optically active, the one with a left-handed, the other with a right-handed twist. But in all other respects they are alike. Their salts have the same solubility in symmetric media, the same specific gravity, and so forth. It is assumed, therefore, that in the original solution right and left-handed molecules exist in equal proportions, and that their equal and opposite optical activities balance each other so as to give apparent inactivity.

If now such a mould as _Penicillium_ be grown in a solution of the ammonium salt of racemic acid, fermentation takes place; and the solution, originally

inactive, becomes optically active. The living substance is able to select all the optically right-handed
moiety of the solution, leaving the left-handed moiety
intact; and from this the appropriate lopsided crystals, of one type only, may be readily obtained. It is
urged, therefore, that there are two modes, and only
two modes, in which the complementary types of molecules commingled in a racemic or analogous solution can
be separated,--either by the selective action of a rational being who has this end in view, or by the action
of living organic matter or its products. The separation cannot conceivably be effected through the chance
play of symmetric forces. The absolute origin of one-
sided asymmetry is a mystery as profound as that of
life itself. "No fortuitous concourse of atoms, even
with all eternity to clash and combine in," says Professor Japp, "could compass this feat of the formation
of the first optically active organic compound." "I
see no escape from the conclusion," he adds, "that, at
the moment when first life arose, a directive force
came into play,--a force of precisely the same character as that which enables the intelligent operator, by
the exercise of his Will, to select one crystallised
enantiomorph and reject its asymmetric opposite."

Such is one of the latest pronouncements of Vitalism. Let us critically consider the evidence; but
before doing so let us endeavor to be quite clear on
certain preliminary matters of broad and general application.

Are we to regard the argument as special and applicable to Vitalism only; or are we to look upon it as
general and applicable also to Chemism, Crystallism,
and an indefinite number of other isms? Are we to look
upon the directive force, analogous to that exercised
by an intelligent operator, which, we are told, was
called into play at the moment when first life arose,
as something essentially different in its nature from
anything which is found in the inorganic world? Is it
alone characterised by its directiveness; or is such
directiveness exercised elsewhere in nature in different modes and under different conditions? Again, is
the inconceivability of the origin of asymmetry from
"the chance play of symmetric forces," special to the
problems suggested by living matter, or is it only a
special example of an inconceivability which faces us
in other regions of our extended survey of nature? Once
more, is genesis by fortuitous concourse of atoms (a
conception in itself bewildering in its irrationality)

183

unsatisfactory where protoplasm is concerned, though satisfactory for inorganic products; or is it to be regarded as intrinsically absurd as a way of accounting for anything in an orderly world of phenomena? The answer to these questions is really of fundamental importance. It makes all the difference whether we are discussing something which is distinctive of life and its origin--distinctive not only in its mode of operation but in its essential character--or whether we are discussing principles which are common to natural phenomena, including those of organic nature, in many of their varying phases. A belief in the former, as implying a supernatural hiatus between the inorganic and the organic, is to be regarded as unphilosophical and misleading; the acceptance of the latter is the logical outcome of a survey of phenomena and the teaching they afford.

I have no wish to imply that Professor Japp in his address intended to limit the application of a "directive force" to the phenomena of life. But I am quite certain that many of those who read that address will read it in this sense. And it is rather to them than to him that I would address the remarks that follow. It will serve to put the matter in a clearer light if we state the question in a somewhat concrete form, and ask: Is there anything in the phenomena of life which differs, not merely in mode of operation but in principle, from what may be discovered in the phenomena of crystallisation? It is convenient to select crystallisation because here also we are presented with certain optical effects.

First let us consider the building up of crystalline forms. All known crystals may be classified in six groups or systems, and their forms being solid geometrical figures, the relations of the faces to each other may be expressed geometrically. To lessen confusion, let us limit our attention to three readily obtainable crystalline forms. If we allow a solution of aluminium-potassium sulphate to evaporate slowly, large ochtohedral crystals of alum will be produced. Each is symmetrical in all crystallographic respects. Each has six points or solid angles, and it matters not which of these points is placed uppermost. Imaginary straight lines drawn from point to point within the crystal are spoken of as the axes. There are three such axes, all at right angles, and all of equal length; and any face of the crystal cuts three of these axes symmetrically at equal distances from the centre of the figure. Next

184

allow a solution of sulphur in carbon bisulphide to
evaporate slowly. Rhombic crystals of sulphur will be
obtained. There are six solid angles as before, but
they are not symmetrical in the same sense. They answer to each other in opposite pairs, but they are not
all alike. There are three axes, and all are at right
angles, but they are all of different lengths. Any
face of the crystal cuts three of them, but at unequal
distances from the centre of the figure. Whether we
take large crystals or small crystals, these distances
are proportional; and the angle between any similar
pair of faces remains constant. Thirdly, let a solution of sulphate of copper evaporate and give rise to
crystals of blue vitriol. The geometric figure is far
less simple and symmetrical. At first it may seem that
all the faces are dissimilar. But closer study shows
that there are pairs of faces, situate opposite and
parallel to each other, which are alike; but no one of
these pairs is like other pairs. There are still three
axes; but not only are they of different lengths, but
no two are at right angles to each other. They are inclined at different angles; hence they are said to belong to the doubly-oblique or triclinic system.

Such, stripped as far as possible of technical details, are the observed facts with regard to these
three kinds of crystalline architecture. The alum, the
sulphur, and the blue vitriol, present us with three
types of crystal; but the crystals of each substance
remain true to their several types. There is no theory
about this; it is merely a statement of facts of observation; for the reference to supposed axes is merely
for convenience of geometrical expression. Apart from
crystallisation there is nothing quite like this method
of building in nature. To say that such crystals result from the fortuitous concourse of molecules is
nothing less than grotesque. But if it is not a fortuitous concourse of molecules, it must be a directed or
(to use a better word) determinate concourse. How then
does the determinism of the crystal, each after his
kind, arise? A science which has learnt the grace of
modesty can only reply: We do not know. To drop into
the colloquial, if not very elegant, prose of Dr.
Watts's hymn, one can but say: For 'tis their nature
to. Such are the facts. We believe that they are the
visible expression of certain attractions or repulsions; and if we like to dip into metaphysics we may
add that the cause of these attractions is crystalline
force. Surely we may say here with just as much (or as
little) cogency as may be said with regard to the

185

phenomena of life, that when the first crystal arose, a directive force came into play--a force of precisely the same character as that which enables an intelligent operator, by the exercise of his will, to build up the model of a crystal.

If it be urged, with an almost desperate appeal to metaphysics, that the potentiality of assuming the crystalline form existed in certain kinds of matter ere ever a crystal was formed, it is difficult to see wherein this assertion differs from Tyndall's celebrated poetic outburst, when he proclaimed that he could "discern in that matter which we, in our ignorance of its latent powers, have hitherto covered with opprobrium, the promise and potency of all terrestrial life." Such appeals to potentialities and potencies do not really help us in any appreciable degree. To say that crystalline polarity is due to the polarity of the molecules merely shifts the question back a step; for we must still ask: How did this molecular polarity arise? At some stage, sooner or later, we are brought face to face with the final answer of science; that such is the observed or inferred constitution of nature. The reference to potency and potentiality is merely a somewhat pompous mode of stating that what does occur under certain conditions can occur under these conditions.

We may now pass to the brief consideration of certain optical effects which are observable in our three crystals. If a number of sections be cut, so as to give us flat plates, some being cut from the crystal in one direction and others in other directions, that is to say, making various angles with the geometrical axes; and if these be placed on a piece of white paper over a minute inkspot thereon; then it will be found that, in the case of the sections or slices of alum, they are all alike in exercising no peculiar influence on the rays of light passing through them from the inkspot. Through every one of them a single image of the inkspot will be seen. There is no double refraction. But in the case of all, or nearly all, of the plates of sulphur or blue vitriol (in all save those which are cut at right angles to two imaginary lines termed the optic axes) two images of the inkspot will be seen, or might be seen if the plates were thick enough and sufficiently transparent. The slices exhibit the phenomena of double refraction. The rays of light which pass through the crystalline plates are divided into two groups. And by appropriate means it can be shown, first that the two groups pass through the plate at

different rates, one group being more retarded than the
other; and secondly that each group consists of polarised rays, or rays the vibrations of which are all parallel to one plane. In the two groups the planes of
polarisation are at right angles; thus if we call the
one N and S the other will be E and W.

It is clear therefore that there is something
about the crystalline plates of sulphur and blue vitriol (and these differ from each other in ways which
need not be entered into) that produces certain peculiar optical effects. Now it is found that a plate of
glass behaves just like a plate of alum and produces no
double refraction. But if the plate be unequally heat-
ed, or if it be subjected to a mechanical twist, double
refraction is induced. Since therefore this optical
effect may be artificially induced by differential
strain it is reasonable to suppose that the plates of
sulphur and blue vitriol are, under natural conditions,
in a state of differential strain, of which double refraction is the optical expression. And since solutions of sulphur and blue vitriol show no double refraction it is reasonable to suppose (on the assumption
that the molecules themselves undergo no change during
solution) that the strain is produced by the interactions of the molecules when they assume the crystallised state. So that, if we are to use the analogy of
the intelligent operator, not only does he build up the
crystals in definite geometric forms, each true to its
system type and to its generic and specific type within
the system, but he introduces the dynamic element of
differential strain itself true to its system type, and
to its generic and specific type within the system.
And these differential strains are not manifested until
crystal forms arise in the course of what we believe to
be a natural process of evolution.

There is one more lesson which the crystal has to
teach. It exercises a further differential influence
which is markedly selective in its nature. If, for example, we take a plate of the mineral tourmaline, cut
parallel to the principle geometrical axis, the light
within the crystal is divided into two groups of vibrations polarised in opposite. planes. But only one group
passes through the crystal and reaches the eye; the
other is quenched within the plate. So that the crystallised substance "selects" one set of polarised rays
for transmission and the other set for extinction.

Some crystals of quartz exhibit small asymmetric faces. The common form of this mineral, with a hexagonal prism capped by a hexagonal pyramid is a familiar object. But sometimes the solid angles between the prism and the pyramid are asymmetrically bevelled off to form these tetartohedral faces. And these faces are situated in some cases to the right and in others to the left. The complementary forms are thus mirror-images of each other. They answer to each other as the right hand answers to the left. They are enantiomorphs. And each has the property of rotating the rays of plane-polarised light to the right or to the left according to the position of the asymmetric faces. These effects may be attributed to differential strains; and since they are only observed in the crystalline condition of quartz, it is held (on the assumption that fusion does not alter the molecules) that the strains are inter-molecular (or between the molecules) and not intra-molecular (or within the molecules). However they arise, there they are, exhibiting a yet further differential effect on the ray of light. We do not know whether the right-handed or the left-handed forms predominate in nature; or whether the numbers, or the joint mass, of the one exactly balance those of the other.

Thus we lead up to the enantiomorphs in crystalline substances of organic origin. As Professor Japp points out, the fact that an optical twist is produced, not only in the crystalline condition but also in solutions, leads us to suppose that the differential strain is intra-molecular and not inter-molecular. His thesis is that, since the enantiomorphs or mirror-types are produced in complementary pairs (right-handed and left-handed rotation being equal and opposite in amount) the selection of either for predominance is "absolutely inconceivable" under the play of symmetric forces. But the teaching of the crystal has made us familiar with the fact that a mode of optical "selection," if not this mode, occurs under the play of natural forces. For the tourmaline plate selects vibrations in one plane for transmission and vibrations in the opposite plane for extinction. And the teaching of the solar system with its predominant anti-clockwise rotation, has made us familiar with the fact that from the play of (presumably) symmetric forces an asymmetric resultant may arise.

Let us however look at the actual facts. We find that from a racemic solution enantiomorphous,

188

mirror-type crystals, up to a size of, say, half an inch, may be produced, some right-handed, others left-handed, in equal amounts. What gives rise to the observed preponderance of right-handed molecules in the one crystal and of left-handed molecules in the other? Must we not reply either that there is a selective influence at work at a stage prior to that postulated, or at any rate emphasised, by Professor Japp; or that chance gave an initial preponderance, here of the one and there of the other, and thus formed nuclei for the further segregation of like to like?[1] Either answer is difficult to square with Professor Japp's essentially vitalistic conception. In any case crystals half an inch or so in diameter, some right-handed and others left-handed, are actually formed. And it is scarcely an extravagant supposition, one certainly not beyond the bounds of conceivability, that, given a finite number of such crystals, a quite indiscriminate mode of destruction might reduce this finite number to one, or to a small uneven number, and thus leave a group with a preponderance of one or the other type of molecule.

Now granting that the first formed organic molecules were possessed of equal and opposite rotatory powers, is there anything inconceivable in the supposition that when these segregated into units of protoplasm, some of these units were right-handed, and others left-handed, in equal amounts? Nay rather, may we not apply the lesson of the racemic crystals here, and urge that the observed segregation in the crystals renders it probable that a similar segregation occurred in the units of protoplasm? And the analogy in the two cases is strengthened when we remember that the rotatory property is not the outcome of the crystallised condition but is (as solution is held to show), of intra-molecular origin. But if this be so the units of protoplasm, the initial starting-points of life (starting-points with some of which existing life is continuous), were individually asymmetric, though in the aggregate of distinct individuals their asymmetry was complementary. And this is just what is denied to be conceivable under natural conditions! So far from being inconceivable it is precisely that which known facts render inherently probable.

Lastly, if we grant that, when protoplasm first came into being, asymmetric molecules had their initial genesis, is there anything here different in principle from that with which the study of inorganic nature has already made us familiar? Such asymmetry is presumably due to differential strain between the atoms, or between subordinate groups of atoms, within the molecule. But the lesson of the crystal tells that certain modes of differential strain, elsewhere unknown in nature, arise under appropriate conditions, and should prepare us to learn, in the succeeding organic lesson, that other modes of differential strain may arise under other conditions. When we remember of what an extraordinarily complex group the molecule of protoplasm in all probability consists, it seems hazardous to assert that circular polarisation cannot be its natural prerogative, just as plane polarisation is a natural property of the much simpler group of molecules in the crystal of sulphur or blue vitriol, especially when we find crystals of quartz and other inorganic substances, possessed of circular polarisation.

And so, after (it is feared) much technicality of discussion,--technicality which can scarcely be avoided if the discussion is to be adequate,--we reach the conclusion that, in so far as the hypothesis of Vitalism merely directs our attention to those new modes of attraction and of intra-molecular strain, together with other concomitant properties, the occurrence of which in living matter is observed or inferred, it is doing good service. But when it asserts that any natural connexion or analogy between these properties and those found elsewhere in nature is inconceivable; when it hints at modes of action not in accordance with the conservation of momentum and what has been described as the basal law of dynamics; when it invokes the special intervention of a directive force, analogous to that exercised by an intelligent operator; then it is not doing good service and must be arraigned at the bar of science and metaphysics. And if vital force is to be placed alongside crystal force, as the noumenal cause of certain observed or inferred attractions and repulsions, we can discuss its validity without doing violence to our conceptions of the universe as a rational whole; but if it is to be regarded, not as immanent and acting within the material system, but as external and introduced from beyond the system, then we must regard it, not as a friend to be welcomed, but as a foe whose insidious attacks must be repulsed lest it hold our weaker brethren in bondage.

Notwithstanding some appearances to the contrary, I venture to hope that the conclusion to which we have here been led is substantially in accord with that which Mr. Herbert Spencer reaches in the new edition of

his Principles of Biology. He there contends for a
principle of activity, elsewhere termed a special kind
of energy, which constitutes the essential element in
our conception of life. He urges that this is conceivable neither as something superadded from without, nor
as something inherent in organic matter. And he regards it as due to that Ultimate Reality which underlies this manifestation as it underlies all other manifestations. He reminds us that the actions of that
which the ignorant contemptuously call brute matter,
cannot in the last resort be understood in their genesis. And in concluding that, on the one hand, we find
it impossible to think of life as imported into the
unit of protoplasm from without, so also, on the other
hand, do we find it impossible to conceive it as emerging from the co-operation of the components; he attributes this to the fact, that while phenomena are accessible to thought, the implied noumenon is inaccessible;
that only the manifestations come within the range of
our intelligence, while that which is manifested lies
beyond it.

We will not stay to inquire how it comes about
that the existence of a noumenon inaccessible to
thought can be implied. Mr. Spencer's meaning, I take
it, here and elsewhere, is, that though noumenal existence is implied, and so far comes into the field of
thought, its nature is unknowable,--a conclusion which
need not here be discussed. The essential point seems
to be that new modes of manifestation imply new modes
of activity in the noumenal cause; and this is just the
conclusion to which our own discussion has led up. At
the same time there are some statements of Mr. Spencer
which may well seem to indicate an interpretation different from that which I have endeavored to present,
and more akin to that against which I have been contending.

On the first page of the Principles of Biology we
are told: "The properties of substances, though destroyed to sense by combination, are not destroyed in
reality. It follows from the persistence of force,
that the properties of a compound are the resultants of
the properties of its components,--resultants in which
the properties of the components are severally in full
action, though mutually obscured." And in the discussion of the dynamic element in life we read: "The
processes which go on in living things are incomprehensible as results of any physical actions known to us;"
and again: "We find it impossible to conceive life as

191

emerging from the co-operation of the components of protoplasm." Now, if these statements be taken to imply that in the organic world an incomprehensible principle of activity comes into operation different, not only in its mode of manifestation, but in its essential nature, from anything to be found in the inorganic world, (and this at first sight does seem to be implied,) then must Mr. Spencer be looked upon as a champion of Vitalism in its unsatisfactory form. I cannot believe that this is the true reading of Mr. Spencer's statements. It does not accord with the broader contention that the Ultimate Reality behind this manifestation, as behind all other manifestations, transcends conception. It must be remembered that Mr. Spencer has (to our great loss) been forced to omit from his System of Philosophy the volumes which should have dealt with inorganic evolution. May we not, from the general tenor of his thought from such statements as are found in the "letter to the Editor of The North American Review," and from other passages of his works,--may we not from these conclude that, had the inorganic volumes been written, it would have been shown that in the genesis of the crystal too a new manifestation of Force came into play? And may we not fairly place parallel to each other the following assertions: first, that we are obliged to confess that life in its essence cannot be conceived in physico-chemical terms,--one which Mr. Spencer does make; and, secondly, that we must similarly confess that crystallisation in its essence cannot be conceived in gravitative terms,--one which Mr. Spencer does not make, but which is, I conceive, nowise contradictory of anything that he has written?

But perhaps I have no right to fly the commodore's flag at the masthead of my own craft; and, in any case, no impertinence to a superior officer is thereby intended. The conclusions reached must be taken for what they are worth; no banner of authority can render them better or worse. Those conclusions are, that, if by Vitalism we give expression to the fact that living matter has certain distinctive properties, it may be freely accepted; but that if by it we imply that these properties neither are nor can be the outcome of evolution, it should be politely rejected; and further that, if by Vital Force we mean the noumenal Cause of the special modes of molecular motion that characterise protoplasm, its metaphysical validity may be acknowledged, so long as it is regarded as immanent in the dynamical system and not interpolated from without in a

192

manner unknown throughout the rest of the wide realm of nature.

FOOTNOTE

[1]Prof. Karl Pearson has, since this was written, adopted a similar line of argument. See <u>Nature</u>. Nov. 10th, 1898, p. 30.

SUGGESTED READINGS

Conwy Lloyd Morgan

Morgan, C. Lloyd. Instinct and Experience (London: Methuen, 1885, 1912).

_____. Spencer's Philosophy of Science (Oxford: Clarendon Press, 1913).

_____. Emergent Evolution (London: Williams and Norgate, 1923).

_____. Life, Mind and Spirit (London: Williams and Norgate, 1926).

_____. Mind at the Crossroads (London: Williams and Norgate, 1929).

_____. The Emergence of Novelty (London: Williams and Norgate, 1933).

* * *

_____. "Physical and Metaphysical Causation," Monist, VIII, 2 (January 1898), 230-249.

_____. "Philosophy of Evolution," Monist, VIII, 4 (July 1898), 481-501.

_____. "Biology and Metaphysics," Monist, IX, 4 (July 1899), 538-562.

_____. "Conditions of Human Progress," Monist, X, 3 (October 1900), 422-440.

_____. "Riddle of the Universe," Contemporary Review, LXXXV (June 1904), 776-799.

_____. "Interpretation of Nature," Contemporary Review, LXXXVII (May 1905), 609-627.

Morgan, C. Lloyd. "Individual and Person," American Journal of Sociology, XXXIV (January 1929), 623-631.

* * *

_____. "The Ascent of Mind," The Great Design (New York: Macmillan, 1934), pp. 115-134. F. Mason (Ed.).

8. PRESENT PROSPECTS FOR METAPHYSICS

Charles Hartshorne

Charles Hartshorne (1897-   ) attended Harvard University where he was an assistant to
Alfred North Whitehead and ably edited the
papers of Charles Sanders Peirce. He has indicated that both men have influenced his own
philosophical perspective. He taught at Harvard, Chicago, Emory, and the University of
Texas at Austin. He has now retired in Austin.

The twentieth century has not been an age of metaphysical systems. What, then, can be the future of the
subject under discussion; namely, "process philosophy?"
Professor Hartshorne argues that the basic problem lies
in certain biases common to the classical metaphysical
systems of Aristotle, Descartes, Spinoza, and Leibniz;
biases from which philosophy today is struggling painfully to free itself. These include the favoring of
being over becoming, identity at the expense of diversity, the absolute to the detriment of the relative,
the non-physical at the expense of the physical, and,
finally, the origins of events at the expense of their
outcomes. The roots of these biases are complex, including the exhaltation of mathematics, the despair of
life with a consequent desire of escape from change and
uncertainty, and the problem of death.

Modern ("neoclassical") metaphysics, if it is to
have the success which Hartshorne believes is possible
for it, must transform its traditional preoccupations
and concern itself with becoming and relativity. It
must study the ways that things become, and the manner
in which their existence is dependent on their mutual
relations. This starting point has the virtue of making otherwise irresolveable classical problems manageable. It now becomes possible to see how God can have
knowledge of contingent truth and yet be all-inclusive
(of both 'relative' and 'absolute' realities). It becomes possible (with the aid of modern science) to attain a more satisfactory conception of individuality

197

than was ever available, say to Aristotle, and a more coherent conception of the relations between determinism and indetermination than has heretofore been conceivable. In spite of these and other advantages, however, neo-classical metaphysics faces challenging problems in the contemporary world. The essay concludes by mentioning several of these.*

---

*The selection is from Creative Synthesis and Philosophic Method (London: SCM Press LTD, 1970), pp. 43-56. The article was originally published in the Monist, 47 (1963), 188-210. Used by the permission of the Monist and Dr. Charles Hartshorne.

Present Prospects for Metaphysics

That classical metaphysics, say from Aristotle and Plotinus to Hegel, Schopenhauer, Bradley, and Royce, was something less than a success is rather widely conceded. However, it might be thought that its failure is no worse than the fate which overtakes scientific views. Classical physics, too, has been set aside. Yet this is chiefly with respect to the very small and the very large in nature. In application to things of middling magnitudes Newton's principles are still largely valid, at least as first approximations. But what can one do today with Aristotelianism, Cartesianism, Spinozism, Leibnizianism, or Hegelianism? Not a great deal, many of us would say. What then was wrong? Why have these systems lost relevance to so great an extent? Here opinions differ considerably.

There are two main possibilities. Either classical metaphysics failed because it was metaphysics or there is a more special reason. On the first view, a metaphysician is one who attempts the impossible or absurd: perhaps he wants answers to unanswerable questions, or non-factual answers to factual questions (or vice versa); or he wants to describe the ineffable and say the unsayable or to give a linguistic proposal the value of a statement about existence. Or again perhaps he is engaged in explaining away the paradoxes engendered by some outrageous overstatement, such as 'nothing changes', or 'only atoms exist', or 'nature is but our (or God's) ideas', or 'other minds (or the past or future) cannot be known'.

Let us grant that metaphysicians have at times discussed questions too ill-defined to have definite answers, or dealt with empirical questions in unempirical ways; also that they have at times strained language to the breaking point and beyond, or have confused linguistic proposals with existential affirmations or negations; and finally, that some of them have presented foolishly one-sided or extreme doctrines--still, do these vagaries constitute all that metaphysics can be, if it is not to dissolve into the sciences, or into the study of language?

I believe that metaphysics has a proper task, which is not that of the special sciences, a task in which, in the near future, a certain measure of success can be attained. Indeed, I think that Peirce's

199

prophecy, 'Early in the twentieth century metaphysics will become a science', has already had some degree of fulfilment--though one must here also take into account Whitehead's prediction in conversation, 'metaphysics will never be a popular science'. In my opinion, however, classical metaphysics suffered from certain handicaps which are not inherent in its task and which we are now for the first time in a favourable position to overcome.

Philosophy early acquired a bias from which it has been painfully struggling to free itself, a bias favouring one pole of certain ultimate contraries at the expense of the other pole, thus being at the expense of becoming, identity at the expense of diversity, the absolute or non-relative at the expense of the relative, the inextended or non-physical at the expense of the physical, origins or causes at the expense of outcomes or effects. This bias is found both in Ancient Greece and in the Orient. It appears to have several roots rather than one. In Greece, at least, it is due partly to the discovery of pure mathematics, and the one-sided enthusiasm for very abstract ideas which this discovery not unnaturally produced. In both Greece and India it arises from a certain despair of the values of concrete living which early civilization produced, especially in the Indian climate. Everywhere and always man's future is uncertain, and in view of death and the fragility of human institutions, no clear limit can easily be set to the scope of this uncertainty and its importance for our values. The simplest remedy is to attack the idea of change itself; if the 'true reality' is immune to change, we have but to identify ourselves in thought with this reality, and all danger and fear are felt to be, in principle, transcended. A similar argument favours identity over diversity. As the Upanishad has it, where there is no Other, there is nothing to fear.

The element of escapism just sketched joins the exaltation of mathematics. The relations of numbers are serenely indifferent to the chances of human life: they are fixed, independent, identical, immaterial. Thus in Augustine's discussion of God as the eternal Truth, mathematical ideas play a strikingly prominent role. The attitude is very Greek; but what is its relation to the Gospels, the God of which seems to respond rather to persons as a person than to abstract ideas as a pure knower or nous? The bland identification of God with the absolute or the infinite today appears to many of us as a species of idolatry.

200

But the roots of the classical bias are indeed
complex. One aspect of this complexity is the following. The universality of death puts man, as it seems,
before a dilemma. Either he lives on individually beyond death, or he becomes identical with a worthless
corpse. The second view seems to make a mockery of all
our intuitions of importance; the first is one of the
most fertile sources of bad metaphysics. It has, for
instance, been shown that Berkeley's one-sided idealism
has as its principal motivation the hope of justifying
the belief in personal immortality. Descartes's interest in the idea of the 'thinking substance' is explicitly connected by him with the same motif, which is
found also in Kant's discussion of the soul. One could
easily multiply these examples many times over. I hold
that in all these cases the influence of the interest
in individual immortality has been destructive of clear
analysis. The notion of an 'immortal soul' or 'spiritual substance' has clarified no theoretical problem,
as both Locke and Kant admitted. What they did not
fully see is the extent to which it has muddled and
confused many problems. If nevertheless the belief is
required for ethical or religious reasons, then so much
the worse for our prospect of a clearheaded metaphysics. But is it required? I do not believe that the
immortality which is implied by our essential values
has anything to do with that notion of soul-substance
which runs through Western philosophy from Plato to
modern Scholasticism.

Substance is a 'being' to which adventures happen,
or experiences occur; to make it the primary conception
is to assume the priority of being. The alternative,
one version of which was taken long ago by the Buddhists but by almost no one else, is to view events or
states (e.g., 'I now') as the concrete realities, and
construe enduring things, substances, persons, as ways
in which events are qualified, and related to other
events. Unfortunately, the Buddhists failed to do full
justice to the relatedness of events. They were not
entirely free from the anti-relativistic bias. A metaphysics of becoming and relativity is the modern philosophical task. It was certainly not accomplished in
former ages.

The reader may be wondering how metaphysics may be
defined, if it concerns itself with becoming and relativity. Is not this the concern of the empirical sciences? I reply: they concern themselves with things
or events which become and are relative, but not with

becoming and relativity as such. Of all the kinds of entities which might become, or stand in relation, what kinds do become and in what particular sorts of relations do they stand? These are the scientific questions. But what is it to become or to be relative? This is a very different query. Metaphysics seeks, I suggest, the essential nature of becoming which does not itself become and cannot pass away; or, it seeks the universal principle of relativity whose validity is absolute. 'Nothing is absolute but relativity'--this saying, which I heard as a student, and which meant nothing much to me at the time, I have come to see as, properly construed, the secret of secrets, just as the man who uttered it claimed that it was (though I shall never know just what this meant to him).

It will perhaps be granted that it is the abstract, as seen in mathematics, which is exempt from relativity and becoming. Upon what does arithmetic depend? Upon nothing in the particular features of the actual world. Any abstraction is similarly independent of the concrete in proportion to its degree of abstractness. Very well, 'relativity' is as abstract a term as one is likely to find, and just as much so as 'absoluteness'! 'Becoming' is also exceedingly abstract. And its independence of circumstances is similarly great. No matter what in particular may happen, happening itself is and presumably will be a reality. That human beings can exist is relative to certain conditions of temperature, etc., but that something relative can exist, to what is that in turn relative? To the Absolute, some will say. Let us grant that relativity as such is correlative to absoluteness as such, the two concepts expressing the same contrast from opposite ends. We shall see later (Chapters VI, XI) how this contrast is illustrated even in the ordinary phenomena. But we shall still maintain that relativity as such is that which could not not be, its existence having no special conditions. Relativity is the absolute principle! Some may feel this proposition to be contradictory. If so, what do they make of Russell's similar statement: concreteness as such is a highly abstract term? And what else is it? Universals need not be, indeed usually are not, instances of themselves. Concreteness is not concrete, relativity is not relative. Indeed, it is as absolute as absoluteness. In a way it is more absolute. If there is such a thing as 'the absolute', it is some ultimate or supreme kind of relativity. And similarly, according to what I call

202

'neo-classical metaphysics', if there is an eternal Being, it is some ultimate form of becoming.

Was this the doctrine of classical metaphysicians?
If so, they certainly chose remarkably indirect and
confused ways of expressing themselves!

Instead of the contraries previously considered,
let us take the pair, necessary-contingent. Classical
metaphysics depreciated the contingent. Spinoza is an
extreme case. But as late as Hegel, 'necessary' is a
work of laudation, and 'contingent', of denigration.
Metaphysics seeks to know what it is that is necessary,
or 'could not be otherwise than it is'. But perhaps
what is necessary is precisely and solely that a certain ultimate form of contingency should have instances.
Perhaps even the 'necessary being' is not one 'without
accidents', but one which is bound to have some appropriate accidents or other. It is no accident that
there should be accidents; rather, there are bound to
be accidents, just as it is predictable that unpredictable events will never cease to occur. In the same
way, the divine being whose existence is not contingent
may escape contingency only because, and only in the
sense that, not only are accidents bound to occur, but
divine accidents are bound to be among them. It is a
defensible view that God is the one being to whom accidents are always bound to happen. Whereas, to the rest
of us, nothing accidental occurred before we were born,
nor will occur after we die, nor had we never been born
would any accident ever have occurred to us, 'divine
accidents', it may be held, are bound always to be.
They form a class which could not ever have been or
ever be empty.

I hope the reader begins to see that this new
metaphysics does have a logic. Many difficulties of
the older metaphysical systems are transformed by this
logic into at least more manageable proportions. For
instance, in those systems there was often the contradiction of a God held to be without accidental properties, although having knowledge of contingent truth.
Thus he knows that a certain world exists which might
not have existed; but surely had it not existed, he
would not have known it to exist; hence he has knowledge which he might not have had. And still, none of
his properties or qualities was admitted to be contingent! This is a typical antinomy of classical metaphysics. In the new metaphysics, where divine accidents are definitely admitted, there is no such

antinomy. Yet, it can be held, there is also no need
to admit divine ignorance or divine error. God, neo-
classically conceived, knows whatever there is to know,
just as it is.

Another customary antinomy was that the supreme
reality, taken to be absolute, must be either all-
inclusive or not all-inclusive. The supposition of inclusiveness involves a choice between the contradiction
that constituents which could have been otherwise contribute to a totality which could not have been otherwise and the contrasting absurdity that neither the totality nor the constituents could have been otherwise,
and thus that everything is absolute--wherewith both
relativity and absoluteness lose all distinctive meaning. The supposition that the supreme reality is not
all-inclusive implies that it is but a constituent of
the totality, and so not the supreme reality after all.
In the new metaphysics, the supreme reality is held to
be supremely relative. It therefore can be all-
inclusive, not only of all relative things, but also
of 'the absolute', which is indeed but an abstract aspect of relative reality, its relativity as such or in
principle (see Chapter VI, XI).

Another advantage enjoyed by metaphysics in our
time is that the concept of mere matter, which haunted
not only Greek and medieval but also Indian thought,
has been shown, far more clearly than ever before, by
the development from Leibniz to Bergson, Peirce, and
Whitehead, to be superfluous. It was always a term for
intellectual embarrassment, as anyone who has read the
history of the concept must, I should think, know.

At this point current science is an asset which
Aristotle and Descartes lacked. The division of nature
into inanimate, vegetable, and animal is plausible
enough in a primitive state of knowledge; for to the
unaided senses that is how things appear to us. But
the microscope and the even more powerful magnifying
power of mathematical manipulation have shown us that
these divisions are superficial. All life is either
unicellular or multicellular, and a cell is a living
individual which in a certain measure determines its
own activities in response to stimuli from without.
The division between vegetable and animal has no deep
significance at this unicellular level. The great contrast between plants and animals, which makes the latter alone seem to have such psychical traits as sensation, feeling, or memory, is due to the fact that the

multicellular plants (which alone are readily perceptible to our senses) are but colonies of cells, compared
to the integration which nervous tissue gives to the
multicellular animals. The visible plant individuals
therefore seem not to have animal 'souls' (a term which
here need only mean individual experiences or feelings),
but this does not constitute any evidence, however
weak, to show that the invisible plant individuals of
which they are composed have none. A crowd of visible
animals is generally not a sentient individual either.
But single-celled animals give behavioural signs of individual sentience. So, I suggest, do single-celled
plants.

Aristotle's expression 'vegetable soul' was his
compromise term to cover at once his sound intuition
that growth implies an internal principle of self-
determination analogous to animal self-control, and his
observation that nevertheless visible plants do not respond as individuals to external stimuli. He was
wrong, first, in referring the principle of growth to
the entire plant. It is cells which multiply and constantly form and reform themselves, and the growth of
the visible plant is but our collective way of seeing
these individually invisible actions. Aristotle was
wrong, second, in referring his denial of individual
sensitive response both to the entire visible plant and
(tacitly and by omission) to its constituents as well.
The absence of any (to us) perceptible behavioural
signs of sensation tells nothing as to the absence of
imperceptible behaviour appropriate to sensation.

As for inanimate nature, the apparent inertness of
a stone, or of water, tells nothing as to the inactivity of its minute constituents. For the general situation is this: all concrete things (and the new metaphysics holds that something of the sort would be true
in any really conceivable world) must react--if not as
wholes then in their constituents--to their environ-
ments, they respond to what in effect are stimuli, and
their responses become in turn stimuli to others. In
our actual world, however, there is a vast difference
between animals, plants, and the minerals in the extent
to which individual agents of response are perceptible
to the unaided senses of such higher animals as ourselves. Only when multicellular animals are observed
is individuality of behaviour clearly discerned; in
plants, individuality of action is hidden from us,
though there is a semblance or illusion of active individuality which caused Aristotle to speak of 'soul';

while below the plants, dynamic individuality is not directly apparent to the senses at all. Either one supposes that the proposition, 'reality consists of active individuals', is true only of animal reality, or at most animal and vegetable reality, or else one must admit that direct perception fails to reveal the constituents of which natural things are composed. The Greek atomists and, much more clearly, Leibniz drew the correct conclusions: perception gives a largely blurred or indistinct outline of the acting physical things. The lack of individual self-activity which these outlines suggest is to be discounted; indirect means of knowledge are alone adequate at this point. Materialism or dualism (they come to much the same) rest on the failure to think through the relation of the category of individuality to the limitations of human perception.

The moral of the foregoing for metaphysical method is this: we must beware of allowing our theory of the categories (i.e., our metaphysics) to be determined by supposed 'facts' whose factuality itself depends upon presupposed decisions as to the categories. Aristotle did not know that nature consists, or could possibly consist, of the animata and the inanimata, in the absolute sense which alone is relevant to the controversy concerning mind as such and matter. He knew, to be sure, that in our perceptions individual agency is distinctly apparent only when we observe animals, or (in much vaguer, more problematic form) when we observe plants. However, before trying to turn this fact about our perceptions into a fact about nature at large, one must decide whether direct perception is to be expected always to reveal things as they are. But this, too, is a metaphysical question. For ultimately, one comes to this: only deity could have perceptions from which the characters of things experienced could simply be read off; and this would be one way and not a bad way, to define deity. (Here, too, is a source of poor metaphysics: men like to play at being God.) Thus it is a metaphysical mistake to decide the perceptual question as Aristotle did. Where individuality is as clearly perceived as it is when the perceived is a vertebrate animal, its presence is to be taken as probably factual, especially since we know our own individuality intuitively in memory, including immediate memory. But where we fail to perceive individuality of action this negative fact, this failure, must not be turned into a positive affirmation, a success, the insight that no such individuality is present in that part of nature.

Rather, to avoid an unintelligible dualism, we should discount the apparent absence of individuality and look for indirect evidence of its presence. Science has turned up a great deal of such evidence.

In sum, scientific progress does not change the essential metaphysical evidence, but only alters its ready availability, its obviousness. Aristotle's metaphysics of mind and matter is at best mediocre, simply as metaphysics, no matter what science one does or does not know. However, it is a lot easier to avoid bad metaphysics if there is no bad science to furnish misleading suggestions as to the 'facts' which have to be accepted. 'Inanimateness' in the absolute sense never was or could be a fact; but it seemed to be so, by a natural illusion of commonsense and primitive science.

It is, I believe, similar with determinism. Newtonian and even Greek science seemed to favour determinism, partly for the reason, pointed out by Clerk Maxwell, that the statistical laws which are, as many of us now believe, the genuine stabilities of nature, were not yet accessible in application to the fine-structure of the world. Beginning with Maxwell's and Peirce's reflections upon the law of gases, and then the discoveries of Gibbs, Boltzmann, Darwin, Mendel, and finally Heisenberg, science has made it easier and easier to see, what metaphysically was always accessible to sufficiently resolute inquiry, that the absolutizing of law and regularity is self-defeating, and like many other modes of unlimited exaggeration finally destroys the meanings which it seeks to preserve or magnify. Here, too, science tells us no truth about the ultimate categories which we might not, if sufficiently intelligent, think out, even without science, from the inherent logic of the categories themselves. But perhaps we human beings could not be so intelligent as all that! At any rate, less intelligence is needed when science ceases to appear to be on the wrong metaphysical side.

It might seem that if relativity is the absolute principle, determination of events by causes must also be absolute, as expressing the way in which phenomena are relative to their antecedent conditions. But this is just what it fails to express! For if to be effect is to be dependent upon, relative to, a cause, to be cause is to be an independent or, in that context and in so far, a non-relative or absolute factor. The intuitive meaning of cause-effect implies one-way

dependence or relativity, or--the same thing--one-way
independence or absoluteness. This asymmetry is contradicted by the deterministic concept which has for so
long been accepted as a harmless definition: 'necessary and sufficient condition'. The first adjective
makes the effect imply the cause, and the second makes
the cause imply the effect. Thus either (or neither)
is relative to the other. Long, long ago in Asia,
Nagarjuna showed the absurdities which result (see
Chapter X). And since causal conditioning is thus
turned into biconditioning or equivalence, it is surprising how few have noted, in this connection, as Meyerson did, that equivalence is a special and indeed de-
generate form of implication. Determinism, taken without qualification, deprives causal relativity of any
contrasting aspect of independence or absoluteness, and
makes temporal relations for all practical purposes
'internal' in both directions. This is the one-sided
monistic extreme to which Hume's pluralism of universal
external relations is the opposite extreme. That Hume
held both doctrines only shows on what a verbal level
his thought, in some aspects, remained. At least one
of the two, absolute causal determination, universal
externality or independence, must be unreal. Neo-
classical metaphysics holds that neither is real; but
only indeterministic yet intrinsic causality, whereby
events are relative to their predecessors but not to
their successors. That a certain measure of prediction
is thereby made possible I have shown elsewhere.[1]

The reader may still be wondering how relativity
can be the absolute principle, if events are not relative to their successors. The answer is as follows:
negative predicates are parasitic upon positive ones;
non-relativity, therefore, upon relativity. When it
becomes true that event B is actual, and is relative to
previous event A (although A is not relative to B),
this truth is made so entirely by the existence of the
relativity of B to A. For 'not relative to B' has no
definite referent until B occurs as successor to A.
All one can say in advance, and all that ever qualifies
A in itself, is that A is not relative to any later
event. And this involves only negation, relativity,
any, and later. And note that the relativity of events
to their predecessors fully suffices to give each event
its place in the time series. If B follows (and thus
is relative to) A, and C follows B, no element of order
is added by saying that B precedes C and A precedes B.
The information is already complete with the statement
of the backwards relatedness. Thus one-way relativity

(positive in one direction, negative in the other) covers the whole story. Relativity as directional or non-symmetrical is the absolute principle, because it includes the idea of its own negative, absoluteness. Similarly, becoming includes being; contingency, necessity (which is merely the universal abstract constituent of the contingent); the complex, the simple (see Chapter VI).

The double advantage of our time, that we have finally seen the need and possibility of giving becoming and relativity their rights, and that many apparent facts of science supporting dualism, and hence destructive of metaphysical coherence, have turned out to be pseudo-facts or artifacts of primitive knowledge, does not quite mean that 'we now have it made'. There are also some new difficulties. Contemporary science is extremely difficult to grasp with any accuracy, and it is hard to know how much grasp we need to have. Certainly someone ought to correlate metaphysics and physics. For instance, if even the supreme reality is a kind of becoming, then it seems there must be a sort of divine time (even Barth says something like this), and the correlation of this with worldly time, as construed by relativity physics, is a neglected and apparently extremely formidable task.[2] Perhaps this is rather a problem in cosmology than pure metaphysics, cosmology being the application of metaphysical principles to what science reveals as the structure of our 'cosmic epoch'. Yet unless either physicists or metaphysicians have erred, there must be an at least possible way of harmonizing what the physicists say is true of our epoch and what metaphysicians say is true of all possible epochs (since it forms the content of ideas of such generality that there is nothing we can think which is not a specialization of this content).

Another difficulty is the technical proliferation of formal logic. To master it is half a life-work. Can metaphysicians afford to know but little of this development? And what, for instance, is one to make of the contention of most logicians that truth is in no way time-bound, in contrast to the neo-classical doctrine that the reality which makes statements true is protean, and partly new each time we refer to it? I believe that the logicians' contention is subject to a qualification which they fail to make explicit. To call factual truths timeless is at best like calling a whole part of itself, a convenient convention, not an insight into the proper or non-degenerate meaning of 'factual truth'. Logicians are beginning to look into this question.[3] Still another difficulty is that although science has destroyed the commonsensical and classical basis of the mind-matter division by removing the supposed evidence for inert matter, it has also tended to give new encouragement to materialistic or dualistic tendencies through the behaviouristic trend in the social and humanistic sciences. A 'methodological materialism' (better, 'physicalism') is in the saddle. What is its relation to the speculative psychicalism which alone can escape dualism without denial of any given aspects of reality? Here, too, is an interesting and difficult problem.[4]

A hopeful aspect of the present situation is the reconsideration being given to the most famous of all metaphysical arguments, Anselm's proof for God's existence. It has been made clear that neither critics nor defenders during eight centuries succeeded in laying bare either the real weaknesses or the real strength of Anselm's discovery. So far, I think, Malcolm, Findlay, Purtill, Hartshorne, and still others, agree. God's existence could not be one fact among others, if fact means contingent truth. Either God is the God of all possible worlds, not just of this one, or he is not even genuinely conceivable, an impossibility rather than an unrealized possibility. Since the idea of God contains implicitly the entire content of metaphysics, as I have argued in various places, the new perspective upon Anselm alone should suffice to open a new era in metaphysics.

Probably the most important function of metaphysics is to help in whatever way it can to enlighten and encourage man in his agonizing political and religious predicaments. Traditional religion is being reappraised; there are metaphysical aspects of religious problems. Some of these were hinted at above. The communist world understands (someone has said) the importance of political unity; the advanced democracies understand the importance of political freedom; how shall we achieve an understanding of both? It might help us if we realized more clearly and at all levels, including the ultimate or metaphysical level, that freedom can never be either absolute or wholly absent, that risk and uncertainty are inherent in existence as essentially creative becoming, with its always partly open future; but that if freedom is to have promise of producing harmony, limits must always be set to the scope of freedom. Yet ultimately it is freedom itself

which sets these limits, divine freedom setting the
cosmical limits, and the free decisions of minorities
or majorities setting the local political limits for
human beings. Sufficient order is a sine qua non, and
technology has made the scale of the necessary order
world-wide, in some minimal respects at least.

These problems, and all problems, are special
cases of the ultimate or metaphysical problems of dependence and independence, or asymmetrical, positive-
negative relativity between forms of more or less creative experiencing. In one sense, a metaphysics of relativity and creativity is very old, rather than a modern
invention. To be relative is to take other things into
account, to allow them to make a difference to oneself,
in some sense to care about them. What else, then, can
the ancient saying, deus est caritas, imply if not the
supremacy of relativity? Yet nearly two thousand years
have been partly wasted in the effort to make this
deepest truth connote its opposite, the supremacy of
absoluteness, i.e., of indifference to others. And so
we have the shameful situation of communists preaching
devotion to a super-individual goal, while Christians
generally fail to reach any clear alternative to an
ethics of enlightened self-interest. (Buddhism in some
respects did better at this point.) It is the Christians, and the heirs of the Christian ethics, who ought
logically to find this alternative. It is time philosophers gave them some assistance. A metaphysics of
love, that is, of socially structured, and thus relative, creative experience is what we need, whether in
ethics, religion, or politics--and indeed, in all our
basic concerns.

FOOTNOTES

[1] "Causal Necessities: An Alternative to Hume," The Philosophical Review, 63 (1954), pp. 479-499.

[2] See John T. Wilcox, "A Question from Physics for Certain Theists," Journal of Religion, 61, 1961, pp. 293-300. Several writers discuss the metaphysical bearings of relativity physics in the Journal of Philosophy, 46 (1969), no. 11, pp. 307-355. The discussion by Paul Fitzgerald is especially relevant.

[3] See A. N. Prior, Past, Present and Future (Oxford: Oxford University Press 1967), ch. 7.

[4] I shall have something to say about this problem in the book on bird song, Born to Sing, which I hope to publish in a year or two.

SUGGESTED READINGS

Charles Hartshorne

Hartshorne, Charles. Anselm's Discovery: A Re-examination of the Ontological Argument for God's Existence (LaSalle, Ill.: Open Court, 1965).

_____. The Logic of Perfection, and Other Essays in Neoclassical Metaphysics (La-Salle, Ill.: Open Court, 1962).

_____. Man's Vision of God and the Logic of Theism (Hamden, Conn.: Archon Books, 1941).

_____. Whitehead's Philosophy: Selected Essays, 1935-1970 (Lincoln: University of Nebraska Press, 1972).

* * *

_____. "What Metaphysics Is," Journal of Karnatak University: Social Sciences, III, (1967), 1-15.

_____. "The Case for Idealism," Philosophical Forum, I, 1 (Fall 1968), 7-23.

_____. "Wittgenstein and Tillich: Reflections on Metaphysics and Language," in Creative Synthesis and Philosophic Method (London: SCM Press, 1970), pp. 131-158.

* * *

Martin, R. M. "On Hartshorne's 'Creative Synthesis' and Event Logic," Southern Journal of Philosophy, VIII, 4 (Winter 1971), 399-410.

Palin, D. A. "Neville's Critique of Hartshorne," Process Studies, IV, 3 (Fall 1974), 187-198.

Capek, Milic. "Natural Sciences and the Future of Metaphysics," Main Currents, XXVIII, 3 (May-June 1972), 167-171.

* * *

Gragg, Alan. Charles Hartshorne (Waco, Texas: Word Books, 1973).

Leclerc, Ivor. The Nature of Physical Existence (New York: Humanities Press, 1972).

Peters, Eugene. Hartshorne and Neoclassical Metaphysics (Lincoln: University of Nebraska Press, 1970).

Reese, W. L., (Ed.). Process and Divinity: The Hartshorne Festschrift (LaSalle, Ill.: Open Court, 1964).

S C I E N C E

"Truths emerge from facts,
there is
no 'universal substance.' "

William James

Jan Christian Smuts
Alfred North Whitehead
Charles Hartshorne
Milic Capek

9. THE HOLISTIC UNIVERSE

Jan Christian Smuts

Jan Smuts (1870-1950) was educated at Vic-
toria College, Stellenbosch, South Africa,
and Christ's College, Oxford, England. He
took his degrees in science and literature,
and later studied law. Returning to South
Africa he committed himself to philosophy
and politics, becoming over the period of
the rest of his life soldier, statesman,
scientist, philosopher, general, state at-
torney and premier.

Jan Smuts, although not a professional philosopher, nevertheless was one who made a significant contribution to the idea of emergent evolution during the
first part of this century. The one idea which forever
captured his thought, he said, was that of the holistic
aspect of the evolutionary process. One of the important aspects of his work was that he was able to go beyond the more or less static imagery of the biology and
evolution of Darwin and Spencer to a more dynamic or
organismic view which he preferred to call Creative Evolution. He was of the opinion that the fields of biology and psychology at that time were tending to divide nature and reality, and in opposition to this
trend he endeavored to pose a view of the wholeness of
the biological organism which would serve as a means of
better understanding the social character of reality.
Smuts saw that biological analysis with its emphasis
upon particular or minor variations was entirely inadequate to the task of explaining the complexity of the
total organism or the dynamic equilibrium called life.
It is "holistic variation or variation of a whole in
any particular respect that is the cause and carrier of
minor variations," he said, and not the minor variations that are "independently selected or conserved."*
Moreover, the former is much more "social" in its

---

*Holism and Evolution (New York: Macmillan Pub-
lishing Company, 1926), p. 213.

activity, and controls, guides and conserves all. Reality is seen therefore as the continual movement toward more complex patterns of various relationships,
yet with each such pattern making up its own "whole."
Smuts came to call this process "Holism" as appears in
his major work Holism and Evolution (1926) of which the
following selection# is the concluding chapter. Holism
represents the emergent episode of the creation of
wholes in the universe which is itself inherently active in the process of whole-making. The movement is
envisioned as beginning with simple chemical mixtures
from which it proceeds through chemical compounds to
living organisms and conscious minds to the unique creative novelty of the human personality which is seen to
be the highest and most evolved of the structures of
the universe. The universe is thus described as one of
interacting organisms which continually develop into
higher and more complex wholes. The creative process
of Holism, he will say, consists in the process of the
intensification of structures. His work greatly contributed to the idea of organism as a way of understanding the universe as a creative holistic process.

#From Holism and Evolution, pp. 319-345. Used by
permission of Macmillan Press.

The Holistic Universe

This is not a treatise on Philosophy; not even on the philosophy of Nature; not even on the philosophy of Evolution. It is an exploration of one idea, an attempt to sketch in large and mostly vague, tentative outline the meaning and the consequences of one particular idea. But that is a seminal idea; indeed it is here presented as more than an idea, as a fundamental principle operative in the universe. As such it is bound to affect our general view of the nature of the universe. I therefore come . . . to consider what Holism means for our general world-view, our Weltanschauung, and as briefly as possible to sum up the bearing which the argument of the preceding chapters must have on such a general conception of the universe.

Holism has been our theme--Holism as an operative factor in the universe, the basic concept and categories of action which can be more or less definitely formulated. I have in the broadest outline sketched the progress of Holism from its simple mechanical inorganic beginnings to its culmination in the human Personality. All through we have seen it at work as the fundamental synthetic, ordering, organising, regulating activity in the universe, operating according to categories which, while essentially the same everywhere, assume ever more closely unified and synthetic forms in the progressive course of its operation. Appearing at first as the chemical affinities, attractions and repulsions, and selective groupings which lie at the base of all material aggregations, it has accounted for the constitution of the atom, and for the structural organising of atoms and molecules in the constitution of matter. Next, after some gaps which are being energetically explored by biology and bio-chemistry, and still operating as a fundamental synthetic selective activity, it has emerged on a much higher level of organisation in the cell of life, and has again been responsible for the ordered grouping of cells in the life-structures of organisms, both of the plant and the animal type, and in the progressive complexifying of these structures in the course of organic Evolution. The synthetic activity in these organic structures has been so far-reaching that the independent existence of the original unit cells has sometimes been questioned, and the organism has been taken as the synthetic unit, of which the cell is but a defined portion of nucleated protoplasm.[1] In other words, the organic synthesis of cells has been

such as practically to lead to the suppression of the
individual cells as such. Next, in the higher animals
and especially in man, Holism has emerged in the new
mutation or series of mutations of Mind, in which its
synthetic co-ordinating activity has risen to an
unheard-of level, has turned in upon itself and become
experience, and has achieved virtual independence in
the form of consciousness. Finally, it has organised
all its previous structures, including mind, in a supreme structural unity in Human Personality, which has
assumed a dominating position over all the other structures and strata of existence, and has in a sense become a new centre and arbiter of reality. Thus the
four great series in reality--matter, life, mind and
Personality--apparently so far removed from each other,
are seen to be but steps in the progressive evolution
of one and the same fundamental factor, whose pathway
is the universe within us and around us. Holism constitutes them all, connects them all and, so far as explanations are at all possible, explains and accounts
for them all. Holism is matter and energy at one
stage; it is organism and life at another stage; and it
is mind and Personality at its latest stage. And all
its protean forms can in a measure be explained in
terms of its fundamental characters and activities, as
I have tried to show. All the problems of the universe, not only those of matter and life, but also and
especially those of mind and personality, which determine human nature and destiny, can in the last resort
only be resolved--in so far as they are at all humanly
soluble--by reference to the fundamental concept of Holism. For this reason I have called our universe "the
Holistic universe," as Holism is basic to its constitution, its multitudinous forms and its processes, its
history in the past, and its promise and potency for
the future.[2]

The scientist, viewing my claims for Holism in the
dry light of Science, might perhaps feel tempted to de-
mur to them. He might object that Holism is a mere assumption which may have a philosophical or metaphysical
value, but that it has no scientific importance, as it
cannot be brought to the test of actual facts and experiments. Holism as here presented, he will say, is
not a matter for Science; it is an ultra-scientific entity or concept. It falls outside the scope of Science, and the explanation of things which it purports
to give is not a scientific explanation. Even assuming
that there is such an activity as Holism at work in the
universe, it would have no value for Science. To be of

222

interest to Science, it must make a difference to actual facts and therefore be capable of experimental verification. But clearly Holism, owing to its pervasiveness and universality, cannot be so tested. As its presence would not be revealed by an examination of the particular facts, mechanisms and phenomena with which Science deals, it is unnecessary for Science to take any further interest in it.

I hope I have fairly summarised the attitude which Science might perhaps feel impelled to adopt towards the claims I have put forward on behalf of Holism. And I would reply by pointing out what seems to me to be the weakness or rather the one-sidedness and partialness in this strictly scientific attitude. Science seems to me to take too narrow a view of her sphere and functions when she confines herself merely to details, to the investigation and description of the detailed mechanisms and processes in regard to matters falling within her province. A description of analytical details, however true so far as it goes, is not yet a full and proper account of the thing or matter to be described. It is not enough; the details must be supplemented by a description which will take us back to the whole embracing those details. The anatomy and physiology of a plant would surely not be sufficient as a description of the plant itself. No description of the parts is a complete description of the whole object; it is only a partial description, and falls short of a true and full account in proportion as the object partakes of the character of a whole; where the object, for instance, is what I have called a biological or psychical whole. We may say generally that wherever an object shows structure or organisation (as every object does) a full description of it would involve at the very least an account of this structure or organisation as a whole, in addition to its detailed mechanisms and functions. And where many objects show similar or related structures, a proper description would involve an account of the ground-plan of organisation affecting them all. Thus in regard to organic and inorganic Evolution, where the whole world of matter and life and mind can be grouped into progressive series of structures from the beginning to the end, a scientific account of the universe would necessarily involve the working out of the universal ground-plan which expresses this Evolution. And it can but add to the value of such a ground-plan that it is not merely descriptive but also attempts to be self-explanatory. A plan or scheme is by its very nature not properly stated unless

223

it is not merely described but also explained and accounted for as far as possible. Now I ask, what else is Holism but such an attempted ground-plan of the universe, which is of a self-explanatory character, a ground-plan which makes the whole scheme the progressive operation and effect of a given cause? It may be objected that ultimate causes lie beyond the purview of Science. But even so the descriptive ground-plan of Holism would remain and would challenge serious consideration on scientific grounds. To me the issue seems quite simple. So long as Science eschewed all wider viewpoints (as she modestly did in her earlier years) and confined her attention to particular areas of facts, such as are embraced by the separate sciences, she was quite entitled to look upon a general explanatory ground-plan of Evolution as too ambitious for her and as falling outside her proper sphere. But once she abandons this sectional standpoint and comes to look upon the entire universe as evolutionary (as she now does), she is bound to examine a scheme such as is here put forward on its merits as falling within her universal province.

Science has been compelled in other instances to complete and support her account of detailed processes by the assumption of factors which lie beyond the area of observation, but without which the detailed processes become unintelligible. Thus the assumption of the ether of space was resorted to as the basis of the undulatory theory for the transmission of radiant energy. Although ether admittedly lies beyond the area of scientific observation and experiment, and no test however delicate has ever revealed its actual existence, it was long accepted as one of the conceptual entities which were necessary to complete the coherent system of Science, and indeed as a real physical element in the universe. It is true that ether seems to have fallen on evil days and that its existence or conceptual necessity is being more and more questioned by various groups of physicists. But it has admirably served its purpose as a scientific hypothesis, and the legitimacy of such a hypothesis was never questioned by even the most rigid school of scientists. And I would submit that the case for Holism is much stronger than that for ether ever was, as ether was meant to account only for one particular group of phenomena in physics, while Holism in the main phases of its development is necessary to account for the facts and phenomena of Evolution, both organic and inorganic. The plain fact is that, as our intellectual outlook widens and the intellectual horizons recede more and more, the domain of Science is undergoing an ever greater expansion, and therefore the formulation of new principles and new concepts embodying them becomes necessary for the support and the coherence of the whole vast scheme of Science. Science is thus for ever encroaching on the domain of philosophy and the other great disciplines of the Reason or the Spirit, and it becomes ever more difficult to confine her activities within the old orthodox limits. Holism no doubt breaks new ground; it is here intended as the basis of a new <u>Weltanschauung</u> within the general framework of Science; <u>it</u> is meant to be the foundation of a new system of unity and inward character in our outlook upon the universe as a whole. But it does not fall outside the province of Science in the larger sense. And it does not introduce strange, alien concepts into the sphere of Science.

I would also point out that the scientific objection to Holism as above formulated would, in fact, be identical with the objection which mechanistic Science has taken to life and mind as operative factors in the universe--an objection which Science is feeling herself ever more strongly compelled to overrule. The difficulty to verify Holism in the detailed mechanisms and functions would be the same as the difficulty to verify life and mind as operative factors in organic and human structures. Holism is really no more than an attempt to extend the system of life and mind, with the necessary modifications and qualifications, to inorganic Evolution, and to show the underlying identity of this system at all the stages of Evolution. In life the character of the system becomes clear, in mind still more so. That is no reason to look upon it as non-existent in the case of matter. The facts submitted in the foregoing chapters disclose a more or less connected, graduated, evolutionary series covering the phenomena of matter no less than of life and mind. Holism is a concept and a factor which formulates and accounts for the fundamental ground-plan of this series. It is therefore very much of the same order of ideas as life and mind, and stands or falls very much by the same lines of reasoning as they.

The graduated serial character of the universe has led to the theory of Evolution. But it is clear that that serial character opens up still greater questions of sources and origins. A connected graduated system of facts implies not only a particular method of their becoming, such as the theory of Evolution formulates,

225

but also a common origin and a common propelling force
or activity behind the system. In life and still more
in mind we get clear indications of this origin and
this activity. All that remains is to take a wider
view and to bring all the facts and phenomena of the
universe within the scope of this common method and origin. We then reach the concept of Holism as embracing
life and mind, but covering a much wider area and forming, in fact, the genus of which they are the species.
All Evolution then becomes the manifestation of a specific fundamental, universal activity.

Having thus attempted to vindicate Holism as a
proper scientific concept in the wider sense, let us
now proceed to sketch the main distinguishing features
of the Holistic universe, in other words, of the conception of the universe which results from the principles discussed in the foregoing chapters. The final
net result is that this is a whole-making universe,
that it is the fundamental character of this universe
to be active in the production of wholes, of ever more
complete and advanced wholes, and that the Evolution of
the universe, inorganic and organic, is nothing but the
record of this whole-making activity in its progressive
development. Let me briefly summarise the main points
in the preceding argument which lead up to this result.

We have seen that this is an essentially and wholly active universe; that its apparent passiveness as
matter is nothing but massed energy, and that activity
is therefore its fundamental character. Indeed, energy
itself is too narrow and metrical a term to do justice
to this character of the physical universe as concrete
activity. Activity in time, energy multiplied by time,
Action as it is technically called in physics, is the
physical basis of the universe as a whole, and nothing
besides. The universe is a flowing stream in Space-
Time, and its reality is not intelligible apart from
this concept of activity. So much the new Relativity
has made us realise; and to this conclusion the profoundest reflections on the nature of the universe also
tend. For us, constituted as we are, the universe
starts and takes its origin in Action. With deeper
meaning than ever before we realise that "Im Anfang war
die Tat." It is, of course, conceivable that much lies
beyond and back of this beginning as it appears to us.
It may be that the universe of Action has itself e-
volved out of a prior order which lies beyond human
ken; that there is an infinite regress of celestial Evolution into time past; and that the physical universe

226

as it now appears to or is conceived by us is the evolved result of inconceivable prior developments. We do not know, and speculation would be barren and futile.

The physical stuff of the universe is therefore really and truly Action and nothing else. But when we say that, when we make activity instead of matter the stuff or material of the universe, a new view-point is subtly introduced. For the associations of matter are different from those of Action, and the dethronement of matter in our fundamental physical conception of the universe and its replacement by Action must profoundly modify our general outlook and view-points. The New Physics has proved a solvent for some of the most ancient and hardest concepts of traditional human experience and has brought a rapprochement and reconciliation between the material and organic or psychical orders within measurable distance. I must refer to the concluding portion of the third chapter for a statement of this far-reaching advance which has been made by Science within this century. That is the contribution of the New Physics to the new outlook.

Action in Space-Time is necessarily structural; indeed Space-Time supplies the co-ordinates, the framework of the Activity which is the ultimate stuff of the world. Space-Time is the structure; hence Action in Space-Time, in the first phase of Holism, is purely structural and mechanistic, as we saw in Chapter VII. The recognition of the fundamental structural character not only of matter but of the whole universe is the contribution of the Relativity theory to the new outlook. The physical world thus becomes at bottom structural Action, Activity structuralised in bodies, things, events. Thus arises the apparent material universe which surrounds us and in our bodies forms part of us.

What is the next step? Action does not come to a stop in its structures, it remains Action, it remains in action. In other words, there is more in bodies, things and events than is contained in their structures or material forms. All things overflow their own structural limits, the inner Action transcends the outer structure, and there is thus a trend in things beyond themselves. This inner trend in things springs from their very essence as localised, imprisoned Action. From this follow two important conclusions. The first is the concept of things as more than their apparent structures, and their "fields" as complementary to

227

their full operation and understanding. A thing does not come to a stop at its boundaries or bounding surfaces. It is overflowing Action, it passes beyond its bounds, and its surrounding "field" is therefore essential not only to its correct appreciation as a thing, but also to a correct understanding of things in general, and especially of the ways in which they affect each other. I have tried, at various points in the foregoing discussion, to emphasise the great importance of this concept of "fields" not only for physics but also for biology and philosophy.

The second and more important conclusion is the great fact and concept of Evolution. The inner character of the universe as Action expresses itself in actuality as a passage, a process, a passing beyond existing forms and structures, and thus the way is opened up for Evolution. The actual character of Evolution can, of course, be concluded and known only from the facts, and is not a matter of logical inference deducible from the nature of the universe as Action. But if activity is the essence of the universe we see more easily why the universe is evolutionary and historical rather than static and unchangeable. There is a passage, a process, a progress, but its characters can only be determined by a study of the facts of the passage. It may turn out to be merely a movement of combinations and groupings; or it may turn out to be an unfolding, explication and filling out, an evolutio in the stricter sense; or it may turn out to be a real creative Evolution such as we have seen it to be. Real Evolution requires other concepts besides those of Action and structure; and these concepts can only be derived from experience. Thus the creativeness of Evolution is a conclusion not so much from theory as from the empirical facts. And the exact nature of this creativeness is unknown in some respects and remains a problem for the future to solve. A still wider survey and closer scrutiny of the facts lead to the conception of Holism which accounts not only for the structural combinations of bodies, things and events, but for all the progressive series of unities and syntheses which have arisen in the cosmic process.

Assuming that Holism and the nature of wholes in the universe have been sufficiently explained in the foregoing chapters, I now proceed to compare the worldview to which Holism leads with those which resemble or touch it at various points and yet are essentially different from it.

The Holistic view agrees with the Naturalistic conception of physical science in giving the fullest importance to the physical aspect of the universe. It does full justice to the structural and mechanistic characters of Nature, and indeed it considers Mechanism simply an earlier phase of Holism, and therefore perfectly legitimate up to a point. It affirms the validity of the fundamental laws and principles of physics not only for inorganic bodies but also for organisms, in so far as they are material. It represents the organic order as arising from and inside the inorganic or physical order without in any way derogating from it. If in the end it erects on the physical a superstructure which is more and more ideal and spiritual, that does not mean a denial of the physical. The idealism of Holism does not deny matter, but affirms and welcomes and affectionately embraces it. If Holism begins as realism and ends as idealism, it does not spurn or deny its own past; in Holism both realism and idealism have their proper place and function and indeed find their justification and reconciliation. It breaks with Naturalism only at the point where Naturalism becomes purely materialistic, and in effect denies the creative plasticity of Nature, presents Nature as an anatomical museum, as a collection of dead and dried disjecta membra, instead of the interwoven body of living, creative, progressive unities and syntheses which she essentially is. Naturalism represents the universe as a vast reservoir of energy, unalterable in amount but steadily deteriorating in character, subject to immutable laws and fixed equations which prevent anything essentially new from ever arising or having arisen. It thus negatives the concept of creative Evolution except as a mere figure of speech. It presents life and mind as mere wandering insubstantial shadows on the shores of this ocean of energy; the great Mirage of Evolution broods over the waters; and Man himself, so far from being a creative factor in reality as a whole, becomes an impotent spectator of this melancholy scene, wrapped up in the illusions of his own self-consciousness. Such a view of the universe seems to me hopelessly one-sided and distorted, and comes into direct conflict with large and important bodies of facts of experience which cannot be denied or reasoned away. To me the rock on which Naturalism must split is the fact of creative Evolution. In the first chapter I pointed out that the old materialistic Naturalism is inconsistent with a clear and frank recognition of the great fact of Evolution, and in the body of this work I have tried to drive the point further home.

Creativeness is the key-word and the key-position,
not only as far as Naturalism is concerned, but also as
regards those other world-conceptions which are most
hostile to Naturalism, such as the various modern forms
of Spiritual Idealism. Naturalism imposes the past on
the present and the future; Idealism, again, imposes
the present and the future on the past. Both implicitly deny that creative Evolution which shows the universe historically as a gradual transformation, as a
real creative process moving from the real structures
of the past to the real structures of the future; and
therefore as a system which in its historical development embraces and gives justification to both contrasted points of view. To view the ideal or spiritual element in the universe as the dominant factor is to ignore the fact that the universe was before ever the
ideal or spiritual had appeared on the horizon; that
the ideal or spiritual is a new and indeed recent creation in the order of the universe, that it was not implicit in the beginnings and has not been reached by a
process of unfolding; but that from a real pre-existing
order of things it has been creatively evolved as a new
factor; and that its importance to-day should not be
retrospectively antedated to a time when the world existed without it. Where was the Spirit when the warm
Silurian seas covered the face of the earth, and the
lower types of fishes and marine creatures still formed
the crest of the evolutionary wave? Or going still
further back, where was the Spirit when in the Pre-
Cambrian system of the globe the first convulsive movements threw up the early mountains which have now entirely disappeared from the face of the earth, and when
the living forms, if any, were of so low a type that
none have been deciphered yet in the geological record?
Where was the Spirit when the Solar System itself was
still a diffuse fiery nebula? The evolutionary facts
of Science are beyond dispute, and they support the
view of the earth as existing millions of years before
ever the psychical or spiritual order had arisen; and
what is true of the earth may be similarly true of the
universe as a whole. The fact that we have to grasp
firmly in connection with creative Evolution is that,
while the spiritual or psychical factor is a real element in the universe, it is a comparatively recent arrival in the evolutionary order of things; that the
universe existed untold millions of years before its
arrival; and that it is just as wrong for Idealism to
deny the world before the appearance of Spirit, as it
is for Naturalism to deny Spirit when eventually it did
appear in the world.

Creative Evolution seems to move forward by small
steps or instalments or increments of creativeness.
Why there should be this discontinuity rather than a
smooth continuous advance we cannot say; we can but
note the fact, which seems to be a universal phenomenon. Not only does matter in its atomic and elemental
structure show this minute discontinuity, but the electric elements in the atom, and in the electric current
generally, and the quanta of heat and radiant energy
show the same remarkable feature. Thus the unit character of Action and Structure is reproduced in the unit
character of Evolution and of nuclear change in the
cell. There is real creation as distinct from mere
combinations of pre-existing units or mere unfolding of
implicit elements; but this creation is not consummated
in one supreme creative Act; nor is it evenly and uniformly distributed throughout all time. Its distribution is unevenly spread in minute parcels over the
whole almost infinite range of evolution. Evolution
thus becomes a long-drawn-out process of creation, in
which the new for ever arises by slow and minute increments from the old, or rather by way of the old, as it
is not known how the new actually arises from the old.
As I have explained in Chapter VII, Holism is the pre-
siding genius of this advance. It determines the direction of the advance, and it incorporates the new
element of advance synthetically with the pre-existing
structure. It thus harmonises the old and the new in
its own unity; it synthesises Variation and Heredity;
and by slow degrees and over enormous periods of time
carries forward the creative process from the most
simple, primitive, inorganic beginnings to the most
exalted spiritual creations. From the atom to the
Soul, from matter to Personality is a long way, marked
by innumerable steps, each of which involved a real
creative advance and added something essentially new to
what had gone before. Such seems to be the nature of
Evolution, and it appears to be fatal alike to the ret-
rospective interpretation of the universe according to
Idealism, and the prospective interpretation according
to Naturalism. Mind or Spirit did not exist at the beginning, either implicitly or explicitly; but it does
most certainly exist now as a real factor.

Another world-conception which may be considered
as having considerable affinities with the Holistic
view is that of Leibniz's Monadology. The resemblance
is, however, confined to certain aspects of the respective central ideas; beyond those aspects the two views
are totally and essentially different. There is a

close resemblance between the central ideas of wholes and monads; that is all. The unities and units which exist in Nature seemed to Leibniz to be of the greatest importance for the interpretation of the universe; not the One but the Many and their intimate nature seemed to him to supply the key to the great riddle. I have in the foregoing reached the concept of wholes by a different process of reasoning from that followed by Leibniz, but the result looks very much like that arrived at by him along different lines. And the convergence of the two views from totally different standpoints would appear to suggest that there is a substantial element of truth and value in the concepts of wholes, as there undoubtedly is in the Leibnizian theory of Monads. They agree in having an innerness, in being little worlds of their own, with their own inner laws of development and with a certain measure of inner self-direction or self-conservation which makes them partial mirrors or expressions of the greater reality. But the monads according to Leibniz are essentially spiritual entities or selves, conceived on the analogy of the human mind, and their activities are of a purely psychical character such as perception. They are, moreover, absolutely closed, isolated, self-contained units, each with its own immutable inner system, uninfluenced by any other monad; and all maintained in harmony with each other by some divine pre-established order outside of them. The greater and lesser selves of the universe lead their own inner self-existences, without any contact between one another, and only the divine interposition maintains a Pre-established Harmony between them. There is a scale of these monads, from the lowest most simple, such as atoms or molecules, whose confused perceptions produce the world of matter, to the highest most complex in the universe, such as human minds, whose clear and distinct perceptions produce the world of spirit. God himself is but the Supreme Monad of monads on this view. It will be seen how different this monadic conception is from that of wholes developed in this work. In the first place, wholes are not all spiritual entities, and the world is not a hierarchy of spirits exclusively, as Leibniz conceived it. Spiritual wholes are merely the apex and crowning feature of the universe, while non-spiritual (material or organic) wholes compose its earlier phases. In the second place, wholes are not closed, isolated systems externally; they have their fields in which they intermingle and influence each other. The Holistic universe is a profoundly reticulated system of interactions and inter-connections rising into a real

232

society in its later phases. In the third place, genetic relationships connect the entire Holistic universe. Wholes from the lowest to the highest are akin
and form one great family, and are derived from one another in the process called Evolution. In the fourth
place, it is the ascertainable character of this evolutionary process which holds all the wholes together
in one vast network of adaptations and harmonious coordinations, and not some mystic assumed Pre-established
Harmony. Leibniz, while he correctly guessed the real
secret in his idea of Monads, missed yet the true explanation through not having any knowledge of creative
Evolution, such as the deeper science of our day has
revealed to us. To him Evolution was a mere unfolding
of an implicit content; he adhered to the traditional
preformation views of his day as well as to the current
belief in the fixity of species. He could not, therefore, realise the idea that monads were genetically related and evolved; and that the order which underlay
the series of monads from the lowest to the highest was
of a creative character. In the absence of genetic relationships and creative Evolution, he had to make
shift with the notions of isolated inner selves and a
pre-established harmony. We may therefore say that
just as both Naturalism and Idealism are shattered on
the rock of creative Evolution, so likewise the Monadology, however valuable and suggestive in other respects, founders on that same rock, which was, however,
still secret and undisclosed to the science of Leibniz's time. But for that ignorance who knows whether
Leibniz might not have elaborated a far more adequate
and suggestive Holistic conception than that contained
in this poor effort!

The astonishing thing is that thinkers of our own
time, who are not only conversant with the idea of creative Evolution but convinced adherents of it, fail to
adjust their view-points to it. Thus the late Professor James Ward, who advocated the view of Evolution as
epigenesis or creative synthesis, and whose Pluralism
has close affinities to the Monadology, seems yet to
have failed to realise that his view of Evolution as
creative was in conflict with his spiritual Pluralism
or Panpsychism. His Pluralistic universe also consisted entirely of spiritual monads or entities, and
this implied the possession of spiritual or psychical
characters not only on the part of the higher monads,
like persons, but also on the part of the most rudimentary monads, such as atoms and chemical compounds.
Spinoza, who otherwise differed widely from Leibniz,

233

had also assumed that all things were in their several degrees _animata_, but he had the excuse of being, like Leibniz, ignorant of the idea of creative Evolution. But Ward, in spite of his fuller knowledge, calmly follows Leibniz and Spinoza in their error. The plain fact, of course, is that psychism or spiritualism can by no stretch of language be ascribed to mere bits of matter or energy or physical entities like atoms or chemical compounds without the gravest confusion. The very idea of creative Evolution or epigenesis is that both life and mind are later creations in the evolutionary series, and cannot possibly be antedated to the mere physical level of Evolution. There is not a great Society of Spirits in the universe, of which Persons and Things, Souls and Atoms alike are members on the same spiritual footing. When the term "Spiritual" is stretched that far and spread that thin, it loses all real value and becomes a mere empty figure of speech. There is indeed no such spiritual Society of the whole universe, but there is the Holistic order, which is something far greater, and stretches from the beginning to the end, and through all grades and degrees of holistic self-fulfilment. Holism, not Spiritualism, is the key to the interpretation of the universe. Mind is not at the beginning but at the end, but Holism is everywhere and all in all. If the universe were a great spiritual Society of lower and higher souls or spirits, Evolution as creative would become meaningless; it would be merely a process of explication of the implicit spirituality (if any) inherent in the universe. The Holistic view thus not merely negatives the far-reaching spiritual assumptions of the Monadology, or Panpsychism, but it is also in firm agreement with the teachings of science and experience. Nor does it, in fact, detract from the value or importance of the universe. It but impresses on us the necessity of that great lesson of humility which is the ethical message of Evolution. It shows that values should not be confused with origins, and that from origins the most lowly may be raised values the most exalted and spiritual in the order of the universe. The Great Society of the universe leaves a place for the most humble inanimate inorganic structure no less than for the crowning glory of the great soul. To conceive the universe otherwise is to indulge in anthropomorphism, which may be pleasing to our vanity, but in reality detracts from the richness and variety of the universe. The Holistic universe embraces all the real structures from the lowest to the highest in their own right and as they are, without decking them in spiritual habiliments which are

234

alien to their true nature. This world, in the noble
language of Keats, is indeed the valley of soul-making;
but it could not be that if the valley itself consists
of nothing but souls. To those who have the deepest
experience of life, this world is not only the upward
path for the soul, but a very hard and flinty one. To
attempt to pave that rugged way with the roses of the
spiritual order would be a profound mistake from every
point of view.

To say this is not to assume that there is anything alien or antagonistic between the human soul and
the natural environment in which it finds itself in
this world. There is not only poetic value but profound truth in the spiritual interpretation of Nature
to which Wordsworth and other great poets of Nature
have accustomed us. And that truth is not merely due
to the creative part which mind plays in the shaping
and fashioning of Nature. It is not merely that we invest Nature with our own emotional attributes. It is,
in fact, to be traced to far deeper sources in our human origins. For we are indeed one with Nature; her
genetic fibres run through all our being; our physical
organs connect us with millions of years of her history; our minds are full of immemorial paths of pre-
human experience. Our ear for music, our eye for art
carry us back to the early beginnings of animal life on
this globe. Press but a button in our brain, and the
gaunt spectres of the dim forgotten past rise once more
before us; the ghostly dreaded forms of the primeval
Fear loom before us and we tremble all over with inex-
plicable fright. And then again some distant sound,
some call of bird or smell of wild plants, or some sun-
rise or sunset glow in the distant clouds, some mixture
of light and shade on the mountains, may suddenly throw
an unearthly spell over the spirit, lead it forth from
the deep chambers, and set it panting and wondering
with inexpressible emotions. For the overwrought mind
there is no peace like Nature's, for the wounded spirit
there is no healing like hers. There are indeed times
when human companionship becomes unbearable, and we fly
to Nature for that silent sympathy and communion which
she alone can give. Some of the deepest emotional experiences of my life have come to me on the many nights
I have spent under the open African sky; and I am sure
my case has not been singular in this respect. The intimate rapport with Nature is one of the most precious
things in life. Nature is indeed very close to us;
sometimes perhaps closer than hands and feet, of which
in truth she is but the extension. The emotional

235

appeal of Nature is tremendous, sometimes almost more than one can bear. But to explain it we need not make the unwarrantable assumption of a universal animism or animatism, and invest inanimate things with souls kindred to our own. Evolution, with the genetic relationships and fundamental kinship it implies, accounts for all this intimate emotional appeal. The idea of the universe as a spiritual Society of Souls is a poetical idealised picture, and not in accord with the sober realistic, scientific view of the facts. This is a universe of whole-making, not merely of soul-making, which is only its climax phase. The universe is not a pure transparency of Reason or Spirit. It contains unreason and contradiction, it contains error and evil, sin and suffering. There are grades and gaps, there are clashes and disharmonies between the grades. It is not the embodiment of some simple homogeneous human Ideal. It is profoundly complex and replete with unsearchable diversities and variety. It is the expression of a creative process which is for ever revealing new riches and supplying new unpredictable surprises. But the creative process is not, on that account, issuing in chaos and hopeless irreconcilable conflict. It is for ever mitigating the conflict through a higher system of controls. It is for ever evolving new and higher wholes as the organs of a greater harmony. Through the steadily rising series of wholes it is producing ever more highly organised centres whose inner freedom and creative metabolism transform the fetters of fate and the contingencies of circumstance into the freedom and harmony of a more profoundly co-operative universe. But though the crest of the spiritual wave is no doubt steadily rising, the ocean which supports it contains much more besides the Spirit. Enough for us to know that the lower is not in hopeless enmity to the higher, but its basis and support, a feeder to it, a source whence it mysteriously draws its creative strength for further effort, and hence the necessary pre-condition for all further advance. Thus beneath all logical or ethical disharmonies there exists the deeper creative, genetic harmony between the lower and the higher grades in the Holistic series.

Reference must be made to one more question or set of questions before we conclude. I have said before that the scope of this work is limited, and that it is not intended to deal exhaustively with the entire subject of Holism. But within the limits of the introductory task which I have set myself here, one problem remains to be mentioned. It is the problem of The Whole,

the great whole itself as distinguished from the lesser
wholes which we have found as the texture of Evolution.
In other words, is there a Whole, a Supreme Whole, of
which all lesser wholes are but parts or organs? And
if there is such a Whole of wholes, how is it to be
conceived? Is it to be conceived on the analogy of an
organism, as Nature? Or is it to be conceived on the
analogy of Mind and Personality as a Supreme divine
Personality? Or are both these conceptions inadmissi-
ble, and is there some other way of conceiving the system of wholes in their actual or possible synthesis?
These are very difficult and thorny questions, but it
is clear that we cannot leave the consideration of
wholes at the present stage of our argument. For that
argument implies clearly something more to complete it,
even in the preliminary way which is all that is intended in this work.

Two points arise from the preceding discussion
which naturally carry us forward to the consideration
of these larger questions. In the first place, where
do we fix the limits of a lesser whole? In a whole we
have included its field; but how far does this field
extend? What limits are there to the field of an inorganic body, or an organism, or a Personality? Leibniz
represented each monad as containing or mirroring the
whole universe in its own way and from its own particular angle; lower monads, of course, more imperfectly
than higher monads; but each in its own degree is a
sort of microcosm or miniature universe. In other
words, each tiniest least monad is in a sense cosmic
and universal. This description would not apply to a
field. As we have seen, a field is of the same character as the inner area of the whole, only more attenuated in its force and influence, and the farther it re-
cedes from that area the greater the attenuation; so
that the field, though theoretically indefinite in extent, is in effect quite limited in practical operation. When we come to consider a group of wholes we
see that, while the wholes may be mutually exclusive,
their fields overlap and penetrate and reinforce each
other, and thus create an entirely new situation. Thus
we speak of the atmosphere of idea, the spirit of a
class, or the soul of a people. The social individuals
as such remain unaltered, but the social environment or
field undergoes a complete change. There is a multiplication of force in the society or group owing to
this mutual penetration of the conjoint fields, which
creates the appearance and much of the reality of a new
organism. Hence we speak of social or group or national

organisms. But as a matter of fact there is no new organism; the society or group is organic without being an organism; holistic without being a whole. The mentality of a crowd as distinct from the number of individuals composing it is a good illustration of the changed and reinforced mental field which results from the meeting of many individuals and the fusion and heightening of their conjoint fields. And the more psychic they are, the more they are under the influence of strong passions or carried away by some contagious idea, the more overpowering the common field becomes. The force of the group field is generally out of all proportion to the strength of the idea or the passions in the individual units composing the group. The group field is so to say the multiplication of all the individual fields. The subject falls under the study of social psychology and is referred to here only for the purpose of illustration. We have in such cases an organic situation but not an organism. Groups, families, churches, societies, nations are organic but not organisms.

Taking all the wholes in the world and viewing them together in Nature, we see a similar interpenetration and enrichment of the common field. When we speak of Nature we do not mean a collection of unconnected items, we mean wholes with their interlocking fields; we mean a creative situation which is far more than the mere gathering of individuals and their separate fields. This union of fields is creative of a new and indefinable spirit or atmosphere; the external mechanical situation is transformed into an inward synthetic, "organic" situation or atmosphere. This "organic" Nature seems in certain situations to be alive to us, to stir strange unsuspected depths in us, to make an appeal to our emotional nature which often "lies too deep for words." Thus we come to consider Nature as an organism; we personify her, we even deify and worship her. But the sober fact is that there is no new whole or organism of Nature; there is only Nature become organic through the intensification of her total field. In other words, Nature is holistic without being a real whole.

Nor is it merely we humans, with our intense psychic sensitivity, who feel this appeal of organic or holistic Nature. All organic creatures feel it too. The new science of Ecology is simply a recognition of the fact that all organisms feel the force and moulding effect of their environment as a whole. There is much

more in Ecology than merely the striking down of the
unfit by way of Natural Selection. There is a much
more subtle and far-reaching influence within the special or local fields of Nature than is commonly recognised or suspected. Sensitivity to appropriate fields
is not confined to humans, but is shared by animals and
plants throughout organic Nature.

There is a second point which emerges from the
foregoing chapters and leads up to the issue now under
discussion.

In Chapter VII we have spoken of a general common
trend of Evolution, of Evolution as not tacking and
veering about, but as moving in one general direction,
as keeping a general course and direction through all
the endless ages of her voyaging. How is this to be
explained? Here again the expedient of personification
is often resorted to for the purpose of finding an explanation. It is said that Evolution discloses a grand
inner Purpose, that Nature or the universe is purposive
or teleological, and that no other category will do
justice to the great fact of Evolution as we see it.
But if there is purpose there must be a Mind behind
that purpose. And thus Mind comes to be personified in
Nature as the source of the great evolutionary purpose
which the world discloses. Cosmic Teleology spells a
corresponding transcendent Personality. Do the facts
warrant or necessitate such tremendous assumptions?
Would it not rather seem that the whole basis of this
reasoning is unsound and false? In all the previous
cases of wholes we have nowhere been able to argue from
the parts to the whole. Compared to its parts, the
whole constituted by them is something quite different,
something creatively new, as we have seen. Creative
Evolution synthesises from the parts a new entity not
only different from them but quite transcending them.
That is the essence of a whole. It is always transcendent to its parts, and its character cannot be inferred from the characters of its parts. Now the above
reasoning, by which a supra-mundane Mind or Personality
is reached, ignores this fact. Such a "Personality"
would be creatively new and unlike the wholes which we
know and which would constitute its parts. It would be
as different at least from human Personality as this
again is from mere organism. To call such a new Transcendent Whole by the same name as human Personality is
to abuse language and violate thought alike. There is
universal agreement with the well-known argument of
Kant, that from the facts of Nature no inference of God

is justified. The belief in the Divine Being rests, and necessarily must rest, on quite different grounds. From the facts of Evolution no inference to a transcendent Mind is justified, as that would make the whole still of the same character and order as its parts; which would be absurd, as Euclid says. From the facts neither an organism nor a Mind of Nature can strictly be inferred; still less a Personality constituted by both.

Nor is it necessary to make these far-reaching assumptions. There is indeed a great trend in Evolution, but it would be wrong and a misnomer to call that trend a purpose, and worse to invent a Mind to which to refer that purpose. There is something organic and holistic in Nature which shapes her ends and directs her courses. Without forming an organism or a mind the totality of wholes which compose Nature develop an organic field which is sufficient to control her creative movement. As a physical field has its lines of force, so the organic field of Nature, which results from the creative interpretation of all fields of wholes composing her, has its own structural curves of progress. In human society we see how the social field or atmosphere becomes a system of control, a moulding influence to which all incoming members are subject. The individual in society is born into a vast network of controls, and from birth to death he never escapes its subtle toils. The holistic organic field of Nature exercises a similar subtle moulding, controlling influence in respect of the general trend of organic advance. That trend is not random or accidental or free to move in all directions; it is controlled, it has the general character of uniform direction under the influence of the organic or holistic field of Nature.

And there is more. Behind the evolutionary movement and the holistic field of Nature is the inner shaping, directive activity of Holism itself, working through the wholes and in the variations which creatively arise from them. We have seen in Chapter VIII that these variations are not accidental or haphazard, but the controlled, regulated expression of the inner holistic development of organisms as wholes. There is Selection, and thus direction and control, right through the entire forward movement, not only in the origin of variations but also at the various subsequent stages of their "selection," internal and external. This organic holistic control of direction, this inner trend of the evolutionary process is really all that is

240

meant by the metaphor of Purpose or Teleology as applied to Nature or Evolution. To infer more is in effect to make the mistake of spiritual Idealism and to
apply later human categories to the earlier phases of
the evolutionary process.

Thus it is that when we speak of Nature or the
Universe as a Whole or The Whole, we merely mean Nature
or the Universe considered as organic, or in its organic or holistic aspects. We do not mean that either is
a real whole in the sense defined in this work. We
have seen that the creative intensified Field of Nature, consisting of all physical organic and personal
wholes in their close interactions and mutual influences, is itself of an organic or holistic character.
That Field is the source of the grand Ecology of the
universe. It is the environment, the Society--vital,
friendly, educative, creative--of all wholes and all
souls. It is not a mere figure of speech or figment of
the imagination, but a reality with profound influences
of its own on all wholes and their destiny. It is the
öikos, the Home of all the family of the universe, with
something profoundly intimate and friendly in its atmosphere. In this Home of Wholes and Souls the creative tasks of Holism are carried forward. Without ide-
alising it unduly we yet feel that it is very near and
dear to us, and in spite of all antagonisms and trou-
bles we come in the end to feel that this is a friendly
universe. Its deepest tendencies are helpful to what
is best in us, and our highest aspirations are but its
inspiration. Thus behind our striving towards betterment are in the last resort the entire weight and momentum and the inmost nature and trend of the universe.

I have now reached the end of my argument. The
reflections embodied in this work lie far removed from
the busy and exciting scenes in which most of my life
has been spent; and yet both of them tend toward the
same general conclusions. It has been my lot to have
passed many of the years of my life amid the conflicts
of men, in their wars and their Council Chambers. Everywhere I have seen men search and struggle for the
Good with grim determination and earnestness, and with
a sincerity of purpose which added to the poignancy of
the fratricidal strife. But we are still far, very
far, from the goal to which Holism points. The Great
War--with its infinite loss and suffering, its toll of
untold lives, the shattering of great States and almost
of civilisation, the fearful waste of goodwill and sincere human ideals which followed the close of that vast

241

tragedy--has been proof enough for our day and generation that we are yet far off the attainment of the ideal of a really Holistic universe. But everywhere too I have seen that it was at bottom a struggle for the Good, a wild striving towards human betterment; that blindly, and through blinding mists of passions and illusions, men are yet sincerely, earnestly groping towards the light, towards the ideal of a better, more secure life for themselves and for their fellows. Thus the League of Nations, the chief constructive outcome of the Great War, is but the expression of the deeply-felt aspiration towards a more stable holistic human society. And the faith has been strengthened in me that what has here been called Holism is at work even in the conflicts and confusions of men; that in spite of all appearances to the contrary, eventual victory is serenely and securely waiting, and that the immeasurable sacrifices have not been in vain. The groaning and travailing of the universe is never aimless or resultless. Its profound labours mean new creation, the slow, painful birth of wholes, of new and higher wholes, and the slow but steady realisation of the Good which all the wholes of the universe in their various grades dimly yearn and strive for. It is the nature of the universe to strive for and slowly, but in ever-increasing measure, to attain wholeness, fullness, blessedness. The real defeat for men as for other grades of the universe would be to ease the pain by a cessation of effort, to cease from striving towards the Good. The holistic nisus which rises like a living fountain from the very depths of the universe is the guarantee that failure does not await us, that the ideals of Wellbeing, of Truth, Beauty and Goodness are firmly grounded in the nature of things, and will not eventually be endangered or lost. Wholeness, healing, holiness--all expressions and ideas springing from the same root in language as in experience--lie on the rugged upward path of the universe, and are secure of attainment--in part here and now, and eventually more fully and truly. The rise and self-perfection of wholes in the Whole is the slow but unerring process and goal of this Holistic universe.

FOOTNOTES

[1]Doncaster: Introduction to Study of Cytology, pp. 3-4.

[2]Professor Lloyd Morgan has made the creative or emergent character of Evolution the theme of his book on "Emergent Evolution," and it has been suggested to me that I should explain my relation to it. The fact is that my views had a different origin from his, and that they had been matured and the whole of this book written before I saw his interesting and suggestive volume. The result is that, in spite of many surprising similarities of thought, there remains an essential diversity in our themes as well as in our emphasis even on those matters on which we apparently agree. To him emergence of the new in the evolution of the universe is the essential fact; to me there is something more fundamental--the character of the wholeness, the tendency to wholes, ever more intensive and effective wholes, which is basic to the universe, and of which emergence or creativeness is but one feature, however important it is in other respects. Hence he lays all the emphasis on the feature of emergence, while I stress wholes or Holism as the real factor, from which emergence and all the rest follow. To me the holistic aspect of the universe is fundamental, and appears to be the key position both for the science and for the philosophy of the future.

Besides, Professor Lloyd Morgan makes the psychical factor the correlate at all stages of the physical factor, thus in effect getting back to the Spinozist position that all bodies, even inorganic matter, are animata in their several degrees. This view seems to be a reversion to the preformation type of Evolution and to be destructive of all real effective "emergence." In any case it is wholly different from the view of creative advance consistently put forward in this book.

SUGGESTED READINGS

Jan Christian Smuts

Smuts, Jan C. Holism and Evolution (New York: Macmillan, 1926). (Viking Press, 1961; Greenwood Press, 1973).

_____. Plans for a Better World (London: Hodder and Stroughton, 1942).

_____. Toward a Better World (Yonkers, New York: World Book Company, 1944).

_____ and Others. Our Changing World View (Johannesburg: University of Witwatersrand Press, 1932).

* * *

Smuts, J. C. Jan Christian Smuts: A Biography (New York: William Marrow, 1952).

* * *

Hancock, W. K. and Jean van der Poel (Eds.). Selections from the Smuts Papers (Cambridge: University Press, 1966-1973), Vols. 1-7.

Bradley, Gen. Omar N. A Soldier's Story (New York: Holt, 1951).

Burtt, B. L. W. Makers of South Africa (Toronto: Nelson, 1944).

Churchill, Winston S. The World Crisis, 1911-18 (London: T. Butterworth, 1931).

Crafford, F. S. Jan Smuts (New York: Doubleday, Doran, 1944).

Levi, N. Jan Smuts (London: Longmans, Green, 1917).

Millan, Sarah G. General Smuts (London: Faber and Faber, 1936).

244

Robertson, Field Marshal Sir William. Soldiers and Statesmen (London: Cassell, 1926).

10. THE ANALYSIS OF EXPERIENCE

Alfred North Whitehead

Alfred North Whitehead (1861-1947) was early
in his life introduced to the Greek and Latin
languages, and consequently, classical thought.
He gained his basic education at Trinity College, Cambridge, where he remained from 1880
until 1910 as first Scholar and then Fellow.
After three years at University College, London, he then served at Imperial College of
Science and Technology, Kensington, before
coming to Harvard where he served from 1924
until 1947.

Whitehead has his beginnings in physics, logic,
and mathematics, but there was a continual progression
in his thought from mathematics to the science of nature and in turn to metaphysics. In his interpretation
of each of these areas, moreover, he never turned loose
of a firm confidence in the validity of 'immediate experience'. He was critical of what he called simple
recourse to metaphysics and the general incoherence
which follows from it. Being very concerned to explicate ultimate notions without the multiplication and
disconnection of first principles, Whitehead conscientiously sought to synthesize the customary dualisms of
subject and object, man and nature, mind and matter.
The interpreters of Whitehead have found the following
section of Adventures of Ideas to be one of his clearest and most constructive protests against the doctrine
of secondary qualities.* Here he argues against the
promotion of quantitative entities in complete disregard of the features of our experience and what is disclosed to us in sense perception; as well as against
the time-worn attempt to explain the elements of nature
by means of something which is said to transcend the

---

*This section is from Adventures of Ideas (New
York: Macmillan, 1933), pp. 225-233, 235, 253-257,
268-282, with certain editorial omissions. Used by
permission of Macmillan Publishing Company.

natural order; namely, the mind. Whitehead therefore places considerable emphasis upon the idea that, as far as natural philosophy is concerned, everything that is perceived is in nature, but he places equal emphasis on the notion that all actual existences are to be viewed as 'occasions of experience'. In opposition to theories of the disconnectedness of experience and the bifurcation of nature he proposes a unification in which the actualities of the universe as objects of external experience are in turn data in the subjective occasion of experiencing. His basic intent is to clarify the term 'object' as always correlative to that of the 'experiencing subject'.[#] Only if we balance the subjective bias with the objective facts of the case, he says, can we hope to have a valid inference with respect to the world of external things in contradistinction to past theories extolling the disconnectedness of experience and/or the bifurcation of nature.

[#]Dr. Hartshorne reminds us that Whitehead's ultimate solution to the bifurcation problem is that concrete objects simply are subjects as given to, prehended by, later subjects. The simple fact that 'object' is always correlative to that of experiencing 'subject' does not necessarily make this point.

The Analysis of Experience

When Descartes, Locke, and Hume undertake the analysis of experience, they utilize those elements in their own experience which lie clear and distinct, fit for the exactitude of intellectual discourse. It is tacitly assumed, except by Plato, that the more fundamental factors will ever lend themselves. for discrimination with peculiar clarity. This assumption is here directly challenged.

No topic has suffered more from this tendency of philosophers than their account of the object-subject structure of experience. In the first place, this structure has been identified with the bare relation of knower to known. The subject is the knower, the object is the known. Thus, with this interpretation, the object-subject relation is the known-knower relation. It then follows that the more clearly any instance of this relation stands out for discrimination, the more safely we can utilize it for the interpretation of the status of experience in the universe of things. Hence Descartes' appeal to clarity and distinctness.

This deduction presupposes that the subject-object relation is the fundamental structural pattern of experience. I agree with this presupposition, but not in the sense in which subject-object is identified with knower-known. I contend that the notion of mere knowledge is a high abstraction, and that conscious discrimination itself is a variable factor only present in the more elaborate examples of occasions of experience. The basis of experience is emotional. Stated more generally, the basic fact is the rise of an effective tone originating from things whose relevance is given.

Thus the Quaker word 'concern', divested of any suggestion of knowledge, is more fitted to express this fundamental structure. The occasion as subject has a 'concern' for the object. And the 'concern' at once places the object as a component in the experience of the subject, with an effective tone drawn from this object and directed towards it. With this interpretation the subject-object relation is the fundamental structure of experience.

* * *

A more formal explanation is as follows. An occasion of experience is an activity, analysable into modes of functioning which jointly constitute its process of becoming. Each mode is analysable into the total experience as active subject, and into the thing or object with which the special activity is concerned. This thing is a datum, that is to say, is describable without reference to its entertainment in that occasion. An object is anything performing this function of a datum provoking some special activity of the occasion in question. Thus subject and object are relative terms. An occasion is a subject in respect to its special activity concerning an object; and anything is an object in respect to its provocation of some special activity within a subject. Such a mode of activity is termed a 'prehension'. Thus a prehension involves three factors. There is the occasion of experience within which the prehension is a detail of activity; there is the datum whose relevance provokes the origination of this prehension; this datum is the prehended object; there is the subjective form, which is the affective tone determining the effectiveness of that prehension in that occasion of experience. How the experience constitutes itself depends on its complex of subjective forms.

The individual immediacy of an occasion is the final unity of subjective form, which is the occasion as an absolute reality. This immediacy is its moment of sheer individuality, bounded on either side by essential relativity. The occasion arises from relevant objects, and perishes into the status of an object for other occasions. But it enjoys its decisive moment of absolute self-attainment as emotional unity. As used here the words 'individual' and 'atom' have the same meaning, that they apply to composite things with an absolute reality which their components lack. These words properly apply to an actual entity in its immediacy of self-attainment when it stands out as for itself alone, with its own effective self-enjoyment. The term 'monad' also expresses this essential unity at the decisive moment, which stands between its birth and its perishing. The creativity of the world is the throbbing emotion of the past hurling itself into a new transcendent fact. It is the flying dart, of which Lucretius speaks, hurled beyond the bounds of the world.

All knowledge is conscious discrimination of objects experienced. But this conscious discrimination, which is knowledge, is nothing more than an additional factor in the subjective form of the interplay of subject with object. This interplay is the stuff constituting those individual things which make up the sole reality of the Universe. These individual things are the individual occasions of experience, the actual entities.

* * *

The particular agelong group of doctrines which I have in mind is: (1) that all perception is by the mediation of our bodily sense-organs, such as eyes, palates, noses, ears, and the diffused bodily organization furnishing touches, aches, and other bodily sensations; (2) that all percepta are base sensa, in patterned connections, given in the immediate present; (3) that our experience of a social world is an interpretative reaction wholly derivative from this perception; (4) that our emotional and purposive experience is a reflective reaction derived from the original perception, and intertwined with the interpretative reaction and partly shaping it. Thus the two reactions are different aspects of one process, involving interpretative, emotional, and purposive factors.

* * *

The process of experiencing is constituted by the reception of entities, whose being is antecedent to that process, into the complex fact which is that process itself. These antecedent entities, thus received as factors into the process of experiencing, are termed 'objects' for that experiential occasion. Thus primarily the term 'object' expresses the relation of the entity, thus denoted, to one or more occasions of experiencing. Two conditions must be fulfilled in order that an entity may function as an object in a process of experiencing: (1) the entity must be antecedent, and (2) the entity must be experienced in virtue of its antecedence; it must be given. Thus an object must be a thing received, and must not be either a mode of reception of a thing generated in that occasion. Thus the process of experiencing is constituted by the reception of objects into the unity of that complex occasion which is the process itself. The process creates itself, but it does not create the objects which it receives as factors in its own nature.

251

'Objects' for an occasion can also be termed the 'data' for that occasion. The choice of terms entirely depends on the metaphor which you prefer. One word carries the literal meaning of 'lying in the way of', and the other word carries the literal meaning of 'being given to'. But both words suffer from the defect of suggesting that an occasion of experiencing arises out of a passive situation which is a mere welter of many data.

The exact contrary is the case. The initial situation includes a factor of activity which is the reason for the origin of that occasion of experience. This factor of activity is what I have called 'Creativity'. The initial situation with its creativity can be termed the initial phase of the new occasion. It can equally well be termed the 'actual world' relative to that occasion. It has a certain unity of its own, expressive of its capacity for providing the objects requisite for a new occasion, and also expressive of its conjoint activity whereby it is essentially the primary phase of a new occasion. It can thus be termed a 'real potentiality'. The 'potentiality' refers to the passive capacity, the term 'real' refers to the creative activity, where the Platonic definition of 'real' in the Sophist is referred to. This basic situation, this actual world, this primary phase, this real potentiality--however you characterize it--as a whole is active with its inherent creativity, but in its details it provides the passive objects which derive their activity from the creativity of the whole. The creativity is the actualization of potentiality, and the process of actualization is an occasion of experiencing. Thus viewed in abstraction objects are passive, but viewed in conjunction they carry the creativity which drives the world. The process of creation is the form of unity of the Universe.

In the preceding sections, the discovery of objects as factors in experience was explained. The discussion was phrased in terms of an ontology which goes beyond the immediate purpose, although the status of objects cannot be understood in the absence of some such ontology explaining their function in experience, that is to say, explaining why an occasion of experience by reason of its nature requires objects.

The objects are the factors in experience which function so as to express that that occasion originates by including a transcendent universe of other things.

Thus it belongs to the essence of each occasion of experience that it is concerned with an otherness transcending itself. The occasion is one among others, and
including the others which it is among. Consciousness
is an emphasis upon a selection of these objects. Thus
perception is consciousness analysed in respect to
those objects selected for this emphasis. Consciousness is the acme of emphasis.

It is evident that this definition of perception
is wider than the narrow definition based upon sense-
perception, sensa, and the bodily sense-organs.

This wider definition of perception can be of no
importance unless we can detect occasions of experience
exhibiting modes of functioning which fall within its
wider scope. If we discover such instances of non-
sensuous perception, then the tacit identification of
perception with sense-perception must be a fatal error
barring the advance of systematic metaphysics.

Our first step must involve the clear recognition
of the limitations inherent in the scope of sense-
perception. This special mode of functioning essentially exhibits percepta as here, now, immediate, and
discrete. Every impression of sensation is a distinct
existence, declares Hume; and there can be no reasonable doubt of this doctrine. But even Hume clothes each
impression with force and liveliness. It must be distinctly understood that no prehension, even of bare
sensa, can be divested of its affective tone, that is
to say, of its character of a 'concern' in the Quaker
sense. Concernedness is of the essence of perception.

* * *

In human experience, the most compelling example
of non-sensuous perception is our knowledge of our own
immediate past. I am not referring to our memories of
a day past, or of an hour past, or of a minute past.
Such memories are blurred and confused by the intervening occasions of our personal existence. But our immediate past is constituted by that occasion, or by that
group of fused occasions, which enters into experience
devoid of any perceptible medium intervening between it
and the present immediate fact. Roughly speaking, it
is that portion of our past lying between a tenth of a
second and half a second ago. It is gone, and yet it
is here. It is our indubitable self, the foundation of
our present existence. Yet the present occasion while

253

claiming self-identity, while sharing the very nature of the bygone occasion in all its living activities, nevertheless is engaged in modifying it, in adjusting it to other influences, in completing it with other values, in deflecting it to other purposes. The present moment is constituted by the influx of the other into that self-identity which is the continued life of the immediate past within the immediacy of the present.

* * *

This doctrine balances and limits the doctrine of the absolute individuality of each occasion of experience. There is a continuity between the subjective form of the immediate past occasion and the subjective form of its primary prehension in the origination of the new occasion. In the process of synthesis of the many basic prehensions modifications enter. But the subjective forms of the immediate past are continuous with those of the present. I will term this doctrine of continuity, the Doctrine of Conformation of Feeling.

* * *

The actualities of the Universe are processes of experience, each process an individual fact. The whole Universe is the advancing assemblage of these processes. The Aristotelian doctrine, that all agency is confined to actuality, is accepted. So also is the Platonic dictum that the very meaning of existence is 'to be a factor in agency', or in other words 'to make a difference'. Thus, 'to be something' is to be discoverable as a factor in the analysis of some actuality. It follows that in one sense everything is 'real', according to its own category of being. In this sense the word 'real' can only mean that some sound or mark is a word with a denotation. But the term 'realization' refers to the actual entities which include the entity in question as a positive factor in their constitutions. Thus though everything is real, it is not necessarily realized in some particular set of actual occasions. But it is necessary that it be discoverable somewhere, realized in some actual entity. There is not anything which has failed in some sense to be realized, physically or conceptually. The term 'real' can also mark the differences arising in the contrast between physical and conceptual realization.

Any set of actual occasions are united by the mutual immanence of occasions, each in the other. To the

254

extent that they are united they mutually constrain
each other. Evidently this mutual immanence and constraint of a pair of occasions is not in general a symmetric relation. For, apart from contemporaries, one
occasion will be in the future of the other. Thus the
earlier will be immanent in the later according to the
mode of efficient causality, and the later in the earlier according to the mode of anticipation, as explained above. Any set of occasions, conceived as thus
combined into a unity, will be termed a nexus. The
unity of such a nexus may be of a trivial description,
if the various occasions are dispersed through the Universe, each with a widely different status from the
other. When the unity of the nexus is of dominating
importance, nexus of different types emerge, which may
be respectively termed Regions, Societies, Persons, Enduring Objects, Corporal Substances, Living Organisms,
Events, with other analogous terms for the various
shades of complexity of which Nature is capable. It
will be sufficient [now] to indicate a few of these
special types of nexus.

We think of Constraint and Freedom in terms of
values realized in connection with them, and also in
terms of the antithesis between them. But there is another way of considering them. We can ask what there
is in the physical nature of things constituting the
physical realization either of freedom, or of constraint, or of a compatible association of both in a
suitable pattern.

In fact we do habitually interpret human history
in terms of freedom and constraint. Apart from the realization of this antithesis in physical occurrences,
the history of civilized humanity is a meaningless succession of events, involving a play of emotions concerned with concepts entirely irrelevant to the physical facts.

The causal independence of contemporary occasions
is the ground for the freedom within the Universe. The
novelties which face the contemporary world are solved
in isolation by the contemporary occasions. There is
complete contemporary freedom. It is not true that
whatever happens is immediately a condition laid upon
everything else. Such a conception of complete mutual
determination is an exaggeration of the community of
the Universe. The notions of 'sporadic occurrences'
and of 'mutual irrelevance' have a real application to
the nature of things. Again the perspective imposed by

incompatibilities of subjective form in another way provides for freedom. The antecedent environment is not wholly efficacious in determining the initial phase of the occasion which springs from it. There are factors in the environment which are eliminated from any function as explicit facts in the new creation. The running stream purifies itself, or perhaps loses some virtue which in happier circumstances might have been retained. The initial phase of each fresh occasion represents the issue of a struggle within the past for objective existence beyond itself. The determinant of the struggle is the supreme Eros incarnating itself as the first phase of the individual subjective aim in the new process of actuality. Thus in any two occasions of the Universe there are elements in either one which are irrelevant to the constitution of the other. The forgetfulness of this doctrine leads to an overmoralization in the view of the nature of things. Fortunately there are a great many things which do not much matter, and we can have them how we will. The opposite point of view has been the nursery of fanaticism, and has tinged history with ferocity.

The understanding of the Universe, in terms of the type of metaphysic here put forward, requires that the various roles of efficient causation, of teleological self-creation, of perspective elimination, of contemporary independence, of the laws of order dominating vast epochs, and of the minor endurances within each epoch, be conceived in their various relations to each other. Another summary expression of this type of understanding is contained in the phrases, Constraint and Freedom, Survival and Destruction, Depth of Feeling and Triviality of Feeling, Conceptual realization and physical realization, Appearance and Reality. Any account of the Adventure of Ideas is concerned with Ideas threading their way among the alternatives presented by these various phrases.

When we examine the structure of the epoch of the Universe in which we find ourselves, this structure exhibits successive layers of types of order, each layer introducing some additional type of order within some limited region which shares in the more general type of order of some larger environment. Also this larger environment in its turn is a specialized region within the general epoch of creation as we know it. Each one of these regions, with its dominant set of ordering relations, can either be considered from the point of view of the mutual relations of its parts to each other, or it can be considered from the point of view of its impact, as a unity, upon the experience of an external percipient. There is yet a third mode of consideration which combines the other two. The percipient may be an occasion within the region, and may yet grasp the region as one, including the percipient itself as a member of it.

A region, analysed in the first way, is thereby conceived as subject to certain Laws of Nature, which laws are its dominant set of ordering relations. In the second mode of consideration, synthesis replaces analysis. The region in question assumes the guise of an enduring unity, of which the essence is a certain complex internal character. This essential character, as it appears in the second approach, is nothing other than the set of Laws of Nature reigning within the region, as they appear in the first approach. Either mode of approach simply lays stress upon the dominant identity of character pervading the concrete connexity of the many occasions constituting the region. The unity of the region is two-fold:--first, by reason of the sheer connexity arising from the mutual immanence of the various occasions included in it, and secondly, by reason of a pervasive identity of character whereby the various parts play an analogous role in any external occasion. Thus the region with its Laws of Nature is a synonym for the enduring substance with its Essential Character.

* * *

The objective content of an occasion of experience sorts itself out under two contrasted characters-- Appearance and Reality. It is to be noticed that this is not the only dichotomy exhibited in experience. There are the physical and the mental poles, and there are the objects prehended and the subjective forms of the prehensions. In fact this final pair of opposites, Appearance and Reality, is not quite so fundamental metaphysically as the other two pairs.

In the first place the division between appearance and reality does not cover the whole of experience. It only concerns the objective content, and omits the subjective form of the immediate occasion in question. In the second place, its importance is negligible except in the functionings of the higher phases of experience, when the mental functionings have achieved a peculiar complexity of synthesis with the physical functionings.

But in these higher phases, the contrast Appearance and Reality dominates those factors of experience which are discriminated in consciousness with peculiar distinctness. Thus the foundation of metaphysics should be sought in the understanding of the subject-object structure of experience, and in the respective roles of the physical and mental functionings.

Unfortunately the superior dominance in consciousness of the contrast 'Appearance and Reality' has led metaphysicians from the Greeks onwards to make their start from the more superficial characteristic. This error has warped modern philosophy to a greater extent than ancient or mediaeval philosophy. The warping has taken the form of a consistent reliance upon sensationalist perception as the basis of all experiential activity. It has had the effect of decisively separating 'mind' from 'nature', a modern separation which found its first exemplification in Cartesian dualism. But it must be remembered that this modern development was only the consistent carrying out of principles already present in the older European philosophy. It required two thousand years for the full implication of those principles to dawn upon men's minds in the seventeenth and the eighteenth centuries after Christ.

The distinction between 'appearance and reality' is grounded upon the process of self-formation of each actual occasion. The objective content of the initial phase of reception is the real antecedent world, as given for that occasion. This is the 'reality' from which that creative advance starts. It is the basic fact of the new occasion, with its concordances and discordances awaiting coordination in the new creature. There is nothing there apart from the real agency of the actual past, exercising its function of objective immortality. This is reality, at that moment, for that occasion. Here the term 'reality' is used in the sense of the opposite to 'appearance'.

The intermediate phase of self-formation is a ferment of qualitative valuation. These qualitative feelings are either derived directly from qualities illustrated in the primary phase, or are indirectly derived by their relevance to them. These conceptual feelings pass into novel relations to each other, felt with a novel emphasis of subjective form. The ferment of valuation is integrated with the physical prehensions of the physical pole. Thus the initial objective content is still there. But it is overlaid by, and intermixed

258

with, the novel hybrid prehensions derived from integration with the conceptual ferment. In the higher
types of actual occasions, propositional feelings are
now dominant. This enlarged objective content obtains
a coordination adapting it to the enjoyments and purposes fulfilling the subjective aim of the new occasion.

The mental pole has derived its objective content
alike by abstraction from the physical pole and by the
immanence of the basic Eros which endows with agency
all ideal possibilities. The content of the objective
universe has passed from the function of a basis for a
new individuality to that of an instrument for purposes. The individual process is now feeling its own
completion:--Cogito, ergo sum. And in Descartes' phraseology, 'cogitatio' is more than mere intellectual understanding.

This difference between the objective content of
the initial phase of the physical pole and the objective content of the final phase, after the integration
of physical and mental poles, constitutes 'appearance'
for that occasion. In other words, 'appearance' is the
effect of the activity of the mental pole, whereby the
qualities and coordinations of the given physical world
undergo transformation. It results from the fusion of
the ideal with the actual:--The light that never was,
on sea or land.

There can be no general metaphysic principles
which determine how in any occasion appearance differs
from the reality out of which it originates. The divergencies between reality and appearance depend on the
type of social order dominating the environment of the
occasion in question. All our information on this topic, direct and inferential, concerns this general epoch
of the Universe and, more particularly, animal life on
the surface of the Earth.

In respect to the occasions which compose the societies of inorganic bodies or of the so-called empty
spaces, there is no reason to believe that in any important way the mental activities depart from functionings which are strictly conformal to those inherent in
the object datum of the first phase. Thus no novelty
is introduced. The perspective elimination is effected
according to the 'laws of nature' inherent in the epoch.
This composition of activities constitutes the laws of
physics. There is no effective 'appearance'.

But the case is very different for the high-grade occasions which are components in the animal life on the Earth's surface. Each animal body is an organ of sensation. It is a living society which may include in itself a dominant 'personal' society of occasions. This 'personal' society is composed of occasions enjoying the individual experiences of the animals. It is the soul of man. The whole body is organized, so that a general coordination of mentality is finally poured into the successive occasions of this personal society. Thus in the constitutions of these occasions, appearance is sufficiently coordinated to be effective. Also consciousness arises in the subjective forms in these experiences of the higher animals. It arises peculiarly in connection with the mental functions, and has to do primarily with their product. Now appearance is one product of mentality. Thus in our conscious perceptions appearance is dominant. It possesses a clear distinctness, which is absent from our vague massive feeling of derivation from our actual world. Appearance has shed the note of derivation. It lives in our consciousness as the world presented to us for our enjoyment and our purposes. It is the world in the guise of a subject-matter for an imposed activity. The occasion has gathered the creativity of the Universe into its own completeness, abstracted from the real objective content which is the source of its own derivation.

This status of 'appearance' in the constitution of experience is the reason for the disastrous metaphysical doctrine of physical matter passively illustrating qualities, and devoid of self-enjoyment. As soon as clarity and distinctness are made the test of metaphysical importance, an entire misapprehension of the metaphysical status of appearance is involved.

When the higher functionings of mentality are socially stabilized in an organism, appearance merges into reality. To take the most conspicuous example, consider the personal succession of experiences in the life of a human being. The present occasion in this personal life inherits with peculiar dominance the antecedent experiences in this succession. But these antecedent experiences include the 'appearances' as in those occasions. These antecedent appearances are part of the real functioning of the real actual world as it stands in the primary phase of the immediately present occasion. It is a real fact of nature that the world has appeared thus from the standpoint of these antecedent occasions of the personal life. And more generally

260

dropping the special case of personality, the objective
reality of the past, as it now functions in the present, in its day was appearance. They may be strengthened in emphasis, embroidered upon, and otherwise modified by the novel appearances of the new occasion. In
this way, there is an intimate, inextricable fusion of
appearance with reality, and of accomplished fact with
anticipation. In truth, we have been describing the
exact situation which human experience presents for
philosophic analysis.

     We are apt to think of this fusion from the point
of view of the higher grades of human beings. But it
is a fusion proceeding throughout nature. It is the
essential mode in which novelty enters into the functionings of the world.

     It is a mistake to suppose that, at the level of
human intellect, the role of mental functionings is to
add subtlety to the content of experience. The exact
opposite is the case. Mentality is an agent of simplification; and for this reason appearance is an incredi-
bly simplified edition of reality. There should be no
paradox in this statement. A moment's introspection
assures one of the feebleness of human intellectual operations, and of the dim massive complexity of our
feelings of derivation. The point for discussion is
how in animal experience this simplification is effected.

     The best example of this process of simplification
is afforded by the perception of a social nexus as a
unity, characterized by qualities derived from its individual members and their interconnections. With some
elimination, the defining characteristic of the nexus
is directly perceived to be qualifying that nexus as a
unity. It often happens that in this perception of the
nexus as thus qualified there is a wavering between the
ascription of the quality to the group as one, and to
its individual components as many. Thus, the orchestra
is loud as one entity, and also in virtue of the perceived loudness of the individual members with their
musical instruments. The transference of the characteristic from the individuals to the group as one can
be explained by the mental operations. There is the
conceptual entertainment of the qualities illustrated
by the individual actualities. The qualities shared by
many individuals are fused into one dominating impression. This dominating prehension is integrated with
the nexus, or with some portion of it, perceived as a

261

unity illustrating that quality. The association of a nexus as one with a quality will, for the experient subject, be in general a mode of exemplification which differs from the mode in which the respective individuals illustrate it. The discipline of a regiment inheres in the regiment in a different mode from its inherence in the individual soldiers. This difference of mode of illustration may be more or less evident. But it is there. It gives another reason for the aspect of the passive inherence of quality in substance. The composite group illustrates its qualities passively. The activity belongs to the individual actualities. This whole question of the transference of quality from the many individuals to the nexus as one is discussed at length in Process and Reality, Part III, Chapter III, Section IV, where it is termed 'Transmutation'. Obviously the transmuted percept belongs to Appearance. But as it occurs in animal experience, it belongs to appearance merged with reality. For it is inherited from the past. It is thus a fact of nature that the world so appears. It is a structural relationship of animate nature on the Earth's surface. In all Appearance there is an element of Transmutation.

For animal life on earth by far the most important example of Transmutation is afforded by Sense-Perception. No doctrine of sense-perception can neglect the teaching of physiology. The decisive factor in sense-perception is the functioning of the brain, and the functioning of the brain is conditioned by the antecedent functionings of the other parts of the animal body. Given requisite bodily functionings, the sense-perception results. The activities of nature external to the animal body are irrelevant as to their details, so long as they have the general character of supporting the existence of the total animal organism. The human body is the self-sufficient organ of human sense-perception.

There are external events, such as the transmission of light or the movements of material bodies which respectively are the normal modes of exciting sense-percepts of particular types. But in the first place these external events are only the normal modes. A diet of drugs will do equally well, though its issue in perception is not so definitely to be predicted. Thus no one type of external event is necessarily associated with one type of sense-percept. Hardly any percept is strictly normal. Gross illusions are plentiful, and some element of illusion almost universal. An ordinary looking-glass produces illusive percepts in almost every room.

Secondly, confining ourselves to the normal modes of excitation, the only important factor in the external event is how it affects the functionings of the surface of the body. How the light enters the eye, and a normal healthy state of the body, are the only important factors in normal visual sensation. The light may have come from a nebula distant by a thousand light-years, or it may have its origin in an electric lamp two feet off and have suffered a complex arrangement of reflections and refractions. Nothing matters except how it enters the eye, as to its composition, its intensity, and its geometric ordering. The body is supremely indifferent as to the past history of its exciting agents, and requires no certificate of character. The peculiar bodily excitement is all that matters.

The conclusion is that the direct information to be derived from sense-perception wholly concerns the functionings of the animal body. The sense of unity with the body does in fact dominate our sense-experiences. But the bodily organization is such as finally to promote a wholesale transmutation of sensa, inherited from antecedent bodily functionings, into characteristics of regions with well-marked geometrical relations to the geometrical structures of these functionings. In this transmutation the experient occasion in question belongs to the personal succession of occasions which is the soul of the animal. The bodily functionings and the nexus relevant to them by geometrical relationship are immanent in the experient occasion. The qualitative inheritance from the individual occasions implicated in these functionings is transmuted into the characteristics of regions conspicuously indicated by their geometric connections. This doctrine is plainly indicated in the analysis of optical vision, where the image occupies the region indicated by geometrical relations within the eyes. It is more obscurely evident in the case of other species of sensa.

It is to be remembered also that along the personal succession of the soul's experiences, there is an inheritance of sense-perception from the antecedent members of the personal succession. Also incipient sense-percepta may be forming themselves in the nerve-routes, or in the neighbouring regions of the brain. But the final synthesis, with its production of

263

appearance, is reserved for the occasions belonging to
the personal soul.

The question of the proper description of the species of qualities termed 'sense' is important. Unfortunately the learned tradition of philosophy has missed
their main characteristic, which is their enormous emotional significance. The vicious notion has been introduced of mere receptive entertainment, which for no
obvious reason by reflection acquires an affective
tone. The very opposite is the true explanation. The
true doctrine of sense-perception is that the qualitative characters of affective tones inherent in the bodily functionings are transmuted into the characters of
regions. These regions are then perceived as associated with those character-qualities, but also these same
qualities are shared by the subjective forms of the
prehensions. This is the reason of the definite aesthetic attitude imposed by sense-perception. The pattern of sensa characterizing the object--that is, those
sensa in that pattern of contrast--enters also into the
subjective form of the prehension. Thus art is possible. For not only can the objects be prescribed, but
also the corresponding affective tones of their prehensions. This is the aesthetic experience so far as it
is based upon sense-perception.

Another point to be noticed is that in sense-
perception a region in the contemporary world is the
substratum supporting the sensa. It is the region
straight-away in such-and-such a direction. But this
geometrical relation of being 'straight-away in such-
and-such a direction' is defined by the operations of
the brain. It has nothing to do with any physical
transmission from the substrate region to the brain.
To judge from some descriptions of perception in terms
of modern scientific theories, it might be concluded
that we perceive along the track of a ray of light.
There is not the slightest warrant for such a notion.
The track of light in the world external to the animal
body is irrelevant. The coloured region is perceived
straight-away in such-and-such a direction. This is
the fundamental notion of 'straightness'.

It therefore becomes necessary for the self-
consistency of this doctrine to enquire whether the
dominant structure of geometrical relations includes a
determination of straightness. The theory requires
that a prehension of a nexus within the brain as exhibiting straightness in the mutual relations of its parts

264

should thereby determine the prolongation of those relations into regions beyond the brain.   In simpler language, a segment of a straight line as prehended within
the brain should necessarily determine its prolongation
externally to the body, irrespective of the particular
characters of the external events.   The possibility of
'Transmutation' involving the 'Projection' of sensa is
then secured.

I have discussed this question elsewhere[1] and have
given a definition of straight lines--and, more generally, of flatness--which satisfies the requirements.
The necessity of basing straightness upon measurement,
and measurement upon particular happenings is thereby
avoided.   The notions of straightness and of congru-
ence, and then of distance, can be derived from those
underlying a uniform systematic nonmetrical geometry.

It may be noticed in passing that, if straightness
depends upon measurement, there can be no perception of
straightness in the unmeasured.   The notion of 'straight
in front' must then be meaningless.

In this way, the inheritance from the past is
precipitated upon the present.   It becomes sense-
perception, which is the 'appearance' of the present.

The 'mutual immanence' of contemporary occasions
to each other is allied to the immanence of the future
in the present, though it presents some features of its
own.   This immanence exhibits a symmetrical relation of
causal independence.   In human experience, the prehensions of the contemporary world exhibit themselves as
sense-perceptions, effected by means of the bodily organs of sensation.   The subjective forms of these
sense-perceptions involve conscious discrimination,
with varying degrees of clarity and distinctness.   Indeed sense-perceptions can exhibit themselves as clear
and distinct in consciousness to a degree unrivalled by
any other type of prehension.   The result is that all
attempts at an exact systematic doctrine of the nature
of things seeks its most obvious verification in the
conformity of its theory with sense-perception.   The
unfortunate effect has been, that all direct observation has been identified with sense-perception.[2]

But sense-perception, as conceived in the isolation of its ideal purity, never enters into human experience.   It is always accompanied by so-called 'interpretation'.   This 'interpretation' does not seem to be

265

necessarily the product of any elaborate train of intellectual cogitation. We find ourselves 'accepting'[3]
a world of substantial objects, directly presented for
our experience. Our habits, our states of mind, our
modes of behaviour, all presuppose this 'interpretation'. In fact the concept of mere sensa is the product of high-grade thinking. It required Plato to frame
the myth of the Shadows in the Cave, and it required
Hume to construct the doctrine of pure sensationalist
perception. Yet even animals share in some 'interpretation'. There is every evidence that animals enjoy a
sensationalist experience. Dogs smell, eagles see, and
noises attract the attention of most of the higher animals. Also their consequent modes of behaviour suggest
their immediate assumption of a substantial world around
them. In fact the hypothesis of a mere sensationalist
perception does not account for our direct observation
of the contemporary world. There is some other factor
present, which is equally primitive with our perception
of sensa. This factor is provided by the immanence of
the past in the immediate occasion whose percipience is
under discussion. The immanence of the past in this
percipient occasion cannot be fully understood apart
from due attention to the doctrine of the immanence of
the future in the past. Thus the past as an objective
constituent in the experience of the percipient occasion carries its own prehension of the future beyond
itself. This prehension survives objectively in the
primary phase of the percipient. Accordingly there is
an indirect prehension of contemporary occasion, via
the efficient causation, from which they arise. For the
immediate future of the immediate past constitutes the
set of contemporary occasions for the percipient. Also
these prehensions of immediate past and of immediate
future operate dominantly in their experience of their
respective subjects. Thus the prehension of contemporary occasions is the prehension of those occasions in
so far as they are conditioned by the occasions in the
immediate past of the prehending subject. Thus the
present is perceivable in so far as it is conditioned
by the efficient causation from the past of the perceiver. The great dominant relationships, fundamental
for the epochal order of nature, thereby stand out with
overwhelming distinctness. These are the general, all-
pervasive, obligations of perspective. Such relationships are what we term the spatial relationships as
perceivable from the standpoint of the observer.

But the particular occasions of the contemporary
world, each with its own individual spontaneity, are

veiled from the observer. In this respect, the contemporary world in the experience of the percipient shares the characteristics of the future. The relevant environment, which is the immediate past of the human body, is peculiarly sensitive to its geometrical experiences and to the synthesis of its qualitative prehensions with these experiences of geometrical relations. In this way, there is a basis in fact for the association of derivates from significant regions in the past with the geometrical representatives of those regions in the present.[4]

The conclusion is that the contemporary world is not perceived in virtue of its own proper activity, but in virtue of activities derived from the past, the past which conditions it and which also conditions the contemporary percipient. These activities are primarily in the past of the human body, and more remotely in the past of the environment within which the body is functioning. This environment includes those occasions dominantly conditioning the perceived contemporary regions. This theory of the perception of contemporaries allows for our habitual belief that we perceive the contemporary world with a general qualitative relevance to the essences of the occasions making up its various regions; and also with a bias of qualitative distortion due to the functioning of the animal body of the percipient.

One distortion stands out immediately. Each actual occasion is in truth a process of activity. But the contemporary regions are mainly perceived in terms of their passive perspective relationship to the percipient and to each other. They are thus perceived merely as passive recipients of the qualities with which in sense-perception they are associated. Hence the false notion of a substratum with vacuously inherent qualities. Here the term 'vacuous' means 'devoid of any individual enjoyment arising from the mere fact of realization in that context'. In other words, the substratum with its complex of inherent qualities is wrongly conceived as bare realization, devoid of self-enjoyment, that is to say, devoid of intrinsic worth. In this way, the exclusive reliance on sense-perception promotes a false metaphysics. This error is the result of high-grade intellectuality. The instinctive interpretations which govern human life and animal life presuppose a contemporary world throbbing with energetic values. It requires considerable ability to make the disastrous abstraction of our bare sense-perceptions

from the massive insistency of our total experiences.
Of course, whatever we can do in the way of abstraction
is for some purposes useful--provided that we know what
we are about.

FOOTNOTES

[1]Cf. Process and Reality, Part IV, Chapters III, IV, and V. The required definition is given in Chapter III, and the theory of the projection of sensa is discussed in Chapters IV and V.

[2]This assumption has been criticized in Chapter XI.

[3]Cf. Perception, by H. H. Price, especially Chapter VI, 'Perceptual Assurance, Perceptual Acceptance'. Published by Methuen, London, 1932. Price in his valuable work gives to sense-perception a more fundamental role in experience than my doctrine allows to it. Cf. also. Santayana's doctrine of 'Animal Faith'.

[4]Cf. Process and Reality, Part III, Chap. III, Section IV, and Part IV, Chaps IV and V.

SUGGESTED READINGS

Alfred North Whitehead

Whitehead, A. N. An Inquiry Concerning the Principles of Natural Knowledge (Cambridge: Cambridge University Press, 1919).

_____. The Concept of Nature (Cam-
bridge: Cambridge University Press, 1920).

_____. The Principle of Relativity
(Cambridge: Cambridge University Press, 1922).

_____. Science and the Modern World
(New York: Macmillan, 1925).

_____. Process and Reality (New York:
Macmillan, 1929), pp. 57ff.

* * *

Felt, J. W. "Whitehead and the Bifurcation of Nature," Modern Schoolman, 45 (1968), 285-298.

Hartshorne, C. "Whitehead's Metaphysics," Whitehead and the Modern World (Boston: Beacon
Press, 1950), pp. 25-41.

Murphy, A. "The Anticopernican Revolution," Journal of Philosophy, XXVI (1929), 281-299.

Northrop, F. S. C. "Whitehead's Philosophy of
Science," The Philosophy of Alfred North Whitehead (Evanston: Northwestern University Press,
1941), pp. 165-207.

* * *

Christian, W. A. An Interpretation of Whitehead's
Metaphysics (New Haven: Yale University Press,
1959).

Emmet, D. M. Whitehead's Philosophy of Organism
(New York: Macmillan, 1932).

Lowe, V. Understanding Whitehead (Baltimore:
    John Hopkins University Press, 1962).

Palter, R. M. Whitehead's Philosophy of Science
    (Chicago: University of Chicago Press, 1960,
    1970).

11. A WORLD OF ORGANISMS

Charles Hartshorne

Charles Hartshorne did his undergraduate
work at Haverford College and Harvard University. While at Haverford his philosophy
teacher was the noted mystic Rufus Jones
who, although influenced by both mysticism
and idealism, taught philosophy in a very
practical and down-to-earth manner. He was
to have a considerable influence upon the
later philosophical career of Hartshorne.

In this essay* Professor Hartshorne argues for
"organic monism," or the doctrine that at all levels
the universe is made up of "organisms." An organism,
in Hartshorne's view, is a whole whose parts (termed
"organs") serve as means to the purposes of the whole.
It is a mistake to believe in mere "dead" matter. Even
such physical existences as electrons, protons and
atoms must be viewed as active and, in their different
ways, purposive. The same is true of the cells and
multicellular organisms which the protons, atoms, and
the like, comprise. Against modern scientific mechanism, therefore, Hartshorne attributes purpose to all
levels of nature. It is in man that purposes become
reflective, self-conscious. The interaction of the
world of organisms and the "cosmic organism"; that is,
God, is described as a process of creative synthesis
which allows to both God and the world a measure of
creativity. God cannot wholly initiate or absolutely
control the actions of the lesser organisms, not

---

*This selection is from The Logic of Perfection
and Other Essays in Neoclassical Metaphysics (LaSalle,
Ill.: Open Court, 1962), pp. 191-215. Used by permission of the Open Court Press and Dr. Charles Hartshorne.
He suggests that for further considerations relevant to
the speculations of this article that one should see
his contribution to the Philosophical Essays in Memory
of Edmund Husserl (Cambridge: Harvard University
Press, 1940).

because of any weakness but because to do so would be to destroy creativity, and hence the very nature of being itself. To the objection that if there were such a thing as God (conscious of the world of organisms) we should have to look for something like a brain and nervous system in the world, Hartshorne replies that God is "co-existent with existence and thus omniscient," that is, directly in contact with the world and therefore not needing the intermediary of a nervous system. The essay concludes with an examination of the place of purpose (teleology) in the Darwinian picture of evolution. While the individual events which make up evolution (for example, mutation and natural selection) are functions of "chance," the maintenance of the conditions under which chance and natural selection can produce evolution may itself be purposive. In any case, chance is only the negative side of the creative spontaneity which is evolution's ultimate explanation.

A World of Organisms

". . . with the magic hand of chance." John Keats.

"I cannot think that the world . . . is the result of chance; and yet I cannot look at each separate thing as the result of design . . . I am, and shall ever remain, in a hopeless muddle."

"But I know that I am in the same sort of muddle . . . as all the world seems to be in with respect to free will, yet with everything supposed to have been foreseen or pre-ordained."

Charles Darwin, writing to Asa Gray, 1860.

An "organism" in this essay is a whole whose parts serve as "organs" or instrument to purposes or end-values inherent in the whole. It is scarcely deniable that organs and organisms exist. A man is aware of realizing purpose, and he is aware of doing so through parts of his body. Hence he is aware that he exists as an organism. It follows that either nature contains two types of wholes, the organic and the inorganic, or all natural wholes are organic. We must choose between a dualism and an organic monism, since an inorganic monism would contradict obvious facts. Is organic monism possible?

It seems not, for just as it is evident that a man is an organism, so it is evident that a mountain is not, although primitive man sometimes thought otherwise. Science exhibits nothing in the behavior of the parts of the mountain to suggest that these parts serve a purpose whose realization is enjoyed by the mountain as a whole. But this fact does not prove that no form of organic monism is possible. There is no evidence that the parts of a finger serve any purpose whose realization is enjoyed by the finger. Not all the parts of an organism are organisms. Yet a finger may in two senses be viewed as organic: it belongs to an organism; and its own parts, at least on one level, the cells, are or may be organisms. That cells literally enjoy health and suffer from injury is a supposition that conflicts with no facts, while there are facts it helps to explain. The mountain, like the finger, may be part or organ of a larger organic whole, perhaps the entire universe as an organism; and the molecules (or if not these, the atoms) composing the mountain may, like cells, though on a still humbler level, be organic wholes. The sub-molecular parts may contribute value, in the form of simple feelings, to the molecules, and the molecules may contribute value to the cosmos.

Organic monism, in the sense just indicated, includes within itself a limited or relative dualism. The assertion is not that all wholes are purposive or organic; but that, first, all well-unified wholes are organic, and second, that all wholes whatever both involve and are involved in organic wholes. But what wholes are well-unified? My suggestion is that any whole which has less unity than its most unified parts is not an organism in the pregnant sense here in question;[1] though, according to organic monism, its most unified parts, and some unified whole of which it is itself a part, must in all cases be organisms.

For example, botanists incline to regard the plant cell, rather than the entire plant, as the primary unit of vegetable activity. A plant is a quasi-organic colony of true organisms, the cells, and not, like the vertebrate animal, itself an organism. Again, a termite colony exhibits definite analogies to a single animal organism, but to an organism with less unity than termites, say a flat-worm. The colony in relation to its members is not a super-organism but an epi- or quasi-organism. There is little reason to suppose that the colony feels, though good reason to think termites feel. Or again, a mountain has inferior dynamic unity to its own atoms. Remove a part from an atom, and the whole responds with a systematic readjustment of its parts, a response to which the activity of the mountain as a whole offers only a feeble analogy, even if the mountain be a volcano. Thus it is reasonable to deny that mountains, trees, or termite colonies enjoy feelings, but not so reasonable to deny that atoms, tree-cells, and termites enjoy them.

Similarly, with all the talk about the "group-mind," there are no good indications that human groups are organisms which could think and feel as individuals. All that one can show is that human beings, like termites and atoms, act differently according to the social environment, the neighbors, which they have. Yet there may be a hidden truth in the group-mind concept. As we shall see, there is reason to think that the cosmic community, the universe, does have a group mind.

The vertebrate organism, as we know it in ourselves, has a group mind, our mind, and this suggests
that quantum mechanics is not the whole account of dynamic action. For this mechanics assumes that nothing
influences what electrons, protons, atoms, and the like
are doing in an organic body except what other electrons and the like are doing. What then of what the
man, say, is doing, for instance, thinking? This
thinking is not just an arrangement of particles and/or
waves; and either the thinking is an effect which produces no effects, a detached miracle in nature, or
electrons in the human brain must move as they do partly because the human being thinks as he does.

However, when one is in deep sleep, what goes on
in the body may indeed be little more than mere group
action--not, to be sure, of particles, but of cells.
And if a cell dies, then what happens in its remains
will be no longer what it is doing, but what its molecules or atoms are doing. Experiments to show the
merely mechanical character of the organism may, in
fact, only show that the organism can at times be reduced to an approximately inorganic state.

Let us return to our main thesis, organic monism.
Part of the justification of this monism is that the
organic principle is sufficiently flexible to explain
the relative lack of organic wholeness found in certain
parts of nature, whereas the notion of absolutely non-
purposive or inorganic wholes throws no light whatever
on the existence or nature of purpose. If there are
wholes which are directly valuable in and for themselves, there can be groups of these wholes which are
valuable not directly, but for the sake of their members, or of some larger whole. Given the concept of
purpose as ultimate, we can restrict its application by
employing the distinction which purpose involves between end and means, or the distinction between simple
and complex purposes, or purposes merely felt and those
consciously surveyed. But given mere purposeless stuff
or "matter," we have not, in so far, any notion of purpose.

The idea of a means or instrument does not require
the notion of mere or dead matter; for an organism can
function as a tool for another organism, and this assumes only that organisms influence each other, which
in turn follows from the notion, to be considered presently, that all lesser organisms are parts of one inclusive organism, the universe. All that dead matter

277

could add to this is the purely negative and empty notion of something that is absolutely nothing but means.
Such an absolute negation seems devoid of philosophical
or scientific utility.

There are, however, some apparent difficulties in
the organismic doctrine. For example, the definition
of organism calls for a whole with parts, and an electron, for instance, is not known to have parts. Even
if it has parts, or if one denies the reality of electrons, must there not be something simple, the ultimate
unit of being, which being without parts is not an organism? We must here reconsider the meaning of the
term "part" as occurring in our definition of the organic. This meaning implies that an organism involves
a plurality of entities contributing directly to the
value of a single entity, the "whole." But the contributing entities need not be internal to the whole in
the sense of spatially smaller and included parts, as
electrons are smaller than and within an atom, or atoms
within a molecule, and as nothing known is smaller than
and within the electron. To render an electron or
other particle an organism it is only necessary that
neighboring electrons or other particles should contribute directly to each other's values, that is,
should directly feel each other. Physics does not assert that particles are in every sense external to each
other. On the contrary, a particle, as inseparable
from its wave-field, overlaps other particles. This
seems to be all the internality that is required by the
general idea of organism. With the simplest organisms
it is the community of neighboring entities that constitutes the plurality contributing to each entity--in
a different perspective, in each case, since no two
electrons, say, will have the same nearest neighbors.
Where there are no smaller entities as parts, there
will be no sharp distinction between internal and external. An ax seems external to a man because the
man's immediate intimate relations are with the parts
of his own body, so that by contrast the ax is something that contributes to his being and value only indirectly, only by first contributing, through several
intermediaries usually, to the parts of his body and
thence to his mind. But perhaps a particle, like a
disembodied spirit, has no bodily parts. Its intimates, if any, will be its equals, the neighboring particles, or the larger wholes which they and it constitute. It will be an organic democrat and proletarian,
but not an organic aristocrat.

278

One may well ascribe intimates, even though "external" intimates, to particles; for such entities respond immediately to neighboring particles. If an
electron feels anything, it must feel its neighbors,
for what else could it feel? We, on the contrary, feel
chiefly our bodies, and through these, other things.
Just this indirectness of feeling, mediated by entities
of lesser power and complexity than oneself, is what is
meant by having a body. To have no body is to have no
inferior servants immediately bound to one's own purposes and feelings. Hence it is the particle, the lowest, not the highest, organism--in spite of what has
often been said about God--that best fits the idea of
an unembodied spirit. The particle, one might say, is
embodied only in its environment, not in itself.

The mention of God brings us to the question at
the opposite extreme from that about particles. If the
simplest of beings can yet have complexity in the sense
required for organic wholeness, can the most complex of
beings, the universe, have sufficient simplicity in the
sense of unity to be an organism, no doubt the supreme
organism? If lack of internal parts does not prevent
organicity, what about lack of an external environment?
The same principle, though in opposite application,
solves both problems. All that an organism requires is
"an immediately contributory complexity." An organic
whole must deal with or "respond" to some field of entities or environment, but the term "internal environ-
men" is not a quibble. An organism can respond to its
parts, if it has them, or its neighbors, if it has
them, or to both, if it has both. An electron has only
neighbors, the universe, only parts, to respond to; but
both may be responsive, and in so far, organic, entities.

It may indeed be urged that the only purpose of
internal adjustments, or responses to parts, is to
serve as basis for desirable external adjustments, responses to neighbors. But it can, with more truth, be
retorted that external adjustments are desirable only
as means for the attainment of the internal organic
state known as happiness. The only error in this second position is that with organisms other than the cosmos the internal field of response fails to include
more than a fraction of the low and high-grade life in
existence. Thus it is not a case of external relations
for their own sake, but of such relations for the sake
of dealing with what would otherwise be missed entirely. The cosmos, which deals with everything through

its internal relations, can perfectly well dispense with external ones (except toward the future, which is never in its concreteness intrinsic to the present). To view this privilege of unique inclusiveness of organic unity as a lack of such unity is simple to lose our way among our own abstractions.

But if the universe has organic unity, where, some have asked, is the world-brain? Fechner long ago, following a trail blazed in the Timaeus, pointed out how unscientific the question is. On each great level of life the basic functions are performed by organs that have only a remote analogy from one level to another. We smile at the lack of generalizing power shown by those men of earlier times who supposed that microscopic animals must have, in miniature, all the organs of macroscopic ones. Is it any less naïve to think that the world, if organic, must have a magnified brain? If any organic level must be a special case, it is the universe, at the opposite end of the scale from that other special case, the particle.

As we have seen, the particle has no special internal organs, because its neighbors serve it as organs. The universe, conversely, has no neighbors as organs, because everything is its internal organ. Everything contributes equally directly to the cosmic value. This means that the world-mind will have no special brain, but that rather every individual is to that mind as a sort of brain-cell. The brain is only that part of the body which most immediately and powerfully affects and is affected by the mind, the value-unity of the whole. The rest of the body is by comparison a house for the nervous system, a quasi-external environment. As the cosmos has no external environment, so it has no gradations of externality, and not even a quasi-external environment, and thus the cosmic analogue of a brain will be simply the entire system of things as wholly internal and immediate to the cosmic mind. A special world-brain, so far from confirming the supposition of a truly cosmic mind, would negate it.

You may object that if the cosmos has no external environment to deal with it does have an internal one, and that the coordination of internal actions requires a brain. But remember that the brain is only a very rough and partial coordinator of internal actions. It has almost no direct control over myriads of actions that go on in the body, even in the brain cavity itself,

and this not because of any deficiency of the vertebrate brain in particular, but as a consequence of
there being a brain at all as a special organ. What is
needed for supreme control is obviously that every organ should be directly, and not via some other organ,
such as a nervous system, responsive to the whole. The
idea of a perfect yet special brain-organ is a contradiction in terms, but the idea of a perfect mind, a
mind co-extensive with existence and thus omniscient,
is not for all that a contradiction. For such a mind
must have, not a world-part as brain, but the whole
world serving as higher equivalent of a brain; so that
just as between a brain cell and the human mind there
is no further mechanism, so between every individual in
existence and the world-mind there is no chain of intermediaries, not even a nervous system, but each and
every one is in the direct grip of the world-value.
The higher the organism, the larger the part directly
responsive to the whole; the highest organism must be
the largest organism as all brain, so to speak.

But what, you ask, would the cosmic organism be
doing? To what end is the coordination of internal activities, where no external action is possible? The
answer is that the end is the prosperity of the parts
and of the whole as the integration of the parts. As
our enjoyment of health is our participation in the
health of the numerous cells, so the happiness of the
cosmos is the integration of the lesser happinesses of
the parts. The benevolence of God is the only way the
psycho-physics of the cosmic organism can be conceived,
as Fechner, one of the first great experimental psycho-
physicists, was at pains to point out. Theologians
have generally missed this valuable argument, for reasons which I believe to be specious. [2]

It has been argued for instance that if the cosmos
were one divine organism there could be no conflict or
suffering. All would be perfect peace, flawless interadjustment. This, I think, is an error.

To show this we must correct the vagueness of our
concept of organism, as so far employed. An organism
is not a "whole which determines its parts," but something more complex and less dialectical. Strictly
speaking, in so far as an organism is a whole, in the
logical sense, it does not even influence its parts. A
collection of agents is not itself an agent; and if the
whole is more than a collection, a genuine dynamic unity, and yet acts on its parts, then since parts

obviously constitute and by their changes alter the whole in certain of its aspects, we should have each part in a relation of mutual determination with the whole, and hence with every other part. How then could we distinguish one part from another or from the whole? Would not every part be the whole? Only if each part is something in abstraction from the whole can we analyze the whole as a collection of parts or members. We can think of a collection distinctly only by adding its members in thought, and this is impossible if the members presuppose the whole.

But surely, you say, an organism is more than a collection, even an organized collection. Yes, but how? Only a creative synthesis of the parts can have its own unity, not identical with the parts and their interrelationships. But the very meaning of such a "synthesis" (see Chapter Eight) presupposes the parts as given, prior to the synthesis, and constituting its materials or data, not its products. Thus any actual whole-synthesis has no influence upon the elements entering into it.

Consider a momentary human experience as a synthesis of events which have just occurred in various parts of the organism, especially the cortical parts of it. This experience does not alter the events which it synthesizes. It may, however influence subsequent events in the brain and hence in the muscles, etc. Only by neglecting the time structure of the situation, as philosophies of being may be expected to do (and they seldom upset our expectations in this regard), have "holistic" philosophies fallen into the confusion of a whole determining its individual parts. The symmetrical idea of "interaction" between whole and parts is due to treating a complex of one-way relations en bloc. What happens in my brain or nerves influences what I feel immediately afterward, and what I thus feel influences what happens in my brain at a slightly later time.

My feeling at a given moment is one, that of my cells is many. The diverse cellular feelings become data for the unitary human feeling, and this feeling is the momentary "whole" summing up the antecedent states of "the parts" and subsequently reacting upon later states of these parts. Thus the many-one action is turned into a one-many action. Not the whole as collection of parts acts upon these very parts, but the one actuality which is my feeling now, and which reflects the actualities previously constituting my body, acts upon the many actualities which subsequently compose that body.

An organism may be viewed as a society--of cells, molecules, or the like. There are two types of such societies. (The distinction goes back to Leibniz.) One type is what might, broadly speaking, be termed a "democracy." It has no supreme, radically dominant member. Certain cell colonies, and probably many-celled plants in general, and some lower forms of many-celled animals, are examples. But a unitary organism in the narrower or more emphatic sense is one with a dominant member, which is the synthetic act, or rather act-sequence, in the vertebrate case corresponding roughly to, or deriving its data from, the nervous system. My "stream of consciousness," an old metaphor which (with reasonable caution) is still usable, is the dominant member in the very complex society of sequences forming my human reality. When I am deeply asleep, there may be no dominant member then actualized. The real agent is always momentary, the stream or sequence of acts being realized only in its members. The abiding ever-identical agent is an abstraction.

In this way we avoid the mysticism of wholes acting on their very own parts, a notion which would imply unrestricted and symmetrical internal relatedness between every part and every other, dissolving all definite structures into ineffable unity, a consequence which has caused clear thinkers to turn away from "holistic" or "organicist" doctrines. To the physiological commonplace which says, the body is a society of cells, we add, not something unknown or speculative, but the given reality of human feelings or experiences, unitary at a given moment (say, during about a tenth of a second), but multiple through time. (They are given not intro- but retro-spectively, in long- or short-range memories.) The cellular processes are not the whole of a man, there is also the process of his experiences. This is not a "ghost in the machine," pace Gilbert Ryle. In the first place, there is no machine, but a society of living creatures, each a sequence of actual events. To this we add, as an empirical fact, the sequence of human experiences. These too are events, influencing other events.

The Cartesian division of events into extended and material, and inextended and psychic, is based on no clear evidence on either side of the division. Nothing

283

shows that the psychical events, the experiences, are point-like, or that they are nowhere; and nothing shows that the extended events are simply without feeling, or are merely material (spatio-temporal). And both obviously have causal conditions and consequences. Ryle's apparent assumption that anyone who believes in psychical events must regard them as non-causal seems wonderfully arbitrary. Experiences must have data and, as I have argued elsewhere, this is the same as to say that they have causes.[3] And since, at least in memory, experiences are data for other experiences, it follows that experiences can be causes as well as effects.

The social view of organic unity is that individuals form organs for other individuals. This proposition is convertible: namely, if individuals are organs, organs are individuals, singly or in groups. Now an individual is self-active; if there are many individuals in the ultimate organism there are many self-active agents in that organism. Being is action, what is really many must act as many. The higher is compounded of the lower, not by suppression but by preservation of the dynamic integrity of the lower. The cosmos could not guarantee that the many individuals within it will act always in concord; for to carry out such a guarantee the cosmos must completely coerce the lesser individuals, that is, must deprive them of all individuality. Existence is essentially social,[4] plural, free, and exposed to risk, and this is required by our conception of organism. For if the action of the parts had no freedom with respect to the whole, there would be no dynamic distinction between whole and parts and the very idea of whole would lose its meaning.

It is true that the many individuals, being organs of the cosmic individual, must, according to our definition, contribute to the value of the one, but this contribution is both negative (in a sense) and positive. It includes suffering as well as joy. The all-inclusiveness of the world-mind means, not that it is exalted above all suffering, but that no pain and no joy is beneath its notice. All things make immediate contribution to the one, but they contribute what they are and have, their sorrow as well as their joy, their discord with their neighbors as well as their harmonies.

A century ago in his Zend Avesta (Ch. II) Fechner argued that an eminent consciousness must resemble all consciousness in containing a contrast between voluntary and involuntary, active and passive, elements. Even eminent volition cannot act in a vacuum, or merely upon itself. But that upon which it immediately acts must be present within it; for action and its material are inseparable. In Fechner's terms, there must be involuntary impulses even in God, or there can be no divine volition or purposive activity. But these impulses must come from something. Why not from the volitions of the creatures, the lesser individuals? Our deliberate acts set up currents, as it were, in the mind of God, as the activities of our brain cells set up currents in our human minds. Each of us is a "pulse in the eternal mind" (Rupert Brooke). God then controls, checks, encourages, redirects, these pulses or impulses. But He cannot wholly initiate or absolutely control them, not because of any weakness on His part, but because absolute control of impulses, or indeed of anything, is a contradiction in terms. God is not limited in His power to do what He wishes to do, but He is not so confused as to wish to destroy the very nature of being, which is its organic character as many individuals in one, the many being as real as the one.

The lesser individuals, being more or less ignorant of each other, act somewhat blindly with respect to many of the effects of their acts. The divine love is not contradicted by the discords which result from this blindness; for love includes tolerance for the freedom of others. The divine perfection lies, not in the suppression of freedom wherever it involves risk, for at all points freedom involves risk, but in the wise and efficient limitation of the risks to the optimum point beyond which further limitation would diminish the promise of life more than its tragedy. Perfection is not to be defined independently of freedom, for then it would be meaningless. Rather perfection is to be defined as the supreme way of mitigating the risk and maximizing the promise of freedom, the optimum of control, beyond which or short of which more harm and less good would result. Statesmen know that beyond a certain point interference with the lives of citizens does more harm than good, and this not solely because of the weakness or stupidity of statesmen but also because of the meaning of good as self-activity. This is part of the reason for the ideal of democracy, that people need first of all to be themselves, and this self-hood no tyrant, human or superhuman, however benevolent, can impose upon them.

285

But is the cosmos genuinely and organically one?
Let us recall that nothing happens anywhere but its effects are communicated with the speed of light in all
directions, that the same basic modes of action, expressed in quantum mechanics and relativity, pervade
all parts of space. But the unity lies deeper than any
such considerations can make clear. All groups short
of the universe can break up, fall to pieces, in various ways and degrees. But from the cosmic community
there is no secession. There is nowhere to go from the
universe. It is the only aggregate that is its own
foundation. This fits to perfection the idea that it
is its own reason or purpose and the integration of all
purposes.

We confuse ourselves in this matter by supposing
that in the cosmos must be summed up all the loose-
jointedness we see in various portions of the cosmos.
This would be true if the loose-jointedness were, at
each point, the whole story. But it is not. A sand-
pile is loose-jointed so far as the pile taken as a
whole is concerned. Its parts serve no imaginable unitary purpose enjoyed by the pile. But it does not follow that they serve no unitary purpose. There is no
unity of action of the sand-pile, but there is unity of
action in the sand-pile, a unity pervading the grains
of sand but referring to a larger whole than the pile.
Physics tells us that the entire universe acts upon
each particle to constitute its inertia. This unity of
action is cosmic, and it is unbroken and all-pervasive.[5]
All looseness and disintegration presuppose and cannot
contradict the cosmic integrity. The one cosmos ar-
ranges and rearranges itself from time to time in subordinate centers of activity (which it can properly be
said to create, in the sense of eliciting as partly
self-determining), but this formation and disintegration of the subordinate centers expresses the cosmic
integrity somewhat as a man may rearrange his thoughts
around different idea-foci, or make different movements
of his body, without ceasing to enjoy the unity of his
personality while doing so.

To all the foregoing, it may be objected that explanations in terms of purpose, teleological explanations, have been discredited in science, above all
through the work of Darwin. This is a contention with
grave implications; for if science, or at least if rational knowledge, cannot deal with purpose, then so
much the worse for purpose, for knowledge, and for human life. But perhaps it is only certain forms of

teleology that have been discredited. One form of teleology that we are, I think, well rid of is the notion of a single absolute world-plan, complete in every detail from all eternity, and executed with inexorable power. The objection is not solely that God would be made responsible for the imperfect adaptations and discords in nature. There is the further objection that the world process would be the idle duplicate of something in eternity. A God who eternally knew all that the fulfillment of his purpose would bring could have no need of that fulfillment or of purpose. Complete knowledge is complete possession: it is just because a man does not know in detail what "knowing his friends better" would be like that he has the purpose to come to know them better. As Bergson and Peirce[6] were among the first to see, even a world-purpose must be indeterminate as to details. For one thing, an absolute and inexorable purpose, supposing this meant anything, would deny individuality, self-activity, hence reality, to the lesser individuals, the creatures.

It follows that ill-adjustments, evils--apart from moral evil, evil deliberately chosen--are not willed but are chance results of free acts. But if evil results partly by chance, so does good. Nevertheless, the idea that adjustments are the result of natural selection among unpurposed or blind variations is not incompatible with that of cosmic purpose. For the maintenance of the general conditions under which chance and competition will produce evolution may itself be purposive. Darwinism derives generally higher forms of interadjusted species from lower; but interadjustment itself and as such is assumed, not explained. Interadjusted atoms or particles involve the same essential problem. Theism can explain order as a general character of existence; can any other doctrine? And an order capable of evolving such a vast variety of mutually compatible creatures seems all that providence could guarantee, granting that freedom is inherent in individual existence as such.

Why should the dinosaurs be any less satisfying to God or to us because they were not specifically predesigned? What after all did the old teleology accomplish, except to swell the problem of evil to impossible proportions, and to make an enigma of the process of human choice? Chance, the non-intentional character of the details of the world, is the only remedy for these two difficulties. But, as Darwin repeatedly declared, chance cannot explain the world as an ordered

287

whole of mutually-adapted parts.[7] It was because of this dilemma that Darwin gave up the theistic problem: purpose could not explain details, and nothing else could explain order as a general fact.

Here I think Darwin showed admirable care and honesty. There must be cosmically pervasive limitations upon chance, since unlimited chance is chaos; supreme purpose or providence is the sole positive conception we can form of this chance-limiting factor. And Darwin actually suggests that perhaps the solution is "designed laws" of nature, with all details, good or bad, depending upon "what we call chance."[8] But the great naturalist could not think this thought through, declaring that he was quite unsatisfied with it. Why? The answer may at least be guessed at. (1) Darwin, like so many others, tended to think of science as committed to determinism. "What we call chance," he explains elsewhere, is not properly that at all, but causes unknown to us.[9] Moreover, (2) it was probably not apparent to Darwin why cosmic purpose should leave anything to chance, at least apart from human free will. Only a philosophy of universal creativity can untie this knot. The "metaphysics" of his day, about which, with his wonderful modesty, Darwin sometimes spoke with quaint respect, did not present him with a clearly-conceived creationist philosophy. For this he was scarcely to blame.

Since Darwin was on the whole committed to determinism, he could admit no genuine element of chance for providence to limit. God must then do everything or nothing; but to do everything is to do nothing distinctive! It is also to leave nothing for the creatures to do. (The long debate about the efficacy of "second causes" remained on an essentially verbal level, since no party to the dispute would make the one concession which alone would give it content.) The "mud" in which Darwin said he was immersed was the opacity which always characterizes a deterministic world-view.

Darwin also illustrated, though this time less consciously, the absurd consequences of overlooking the truth, so much stressed in this book, that divine perfection cannot exist as a contingent fact only. Thus he worries about the question, what could have been the origin and genesis of the first cause, if we postulate one--as though its existence would be a "fact" among facts, something made whose manner of making we should inquire into.[10] Or, when asked by Gray what would

convince him of cosmic Design, he says that this is a
"poser," and tries to imagine experiences which would
be convincing. Then he gives up the effort as "childish."[11] I suggest that it is indeed childish, because
it implies that "God" stands for some great special
fact, to which lesser special facts might witness, and
thus it fails to grasp, as adult thinking about this
matter should, the impossibility that the "creator of
all things, visible and invisible," the ground of all
possibility, should itself be among the things created,
or actualized out of some possibility. Or, if not created, actualized out of possibility, in what intelligible sense could it be contingent, or what could its
factuality have in common with that of any facts which
we know to be such? I labor this point once more, for
it seems to me that the learned world, with almost insignificant exceptions, has been missing it "as if by
magic," and I know not how to startle, coax, or lead it
gently to take a candid look, at last, at the logic of
the concepts involved. (This is also my excuse for
certain other cases of repetition in this book: I repeat not what nearly everyone in the intellectual world
is saying, but what they are ignoring or denying without careful consideration. The same excuse must serve
for the polemical tone of much of this book. The theories I attack have so many friends that no one, it
seems, need feel badly because of my rather isolated
onslaughts.)

The reader may still not quite see why, if teleology, as conceived all along, was a "hopeless muddle,"
Darwin's contributions made such a difference. Darwin
seemed to show that creative potentialities were inherent in the general features of living things. Since
teleology had been thought of as unilateral creativity
on the part of deity, unshared in any appreciable degree with the creatures, indications that the world had
far-reaching potentialities for self-creation were naturally startling. But only because creativity had not
been grasped in its proper universality, as the principle of existence itself.

Darwin saw all this, but as through a glass dark-
ly. And he was misled, like many another, by the apparently factual character of the problem. The facts
of evil, which he repeatedly mentions as conflicting
with the belief in Design,[12] and the at least alleged
fact of human freedom (it is not easy to say in what
sense Darwin accepted this as a fact) were the obstacles to teleology, plus only the one new difficulty

289

that in fact variations seem not designed but rather random, in all directions, good, bad, or indifferent. However, freedom, chance, and evil in general are inherent a priori in the mere idea of existence, construed as a multiplicity of creative processes; and it is arguable that no other construction makes sense (see the previous and the following chapters). As for the randomness effect, neither monolithic design nor rigorous law throws any light upon it. Analysis shows, as Peirce and others have argued, that without chance, its opposing term necessity is unintelligible, and indeed everything is unintelligible. Even in mathematics, one must at some point accept arbitrary decisions, if there is to be any rational necessity. If chance is merely a word for our ignorance, then we are ignorant indeed!

It is true that chance is not something positive, or a cause of anything. It is but the negative aspect inherent in creative spontaneity (to use a phrase whose redundancy is excused by the supposition of many that it is not redundant). Chance is an aspect of the production of additional determinateness, or more simply, of determination as an act: not merely being, but becoming, definite. Determinists want things just to be definite without ever becoming so. This is in effect the denial of becoming itself, or at least its trivialization. Moreover, and this, too, Darwin dimly saw, if the universe is taken as one absolute causal system, while theism is rejected, then it follows that the system as a whole exists only by true and mere chance, that is, neither by intention nor (on pain of an endless regress) thanks to any further cause. So chance is not escaped.

What integrity there was in the honest facing of this impasse, without favoring either of the cheap and easy pretended escapes, by a man who liked to please and console, more than to upset or startle!

Another respect in which Darwin showed wisdom was in his refusal to claim that he had found the solution to the problem of the origin of life on earth. As mere chance cannot explain order, so mere matter cannot explain life and mind. The reason is the same in both cases: chance and matter are essentially negative conceptions which imply but do not explicate something positive. This is overlooked in the case of matter because "extension," spatio-temporality, is positive; but since analysis shows that mind must have this positive character, what distinguishes matter from mind remains merely negative, and therefore the first concept cannot in good logic explain the second. There must be something positive limiting chance, and something more than mere matter in matter, or Darwinism fails to explain life.

Today, some eminent contributors to evolutionary theory--Wright, Huxley, Teilhard de Chardin, and others --meet the second requirement by denying the self-sufficiency of the concept of matter, which they hold is "mere" only as observed from without, and known only in its bare spatio-temporal relationships, while in its intrinsic qualities it is mind or experience on various levels and scales of magnitude and temporal rhythm, vastly different mostly from our own. Darwin lacked this explanation of matter, hence he could only confess his ignorance by referring to the "creator" (in the famous closing passage of the Origin of Species).

By admitting that mind is primordial and only its species emerge, we surmount various difficulties in a more materialistic Darwinism. We then do not have to explain how from a world without any positive principle of organization (would this be a world or anything conceivable?) organic forms are derived. We have only to explain how some forms of integration come from others, or how such forms alter gradually through long ages. Mind is intrinsically and by its essential core of meaning a principle of integration. Any mind is at least a felt unity, in which various data are responded to in such a way as to attain enjoyment or satisfaction, in some degree, through unity in contrast. The orderliness of the entire world can then be interpreted through this same principle of responsiveness operating on many levels at once, as will be discussed somewhat further in the next chapter. Moreover, if the materialist wants to say that his matter has tendencies toward integration, and so mind is not needed for this, then he can be led to face the other horn of the dilemma of materialism: how to distinguish those forms of integration which show the presence of mind somewhere in a system from those which do not. Any criterion, I affirm, will either be arbitrary or will fail to divide nature into an older portion without mind and a newer with mind. Since Darwin (like most of his critics) knew little about such possibilities for reducing matter to mind (a topic regarding which much progress has been made during the last hundred years), and almost nothing about the microstructure of physical reality which has since been so extensively explored, he was

well justified in refusing to deal with the origin of
life, save by vaguely attributing it to the power responsible for the world-order generally.

The Vitalists of several decades ago have in a way
gained their cause, though in other ways they have been
proved mistaken. They have gained their cause in that
a living thing is now seen not to be mechanical, if
that means anything like, consisting of parts which
touch and push or pull each other, and in this manner
constitute the actions of the whole. Digestion, metabolism, growth, and nerve action are not essentially mechanical. But then neither are chemical processes generally. The gratuitous denial of organismic characters
to the "inanimate" was the first basic error of vitalism. The inanimate is that part of nature in which organic wholeness is confined to the ultra-microscopic
level, where it eludes the competence of the human
senses. The second mistake was to see in life a third
"force," distinct from matter, on the one hand, and
mind on the other. But a process either involves sentience (sensation, feeling, memory, and the like) or
does not involve it, there is no third possibility; and
apart from spatio-temporal structure or behavior, and
modes of experience or feeling, there is nothing positive with which we can be acquainted whereby phenomena
may be explained. The third mistake was the converse
of the first, for just as primitive, minute organisms
may be loosely associated to form an apparently quite
inorganic assembly or whole, so on a higher level they
may also be associated in a somewhat more integrated
way which simulates but does not quite constitute an
individual organism. Thus a nation may be viewed as an
organic individual, but this is generally regarded as a
metaphor or illusion. Similarly an embryo in Driesch's
experiments seemed to be doing remarkable things, as
though inspired with a plan of its growth-aim, when really it was the cells which were doing whatever was
done, and any "entelechy" should have been sought on
the cellular level.

While there is no third force, there is a third
level, or group of levels, or organization, between ordinary atoms or molecules and ordinary perceptible animals and plants: the level of cells, nuclei, and those
giant molecules whose chemistry and arrangements constitute the gene-characters by which life is guided.
Here things are even more wonderful than anything
Driesch observed. Myriads of activities, simultaneous
or overlapping in time, effectively coordinated and

controlled! It is cells, genes, and things of that order of magnitude which, as it were, "know" (feel) something of what they are up to, not embryos (except when
and as they turn into animals with functioning nervous
systems). The problem is one of cellular psychology,
sociology, or ecology, and then of molecular psychology
and ecology. Finally, everything is a matter of individual and social psychology, on we know not how many
levels. But this picture cannot be made clear unless
it is firmly grasped that the cells of a tree, for instance (or the atoms or molecules of a solid), may be
the highest form of dynamic individual in the tree (or
solid). Thus the "vegetable soul" (or growth factor)
of Aristotle may be like the "soul of the state," a
metaphor or illusion. Cellular souls are another matter, for cells really do the growing, while the "growing tree" is merely the overall view of the process.
But the cellular souls are almost rather "animal" than
vegetable, in Aristotle's sense, for they respond to
internal and external stimuli, and control their activities accordingly. They should therefore probably be
viewed as sentient, as sequences of feelings, in addition to their molecular constitutions.

The problem of mind and matter is a problem not of
two kinds of stuff or force but of the one and the
many, and of numerous levels or kinds of one-ness and
many-ness. Leibniz, with a flash of the highest genius, discovered this, two and one half centuries ago,
after all mankind, so far as I can find out, in East
and West, had missed it from the beginning. Many, however, are still pre-Leibnizian in their thinking. This
is the sad aspect of the story. Here truly is a "cultural lag," and one affecting the scholar almost as
much as the plain man.

The great mistake of "teleology" consisted in never seeing clearly the one-many problem in relation to
purpose. (At this point Leibniz was not a Leibnizian.)
An absolutely controlling purpose would be the sole
purpose, and could not have as its aim the creation of
other purposes. If there be even two purposes, two decisions, then the conjunction of these two into a total
reality must in some aspect be undecided, unintended, a
matter of chance. Since a "solitary purpose" is meaningless or pointless, chance is inevitable, granted
purpose.[13]

Without the recognition of chance, no teleology!
Paradoxical as it may sound, only good things which in

details come about by chance may concretely fulfill
purpose. A man who goes to the theater to be amused
can say that he has accomplished his purpose without
implying that he knew in advance just what jokes he
wished to hear! And so can a parent whose children
think and feel in a spontaneous and unforeseen fashion,
just as the parent wished they should do. Must God be
without analogy to us in this? And if without analogy,
could he be God?

The conception of the ultimate or cosmic organism
is the remedy for two great errors of political thought,
abstract individualism and abstract or mythical collec-
tivism. Neither the human individual nor any human
class or race is an absolute end, but only that whole
in which men and nations and all existences have their
place and value. We are members one of another because
we are members of one ultimate body-mind, one inclusive,
unborn, and imperishable organism.

But is the cosmos imperishable? What about the
"heat death"? The present world-order, as an arbitrary
choice out of the infinity of possible orders, is doubtless perishable. For as Goethe put it, in the mouth of
Mephistopheles, "Whatever comes to be, deserves to be
destroyed" (except in one sense--see Chapter Nine).
All definite patterns lose their appeal after sufficient reiteration. The history of art and all aesthetic experience show this. It is absurd to suppose that
God would be satisfied with less variety than we ourselves require, when we stretch our imaginations sufficiently to see what is involved. So (in spite of as-
tronomers Hoyle and Bondi) I do not doubt that the
present quantitative system of the cosmos is doomed.
But this is compatible with there being a deeper qualitative identity through change whereby the universe as
the "living garment of deity" retains this status forever.

FOOTNOTES

[1] The reasons for this principle are given in my essay on "The Group Mind" in Social Research, IX (May, 1942), 248-265.

[2] See my Man's Vision of God, especially Ch. V.

[3] "The Logical Structure of Givenness," The Philosophical Quarterly, VIII (1958), 307-316

[4] This essay could have been written as a generalization of "social" instead of "organic." Cf. Whitehead, Adventures of Ideas (New York: The Macmillan Company, 1933, 1948), Ch. XIII.

[5] The action is not, according to physics, instantaneous. This is a serious complication, though not, I believe, an insuperable difficulty for our thesis.

[6] Peirce seems to hesitate between a classical and a neo-classical idea of God. Compare, in The Collected Papers of Charles Sanders Peirce, edited by Charles Hartshorne and Paul Weiss (Cambridge: Harvard University Press, 1934, 1935), pars. 5.119, 588; 6.157, 346, 465f., 489, 508. As a contrast to Einstein's disbelief in a "dice-throwing God" note 5.588! See also "A Critique of Peirce's Idea of God," Philosophical Review, L (1941), 516-523.

[7] See F. Darwin, The Life and Letters of Charles Darwin (New York: Appleton, 1898), II, 146; I, p. 276. I first came upon this quotation in that fine book, Charles Darwin and the Golden Rule, by W. E. Ritter (Washington: Science Service, 1954), p. 75.

[8] F. Darwin, II, 105.

[9] See the 2nd and last sentences of Ch. V of the Origin, 6th Ed.

[10] F. Darwin, I. 276.

[11] Op. cit., II, 169.

[12] II, 105; I, 276, 284.

[13]I find it very odd that Pollard, in the book already referred to (footnote 12, Ch. 6), after giving a brilliant exposition of the irreducible role of chance in science, should relapse into precisely the old "muddle" of attributing details (or have I misunderstood him?) to providence. At least he wants to attribute some details. And so it is to be expected that he should ignore the problem of evil and pass off the question of freedom by the old denial that we could hope to understand such things.

SUGGESTED READINGS

Charles Hartshorne

Hartshorne, Charles. Beyond Humanism: Essays in the New Philosophy of Nature (Chicago: Willett, Clark and Company, 1937; Lincoln: University of Nebraska Press, 1968).

_____. Born to Sing: An Interpretation and World Survey of Bird Song (Bloomington, Ind.: Indiana University Press, 1973).

_____. A Natural Theology for Our Time (LaSalle, Ill.: Open Court, 1967).

_____. The Philosophy and Psychology of Sensation (Chicago: University of Chicago Press, 1934; Port Washington, New York: Kennikat, 1968).

* * *

_____. "Perception and the 'Concrete Abstractness' of Science," Philosophy and Phenomenological Research, XXXIV, 4 (June 1974), 465-476.

* * *

Ayala, F. J. "Teleological Explanations in Evolutionary Biology," Philosophy of Science, XXXVII, 1 (March 1970), 1-15.

Burgers, J. M. "Causality and Anticipation," Science, CLXXXIX, 4198 (July 1975), 194-198.

Capek, Milic. "The Myth of Frozen Passage: The Status of Becoming in the Physical World," Boston Studies in the Philosophy of Science, Vol. II, in Honor of Philipp Frank (New York: Humanities Press, 1965), pp. 441-463.

Harris, E. E. "Mechanism and Teleology in Contemporary Thought" Philosophy in Context, II (1973), 49-55.

297

* * *

Agar, W. E. A Contribution to the Theory of the
   Living Organism, Second Edition (Cambridge:
   Cambridge University Press, 1951).

Burgers, J. M. Reflections on the Concept of Life
   (Santa Monica, Cal.: Rand Corporation, 1969).

Minor, W. E. (Ed.). Charles Hartshorne and Henry
   Nelson Wieman (Carbondale, Ill.: Foundation
   for Creative Philosophy, Inc., 1969).

12. THE SECOND SCIENTIFIC REVOLUTION

Milic Capek

Milic Capek (1909-   ) was born in Trebecho-
vice, Czechoslovakia. In 1935 he received a
Ph.D. in philosophy from King Charles University in Prague, and in 1936 was awarded an M.Sc.
in physics by the same University. He taught
physics from 1944 through 1948 at the University of Nebraska and the University of Olmutz.
From 1948 through 1976 he has taught philosophy at Carleton College and Boston University.

Modern science has had a powerful impact on our
ways of viewing ourselves and our world. It is interesting to note, however, that this impact has to date
been conceived almost entirely in terms of the "First
Scientific Revolution," i.e., the conceptual reform
initiated by Galileo and Newton and culminating in
nineteenth century mechanism. The twentieth century,
by contrast has produced a "Second Scientific Revolution" whose results are more revolutionary than the
first, and whose results are only beginning--against
considerable resistance--to be grasped. In this essay
Professor Milic Capek analyzes the character and implications of this latter revolution.* The difference between nineteenth century and twentieth century physics
can be spelled out in terms of five basic claims made
by mechanistic philosophers: (1) Nature consists of
material particles, which move through Euclidian space
according to the laws of mechanics. (2) Qualitative
differences in the world are due to the motion and configuration of particles. (3) Qualitative changes are
surface effects of the motion of particles. (4) Change
is due only to the direct impact of particles. (5)
Qualitative characteristics and changes exist only in
the mind of the perceiver. Though the fifth of these

*This article is taken from the journal Diogenes,
63 (1968), 114-133. Used by the permission of Diogène:
Revue internationale des sciences humaines and Professor Capek.

claims always provoked epistemological doubts, these doubts did not shake the prevailing mechanical assumptions. Twentieth century physics, however, shakes each of them in turn. For relativity theory matter becomes "fused" with the variable (non-Euclidean) curvature of space-time, and the simple particle disappears. Quantum physics also erases the concept of the simple material particle, while negating the strict determinism of Newton. In all of these cases, and others, qualitative characteristics are reintroduced into nature. Professor Capek concludes his essay with a discussion of the implications of the second scientific revolution for biology, sociology, and psychology. We are on the threshold of a new era in the intellectual history of mankind.

The Second Scientific Revolution

It is easy to guess from the title of this article that its content will deal with the current changes in the foundations of physical sciences--the changes which are far-reaching enough to be called revolutionary. But the full significance of this intellectual upheaval will become clear only if we compare it to <u>another</u> scientific revolution which took place in the sixteenth and seventeenth centuries. The significance of this first scientific revolution is fully recognized by the historians of science and historians in general; if I shall recall its main features, it will be only to provide us with a <u>contrasting backdrop</u> against which the salient features of the contemporary transformation of physics will stand out more vividly and more suggestively. The comparison between what is going on now and what went on three centuries ago will clearly show that the distance along which physical science moved in the last fifty years is not only greater than that covered in the last three centuries, but also--and this is far more significant--greater than the distance separating the science of Newton from that of Aristotle. In other words, the twentieth century revolution is far more profound than what was rather inappropriately called "the Copernican revolution"; the intellectual distance between Aristotle and Newton is <u>far smaller</u> than the distance separating the world of Newton and Laplace from that of Einstein, Planck, de Broglie, and Heisenberg.

This may appear as a hasty and paradoxical statement for various reasons. In the first place, we still teach Newtonian physics on a high school level and in the elementary college courses; and for the reasons which will be mentioned we shall continue to teach it. This seems to indicate that the break between Newtonian and modern physics is perhaps not as sharp as I claimed, and seemingly not as sharp as between Aristotelian physics and the physics of Newton. This objection is also seemingly supported by the fact that Newtonian physics was born painfully and laboriously because it faced the sharp opposition of the previous solidly entrenched medieval view. There is hardly any need to recall how Copernicus' book was placed on the index of prohibited books, how Giordano Bruno died, how Galileo was forced to recant, how extremely cautious Descartes had to be. In contrast to this, modern physics was born in the state-supported institutions, endowed by

generous grants, hailed by a large public, appreciated
by the military circles, respected even by the churches.
The transition from the Newtonian to the Einsteinian
physics went on in this respect smoothly and without
external interference, at least if we disregard Nazi
Germany whose opposition to the relativity theory, however, was more an opposition to its author rather than
to its content. Closest to the medieval oppression
came the policy of Stalin's Russia where the materialistic scholastics, even today well entrenched in the
university circles, regarded the collapse of classical
physics as a serious threat to its main dogmas. But if
we consider the normally functioning free society--and
it was in such society that modern physics was born--
there was clearly no interference remotely comparable
to that which tried to stifle the incipient classical
science more than three centuries ago.

I am perfectly aware of all these objections. But
they prove really only two things: (a) that the external obstacles which interfered with the development of
the Newtonian science, are absent today, at least in
the free part of the world; (b) that what was so revolutionary in the first scientific revolution was less
its ideas than their implications. Let me explain
these two points in detail. It is understandable that
the cultural climate in the twentieth century is different from that in the sixteenth or seventeenth century. Although there is no guarantee that free inquiry
will not be again restricted--we have seen this in the
Germany of Hitler, in the Spain of Franco, and still in
Eastern Europe and China today--it still remains one of
the basic presuppositions of experimental and theoretical research which even totalitarian regimes eventually
are forced to respect, at least in a limited degree.
In this respect, it is almost ironical that the idea of
freedom for which Bruno and Galileo were persecuted enables the contemporary scientists to question the very
same ideas for which these two men suffered; today we
are much less sure of the infinity of space than Bruno
was, and we are certain that Galileo's dynamics is only
approximately valid. But the fact that the circumstances under which contemporary physics was born were
much less dramatic than those in which the astronomy of
Kepler and the physics of Newton has nothing to do with
the ultimate revolutionary impact of the present transformation of physical sciences. This leads me to the
second point. I said that the implications of the
first scientific revolution were more revolutionary
than the ideas themselves which constituted it. It is

302

true that these implications were fairly obvious and
that they can hardly be separated from the ideas themselves; this is the reason why their dangerous charac-
ter--dangerous to the medieval world view--was soon noticed. But what do we know about the implications of
modern physics? And--let us ask more bluntly--how much
do we care about them? The technological applications
of the present revolution in science are so spectacular
that they tend to obscure its theoretical significance.
There are other additional factors which tend to obscure it. In the first place, there is a deep crisis
in contemporary philosophy which can be compared to the
crisis of Greek philosophy at the time of Socrates. We
know that both Socrates and the sophists simply turned
their back to nature, that is, to the cosmological
speculations which so fascinated their Ionic predecessors. When Socrates, during his trial, was accused by
Meletus that he regarded the sun and the moon not as
divine beings, but as pieces of stone, he answered that
these ideas were not his own but those of Anaxagoras.
He did not say that Anaxagoras was right; nor did he
say that he was wrong; he was simply not interested in
this question at all. And immediately before his death,
according to the dialogue Phaedo, he again emphasized
that he had no interest whatever in the problems of
physical nature. Although I would hesitate to compare
modern existentialists and phenomenologists to Socrates,
there is no question that they share with him his complete lack of interest in the problems of science and
that their interest is narrowly confined to the problem
of man, of human knowledge, and of human values. I
would be less hesitant to compare contemporary linguistic analysts to the Greek sophists; perhaps they would
even be proud of this comparison. If we remember the
circumstances in which the sophistic movement originated, it is difficult not to see the analogy: the same
general intellectual fatigue and frustration generated
by the discouraging diversity of philosophical systems;
the same increase in virtuosity of philosophical argu-
mentation, the same creation of artificial problems,
the same blossoming verbosity and hairsplitting trivi-
alities. We know the harsh pronouncement of Bertrand
Russell who wrote in The British Journal for the Philosophy of Science in the early fifties that the excessive interest in language, which is so characteristic
of the present philosophical scene in England and in
the English-speaking countries in general, is merely an
easy excuse for not being interested in the problems of
contemporary science.[1] Perhaps we may find Russell's
judgment too harsh; there is hardly any question about

303

the usefulness of the linguistic analysis as long as it is applied to the language of science; but I fail to see any particular relevance in the analysis of ordinary language whose shortcomings and inadequacies have been pointed out long ago by pragmatists and even earlier; and I would especially distrust the common usage which is so obviously conditioned by the social media and the whole macroscopic environment to be a reliable tool in philosophy and, in particular, in philosophy of nature.

Thus the only philosophy which is genuinely concerned about the second scientific revolution is logical positivism; ironically enough, it is too much burdened by its intellectual nineteenth-century heritage to be well prepared for this task. In the first place, the agnostic and antimetaphysical tradition of the early positivism of August Comte and Herbert Spencer is still present under different terminological garbs in contemporary positivism; at least their antimetaphysical effusions are as eloquent as those of Auguste Comte, even when hardly anybody among them dares to mention his name in order not to look old-fashioned. This antimetaphysical or, if you prefer, antiontological orientation leads contemporary positivists to ignore or at least to de-emphasize the fact that the present crisis in physics is in the first place the crisis of the classical picture of reality, far more radical than the crisis of the Aristotelian picture of the world. Moreover, the positivists today, like the positivists of the last century, are consciously or semi-consciously committed to the mechanistic view of reality; their agnosticism and phenomenalism is largely verbal since it merely hides their definite mechanistic commitment. (We shall return to this point in due time.) All these factors led the Vienna circle and its prolific Anglo-American progeny to concentrate on the questions of methodology almost exclusively; hence, philosophy of science is equated by them with methodology; and, since there is a perfect continuity between the methodology of classical science and that of modern physics, the revolutionary character of the latter again is naturally overlooked or at least played down.

A few additional factors should be mentioned. First, to measure the distance between classical and modern physics a certain degree of historical awareness is necessary. And this is largely lacking, at least in the United States. As the physicist Dyson wrote some years ago: for those physicists who have grown up

after 1940 and have accepted quantum mechanics as a
fait accompli, it is extremely difficult to imagine the
state of mind of the men who were creating the theory
before 1926.[2] And let us not forget that in 1926 the
second scientific revolution was already a quarter of a
century old. On the other hand, an excessive historical awareness may seriously interfere with the understanding of new and fresh ideas. An extensive acquaintance with the ideas of the past may have an en-
slaving influence on human minds. We have two striking
illustrations of it in the persons of Léon Brunschvicg
and Ernst Cassirer, both with impressive knowledge of
the history of ideas and a deep understanding of their
logical as well as genetic relations. Yet, this knowledge was for them a handicap rather than an advantage
when they were dealing with the twentieth-century revolution in science. This handicap showed itself in a
lesser degree in Cassirer than in Brunschvicg,[3] it is
not entirely absent even in the interpretations of
Émile Meyerson,[4] whose writings still remain among the
most wonderful specimens of historical scholarship
joined to scientific and philosophical erudition. Yet,
a certain degree of historical perspective is inevitable for any attempt at interpreting the current changes
in physics; otherwise, we can easily slip into intellectual traps by committing fallacies analogous to the
fallacies of the past which we could have avoided by
having a more solid historical knowledge. It is true
that it is very difficult to acquire a proper historical perspective which would free us from what Whitehead
called "provincialism in time" and at the same time not
to be submerged by sheer weight of historical scholarship. To escape the curse of specialization and the
irresponsibilities of dilettantism--to steer our intellectual course between these two dangers--is one of the
most challenging tasks of a philosopher of science.

    In what, then, does the revolutionary character of
the contemporary scientific revolution consist? We
pointed out that there were no external obstacles and
oppositions comparable to those which the first scientific revolution faced. But the absence of external
obstacles does not mean that there are no obstacles at
all. As I am going to show, the obstacles and resist-
ances which a modern philosopher of science faces are
of more subtle and more elusive, but also of a more insidious kind; they seem to be due to the factors inherent in the very nature of human understanding or, more
accurately, the present historical form of human understanding. A brief comparison with the first scientific

revolution will show it quite clearly. What was the meaning of that revolution associated with the names of Galileo and Newton? The earth exchanged its place with the sun, and the last celestial sphere--the sphere of the fixed stars--which was still retained by Copernicus, Tycho Brahe, and Kepler, was swept away by Giordano Bruno; thus the sun became a star and the allegedly fixed stars became very distant suns floating freely in the limitless space. The intellectual effort involved in this imaginative transition "from the closed world to the infinite universe"--to use Professor Koyré's phrase--was relatively small. The difficulties involved in this step were mainly due to the emotional resistance to give up the medieval geocentric scheme, especially since this resistance was embodied in the institution of the medieval Church and of Aristotelian science.

But intellectually this step was not hard to achieve; in truth, it was fully anticipated by Greek science. We must not forget that Greek atomists explicitly insisted on the infinity of space, on the plurality of the worlds, and on the unity of nature in space in contrast to the Aristotelian dualism of the terrestrial and celestial realm which dominated the Western world for nineteen centuries. This explains why the protagonists of seventeenth-century science had merely to repeat the argument of the ancient atomists against the impossibility of finite space: "If I were on the alleged edge of the world and shot an arrow outwards, where would an arrow fly?"--asked Giordano Bruno, and one century after him, John Locke, repeating thus the question which Lucretius asked so many centuries before them. Even Copernicus had his Greek predecessors: not speaking of Philolaus who dislodged the earth from the center of the universe, there was Heraclides of Pontus who taught the rotation of the earth around its axis and Aristarchus of Samos who asserted that the earth besides rotating around its axis also revolves once in a year around the sun. This only shows how unfortunate the influence of the established scientific or philosophical authority--in this case of Aristotle--can be. This also explains why Gassendi was so earnestly reviving the ancient atomism; why Francis Bacon wrote a Latin work in which he tried to rehabilitate Democritus; why in the middle of the seventeenth century Johannes Christopher Magnenus wrote a book with a characteristic title Democritus reviviscens--"Democritus revived"; this explains why Newton in the concluding part of his Optics wrote that "God in the beginning created matter in solid, hard, impenetrable, moveable particles of such sizes and figures and with such other properties, and in such proportions in space as most conduced to the end for which he formed them . . .," adding a few lines later the characteristically Lucretian argument that "should they (i.e., atoms) wear away, or break in pieces, the nature of things depending on them would be changed. . ." It was this passage of Newton which John Dalton, one of the founders of modern chemistry, quoted, showing again the persistence of the atomistic inspiration through the whole history of Western thought. About the fundamental identity of the corpuscular-kinetic model of nature from Democritus to Lorentz no doubt is possible; neither can we doubt its historical continuity. It is true that under the pressure of the institutionalized Aristotelianism the atomistic tradition was suppressed and nearly forgotten in the Middle Ages; but, as Kurt Laswitz showed convincingly, it has never been entirely suppressed or forgotten, and survived in a sort of intellectual underground until its triumphant revival in the first scientific revolution.

Why was it so? Was it accidental that so many important ideas of the corpuscular-kinetic scheme were anticipated by the early thinkers? Is there any natural tendency within the human mind to prefer the Euclidian space to any other types of space or to regard solidity as the primary constituting property of matter? Why did the human mind almost spontaneously return to the rejected ideas of atomists as soon as it was free from the pressure of external authority and from the inner pressure of religious prejudices? This is the question which we are facing now and on the way we shall answer it, our attitude to, and understanding of, the second scientific revolution will depend.

Despite the profound differences between the Aristotelian and Newtonian world views, they both had one fundamental feature in common: they were built of the elements borrowed from our sensory perception, and thus it was easy to imagine them, i.e., to construct in our mind their mental picture. The helio-centric system of Copernicus was perhaps less familiar, but in principle as easily imaginable as the geocentric medieval view; both views were characterized by the preponderance of visual elements; Copernicus' circles and Kepler's ellipses were as visualizable as Ptolemy's epicycles and Aristotle's spheres, having furthermore an advantage of lesser complexity and greater aesthetical appeal. Both

307

views accepted Euclidian space; but while Aristotle failed to see that the geometry of Euclid implied the infinity of space Bruno and Newton saw this consequence clearly. Another significant difference was that while the Aristotelian physics still objectified the secondary qualities, the physics of Galileo and Newton excluded them from nature and retained only the basic geometrical and mechanical attributes of matter like position, size, shape, motion and mass. In other words, the only building material which was used in constructing the classical picture of the world was derived from the sensations of sight and touch. Thus the impenetrability of matter was based on the sensation of touch; the geometrical properties of matter were abstracted from the visual sensations and the kinesthetic sensations of the eye-muscles. Not all the visual and tactile sensations were objectified; thus the sensations of color were excluded from physical nature as much as the sensations of dryness and moisture which Aristotle still objectified. It is clear that in accepting the distinction between primary and secondary qualities the physics of Galileo and Newton was consciously returning to the tradition of ancient atomism, i.e., to the corpuscular-kinetic model of nature. Its basic constituent ideas are:

1. Matter, which is discontinuous in its structure, moves through the Euclidian space according to the strict laws of mechanics.

2. All apparently qualitative differences in nature are merely surface effects of the difference of either motion or configuration of the basic units of matter.

3. All apparently qualitative changes are merely surface effects of the displacements of the same units.

4. All interaction between the basic particles is due exclusively to their direct contact. There is no action at a distance.

5. Qualitative varieties and qualitative changes are in the perceiving human mind only; they do not have any objective status.

Time is lacking to consider the richness and fruitfulness of the classical scheme even in a cursory way. The whole history of physics from 1600-1900 bears an eloquent testimony about it. Only about sixty or seventy years ago, difficulties began to appear which grew in number and seriousness. But I would like to call attention to one point which was obscure right from the beginning. It was the point five: the status of secondary qualities and of qualities in general. They were excluded from the objective world; in this sense they were illusory. But what then was their status? Clearly they were regarded as existing in some sense; even an illusion must have some sort of status-- if it did not exist, we should not worry about correcting it. There were two solutions, both not very satisfactory; the first one was to locate them outside of space in an unextended entity, in the "thinking substance," mysteriously associated despite its non-spatial character with a particular organism. This was the solution of Descartes; and although he was basically right in insisting that the introspective qualities cannot be denied without making a self-contradictory statement or, to use Professor Lovejoy's phrase, without creating a "paradox of thinking behaviorist,"[5] he was clearly helpless in trying to construct any rational model which would relate the qualitative realm of consciousness to the mechanistic realm of matter. The second solution was no solution at all: it consisted in a simple and flat denial of those qualities. The mental qualities, according to this view, do not exist because they do not fit into the mechanistic scheme and they are entirely superfluous. This was the solution proposed by materialists and behaviorists; it is very attractive by its simplicity and economy. But it sins by using an Occam's razor which is too sharp--so sharp that it cuts the very branch on which the materialists are sitting. For in no scientific or philosophical explanation should any fact, no matter how embarassing for the symmetry of the system, be simply suppressed. Consciousness cannot be suppressed for it reemerges in the very act by which it is denied. For this reason a consistent behavioristic position is self-contradictory, as it always ends in the paradox of thinking behaviorist or in the absurdity of the self-denying thought. Even such a radical sceptic as Santayana conceded "the solipsism of the mental present" as the only absolute certainty.

It is true that there was the third solution which tried to reconcile the Cartesian certainty of introspection with the data of classical physics. This was the famous identity or double-aspect theory, first formulated by Spinoza, and later very popular in the second half of the last century and among positivists even

309

today. In this theory, consciousness was not denied;
but it was deprived of its causal efficacy. An embarassing question for this theory was: why the cosmic
mechanism ever indulges in a very peculiar luxury to
produce an idle entity of consciousness which does not
interfere with the cerebral processes at all and consequently is entirely superfluous in the whole scheme of
nature? It is strange that this view was and still is
defended by positivists; apparently, in their view, nature itself ignores the rule of Occam in creating a
completely idle and superfluous entity which we call
"consciousness."

I purposely engaged in this digression to indicate
that prior to 1900 the only doubts about the mechanistic scheme of nature were of epistemological kind.
Some epistemological uneasiness was also felt about the
famous distinction between the primary and secondary
qualities. Is not the sensation of touch and hardness
just as subjective as any other sensation? Why should
we believe that the very nature of matter should disclose itself more adequately in the sensation of hardness rather than in the sensation of sound or scent?
Is a solid atom, as Bergson asked a few years before
the second scientific revolution began, anything more
than an objectified sensation of touch?[6] But physicists themselves were naturally unconcerned about these
questions and confidently and with great success extended the mechanization of the world picture far beyond the limits of physics. Darwin's explanation of
evolution as a result of a mechanical sifting process
by which the unsuitable incidental variations are eliminated so that only "the fittest survive" is as mechanistic in its spirit as the physiological psychology
and cerebral reflexology of the nineteenth and twentieth centuries.

I purposefully spent so much time in describing
the classical model of nature to convey the idea what
is at stake when this model, so impressive by its unity
and by its coherence is now shaken to its very foundations. Let us take the concepts of classical physics
one by one to see how profoundly each of them was
transformed. Let us begin with the concept of space.
The space of the Newtonian physics was Euclidian, that
is, infinite, infinitely divisible, absolute, i.e.,
independent of its physical content, and rigid, i.e.,
its structure was independent of time. The space of
modern physics seems to have the very opposite features: it is only approximately Euclidian if we accept

310

the general theory of relativity; in other words, the non-Euclidian curvature of space is practically negligible when we consider our biological surrounding or even our whole solar system; in the same way as a small portion of the spherical surface is flat, a small portion of the cosmic space is Euclidian. The space of modern physics, though still very, very large, is quite possibly finite, though without limits; although it can be subdivided into very small regions, very probably it is not infinitely divisible and the length of 10^{-13} cm may well be the smallest possible length. It is not absolute, i.e., independent of its physical content; if we accept the general theory of relativity, its relation to matter is not the relation of the container to its content, since matter itself, including its dynamic manifestations, is merged with the non-Euclidian structure of space. Finally, its structure is not rigid as that of the classical Newton-Euclidian space, but it varies from place to place and from time to time, not speaking of the over-all expansion of space which causes the recession of galaxies. But even prior to the general theory of relativity the inseparability of space from time found its expression in Lorentz transformation and Minkowski's formula for the world-interval.

From what I just said it is clear that the concept of matter was as much revised as that of space. The classical physics regarded matter as impenetrable and inert stuff occupying certain regions of space. But the general theory of relativity does not regard the relation of matter to space as that of the content to its container; matter is fused with the changing and locally variable structure of space-time. Thus the inertial or gravitational field--both being one and the same reality according to the principle of equivalence-- should not be regarded as being located in the unchanging and physically indifferent Euclidian space-time. Energy and mass, which were traditionally separated, are now merged together according to the famous equation which the whole world knows: $E = mc^2$; and I do not need to refer to the spectacular way in which this equation was verified nearly twenty years ago. This equation tells us that every mass, even when completely at rest, possesses a tremendous energetic content; and that every energy, no matter how disembodied it may appear, has a tiny mass. It means that even the energy of radiation, having a certain mass, must exert a tiny pressure; and must be subject to the action of gravity; the first consequence was verified by the Russian

311

physicist Lebedev even prior to the formulation of the
special principle of relativity (1900), while the confirmation of the latter in 1919 made general relativity
known to the wider public. It is thus conceivable that
under certain conditions the whole mass may be converted into radiation or vice versa; this was indeed con-
firmed in 1932, when the positive electron was discovered. This particle is literally born out of gamma radiation together with a negative electron; thus the law
of conservation of charge is not violated; neither is
there any formal violation of the law of conservation
of mass--for the mass of created particles in a sense
preexisted in the "mass" of the radiation. The oppo-
sit phenomenon--the dematerialization of particles--was
found at the same time, for a positive electron lives a
very short time and disappears after one-hundred-
millionth of a second. We really should not say "disappears" for, again, its mass is preserved in the
"mass" of the radiation into which it is converted.
Both the materialization and dematerialization of particles were not unexpected since they both exemplify
the equivalence of mass and energy; but what was unexpected was the alarming rate with which more and more
new particles were discovered so that Professor Oppenheimer, in 1955, could speak of the whole "sub-nuclear
zoo."[7]

   Philosophically, the most interesting and also
most puzzling feature of these recently discovered
"particles" is that they are, strictly speaking, no
particles at all. The word "particle" or "corpuscle"
suggests something solid, unchangeable, and permanent:
this was the connotation which this word had for Democritus, Lucretius, Gassendi, Newton, Dalton, Boltzmann,
and even for Lorentz: something indestructible and uncreatable. How can such a word be meaningfully applied
to these new strange entities some of which last only a
trillionth or even a quadrillionth of second? Are we
not stretching the meaning of the word "corpuscle" a
bit too far when we apply it to such evanescent entities? Are we not simply yielding to the sheer inertia
of our traditional language? Would not the term
"event" be much more appropriate? Nothing illustrates
more strikingly the profound difference between the
rigid and permanent atoms of the classical kinetic view
of nature and these new event-like entities which are
born out of radiation and disappear in a puff of radiation and whose strange behavior is described by such
terms as "decay" or "multiplication," which certainly
would have made the great Newton shudder in disbelief.

It may be objected that these strange entities possess the corpuscular character at least during their own short life. But even this is not true. For the word "particle" or "corpuscle" means--if it means anything at all--an association of two features: definite position and definite momentum. Yet, if we take Heisenberg's indeterminacy principle seriously, we cannot meaningfully speak of anything of this kind, not because anything of this kind cannot be found in nature, but because it does not exist in nature. Another article would be necessary to discuss two conflicting interpretations of the principle of indeterminacy and, because of the space limitation, I have to make a very concise and dogmatic-sounding statement: the hope that classical determinism and the classical corpuscular model will be recovered on the sub-quantum level, although not entirely unreasonable, seems to the majority of physicists highly unrealistic, especially when we realize that this hope is mainly due to the persistence of the traditional modes of thought.

What then is left of classical physics? Remember that we said it will always be taught on a high school level and in the elementary college courses for one simple reason: that the classical laws are valid in the world in which we live. And this undoubtedly accounts for the fact that classical physics, and the modes of thinking which characterize it, will always appear to the human mind as inherently more attractive and more natural. For our thinking draws nearly all its material from our sensory perception; and our sensory perception is macroscopic. In other words, what we perceive is not matter itself, not reality itself but the macroscopic surface of reality, or, to use Reichenbach's word, the world of middle dimensions which is situated half-way between the electrons and galaxies. We perceive only what has a biological importance for the preservation of individuals or species; for this reason it would be biologically uneconomic if we would perceive the vanishing non-Euclidian curvature of space or negligible microphysical indeterminacy. Although we know that solidity is not the attribute of the ultimate elements of the physical world, it still remains a real quality of our sensory perception which, so to speak, condenses into one single quality of touch an enormous number of the microphysical events in a similar way as our sight condenses in a single quality of color an enormous number of successive electromagnetic vibrations. It would be thoroughly uneconomical if we would perceive each photon

313

and each electron separately; thus the world of sensory
perception is a highly useful, but also a highly selective simplification of the tremendously complex physical reality.

Out of this sensory perception grew classical
physics and to a great extent classical philosophy.
That classical physics was essentially the physics of
solid bodies can hardly be doubted; the persistent
tendency to reduce all phenomena to mechanics, i.e., to
the motion of solid units, indicates it clearly. But
what about classical philosophy? Certainly atomism was
not the only philosophical tradition. But if we take
into account how the traditional concept of Being developed from the Eleatic notion of the solid sphere; if
we remember how the Being of philosophers shared its
rigidity and its static character with the matter of
Democritus and Newton; if we bear in mind the permanent
fascination which this idea of rigid Being exerted on
the imagination of philosophers from Parmenides to
Sartre and Paul Tillich--then perhaps Bergson's nearly
forgotten claim that our logic is a logic of solid bodies would sound less strange. This is made even more
probable by the following consideration: the mechanistic, i.e., corpuscular-kinetic model of nature remained
amazingly successful as long as its application was
confined to the world of middle dimensions, to the
world of our daily life, to the world where the veloc-
ities are negligible, and the quantum discontinuities
can be safely disregarded. Was not this success due to
the fact that our thinking and imagination with its instinctive preferences for the atomistic and kinetic explanation was a result of adjustment to this middle
sector of reality? And that the paradoxes and oddities
which our imagination and even our thought faces are
due to our instinctive attempt to apply our mechanistic
modes of thought even outside of the area to which they
were originally adjusted? Time is lacking to outline
in a more detailed way the biological theory of knowledge which in my view is the only one explaining satis-
factorily both the amazing fruitfulness and applicability of the mechanistic and visual models within certain
ranges of experience and their complete failure and inadequacy outside of the same range.

But does not this sound rather discouraging and
intellectually defeatistic? If our thought is hopelessly contaminated by our macroscopic perception, does
it mean that it will be forever confined in its understanding to the world of middle dimensions? Certainly

not. Although I said that our thought is macroscopi-
cally conditioned, I did not say that is is hopelessly
so. The whole development of post-Newtonian physics
indicates the very contrary. I do not mean only the
fact that physicists are now so intellectually emanci-
pated that they are not and will not be surprised by
any new discovery, no matter how surprising and contrary to their intellectual habits it may be. This may
be just an effect of a new habit; one eventually gets
used to everything, even to the miraculous. And the
state of intellectual apathy which is thus created may
be even dangerous because it is incompatible with the
capacity of wonder, of astonishment, which--in this respect I would side with Aristotle--is one of the basic
presuppositions of philosophy, including philosophy of
nature. What I mean is a wonderful flexibility of the
mathematical formalism which helped the creators of the
new theories in physics to free themselves of the exclusive sway of the Newton-Euclidian intellectual
habits. Whether this will be sufficient remains to be
seen. One can object that even the most abstract mathematics is not entirely free of the original biological
tinge; does not the process of counting presuppose the
permanence of the objects counted, as Helmholtz pointed
out in one of his essays? And with regard to Georg
Cantor's definition of set (in German Menge) as a "collection of definite and separate objects,"8 it can
hardly be denied that we can discern behind the apparently abstract concept of "object" its sensory root--a
solid body of our macroscopic experience, the concept
of which is so utterly inapplicable to microphysics.
But we should not despair. Although our present
thought even in its most abstract forms is conditioned
by the macroscopic environment, it is never completely
dependent on it. I find it highly significant that
just about at the same time when modern physics was
born--at the beginning of this century--psychologists
rediscovered what they called imageless thought which
clearly transcends the limits of sensory thought;9 and
it will be along the line of imageless thought that in
my view--or should I say in my hope?--a deeper understanding of the paradoxical structure of matter will
eventually be obtained.

One may ask: what practical significance can the
second scientific revolution have besides the well
known spectacular technological achievements which certainly are not an unmixed blessing? Such a question
reflects the very widespread superficial view which
tends to equate science with technology and which

completely disregards intellectual curiosity which is
the basic motive of any search for truth, whether in
science or in philosophy. I can hardly imagine a more
significant and more far-reaching intellectual event
than what d'Abro called "the decline of mechanism" in
physics. For three centuries the mechanistic view of
nature ruled unchallenged; and for more than two millennia strict determinism, whether in its theological
or naturalistic form, dominated the majority of the
greatest minds. We are hardly in a position to measure
adequately the implications and possible effects of the
fact that mechanism as well as strict determinism are
now seriously questioned within the science which was
always regarded as the stronghold of both views.

Again I hear the objection: what can the revision
of microphysical determinism conceivably have to do
with determinism in biology, psychology, and social or,
as it is fashionable to say today, behavioral sciences?
Is not man a part of the world of middle dimensions
where the statistical regularities of the microphysical
processes converge asymptotically to the certainty of
classical causality? Or in more simple words: is not
the human and social realm, even according to modern
physics, still ruled by strict determinism?

This, in my view, would be a dangerous half-truth.
It is true that generally the indeterminacies of micro-
events cancel each other in large macroscopic aggregates whose behavior thus can be described for all
practical purposes by the classical deterministic laws.
Only in such a way can the statistical laws of microphysics produce the orderly and almost strictly determined world of matter as we know it from our daily experience. But we must not overlook the crucial importance of the qualifying word "almost." We must not
forget that, although the physical universe is made of
heterogeneous strata--that is of the microcosmos, of
the world of the middle dimension, and of what may be
called megacosmos--these strata are not separated by
sharp boundaries and that they are in perpetual interaction. There is no question that under special conditions a microscopic indetermination can produce a spectacular effect in the world of the middle dimensions,
possibly even on the astronomical scale. While this is
rather an exceptional spontaneous occurrence in the inorganic world, it may be, according to some physicists
and biologists, a regular occurrence in the organic
bodies which were characterized by the physicist

Pascual Jordan as "multiplicators of microphysical indetermination."

Jordan's hypothesis was much criticized by the
positivists of the Vienna Circle, and their criticism
was to some degree justified; for Jordan rather naïvely
identified a single microphysical indeterminacy within
the brain with free voluntary decision. On the other
hand, it was fairly obvious that the generally hostile
attitude of Jordan's critics was mainly due to their
conscious or semi-conscious commitment to the mechanistic modes of thought. With the single exception of
Reichenbach, all of them--Schlick, Zilsel, Frank--were
made visibly unhappy by the very thought that the classical settlement of the controversy between determinism
and indeterminism is perhaps not beyond dispute and
that recent physics created the conditions for new solution.[10] To consider possibility open-mindedly does
not mean to be committed to Jordan's inadequate formulation. John Dewey, who certainly cannot be accused of
supernaturalism, and who reacted very promptly to the
discovery of the indeterminacy principle in his book
Quest for Certainty (1929) formulated this view more
cautiously in saying that microphysical indeterminacy
is merely a necessary, though not sufficient, condition
for freedom.[11] Is not angry impatience and intolerance
which is shown--more by some philosophers than scien-
tists--toward this idea a symptom--I would say almost a
psychoanalytical symptom--of their unconscious loyalty
to the nineteenth-century modes of thought?

I am only raising this question; I am only stating
my personal belief that we are at the threshold of a
new era in the intellectual history of mankind when we
begin to guess only remotely the implications of the
present upheaval in physics. Personally, I find fasci-
nating the possibility that the era of our belief in
psychological determinism and historical necessity,
which was clearly a heritage of classical physics, is
coming to an end. I am fascinated by the possibility
that the era of mechanization of the world picture, by
which the human mind was either eliminated or exiled
into the limbo of casual inefficacy, is coming to an
end. Mechanistic determinism had its positive effects
in the increase of our control of physical nature; but
in human affairs its influence was mostly disastrous.
The superstition of historical inevitability produced--
and still produces--two different effects both of which
are clearly negative. The totalitarian movements of
both rightist and leftist orientation cheerfully

317

identified themselves with historical necessity. No cliché was more worn out than that of the inevitable expansion and victory of the Nordic race as envisioned by Pangermanism and the Nazi racist theories; no cliche is today more tiresomely familiar than that of "the inevitable victory of scientific socialism" or "socialistic humanism"--which is neither scientific nor humanistic. It was not without reason that Karl Popper, who borrowed the term "open society" from Bergson while leaving out its philosophical context, dedicated his book, The Poverty of Historicism, to "all the victims of the superstition of historical determinism who died in the Nazi and Communist concentration camps." The attitude of democracy toward the same idea was not much different. Before the First World War Herbert Spencer identified the progressive democratization of mankind with allegedly inevitable progress, and this belief persists in spite of the tragic frustrations of both World Wars, in spite of the fact that the alleged historical inevitability brought about instead of a greater freedom the worst types of tyranny encountered in history. Yet, the superstition of historical necessity still dominates the leading minds of the Western world. Instead of questioning this superstition itself, they prefer to question the value of the democratic ideals and institutions; thus every expansion of tyranny is hailed as "a historically inevitable social development" while every opposition to it is cursed as an interference with the historical necessity itself--as if such necessity could be interfered with. It is time to realize that the road to democracy, that is, the transition from the closed to the open society, will not take place in a necessary inevitable way, but that it can be realized only by an active effort the result of which remains highly uncertain and is not sanctioned by any historical fatality. This should only increase our feeling of responsibility.

I am not making any dogmatic predictions about an inevitable coming of a certain type of philosophy; to make such a prediction would be incompatible with my disbelief in historical necessity. I mentioned some instances showing that anticipatory insights may be delayed by the natural inertia of human thought and may be even wilfully suppressed by the intervention of external authority. But as long as we succeed in keeping our open society, we should remain alert and keep our mind open to new and far-reaching implications of the second scientific revolution, no matter how sharply they may clash with the cultural heritage of the past.

FOOTNOTES

[1]"The Cult of 'Common Usage,' " British Journal for the Philosophy of Science, (III) 1952-3, pp. 303-7.

[2]F. J. Dyson, in Scientific American, vol. 120 (March 1954), p. 92.

[3]Cf. on this point the article of Louis de Broglie, "Léon Brunschvicg et l'évolution des sciences," in Revue de métaphysique et de morale, vol. 50 (1945), pp. 72-6.

[4]This was pointed by Gaston Bachelard, Le nouvel esprit scientifique (P.U.F., 1946), pp. 131-3; 175-6.

[5]A. O. Lovejoy, "The Paradox of Thinking Behaviorist," The Philosophical Review, XXXI (1922).

[6]Matiére et memoire, 28th ed. (1934), p. 241: "Les atomes qui se poussent et s'entrechoquent ne sont point autre chose que les perceptions tactiles objectivées, détachées des autres perceptions en raison de l'importance exceptionnelle qu'on leur attribue, et érigées en réalités indépendantes . . . ."

[7]Robert Oppenheimer, The Constitution of Matter (Condon Lectures, 1956).

[8]"bestimmte und wohlunterschiedene Objekte" in Georges Cantor's terminology.

[9]Alfred Binet's article "La Pensée sans images," appeared in Revue Philosophique, 1903.

[10]Jordan's articles appeared in Naturwissenschaften, XX (1932) and Erkenntnis, IV (1934), pp. 215-252; the resulting discussion in Einheit der Wissenschaft (1935), pp. 178-184.

[11]John Dewey, The Quest for Certainty. Gifford Lectures, 1929, Reprinted in 1960 in Capricorn Books (G. P. Putnam's Sons, New York), pp. 249-250.

SUGGESTED READINGS

Milic Capek

Capek, Milic. The Philosophical Impact of Contemporary Physics (New York: Van Nostrand, 1961).

_____. Bergson and Modern Physics (New York: Humanities Press; Dordrecht, Holland: Reidel, 1971), Vol. VII, Boston Studies in the Philosophy of Science, Synthese Library.

_____. Ed. The Concepts of Space and Time: Their Structure and Development (Boston, Mass.: D. Reidel Co., 1975).

* * *

Schlegel, Richard. "Quantum Physics and Human Purpose," Zygon, VIII, 4 (September-December 1973), 200-220.

Gunter, Pete A. Y. "Review of Bergson and Modern Physics by Milic Capek," Southwestern Journal of Philosophy, VI, 1 (Winter 1975), 155-166.

Leclerc, Ivor. "The Necessity Today of the Philosophy of Nature," Process Studies, III, 3 (Fall 1973), 158-168.

Waddington, C. H. "The Practical Consequences of Metaphysical Beliefs on a Biologist's Work: An Autobiographical Note," in Towards a Theoretical Biology, Vol. II, Sketches, C. H. Waddington, Editor (Chicago: Aldine, 1969), 72-81.

* * *

Von Weizsacker, C. F. The History of Nature (Chicago: University of Chicago Press, 1966).

Hesse, Mary B. Models and Analogies in Science (Notre Dame, Indiana: University of Notre Dame Press, 1966).

Harris, Errol E. The Foundation of Metaphysics in Science (New York: Humanities Press, 1965).

ETHICS

"To be ethical
is to seek aesthetic optimization
of experience for the community."

Charles Hartshorne

Bernard Eugene Meland
by John B. Spencer
Daniel Day Williams
Henry Nelson Wieman
Charles Hartshorne

13. MELAND'S ALTERNATIVE IN ETHICS:

AN AESTHETIC APPROACH

John B. Spencer

John B. Spencer received his education at
Franklin College (A.B., 1940), Indiana University, Colgate Rochester Divinity School
(D.B., 1945), and the University of Chicago
(Ph.D., 1966). He taught at Keuka College,
Keuka Park, New York (1961-62), and since
that time has taught in the Religion Depart-
ment of Kalamazoo College, Kalamazoo, Michigan.

This essay by John Spencer was suggested by Dr.
Meland as expressing well his ethical position.* We
consider its inclusion here to be important for several
reasons. First, Meland considers it as a very fair
presentation of his thinking with respect to ethics,
and is most appreciative of it in as much as he no
longer considers his ideas expressed much earlier in
"Two Paths to the Good Life" to be entirely representative of his ethical views. Second it not only shows
that Dr. Meland possesses a definitive ethic, but indicates that he has a very substantial and significant
one. And thirdly, an explication of Meland's aesthetic
approach to ethics helps to illustrate the real contribution process philosophy can make in constructing a
realistic and relevant ethic for man in the contemporary world. Spencer indicates that the term 'ethics'
is used here in the broad sense, roughly equivalent to
"the study of how best to act as a human being," and
the terms 'morals' and 'morality' refer to a definite
program of principles or directives enjoined as "the
way of life." Thus a moral code, of which there are
many, is considered as a species of answers to the
question of ethics. The author finds a much more

---

*Essay also appears in Process Studies, VI, 3
(Fall 1976), 165-180. Used by permission of John
Spencer and Process Studies.

radical approach to ethics in the writings of Meland, however, than that found in the growing systems of ethical theory which emphasize moral principles and directives. Rather he sees Meland rejecting morality as the sole, or even primary, content of ethics, and proposing an ethic which has its importance in relationship to a devotion to beauty.[#] This ethic, which expresses the aesthetic unity of reality, is then seen as the key to interpreting and fulfilling the characteristic weaknesses of the teleological, deontological, and the cathekontic types of ethics. The ethic is in turn based upon an aesthetic metaphysic of internal relations. The metaphysical characteristic of these relations is feeling; that is, the ultimate creativity is a matrix of concerns and feelings of valuation out of which grow coordinations of various levels of complex experiences that in turn provides the individual with a 'structure of experience' for his own personal character formation and decision making--in relationship, of course, to the total community.

[#]The beauty which justifies ethical judgements for Meland is not to be confused with the aesthete's "mere qualitative harmony." He has in mind that kind of beauty which Whitehead calls "truthful beauty," and to which he refers as "provocative of a noble discontent" and the "critical discontent which is the gadfly of civilization." Cf. Adventures of Ideas, pp. 12, 13, 309-381.

Meland's Alternative in Ethics:
An Aesthetic Approach

We will begin by noting a typology of ethical systems. These will then be related to a Whiteheadian
aesthetic analysis of an occasion of choice. It will
be discovered that the various types of ethical theory
can be reconciled when they are adequately related to
the aesthetic structure of choice. Then we will note
the distorting effects upon each type when the essential reference to the aesthetic ground is ignored.

H. R. Niebuhr, in The Responsible Self, uses a
typology which should help us in this project. He refers to three types of ethical theory: the teleological, the deontological, and the cathekontic. As he
indicates:

> Purposiveness [teleology] seeks to answer the
> question: "What shall I do?" by raising as
> prior the question: "What is my goal, ideal,
> or telos?" Deontology tries to answer the
> moral query by asking, first of all: "What
> is the law and what is the first law of my
> life?" Responsibility [cathekontic ethics],
> however, proceeds in every moment of decision
> and choice to inquire: "What is going on?"
> If we use value terms then the differences
> among the three approaches may be indicated
> by the terms, the good, the right, and the
> fitting; for teleology is concerned always
> with the highest good to which it subordinates
> the right; consistent deontology is concerned
> with the right, no matter what may happen to
> our goods; but for the ethics of responsibility
> the fitting action, the one that fits into a
> total interaction as response and as anticipa-
> tion of further response, is alone conducive
> to the good and alone is right.[1]

Ethical obligation is dependent upon aesthetic obligation. It is a specialized form of the metaphysically general obligation which characterizes every actual thing, and thus every act of choosing.[2] Since
experience as it occurs concretely is always actually
in process, it can best be understood in terms of the
following three sets of relationships: the relationship to the past is its inheritance; the relationship
to the future is its anticipation and the locus of its
influence; and its internal set of relationships in the

present constitutes its combined response to that particular inheritance and that particular anticipation whereby that particular occasion is something for itself. In other words, every occasion of experience (and there are for Whitehead no other actual things at all) is responsible to the givenness of its past, imposes its preferences on those other occasions into whose existence it subsequently merges, and creates itself in its own pattern of response to both of the other sets of relationships.

These sets of relationships constitutive of an occasion of experience express categories of obligation. Each set gives rise to a type of obligation; from these in turn are derived the types of ethical theory described in Niebuhr's typology. The decision of the present moment of experience is obliged to the given structures of the past which constitute its inheritance. These structures causally define its basic character and limits and thus set its task, though this determination always leaves the present moment free with respect to _how_ it will constructively carry out the imperatives in this situation. The fundamental obligation which the concrescence owes the past in the present is faithfulness to the richness of possibility given by the past, thus fulfilling it. The obligation is categorical precisely because it is the ineluctable presence of the past which constitutes the obligation. To be included is to require being taken account of, to present a claim (that is, to obligate).

Likewise, that this present moment will be included in the future sets up an obligation toward the future. In this future which is coming into being, the imprint of the decision of the present moment of experience is indelible. It will require being taken account of, being completed. The creativity of the occasion becomes a creative influence on the future. The power to shape the future constitutes a claim against the present to consider the consequences of its choice. These consequences for the future are the causal impact of the present occasion upon the world which _must_ receive it. Here, too, there is freedom toward the future as to _how_ the present will exert its influence. But there is no freedom from the obligation of exerting _some_ _one_ particular influence.

Finally, the internal set of relationships which is the becoming of the present occasion is the response of that occasion to the totality of inheritance and the

totality of anticipation which present themselves for
decision. To become as a fully concrete participant in
the creative passage means to respond to this totality
in such a way as to emerge as something for oneself.
Without unifying the multitude of claims presented by
the givens and by the possibilities into one response,
there can be no one actual occasion at all. But there
are always more ways than one of settling these relationships to the universe as a whole. These various
possible patterns of total response and contribution
differ in the degree of their adequacy to the full reality of that total situation. Thus they also differ
in depth and intensity. The universe in its total unity thus obligates the particular occasion in its total
unity.

In other words, every act is constituted: (1) by
the obligatory relation to the past, which in its determinacy demands of it relevance and continuity with
the basic given structures; (2) by the obligatory relation to the future, which in its indeterminacy lures by
visions of the control of the future through influential action taken in the present; and (3) by the obligatory unity of response to what is going on, which requires imaginative creativity with relevance and responsibility for consequences. Thus every occasion is
a product, an influence, and a response. And every
product, every influence, and every response requires
normative decision.

Now it can be seen how these sets of relationships
and their corresponding types of obligation suggest
four kinds of ethical theory, three of which have been
captured in Niebuhr's typology.

The first interpretation sees the occasion of ethical decision essentially as a product with a general
character determined by what is already settled. Its
good will consist of accepting the obligation of conformity with the given basic structures, which are presented in the form of natural or other general laws.
Some type of deontological ethical theory will result
from this emphasis.

The second interpretation sees the occasion of
ethical choice essentially as an influence with a future role as shaper, improver, controller. Its good
will be to perfect future phases of the presently indeterminate future according to evaluations made in the
present but having the character of an ideal. Some

kind of teleological ethical theory will result from this emphasis.

The third interpretation sees the occasion of ethical choice essentially as a <u>response</u> to a universe composed of both givens and possibilities. Its good will consist of acting in the manner most fitting to the ultimate character of the situation which holds it in being. Some kind of cathekontic or situational ethic will result from this emphasis.

This would seem to exhaust the ethical alternatives. However, it is here that Meland makes his key suggestion. He pleads in many books and articles for seeing the occasion of ethical choice as essentially a moment in the creative adventure of a <u>spirit</u> in a community of other spirits. Its good consists of appreciating and serving the richest beauty, in company with others whose love of beauty holds them all in common gratitude, working together, contending with each other in courageous devotion to the vision of beauty held by each, forgiving one another in trust, celebrating together their common devotion expressed in different ways, thus fed by, contributing to, and fighting for the increasing intensity and significance of their communal existence which occurs when it is understood as essentially a matter of individual solution to existence posed as a moral problem, regardless of whether that problem is seen as how to be faithful to the given structures of human life, or how to be faithful to the vision of the ideal human life, or how to be faithful to the specific facts of the total situation of the present.

The most specialized ethical emphases of obligation to the given past, to the perfectible future, and to the most inclusive reality are caught up and transformed in this aesthetic ethic of the final importance of devotion to beauty. The richest beauty justifies the continuity, orderliness, and fullest expression of the inherited structure stressed by deontological ethics. It also justifies the imaginative dedication to entering the future as a contributor to the kind and degree of beauty possible there. It also justifies discriminating with the matrix of internal relations the actual character of the inclusive meanings and making a fitting response to this character. Thus the key interpretation is the aesthetic one. "Beauty" is the answer we get when we ask the ultimate "why?" The more specialized ethical emphases are themselves fulfilled and interrelated from this standpoint.

The characteristic weaknesses of these other ethical theories are illuminated by considering them as the result of the fragmentation of the aesthetic whole. Each of the fragmented emphases tends to lack a full appreciation of the full nature of obligation. Deontological ethics tends toward the absolutizing of the apodictic authority of the given order. Teleological ethics is threatened with the abstract irrelevance of the ideal to the rich concrete givenness of the conditions. And cathekontic ethics lacks objective direction, lapsing into the unintended absolutizing of the set of conditions which happen to present themselves to that person at that moment as the ultimate character of the situation. Another way of putting this same point is to notice how ethics loses its dialectical character when the aesthetic unity is forgotten. Deontological and teleological ethics absolutize one of another kind of static perfection, given or to be achieved. Cathekontic ethics loses its reliability and prescriptive power because there can be no training in "fittingness," nor is there a stopping point in the analysis of the situation at which one has now discovered how it really is, so that his response may be appropriate. A successful attempt on the part of any one of these types to overcome its characteristic weaknesses will move in the direction of supplementation by the other types of obligation. But no amount of mere supplementation seems to add up to the reconception which is needed.

Since moral obligation is rooted in the aesthetic character of reality, it fragments into competing claims for ultimate ethical authority when divorced from this aesthetic ground. Those claims which stress the obligation of the present to the past see moral obligation as imposed by given structures, and thus demand continuity with them (obedience). Those which stress the obligation of the present to the future see moral obligation as the claim of an ideal to direct sacrifice, improvement, and change, and thus demand discontinuity with the past and achievement of a new society. Those which stress the creative responsive role of the present moment see moral obligation as emerging new from each present context of givens and ideals, and thus demand an attitude of "love," indecisive "openness" as the permanent stance, loyalty to the Leader, or complete analysis of the factuality in each situation.

In all of these truncated interpretations the individual is set over against a reality which makes demands on him in the face of which his worth as a person
depends upon his individual response. He must accomplish the goodness either by conformity or by achievement or by the fitting response, directed by the demand.
He is constantly on trial morally, and every good thing
in his life depends upon his sole adequacy in act. In
addition, the goodness which is incumbent upon him must
be that which he and his fellows can and do readily understand. He is not morally obligated by anything
which he does not already accept as obligating him.
Finally, the problematic moments of choice tend to be
assimilated to the kinds of issues for which there are
already principles, projects, and/or attitudes specifying kinds of response and action. Obligations individual are subsumed under obligations general, to which
moral answers can be clearly given. Complicated, rich
situations are trivialized and contorted into the mere
material of the moral conflict and the weighing and
reconciling of moral categories. The rich possibilities and actualities of living are reduced for the sake
of the harmony that can be readily achieved. In this
way moral demands are clearly identified and satisfied--
at the expense of the attenuation of significance.

II

An aesthetic ethic is a matter of feelings. Its
two basic virtues are openness to the universe of interrelated feelings and discrimination of quality. The
good is quality of experience, or beauty. It does
emerge into human existence, but it is not simply the
product of human intention.

The infinite variety in the universe of feelings
is graded in degrees of intensity and of harmonization.
The actual world is a complex of structured feelings,
internally linked into a bewildering maze of social
orders, each of which endures by obligating its member
entities to transmit its pattern. Also each such member entity of any such society is also a member in
other respects of many other such societies. All past
entities must be taken into account by present emerging
experience in some fashion.* And every society likewise

---

*This is merely the recognition of the principle
of causality.

presses its own claim. It is these claims of the past actualities and societies which constitute the first and basic aesthetic obligation. They are all felt, not merely as objects to be known, but as values which are of concern to the emerging individual occasion. From this arises the second aesthetic obligation, that of finding one response or act which will acknowledge these many claims in the way of greatest satisfaction. But, in order to receive the greatest satisfaction and participate in the greatest beauty, the future effects of this decision must be taken into account, and this is the third aesthetic obligation.

When this moment of self-constituting action resolving the claims and consequences of the whole universe is considered in all of its actual complexity, the pretense of moralistic ethics to judge by its handful of principles, or to take responsibility for control of the future of the universe in the name of its one ideal or single pattern of ideal perfection, or to identify the "reality" to which one should make the relevant response, seems naively presumptuous, and at the same time a hopeless enterprise. There is mounting evidence that this typically Western mode of approaching the ordering of existence has had a direct bearing upon some of the most hideous injustices of our civilization and of the world. Action which is aware of its responsibility only to one authority--whether this be a prescriptive principle or set of principles, or a reigning ideal of perfection, or even one God whose will is known--disconnects action from the fullness of aesthetic reality, from minority claims, from emerging creative novelties, from the richness. ambiguity, and mystery of the present reality. In fact, this is what it is intended to do, for who can consciously weigh, or even become aware of, such a bewildering and disordered and discordant reality? The result of the dominance of this moral way of life tends to be the withering away of sensitivity and the brutalizing of the dominant powers of a given region.

III

The preeminent resource for the elaboration of an aesthetic ethic is Bernard Meland, who has for years protested against the brutalizing, desensitizing, and dehumanizing course of human affairs under the leadership of the moralistic and idealistic ethics of the West. Even Meland, however, is still learning the

dimensions of this tragedy. There is an especially
striking instance of this recorded in his Roger Williams
Fellowship lecture in which he speaks of the aesthetic
reality of the white man's burden:

> I must say that, in my initial encounter with
> people of India and the Far East, I strongly
> resented the charge of imperialism that was
> continually made against us as Westerners.*
> On subsequent reflection I have come to real-
> ize that the impact of imperialistic powers
> on the East and other cultures is the one stub-
> born fact of our Western history that will not
> die. And now that it is in the open and made
> stark and unsettling to every sensitive West-
> ern conscience, it tends to put the lie to our
> pretensions of idealism and moral concern for
> humanity; or at least to question it. The
> demonry of the West's imperialistic history
> in the East has been matched only by our own
> enslavement of a whole segment of our people
> in America; and by the eruptions of massive
> acts of inhumanity within Western culture in
> recent history, notably among a nation of peo-
> ple acclaimed to be the principal fashioners
> of modern idealism and its liberal faith.[3]

But in what way can an aesthetic ethic be not only
aesthetically adequate to the fullness of actuality,
but also ethical; that is, a guide in some sense for
living? The aesthetic ethic must indicate at least
general directions for the adequate and selective response upon which it insists, or it is no ethic.

It is clear that an aesthetic ethic must presuppose an aesthetic metaphysic. The inadequacy of moralistic and rationalistic ethics, as we have seen, is
intimately related to the inadequacy of the metaphysic
presupposed. As the artists have known all along, the
situations talked about by the professional moralists
are constructed for that very purpose, and do not correspond to "the way things really are." Analyses of
such constructions can be counted on to show just those
factors which the advocated theory needs for its support. But decisions actually made in passage seem

---

*Meland feels he also reflects this in The Reali-
ties of Faith. Cf. pp. 3-74.

always to reflect the "undue" influence of factors that are not ordinarily thought of as moral at all.[4]

The aesthetic ethic rests on an aesthetic metaphysic. This understanding of the ultimate structure of things allows for no sheer irrelevance. It distinguishes between the simplified edition of reality which is the context of conscious decisions and the actual causal efficacy with which in our actions we are actually dealing. There can be no "eternal" principles or ideals which unfailingly define for us the good in each situation. The crude approximations in terms of which conscious moral judgements must be made "have their day" and are refined or superseded as the shifting patterns of good and evil shape our viewpoint on the significance of our inheritance, the total situation, and the ultimacy of our goals. Each situation in its full concreteness has its own structure, not to be adequately judged simply by comparison with some general prescription nor with some perfect ideal; in fact not by any conscious assessment. The more adequate judgement must come from a more adequate sensitivity to the felt importance, beauty, and intensity actually resident in the moment of experience and likely to contribute an increase of such enhancement of life for the future.

The appreciative consciousness is the indispensable guide to understanding any problem, situation, crises, or impending peril, as well as to dealing constructively with events of scope or of imaginative proportions. For the facts of crucial importance in any such situation are always relational within a dynamic context. The wrong decisions generally proceed from an inadequate grasp of the moving and changing status of facts and relationships. What was unanticipated overwhelms the calculations; and the unexpected happens, often not because the facts gave no hint of the outcome, but because there were no eyes to see or to attend to these relational and transitive factors that formed the pattern of emerging events which generated its movement . . . . Once complexity is acknowledged to be the actual status of any living or dynamic situation, denying the complexity or ignoring it through measures of simplifying the data in order to assure exact scrutiny, can only lead to a false perspective, idealizing the implications. In a world of complex meanings, plagued by forces of

incalculable possibilities, and of ambiguous
intent, there can be no realism of judgement
or of understanding except as facts are seen
in their relations and in their condition of
becoming, and in terms of the intimations of
meaning which these relations and tendencies
imply. This is the realism of the appreciative mind.[5]

Thus Meland has developed a metaphysical description which grounds such an aesthetic ethic.

He begins with the connectedness of existence, re-
lying here on the doctrine of internal relations as
Whitehead developed it:

Deeper than the self is the creative passage,
the creativity, the ongoingness, the space-
time continuum, where the event seems indistinguishable from events. All living is
contained in this medium and is sustained
as a temporal-spatial event by reason of
being continuous with it . . . . There is
this depth in our nature that brings our
subjective life into creatural rapport with
all creatures, and with the creative Source
of our being.[6]

This "realm of internal relations" contains everything. Whitehead refers to it as the "Receptacle." It
constitutes for man the flow of experience of which he
is a part, the inexhaustible river of feeling bearing
him along. The metaphysical character of these relations is feeling and even "concern."[7] That is, the ultimate creativity is a matrix of concerns and feelings
of valuation out of which grow coordinations of various
levels of complex experiences.

Relations are thus seen to suggest not simply
the notion of pattern but the interaction of
structures in a way which makes for a subtle
progression from lower to higher organizations
of events. A binding factor, which is at the
same time a thrust toward the advancing sensitivity of structures, is thus noted as a persisting horizon of mystery and promise attending each actualized order or structure.[8]

Thus the flow of events of feeling is partially
ordered and these orders are structures of value; that

is, they embody values which are the modes of synthesis
of past values coordinated into fresh intensities, only
to pass on themselves to future events for which they
are given. Bare creativity ensures that the past will
be inherited as an obligation in the present of the
values of the past. The present arises as a necessary
response to that past with its value, partly compatible
and partly not, far too complex and mysterious for conscious sorting or understanding, yet with determinative
power in the present.

> Depths of actuality, inaccessible to conscious
> experience, will escape awareness and intelli-
> gibility, and thus be beyond demonstration of
> truth; yet be able to determine or destroy in-
> telligibility itself.[9]

The richness, the mystery, the complexity, the
depth of inheritance into which man is born is beyond
comprehension. It is the universe in that moment, with
all of its particularities of past events and their interconnections and their meanings and values and possibilities. It is at this point, perhaps, that the question arises as to the very possibility of an aesthetic
ethic, for the sensitive awareness of this flux with
its bewildering variety of claims would surely tend to
incapacitate action altogether. How could there be
ethical direction from an appreciative awareness open
to this only partly coordinated flood of causal efficacy? It may be that what Fry refers to as "Establish-
ment ethics" does fail to do justice to the "rationally
unaccountable, ethically nonnormative purely evanescent,
absolutely local, hence crucial shape of circumstances,"[10] but can any ethic? Is it not necessary
to posit even inadequate principles to contribute stability and direction, even though they can now be seen
for the abstract and insensitive systems that they are?
After all they do impose some order and direction.
Openness would seem to guarantee only bewilderment.

IV

Meland's response to this crucial question of an
ethic based upon aesthetics is to point out that the
past of a particular event is not all that chaotic.
The individual is born into a particular tradition.
His relationship to the total past is by way of an actual sequence of events within which there has emerged
a certain general character. The person making moral

choices shares along with the other members this same
order of cultural inheritance. Meland's term for this
key concept is the "structure of experience."

When this notion becomes clear in reading Meland's
work, many other things fall into place. For it is the
complex relationship between the individual and the
depth of his own cultural and natural concrete accumulation that provides the basis for the meaningfulness
of an aesthetic ethic. The structure of experience
furnishes the definiteness in experience required for
individual orientation for any decision. The massive
inheritance out of which each individual comes and from
which he derives the depths of his own present existence thus already has definite character. This character is the outcome of a long accumulation of former
decisions. It gathers itself around a core of significant meanings, with formative images. These images
bear the meanings from generation to generation. They
also furnish the terms by reference to which modifications of insight can find their places in the living
development of a structure of experience. In other
words, the problem of making sense out of the bewildering variety of causal inheritance does not present itself in an ultimately disabling way because, as a matter of empirical fact, the past bears in itself the
fundamental meanings out of which the individual makes
sense of himself and his situation. The claims of the
past and the future are already coordinated into mutually reinforcing societies, which are dominant and
dominating accumulations of value.

This does not, however, mean that acquaintance
with the cumulative environment calculates the single
appropriate action to take in a particular moment. It
might, but it very likely will not. It does mean that
the individual, to the degree that he participates in
the structure of experience which is his own depth, is
given a general set of valuations which he inherits
along with the situation itself, and which will flow
into that situation and carry him along with them.

Within any nation's or community's history,
then, the present moment of time is laden with
qualitative meaning so complex in character,
being the living distillation of decisions and
resolutions of ages, so profound in implication for all existence and for all present
events, that no single center of consciousness is equal to discerning its burden and

338

its opportunity. Each new generation comes
into an organized inheritance greater in
depth and range than the perceptions of any
living person who is a member of it. Thus
people live in a context of feeling and awareness that is always beyond their grasp emotionally or cognitively. They are not auto-
matically bound by this heritage or by these
relationships; for they, too, are creative
of its emerging structure in the way that
all concrete events have influenced it.
Nevertheless, all living persons carry within their nature something of the hidden drives
and aspirations that rise from accumulative
structure of experience.[11]

That is, every moment starts out equipped with an inherited general character already operative with the
energies of the past valuations fashioned by past decisions into a fairly well-integrated pattern of valuation.

In our bodies, as evidenced by the turn of
the head, the look, the stance, the way we
receive other people, and more hiddenly still,
the probabilities of response, the apprehensions, the concerns, yea the sensibilities--
in all that gives character to the person--we
carry the fund of valuations that give the
total, existential meaning of ourselves as
persons.[12]

This inheritance of a basal character as a member
of a culture, with its valuations as my valuations, and
with my meaning fundamentally given to me, is one side
of the structured freedom of the aesthetic ethic. Freedom is expressed by a structured reality; the richer
the structure, the greater the possibilities for creative decision. But there is on the other hand the work
of the critical intellect of the individual in deciding
the role which this inheritance will play in the actual
events of the course of his particular life. The passage of events compels the present moment to transmit
the past through this particular existence, picking up
its additional increments of qualitative meaning. Acts
of conscious perception and apprehension, and critical
intellection, involve decisions about the kind of effect which the inherited meanings and values will have
in specific situations. The human consciousness abstracts from the fullness of meaning borne by the

339

structure of experience. Its primary function is to
select and heighten experience by emphasis. It can
even become the means of actual dissociation of the
conscious awareness from the structure of experience.
One of the main warnings Meland makes everywhere in his
writings is against the excessive reliance upon the abstractions of the moral and rational consciousness.[13]
An overly moral and rational conscious world is separated from the depth of human existence and is therefore a poverty-stricken one, even involving demonic
illusion.

However, consciousness in its various functions
can also provide the structure of experience with appropriate focus and power. In so doing significance is
heightened by attention to the objective goodness discovered in the values presented for choice in the immediate and future situation. This capacity for emphasis
within the flow and the tension of the structure of experience modifies the inherited structure to some extent. However, the modification is never as simple and
direct as moral and rational exhortations assume.

Our understanding of the life-process as
a structure of experience in which formative
elements of great depth and antiquity continue
to cradle and nurture the human spirit leads
us to grasp more readily the way in which
faith as a cultural energy operates to fulfill human life and culture. In part we are
subconsciously molded as persons and as a
society in the way that a mythos invariably
imposes a distinctive character upon any people. In part, however, we are shaped by whatever decisions we make to selfconsciously
appropriate the valuations that are thus
transmitted.[14]

This power of discrimination for emphasis is the
power to affect the structure of experience and the institutions which arise from it in human civilization is
the fateful power. It generates new forms of experience. These new forms are eventually absorbed into the
accumulated experience, transforming it in significant
(but not always better) ways.

The saint and mystic, as well as the creative
artist, have always been enigmas to the common
life and have generally been considered as
people apart from the accepted mores and

customs of society, sometimes persecuted,
but usually tolerated until circumstances
favored their being revered. Then the special mode of experience which had been exclusively and narrowly cherished became the
course of a new communal experience at a
level at which it could be assimilated into
the common experience.[15]

The process of individuation, which centers a personal life through the particularity of his situation
and exercises the powers of discriminatory response,
enables the person to extend the intensity of his existence through the interplay of persons.

Out of [this] emerges the various patterned
existences which we recognize as companionship, the family, the gang, the club, the
religious fellowship, the community; all of
which widen into a well-defined culture, the
bounds of which are usually geographically,
economically, and politically determined.
. . . It is literally true that human nature,
like creature life at every level, is defined
by this interdependence and mutuality of existence.[16]

Interpersonal existence greatly enhances the intentional power of the individual through the development of symbolization in language. The conceptualizing
power of language conveys comparatively greater freedom
by widening the range of recognizable alternatives. At
the same time, however, it makes more specific, and
thus limits, the access of that person to the fullness
of his own depths.

The deepening of life and the reaping of goodness
are not, however, to be recovered by avoiding individuation, reducing human existence to the nonindividuated
or nonrational "lethargic dependence upon the habitual
routine judgements and valuations persisting as duration," for this, if possible at all, would be a "domesticated animality breathing the bovine contentment of
the pastorale."[17] Rather, human creativity and fulfillment depend upon combining disciplined inquiry and
appreciative awareness. Disciplined inquiry acquaints
one with the facts with precision; appreciative awareness is a heightened and disciplined sensitivity to the
richness of concrete human existence. The effectiveness and honesty of human existence in its endeavors

341

require precise factual knowledge. Wisdom and relevance require the openness and sensitivity of appreciative awareness. Appreciative awareness, because it
encounters actual objective goodness at work in the
depths of existence, discovers redemptive end, aim,
and ultimate meaning for the lives that serve that
goodness.

In this essay, I have chosen to introduce the concept of actual objective goodness at work blessing sensitive human endeavor rather abruptly as an empirical
fact of human existence. Meland treats it as such,
usually in the context of Christian interpretation.
However, it is not only the Christian who participates
in the goodness upon which our human fulfillment depends. This goodness he often describes empirically
in general terms:

> It is this abundance of concrete good in the
> tenuous relationships between people, in the
> depths of men's dedications where they have
> envisaged good beyond themselves, in the
> beauty that unsuspectedly crowds our path,
> in memory of one life or of one people that
> gathers 'the greatness incarnate' of a cul-
> ture into an acknowledged and cherished
> tradition--it is this abundance of goodness
> that saves man from his frustrations, his
> failures, and from tragic loss which every
> life, in some measure, encounters. These
> abstract goods which we call relationships,
> dedications, beauty, memory, always meet us
> in vividly concrete form; in our love for
> some person, or in our oneness with friends,
> in our feelings for the Christ, or in some
> clear glimpse of ultimate truth; in the curve
> of a hill or a certain path that has become
> as a shrine in our thought; in particular
> events in history or some moment in our life-
> time when life's meaning was illumined--
> experiences such as these are for every man
> the means of access to this redemptive good
> that hovers about him daily. In grief, in
> times of desolation, these are the structures
> through which the grace of God is mediated
> as a healing force.[18]

Meland's approach to the analysis of ethics is
similar to that of Richard Niebuhr:

> The object of the inquiry is not, as in
> the case of Christian ethics, simply the
> Christian life but rather human moral life
> in general . . . . My concern here is with
> the understanding of our human life from a
> Christian point of view.[19]

This statement serves to describe Meland's aim, too.
The description of human existence is a metaphysical
one, and the affirmation of the goodness borne along
by the structure of experience is empirical. The
Christian faith is the myth which does in fact convey
"the feeling tone of [Western] culture with regard to
its ultimate dimensions."[20] However, the aesthetic
ethic itself, as an ethic, also calls for the education
of the sensitivities so that there can be the reorien-
tation of the way of life toward the goodness not our
own, where the myth of the Christian faith does not,
for whatever reason, perform this illumination. Sensitive persons in non-Christian cultures participate
knowingly in this grace of the structures of goodness
not of our own devising or controlling.

> The freedom of God would argue that God has
> to do with all men, all cultures, all stages
> of human history, in His way, in His time.
> The depth and scope of this Infinite dealing
> with men of all ages and all races is a mys-
> tery which no one human mind can apprehend,
> and no one culture may engineer or supervise.
> God creates them, and redeems them as the
> sensitivity and ripeness of occasions permit
> and demand.[21]

As an ethic, the aesthetic ethic requires faith in
the goodness not our own and seems clearly to imply a
creative Source of such goodness. However, it does not
itself presuppose a particular religion as its ground.
Meland uses many forms of neutral phrases to emphasize
the empirical character of the experience of a source
of goodness not our own: "the encounter with Spirit,"
"the matrix of sensitivity," "the realm of spirit,"
"stratum of sensitive meanings," "the creative activity
which constantly presses [upon] the human organism,"
"the sensitive nature," "structure of sensitivity,"
"transcendent life of spirit," "order of transcendent
good," "matrix of sensitive relations," "order of sensitivity," "sensitive, communal ground," "sensitive
order of spirit," and so forth. The interpretation of
the faith in objective Goodness can be various; but

without this faith in some form there can be no aesthetic ethic. The interpretation of the faith is not, strictly speaking, a part of the ethic.

V

We have looked at four kinds of ethical theory: deontological, teleological, cathekontic, and aesthetic. The superiority of the aesthetic type of ethic lies in its adequacy to the peculiar concerns of each of the other three, without collapsing into any or all of them. Each such special concern emerges in the aesthetic ethic as properly moral, but not the final ethic. The aesthetic ethic acknowledges the value, though limited, of the moral obligations of continuity and faithfulness to the inherited good from the structure of experience (deontological concern). But it does not need to insist upon any given unchanging structure not itself subject to critical inquiry (that is, apodictic).

The aesthetic ethic acknowledges the legitimate but limited values of the moral obligations of influencing the future toward a better form of existence (teleological concern). But it does not find any final perfection which evaluates the elements of the given situation solely and ruthlessly in terms of its role in bringing this ideal to actualization. Therefore it does not tend to blind the devotee to other kinds and depths of goodness with which such an ideal may well be in severe tension. It can therefore recognize genuine tragedy in the human situation and be open to a real creative transcendence of any particular impasse.

The aesthetic ethic acknowledges the limited value of the moral obligations of loyalty to the reality of the present ultimate context. But it is not required to see itself as the focus of active solutions to this situation. The person whose way of life could be described as an aesthetic ethic searches first for the active, objective goodness which is there in the situation. He serves this active goodness in both its immediate and its general indications. This service is not mere obedience or dedicated vicegerency, but creative, zestful contribution to the communal experience.

Beyond the virtue of including and transcending other kinds of ethical theory the aesthetic ethic encourages wonder, growth, appreciative awareness, imaginative understanding of emerging novelty, and the

344

critical refining of the accepted moral regularities
which do provide the minimum of cooperative order basic
to the exercise of man's spiritual calling--devotion to
beauty and goodness not our own. As Meland indicates:

> Moral and legal codes are the human formula-
> tions through which we tentatively define
> the manageable bounds of behavior. They are
> clearly limited in vision and concern to the
> human community that formulates them. To
> elevate these formulations to the status of
> an ultimate measure is to do precisely what
> theologians and churchmen have often done
> with doctrines and other theological state-
> ments; namely, to confuse the realities of
> faith with human formulations about these
> realities. Legal and moral judgements are
> protective measures undertaken in behalf of
> associated living; but they are subject to
> the judgement of a good not our own, which
> comes as a new creation out of the possibil-
> ities of the immediacies of existence as they
> are made open and transparent to what is ul-
> timately involved in the spontaneous occasion.
> Moral codes cannot anticipate these spontane-
> ous openings of goodness beyond their own
> good, or make binding rules to cover them;
> but they can provide for our human response
> to them by holding law and the moral judge-
> ment subject to their occurrence. To some
> extent this is accomplished in the act of
> interpreting the law or in exercising moral
> judgement in any given situation. Where law
> and moral measure are made inflexible or un-
> yielding as to tolerate no good other than
> what appears to be literally implied in the
> formulations of their own making, they are
> no longer simply protective measures against
> disorder, dissoluteness, and tyranny; they
> have themselves then become obstructive to
> the new creation as a work of grace and judge-
> ment in relationships.

The temptation among those who are awak-
ened to the power of the new creation is to
depreciate law and morals and to see them
solely as being insensitive and obstructive
toward the work of the spirit. I see the
same problem here of relating our human formulations to the depth of realities that

exceed our human measure. These human formulations are to be simultaneously affirmed
and held under judgement of that which is
more than human. Clearly they are occasions
of closure for purposes of decision and direction in human action, and as such they
both protect the good that is discerned within our human vision and define it. Living
faithfully within the human measure is simply
living responsibly within our human structure.
But this faithful existence can be responsive
to the new creation only as it can be open to
the demands or opportunities of the spontane-
ities of existence, which come to us as a
work of grace of judgement out of novel and
creative possibilities in relationships, in
the crises of history, or even in more commonplace circumstances of new occasions.[22]

#

FOOTNOTES

[1]Niebuhr, H. R. The Responsible Self (New York:
Harper and Row, 1963), pp. 60ff. Edward Long, Jr.,
uses a very similar list of 'motifs' in A Survey of
Christian Ethics (New York: Oxford, 1967). Long compares his motifs (deliberative, prescriptive, and relational) with the typology of Niebuhr in an appreicative
critique. Cf. pp. 75ff, and 118-123.

[2]The following analysis of "an occasion of choice"
follows Whitehead.

[3]Meland, B. E. "Narrow is the Way Beyond Absurdity and Anxiety," Criterion, V, 2 (1966), 2. Cf. also
Meland, B. E. The Realities of Faith (New York: Oxford, 1962), pp. 3-74.

[4]Fry, John R. The Immobilized Christian (Philadelphia: Westminster, 1963), for a vivid statement of
this point.

[5]Meland, B. E. Higher Education and the Human
Spirit (Chicago: University of Chicago Press, 1953;
Paperback, Chicago: Seminary Cooperative Bookstore,
1965), p. 78.

[6]Meland, B. E. Faith and Culture (New York: Oxford, 1953; Paperback, Carbondale: University of Southern Illinois Press, 1972), pp. 142-143.

[7]Whitehead, A. N. Adventures of Ideas (New York:
Macmillan, 1933), pp. 226, 232.

[8]Meland, B. E. "Interpreting the Christian Faith
within a Philosophical Framework," The Journal of Religion, XXXIII, 2 (April 1953), 92.

[9]Meland, B. E. Faith and Culture, p. 118.

[10]Cf. Fry, John R. The Immobilized Christian, p.
28.

[11]Meland, B. E. Realities of Faith, pp. 195-196.

[12]Meland, B. E. Faith and Culture, p. 37.

347

[13]Meland, B. E.   Higher Education and the Human Spirit, Chap. 13.

[14]Meland, B. E.   Faith and Culture, p. 131.

[15]Meland, B. E.   Realities of Faith, p. 212.

[16]Meland, B. E.   Faith and Culture, p. 130.

[17]Meland, B. E.   Higher Education and the Human Spirit, p. 3.

[18]Meland, B. E.   Faith and Culture, p. 196.

[19]Niebuhr, H. R.   The Responsible Self, p. 45.

[20]Meland, B. E.   Faith and Culture, p. 87.

[21]Meland, B. E.   Realities of Faith, p. 354.

[22]Meland, B. E.   "A Voice of Candor," Religion in Life, 33 (1964), 26-27.

SUGGESTED READINGS

Bernard Eugene Meland

Meland, Bernard. Modern Man's Worship: A Search
for Reality in Religion (New York: Harper
and Brothers, 1934).

_____. Fallible Forms and Symbols:
Discourses on Method for a Theology of Culture (Philadelphia: Fortress Press, 1976).

* * *

_____. "The Social Ideal of Our Age,"
World Unity, 14 (1934), 225-231.

_____. "Mystical Naturalism and Reli-
gious Humanism," The New Humanist, 8 (1935),
72-74.

_____. "The Faith of a Mystical Natu-
ralist," Review of Religion, 1 (1937), 270-
278.

_____. "Growth Toward Order," The Per-
sonalist, 21 (1940), 257-266.

_____. "At Home in the Universe," Con-
temporary Religious Thought: An Anthology,
T. S. Kepler (Ed.), (Nashville: Abingdon-
Cokesbury, 1941), pp. 284-289.

_____. "The Tragic Sense of Life," Re-
ligion in Life, 10 (1941), 212-222.

_____. "Why Modern Cultures Are Uproot-
ing Religion," Christendom, 6 (1941), 194-
204.

_____. "The Creation of a World Cul-
ture," Current Religious Thought, 5 (1945),
1-4.

_____. "Education for a Spiritual Cul-
ture," Journal of Religion, 26 (1946), 87-100.

Meland, Bernard. "How is Culture a Source for Theology?" Criterion, 3 (1964), 10-21.

_____. "The Self and Its Communal Ground," Religious Education, 59 (1964), 363-369.

_____. "A Voice of Candor," Religion in Life, 33 (1964), 19-27.

_____. "Narrow is the Way beyond Absurdity and Anxiety," Criterion, 5 (1966), 3-9.

_____. "Language and Reality in Christian Faith," Encounter, XXXIV, 3 (1973), 173-190.

_____. "Grace, a Dimension of Nature?" Journal of Religion, 54 (1974), 119-137.

* * *

Berdyaev, Nicholas. The Destiny of Man (New York: Charles Scribners, 1937).

Bertocci, Peter. Free Will, Responsibility, and Grace (Nashville: Abingdon, 1957).

Polanyi, Michael. The Study of Man (Chicago: University of Chicago Press, 1959).

* * *

Alexander, Samuel. "Natural Selection in Morals," International Journal of Ethics, 2 (1892), 409-439.

Boodin, John Elof. "Value and Social Interpretation," American Journal of Sociology, 21 (1915), 65-103.

Garnett, A. Campbell. "Reality and Value: An Introduction to Metaphysics and an Essay on the Theory of Value," Journal of Philosophy, 34 (1937), 713-717.

Hartshorne, Charles. "Philosophy After Fifty Years," Mid-Twentieth Century American

Philosophy, Peter Bertocci (Ed.). (New York: Humanities, 1974), pp. 140-154.

Peden, W. Creighton. "Meland's Philosophical Method--Part One," *The Iliff Review*, 31 (Spring 1974), 43-53.

_____. "Meland's Philosophical Method--Part Two," *The Iliff Review*, 31 (Fall 1974), 35-45.

Sibley, Jack R. "A Christian Theology of Culture," *Quest*, 8 (1964), 50-64.

Spencer, John B. "Whitehead as a Basis for a Social Ethic," *Unitarian Universalist Christian*, XXX, 4 (1975-76), 44-55.

Williamson, Clark M. "The Road to Realism," *Criterion*, 3 (1964), 22-24.

Sibley, Jack R. "The Concept of Depth in the Thought of Bernard E. Meland as It Illumines His Understanding of Faith and Reason," Doctoral Dissertation, the University of Chicago Divinity School, 1967.

Spencer, John B. "The Ethics of Alfred North Whitehead," Doctoral Dissertation, the University of Chicago Divinity School, 1966.

14. MORAL OBLIGATION IN PROCESS

PHILOSOPHY

Daniel Day Williams

Daniel Day Williams attended the University
of Chicago, Chicago Theological Seminary and
Columbia University. He taught at Colorado
College and Chicago Theological Seminary and
the Federated Theological Faculty of the University of Chicago before going to teach at
Union Theological Seminary in New York City
where he was Roosevelt Professor of Systematic Theology at the time of his death in
1973.

Dan Williams possessed a strong commitment to
process philosophy, especially as represented by the
thought of Alfred North Whitehead and Charles Hartshorne, his former teacher. He conscientiously used
the metaphysical categories found in process philosophy
as a means to enhance and enliven theology and psychi-
atry. As the following article will show,* Williams
always combined a disciplined grasp of metaphysical issues with a sympathetic and knowledgeable concern for
its practical application to problems of life. Here he
endeavors to show that ethics is actually inseparable
from metaphysics, and that process philosophy is indeed
justified by its capacity to explicate problems of
moral decision. For him philosophical and theological
inquiry are not ends in themselves but are to be pursued as disciplines for enlarging and strengthening
one's understanding and living of the good life.# He

---

*From The Journal of Philosophy, LVI, 6 (March
1959), 263-270. Used by permission of The Journal of
Philosophy.

#Cf. Bernard E. Meland, "The Empirical Tradition
at Chicago," The Future of Empirical Theology (Chicago:
The University of Chicago Press, 1969), pp. 45-47. Cf.
also Daniel D. Williams, "Suffering and Being in

takes a definite metaphysical stance, therefore, which
presumably extends his empirical-rational method to a
consideration of the structures of all experience, and
assumes at the same time that a doctrine of the being
of God is necessary because he believes the human
search for meaning involves questions about the metaphysical order manifested in all things. In the tradition of Socrates, he endeavors to show that the relativism of our individual perspectives is not the end of
the ethical quest, but that this very relativism points
beyond itself to the absolute obligation derived from
the integrity of God's aim for his creatures. An understanding of the integrity of the world in the midst
of its diversity--wherein events or patterned forms of
energy are seen to be the basic realities of our world
and creativity becomes the category of categories--will
contribute significantly to the capacity of man for
ethical integrity in the midst of the ambiguous flux
of occurrences which go to make up the concrete experiences of his life. The task is difficult, he has
said, but faith for human living cannot do without it.

Empirical Theology," pp. 175-194 in the same work; and
chapter 6 of The Spirit and the Forms of Love (New
York: Harper & Row, 1968).

Moral Obligation in Process Philosophy

The purpose of this paper is to examine the nature of moral obligation from the perspective of process philosophy by showing how this philosophy may deal with two specific problems in the moral life: first, the problem of choices which involve the doing of evil; and second, the aspect of temporal spread in the situations which require moral decision. It is an implicit concern of the paper to show that ethics is inseparable from metaphysics. One way a metaphysical perspective may justify itself is to show that it can illuminate problems of moral decision.

I

1. Everything actual is a concrete process. That is, every moment of its being involves reference to a past from which there is a route of inheritance, and a future which involves possibilities. Everything actual has a structure which relates it to the past, to other entities, and to the future.

2. God is the supreme actuality by virtue of which there is a world of finite concrete actualities held together in a societal relationship exhibiting order, relatedness, and definiteness.

3. God's essential nature, here called his primordial nature, is the realm of ordered possibilities. It is abstract, and therefore never exhaustive of any achieved actuality or state of God's own being.

4. God's primordial nature involves the integrity of this vision of the Good; that is, it involves an order and gradation of value. God is that function in the world by virtue of which every occasion is either positively or negatively related to the possibility of increase of value.

5. Increase of value is the enlargement of the scope and depth of community of actualities. It involves depth of feeling-awareness including qualitative richness, ordered harmony, appreciative communion, and creative advance. Creative advance is the bringing of new structures of value to the enrichment of established orders. It may involve displacement of the old.

6. Some creatures have freedom to make decisions which take into account alternative possibilities for future actualization of value, or which involve destruction of value.

II

From the standpoint of these assumptions the following statements follow with respect to the nature of moral obligation:

1. Moral obligation is the claim of possible good upon the free decision of any creature who is able to consider the effect of his action in relation to that good.

2. God is the source of moral obligation since God is the sole reality by virtue of which there is a unified structure of possible good in any situation.

3. There is a double aspect of moral obligation derived from the two aspects of God's being:

(a) There is the absolute obligation derived from the integrity of God's aim for the creatures. This means that freedom should always be used toward the actualization of the wider, more complete creative order of good. This obligation is absolute, eternal, and in its essential nature does not change. It is implied in every moral choice; and it means that principles of moral action cannot be derived from the analysis of particular historical processes alone. Beyond the definable possibilities of any specific historical situation there stretches the inexhaustible possibility of completion in a wider frame of reference, and that frame of reference ultimately lies in the vision of God.

This position agrees with Immanuel Kant that there are absolute moral requirements implied in human freedom, and with the platonists that the Form of the Good gives the final law to all being.

But there is also a radical difference from these philosophies. The structure of the absolute good is abstract. It is an order of possibilities which does not exhaust the nature of its exemplification in any concrete actuality, not even in the being of God.

Therefore, the second aspect (b) of moral obligation is the requirement for the concrete appraisal of the historical situation in which decisions are taken. What we ought to do here and now can never be derived solely from the statement of principles, whether ultimate principles or derivative ones. Moral decision is a response to the concrete working of God in a situation riddled with the ambiguities of historical good and evil, and with the mysteries of as yet unapprehended qualities and possibilities.

Therefore, the nature of moral obligation has to be stated in a somewhat more complex way. It includes the obligation to participate in the present situation by making such decisions as will reflect both basic integrity of aim, and relationship to the concretely given. Thus there is an absolute moral obligation to do more than acknowledge and obey moral principles, though that is never set aside. There is the absolute obligation to make decisions which bring the good into actuality in those present processes within which one stands.

It follows that there is in every moral decision an aspect which transcends all prediction of what, concretely, will be required. Ethical behavior is genuinely creative in that the very act of decision brings into being a concrete good which cannot be wholly predicted or recognized on the basis of any vision of abstract possibilities, not even the divine vision itself, though nothing the creatures can do can affect the ultimate unity and integrity of the divine vision. In the strange words of the book of Genesis: it is after the world is created that God declares it good.

III

There are endless problems in elaborating a moral doctrine (including the relation of "moral" value to other kinds of values). I shall try to show that this position can cope with the problems involved in two special aspects of the moral life. Any moral theory must prove itself by showing its relevance to specific choices. Indeed, one advantage which may be claimed for the present position is that it anticipates an infinite series of situations involving moral choices which have their unpredictable aspects. Moral theorists will always have new problems to solve.

357

The first problem dealt with here is that which
concerns the choices in which acceptance of the doing
of positive evil seems necessary in order to preserve
any good. The problem is so clearly stated by Dr.
Henry N. Wieman from a perspective closely related to
the one here developed, that I refer to his analysis in
The Source of Human Good. In discussing types of evil,
Dr. Wieman analyzes the role of "protective hierarchies" in human society.

Hierarchical structures in government, economic
life, and systems of status and privilege, including
those which make possible the intellectual life, represent an ordering of life "which is a hard necessity,
but it is evil" (p. 118).

It is necessary to enable the creative event
to produce the richest fulfillment of value
with those most capable of engaging in that
kind of communication. It is evil because it
imposes upon many an undue protection from
pain and discomfort; upon some an undue fatigue from hard labor . . . and so on (pp.
119-120).

The moral problem here is a difficult one; but I
do not see how it can be left just where Dr. Wieman
leaves it. For he holds that the absolute obligation
is to give oneself to the transforming power of the
creative event or process (p. 124). Yet the maintenance of the hierarchies is essential to the working
of the event itself. How can anything be necessary to
the working of the creative process which is not ingredient in that process itself? The obligation which God
lays upon the world is the fulfillment of all the conditions necessary to the achievement of his creative
aim. If one of those necessities is the device of the
protective hierarchy, then surely in a concrete situation there is an obligation to respect that element of
value in the hierarchy. It cannot be simply evil. It
is certainly ambiguous in relation to good and evil,
but not sheer evil. I am not sure but what my conclusion here coincides with Mr. Wieman's regarding the
practical obligation to respect the function of the
hierarchies; but once this obligation is recognized it
seems to me to have implications for the doctrine of
how God works in the world. This cannot be restricted
to that "high peak of creative transformation [which]
will continue to soar far above the mass of people with
only a few finding a place there" (p. 124). God is

also involved in more humdrum tasks. Whatever constitutes a necessity for man constitutes in some way a
necessity for God also insofar as God is involved in
promoting human good.

This position does not in any way relieve us of
the problem of dealing with moral choices in ambiguous
situations. That there are such ambiguities in which,
so far as we can see, any choice involves at least the
risk of evil and perhaps the certainty of it, is certainly recognized by Mr. Wieman. Some way must be
found to assert the absolute element in moral obligation and yet to take account of such ambiguity. Otherwise moral obligation is split up among the conflicting
claims of alternative values. Love is torn apart into
sacrificial and mutual love; justice and brotherhood
are made mutually exclusive opposites.

The doctrine of process philosophy that the absolute obligation to participate in the integrity of
God's aim toward the fuller good also involves the obligation to reckon with the concrete possibilities in
actual processes, throws some light on the moral problem here.

It may be that actualization is always involved
in the ambiguities of good and evil. For one consideration, every advance includes a possible risk of new
evil. The most honest moral intention can create a new
situation riddled with evil. But we need not point
only to cases where the purity of our motives might be
assumed. We have to recognize the possibility that
every choice we make is tainted with an interest either
in self-satisfaction or self-destruction which cannot
stand before the claim of God upon us. But if this be
the case, then it is our moral obligation to recognize
our actual state, to allow for it, and to make our
moral choices in the light of our self-knowledge with
its confession of the evil that we do. Since our self-
knowledge is not complete, our confession of it can
never be. But there are degrees. When one who wields
power submits his judgments to a wider criticism, he
may be acknowledging that his own bias needs such a
corrective. We have no moral obligation to act as if
we were morally incorruptible. Quite the contrary, we
have an absolute obligation to make decisions which
take account of our own fallibility.

This is not to deny but rather to underline the
tragic problem of the necessities of our existence

such as those imposed by decisions concerning the development of weapons which potentially can destroy the whole human race. But it is to hold that moral obligation is not set aside by these necessities; rather it is a service of the creative event to make decisions in the light of whatever wisdom we can muster about the concrete factors, and to do with them what expresses, however obliquely, the affirmation of the wider and deeper good which God is creating.

IV

A second aspect of the problem of moral obligation has to do with the fact that what we decide about is, in every case, not a static situation, but a process. This becomes clear in the analysis of the dilemmas just discussed; for part of the problem of the "necessities" has to do with questions of the outcome of a historic process. Necessary for what end? for how long? with what result? All these are questions which are pertinent to moral choice.

In the view of process philosophy every moral decision is itself a process and involves a relationship to the "becoming" of other actualities. Here some of the deepest perplexity of moral choice arises, for we cannot see the end of our actions; and we are dealing with realities which do not disclose their full being to us except through the spread of time. Since there are no discernible limits to the future in which our actions may have some relevance, we are obligated to ask about the effects of our acts "in the long run"; but how long is this?

I suggest that we begin the analysis here with some aspects of the effect of the time dimension on specific moral choices where we can within limits take account of the historic route along which our choices lie. A concrete example is at hand in the recent decision of the Supreme Court bearing upon the desegregation of public schools. Professor Edmond Cahn has pointed out the significance of the method of handling the case and its decision. Having made its decision the court allowed time for consideration of means of implementing it. In its second decision, after hearing arguments concerning implementation, the Court revealed a preference for "an effective gradual adjustment"; and took account of possible differences of timing in local situations. It is in this decision that the District

Courts are ordered to proceed toward the abolition of racial discrimination in the schools "with all deliberate speed." The qualifying word, "deliberate," surely contains a moral injunction to hold to the goal; but also to move with a certain caution toward the taking of specific steps.

Professor Cahn's comments on the principle involved here are highly pertinent to the analysis of moral problems in the perspective of process philosophy. He points out the important difference between "time when" something is to be done and "time during which." And he says:

> The duration or "time during which" a transaction occurs is one of the critical dimensions of the transaction itself. Frequently its inmost nature is determined by how long it lasts. . . . Duration is a moral dimension.

Thus the Supreme Court found that duration could be inserted as a wedge between "either and or."[1]

There are, of course, factors involved in every legal decision which go beyond the range of any moral theory. What "deliberate speed" means in the language of the Supreme Court will have to be argued and determined by lawyers and courts within their frame of reference. But the moral problem here is clear. It is the question of the way in which the timing of any action is related to our obligation to perform it. That moral theory has had so little to say about this problem is a puzzling fact. It is John Dewey preëminently in contemporary philosophy who has pointed out how sterile and irrelevant much traditional discussion of the means-ends relationship has been, precisely because the continuum of concrete process in which means and ends function has been overlooked.

In the perspective of process philosophy the fact that moral principles are guides to action within processes is a fundamental aspect of the whole viewpoint. To insist on decision according to principle without reference to the historic routes of becoming in the lives of those affected is irresponsible. "Insistence on birth at the wrong season is the trick of evil," says Whitehead (Process and Reality, p. 341). In a sense this doctrine lends itself to a certain conservatism in personal and social ethics; "take your time," "don't rush me," "let it work itself out" are homely moral maxims with a wisdom greater than much arbitrary moralizing.

But the principle is equally valid that the concrete nature of process requires action "before it is too late." Historic processes which lead to monstrous evil can be arrested at a certain point, beyond which there is no return. To fail to act at the point where arrest is possible may be the great moral error, no matter how heroic the too late attack may be. It also is clear that there are times and seasons for the beginning of relationships, in individual and social histories, when to fail to seize the right time means to lose all hope for that future good.

There is a further reply to be made to the criticism that this view can become a rationale for an indefinite postponement of deliberate social change. One hears it said: "in another generation we will have public school integration; but not now." But in the view here being defended there is always a question of the integrity of the fundamental aim. Moral obligation means present identification with a line of creative advance, or resistance to an evil tendency. The fundamental decision, made in the core of the personality, may not be observable in overt action at once; but the decision is there. To refuse the basic decision by postponing to some future generation or situation the actual crisis is morally self-destructive.

There will always be some consequences of decision, even if they affect only the inner structure of the personality. In a social universe they also begin to affect the network of relationships in which one stands. It should be pointed out that the view here taken does not exclude the possibility of a situation where nothing whatever can be done except the expression of the integrity of an absolute aim. There are situations created in which it is too late for anyone to do anything to arrest the historic developments which lead to catastrophe. The only moral requirement may be simply recognition of the realities and personal acknowledgment of the absolute will to the good which resides in God.

The recognition of such situations underlies much of the existentialist ethics. The alternatives often seem to be either sheer witness to integrity when no significant moral choice is possible, or reliance on the creativity of the personal decision beyond all

362

rules and norms. We need not deny such situations; but the decisions taken within them are still taken within the context of the historic life of a community and they have their consequences for the new orders of existence as yet unknown.

V

Process philosophy offers a metaphysics and theory of value which holds together absoluteness of moral obligation with acknowledgement of the creative and the tragic factors which attend ethical decision in an unfinished world.

FOOTNOTE

[1]Edmond Cahn, <u>The Moral Decision</u>, Indiana University Press, 1955, pp. 274-277.

SUGGESTED READINGS

Daniel Day Williams

Williams, Daniel D. The Andover Liberals (New York: King's Crown Press, 1941).

_____. God's Grace and Man's Hope (New York: Harper and Brothers, 1949, 1965).

_____. What Present Day Theologians are Thinking (New York: Harper, 1952, 1959, 1967).

_____. The Spirit and Forms of Love (New York: Harper and Row, 1968).

* * *

_____. "Ethical Foundations of the Law: A New Interpretation," Christianity and Crisis, XVII (1957), 99-101.

_____. "Christianity and Naturalism: An Informal Statement," Union Seminary Quarterly Review, XII (May 1957), 47-53.

_____. "Deity, Monarchy, and Metaphysics: Whitehead's Critique of the Theological Tradition," Ivor Leclerc (Ed.), The Relevance of Whitehead (New York: Macmillan, 1961), pp. 353-372.

_____. "How Does God Act? An Essay in Whitehead's Metaphysics," W. L. Reese and E. Freeman (Eds.), Process and Divinity (LaSalle, Ill.: Open Court Publishing Company, 1964), pp. 161-180.

_____. "Theology and Truth," The Journal of Religion, XXII (1962), 382-397.

_____. "Truth in the Theological Perspective," The Journal of Religion, XXVIII (1948), 242-254.

Williams, Daniel D.   "The Victory of Good," The
    Journal of Liberal Religion, III (1942),
    171-185.

_____.   "Suffering and Being in Em-
    pirical Theology," B. E. Meland (Ed.), The
    Future of Empirical Theology (Chicago: Uni-
    versity of Chicago Press, 1969), pp. 175-194.

15. CREATIVE GOOD

Henry Nelson Wieman

Henry Nelson Wieman (1884-1975) was educated
at Park College, the San Francisco Theological
Seminary, and Harvard University. He taught
at Occidental College, Los Angeles, from 1917
until 1927, and as professor of philosophy of
religion at the University of Chicago Divinity
School from 1927 until his retirement in 1947.
He was visiting lecturer at numerous Universities, and continued to teach and write until
his death in 1975.

Henry N. Wieman was veridically one of the earli-
est and most formidable of the interpreters of process
thought on the American scene,* even though it seems he
may have later moved closer to the empiricism or pragmatism of Dewey and away from what he considered to be
excessive metaphysical speculation in Whitehead's
thought. Be this as it may, Wieman has shown himself
to be an original and creative thinker, and few have
done more to limit undue speculation and transcendence
in modern philosophy. No transcendent reality, he
said, can ever do anything, and when the transcendent
becomes an event, it is no longer transcendental. His
ontology, very similar to Whitehead's, is based upon

---

*The story of Wieman's early introduction of
Whitehead at the University of Chicago is admirably
told by Bernard E. Meland in his informative article
"From Darwin to Whitehead:" in The Journal of Religion,
XL, 4 (October 1960), 229-245. For an introduction to
Wieman's ontology and theological methodology cf. "Wie-
man's Stature as a Contemporary Theologian" by Bernard
M. Loomer in The Empirical Theology of Henry Nelson
Wieman (New York: Macmillan, 1963), pp. 392-397, R. W.
Bretall (Ed.); John B. Cobb, Living Options in Protes-
tant Theology (Philadelphia: Westminster Press, 1962),
pp. 91-119; and D. Brown, R. E. James, Jr., and G.
Reeves (Eds.), Process Philosophy and Christian Thought
(New York: Bobbs-Merrill, 1971), pp. 24ff, 35ff.

the premise that nothing is real that is not of the order of experienced reality, and his difference from Whitehead is perhaps more than anything else one of emphasis. Wieman has as his major concern the matter of value or the good because he emphasizes the creative rather than the preserving aspect of the concrete process, and makes this decision on what he considers to be empirical evidence, or the lack of it, within the natural world. His major endeavor throughout his life, therefore, has been to give expression to a value theory which might discover and define the source of good in the world and for man. Although he never published his various considerations pertaining to value theory, the following selection is indicative of his most mature thought with respect to that subject.[#] In it he simply states that the source of all value is the creative event, the creative process. By process is intended reality, and by good he means "qualitative meaning." This selection forms the basis of his value theory in that here Wieman explicates the four aspects of those events in which qualitative meaning grows. When this transpires in felt quality or human satisfaction it becomes "creative interchange" which in turn encourages and guides our commitment to the good.

[#]From The Source of Human Good (Chicago: University of Chicago Press, 1946), pp. 54-70. Used by permission of Southern Illinois University Press, Carbondale, and Mrs. Henry Nelson Wieman. Dan Williams said of this selection that it was one of the most notable contributions to value theory that he knew of within the context of process philosophy.

Creative good is distinguished from two kinds of created good, one of which is instrumental and the other intrinsic. Instrumental and intrinsic created good are alike in the sense that both are made up of events meaningfully connected; but in the instrumental kind the quality of the events is either negligible or irrelevant to their positive value. Eating tasteless or nauseating food might have the instrumental value of providing me with energy for participation later in events yielding intrinsic value. If the food is tasteless, the quality is negligible; if nauseating, there is quality, but the quality is irrelevant to the instrumental value. The eating of such food might, however, take on intrinsic value through other meaningful connections then and there experienced--the friendliness of associates, memories recalled, and happy anticipations. All these qualities flood in upon me from near and far and are experienced in the very act of eating with these people at this time and place. In such an event the eating ceases to be instrumental by taking on rich quality through meaningful connection with many other happenings. The same system of events may be in one reference an instrumental, and in another reference an intrinsic, good.

The shift from instrumental to intrinsic value, through acquisition of qualitative meaning, is a common occurrence in human life. For example, when I chop wood to sustain that other structure of happenings called "the life of my family in our home," the values of the activity may be purely instrumental if the qualities pertaining to life in my home cannot freely enter conscious awareness as I chop. However, if bonds of meaning are developed between my chopping of the wood and the life of my home, so that the lives of the children and the affection of the wife are vivified in conscious awareness by the very act itself, then the activity ceases to be merely instrumental. Then chopping the wood has taken on those qualities pertaining to the total structure of events called "the life of my home." It is an intrinsic good, no matter how fatiguing it may be.

Therefore, intrinsic value may be defined as a structure of events endowing each happening as it occurs with qualities derived from other events in the structure. On the other hand, instrumental value is a structure of events whereby each happening as it occurs does not acquire qualities from other events in the structure, or, if it does, these qualities are irrelevant to the value of the structure in the reference under consideration.

When there is a break between two or more systems of events such that the qualities of the one system cannot get across to the other, the only meaningful connection between the two must be nonqualitative and instrumental. It is nonqualitative either because the qualities of these connecting events are negligible or because they are irrelevant to the good that is served.

Life can break apart into separate systems of qualitative meaning, when each system is an intrinsic good and when the disjunctions between them are bridged by instrumental good. Any meaningful connection between events which does not carry the qualities from one part of life over to the other parts is, on that account, instrumental in respect to this connective function. It is possible that life might break up into smaller and smaller units of intrinsic good, each unit being separated further and further from the others by longer and longer stretches of instrumental value, relatively barren of qualitative meaning. These instrumental stretches might include events that had intense quality in themselves as bare and isolated events. But value as here interpreted is not merely events having intense quality, even when the quality is pleasant; it is events having rich quality derived from other events through meaningful connection with them. Of course, the quality peculiar to the event now happening may make its own contribution; but it is qualitative meaning, not merely events having quality, which is the good distinctive of human existence. Such good is our concern here.

When good increases, a process of reorganization is going on, generating new meanings, integrating them with the old, endowing each event as it occurs with a wider range of reference, molding the life of a man into a more deeply unified totality of meaning. The wide diversities, varieties, and contrasts of all the parts of a man's life are being progressively transformed into a more richly inclusive whole. The several parts of life are connected in mutual support, vivifying and enhancing one another in the creation of a more inclusive unity of events and possibilities. This process of reorganization is what we shall call the "creative event." It is creative good, standing in contrast to both kinds of created good we have been considering. By means of this creative good, systems of meaning having intrinsic value, previously disconnected so that the qualities of the one could not get across to the other, are so unified that each is enriched by qualities derived from the other. Meaningfully connected events, once instrumental, now become component parts of a total meaning having intrinsic value.

In contrast to the disintegration of life previously sketched, the opposite occurs when creative good is dominant. Under the control of this creativity the life of an individual might, in theory at least, be progressively organized so that the qualities of each part could be experienced while the individual was engaged in some minor role, like walking to town. If this were the case, one's whole life could be qualitatively tasted by way of meaning when one was engaged in any part.

This creative good has kinship with instrumental value, but it is very different from the kind of instrumental value we have described as one kind of created good. It has kinship because it produces more intrinsic created good, and in many cases its own qualities are negligible or are not discriminated and appreciated. Yet it is not instrumental because it transforms the mind and purpose so radically that what it produces is never what the initiating mind intended. Therefore, the initiating mind cannot use it as a means for achieving any anticipated consequence of value that can be foreseen in its specific character. The creative event cannot be used to shape the world closer to the heart's desire because it transforms the heart's desire so that one wants something very different from what one desired in the beginning.

The creative event also has kinship with intrinsic value and yet is very different. It has kinship because in some instances the qualities of the creative event have maximum abundance. The creative event in the life of the artist is sometimes an ecstasy. So also the emergence of new transformative ideas in the mind of the creative thinker, the moment of vision for the prophet, the "rebirth" of the religious convert, or the communion of friends may stand forth as a peak of qualitative meaning. However, in the ordinary run of life, for the most part, the creative event reorganizes

371

the mind and transforms its appreciable world without the qualities of the creative event being themselves discriminated and distinguished from the newly emergent meaning. Rather it is the newly created good that is qualitatively appreciated and not the creative event producing it.

The creative event is so basic to all our further interpretation of value that we must examine it with care. It is made of four subevents; and the four working together and not any one of them working apart from the other constitute the creative event. Each may occur without the others and often does, but in that case it is not creative. We have to describe them separately, but distinctions made for the purpose of analysis must not obscure the unitary, fourfold combination necessary to the creativity.

The four subevents are: emerging awareness of qualitative meaning derived from other persons through communication; integrating these new meanings with others previously acquired; expanding the richness of quality in the appreciable world by enlarging its meaning; deepening the community among those who participate in this total creative event of intercommunication. We shall examine each of these subevents in detail.

. . .

Let us remember that qualitative meaning consists of actual events so related that each acquires qualities from the others. Every living organism so reacts as to break the passage of existence into units or intervals called "events" and to relate these to one another in the manner here called "qualitative meaning." So long as this is done by the organism without the aid of linguistic communication, the range and richness of qualitative meaning is very limited. Not until the single organism is able to acquire the qualitative meanings developed by other organisms and add them to its own can the world of meaning and quality expand to any great compass. Therefore the first subevent in the total creative event producing value distinctively human is this emerging awareness in the individual of qualitative meaning communicated to it from some other organism.

Interaction between the organism and its surroundings, by which new qualitative meaning is created without communication or prior to communication, is

certainly creative. If we were studying the creative
event as it occurs at all levels of existence, this
creativity at the subcommunicative level would be included. But we have chosen to give attention to what
creates value at the human level. What creates value
at the biological level is basic to human existence,
but it is not distinctively human. We shall give some
attention to it, but only for the purpose of seeing
more clearly the character of the creative event as it
works through intercommunication in human society and
history. It is here, where one organism can acquire
the meanings gathered by a million others, that the
miracle happens and creativity breaks free from obstacles which elsewhere imprison its power. Only at this
level can the creative event rear a world of quality
and meaning expanding beyond any known limit, sometimes
by geometrical progression.

. . .

The individual becomes more of a personality when
these meanings derived from others are integrated with
what he already has. His thoughts and feelings are enriched and deepened. This integrating does not occur
in every case of communicated meaning, since there is
much noncreative communication in our modern world by
way of radio, television, movies, newspapers, and casual interchange between individuals. The mere passage
through the mind of innumerable meanings is not the
creative event. These newly communicated meanings must
be integrated with meanings previously acquired or na-
tively developed if the creative event is to occur.
This integrating is largely subconscious, unplanned
and uncontrolled by the individual, save only as he
may provide conditions favorable to its occurrence.
This integrating is, then, the second subevent in the
four, which together make the total event creative of
all human value.

It is in this second subevent that man seems most
helpless to do what must be done. The supreme achievements of this internally creative integration seem to
occur in solitude, sometimes quite prolonged. When
many meanings have been acquired through communication
and through much action on the material world, there
must be time for these to be assimilated. If one does
not for a time draw apart and cease to act on the material world and communicate with others, the constant
stream of new meanings will prevent the deeper integration. A period of loneliness and quiet provides for

incubation and creative transformation by novel unification. If new meanings are coming in all the time,
the integration is hindered by the new ingressions.
The creative integration may be greatly aided by worship when worship allows a supreme good to draw into
a unity of commitment to itself all the diverse values
that have been received from many sources.

Jesus in the wilderness of "temptation" and in
Gethsemane, Buddha alone under the Bo tree, Paul in the
desert on the way to Damascus, Augustine at the time of
his conversion--all these exemplify creative integration in solitude. Many of the great innovating ideas
in literature, philosophy, and science have come to men
in their loneliness. Also it seems that the individuals through whom the creative event has done most to
transform and enrich the world with meaning have been
more lonely than other men and have spent more time in
lonely struggles. Yet with equal emphasis it must be
said that they have had profound communication with
others, if not face to face, then through writing and
meditation on written words.

But mere solitude is not enough. Nothing can be
more deadening and dangerous to the human spirit than
solitude. If the mind degenerates into a state of torpor, as it generally does when isolated from communication with others, solitude is not creative. If the
mind wanders in vagrant fancy, one idea following another by accidental association, there is no creativity.
Or if one engages in minute and intensive analysis of a
particular problem or is harassed with many worries,
fears, and hopes, solitude may yield nothing. What is
required of one in solitude that it may be fruitful?
We do not know. We only know that one who is continuously in association with others is not likely to be
the medium through whom great creative transformations
occur. They who struggle in loneliness to overcome
conditions that seem to block the good of human existence are the ones through whom this second stage in the
creative event can be fulfilled. Whitehead has said
that religion is what a man does with his solitude, and
this is profoundly true, even though it be but part of
the truth, since much more than solitude is needed.
But one of the major unsolved problems of our existence
is to learn how to make solitude creative instead of
degenerative, as it most commonly is.

The creative event, in all four of its stages, is
going on all the time in human existence. When we

374

speak of prolonged solitude, on the one hand, and intensive and profound communication, on the other, as being prerequisite to creative transformation, we refer only to the more striking examples of it. In obscure and lowly form it is occurring continuously in human life, even when decline and disintegration also occur. The latter might be more rapid than the creative process until human life itself disappeared. Nevertheless, the creative event must continue so long as human life goes on because it is necessary to the human level of existence.

. . .

The expanding and enriching of the appreciable world by a new structure of interrelatedness pertaining to events necessarily follow from the first two sub-events. It is the consequence of both the first two, not of either one by itself. If there has been inter-communication of meanings and if they have been creatively integrated, the individual sees what he could not see before; he feels what he could not feel. Events as they happen to him are now so connected with other events that his appreciable world has an amplitude unimaginable before. There is a range and variety of events, a richness of quality, and a reach of ideal possibility which were not there prior to this transformation.

This creative increase in qualitative meaning may not be dramatic and sudden; it may be imperceptible, except as one compares the world accessible to the man of thirty with what he could see and feel and do when he was one year old. However, one must remember that mere expanse in range and complexity of events is not an increase in qualitative meaning. Mere expanse may be achieved by multiplying and lengthening instrumental connections so that life becomes a burden and a weariness. When this happens, it is due to conditions which prevent the creative event from producing increase in intrinsic value. These conditions may be physiological, psychological, social, or historical and most probably are a combination of all of them.

Also it should be noted that this expanded world of qualitative meaning does not continue as a steady vision. The appreciable world in which each man lives from day to day expands and contracts through great variations. Yet the expanded world, once acquired, is not entirely lost, unless some degeneration sets in.

375

It is not always immediately accessible, certainly not in the torpor of sleep and under many other conditions; yet one can at times recover what has been achieved if he retains his vitality and conditions are not too unfavorable. It is at least a memory and a conceivable hope, as it was not prior to the creative transformation.

One important thing to note is that this expanding of the appreciable world may make a man more unhappy and more lonely than he was before; for now he knows that there is a greatness of good which might be the possession of man but is not actually achieved. One is reminded of the man who preached through all his life: "God is my Father and all you are my brothers," declaring continuously the blessedness of all-encompassing love and yet living in a world so barren of love that he must have been heartbreakingly lonely through all the days of his life. This loneliness comes to agonized expression in the story of the temptation, Gethsemane, and the cry on the Cross.

Such a profound sense of loneliness is difficult for any man to bear, and yet it is the hope of the world because the man who feels it is aware of a greatness of love that might be but is not. Such loneliness indicates a vast emptiness which love between men might fill. This loneliness might become so deep and so intense that a man could not endure it unless he were permitted to die upon a cross for love; he might then fill an emptiness no actual love can fill by a sacrificial expression of love. This seeking for a love that is never fulfilled might become so deep and so intense that a man would spend all his life preaching the principles of a kingdom of love that would sound like the beatitudes of madness in a world like this. They could be made intelligible only by attributing them to an illusion that the world was shortly to come to an end and would be transformed miraculously into such a kingdom. Perhaps such loneliness, born of such craving for love between men, would drive a man to that desperate madness in which he dreamed that by dying on a cross he could somehow bring this kingdom of love into existence.

This expanding of the appreciable world, accomplished by the third subevent, is not, then, in its entirety the actual achievement of an increase of value in this world, although it will include that. But it is also, perhaps even more, an expansion of the individual's capacity to appreciate and his apprehension

of a good that might be, but is not, fulfilled. It is
the awakening of a hunger and a longing which, in one
aspect at least, is a craving for more love between men
than ever can be in the compass of his life.

. . .

Widening and deepening community between those who
participate in the total creative event is the final
stage in creative good. The new structure of interrelatedness pertaining to events, resulting from communication and integration of meanings, transforms not only
the mind of the individual and his appreciable world
but also his relations with those who have participated
with him in this occurrence. Since the meanings communicated to him from them have now become integrated
into his own mentality, he feels something of what they
feel, sees something of what they see, thinks some of
their thought. He may disapprove, deny, and repudiate
much that has been communicated to him from them, but
this is a form of understanding and community. Perceptions and thoughts that are denied are as much a part
of one's mentality as those affirmed. They may contribute as much to the scope and richness of one's mind,
to one's appreciable world, and to the depth of one's
community with others as perspectives which we affirm
and with which we agree.

This community includes both intellectual understanding of one another and the feeling of one another's
feelings, the ability to correct and criticize one another understandingly and constructively. It includes
the ability and the will to co-operate in such manner
as to conserve the good of life achieved to date and to
provide conditions for its increase.

Paradoxical as it may sound, this increased community between persons may bring with it a sense of alienation and wistful hunger and even anguish, because
one is now aware of misunderstandings in the other. He
apprehends in the mind of the other, as he could not
before, bitterness, fear, hate, scorn, pride, self-
concern, indifference, and unresponsiveness when great
need and great issues call. Likewise, the other may
apprehend in him in somewhat different areas these ail-
ments of the human spirit. Increase in genuine community, which is not mere increase in backslapping geni-
ality, will include all this discernment of illness and
evil in one another. Increase in community is not necessarily pleasant; the good produced by the creative

event brings increase in suffering as well as increase in joy; community brings a burden as well as a release. Those who cannot endure suffering cannot endure the increase of human good. Refusal to take suffering is perhaps the chief obstacle to increase in the good of human existence.[1]

These are the four subevents which together compose the creative event. They are locked together in such an intimate manner as to make a single, total event continuously recurrent in human existence. The creative event is one that brings forth in the human mind, in society and history, and in the appreciable world a new structure of interrelatedness, whereby events are discriminated and related in a manner not before possible. It is a structure whereby some events derive from other events, through meaningful connection with them, an abundance of quality that events could not have had without this new creation.

If by "new creation" one simply means something new in the world, a new event that never occurred before, then, of course, every event is creative. But that is not what is here meant. We are limiting our study chiefly to creative event as it occurs in communication between human individuals, and not even all communication displays it. It is true that there is a creative process that has worked through many centuries to bring forth the kind of organism that can participate in the creative event of human communication. The subhuman organism and the human organism at the submental level can have creative interaction with environment. This creative interaction which underlies the creativity of linguistic communication is (1) emerging awareness of a new structure of interrelatedness pertaining to events through a new way of interacting between the organism and its material situation; (2) integrating of this newly emergent structure with ways of distinguishing and relating events that had previously been acquired by the organism, thus achieving a more complex system of habits; and (3) consequent expanding and enrichment of the world of events having quality relative to the discriminating feeling-reactions of the organisms.

The thin layer of structure characterizing events knowable to the human mind by way of linguistic specification is very thin indeed compared to that massive, infinitely complex structure of events, rich with quality, discriminated by the noncognitive feeling-reactions

378

of associated organisms human and nonhuman. This infinitely complex structure of events composing this vast
society of interacting organisms and their sustaining
or destructive environment is like an ocean on which
floats the thin layer of oil representing the structures man can know through intellectual formulation.
These structures knowable to the human mind can have
depth and richness of quality only if they continue con-
junct and integral with this deep complex structure of
quality built up through countless ages before even the
human mind appeared and now accessible to the feeling-
reactions of the human organism. But when the human
mind in its pride tries to rear its knowable structures
as supreme goals of human endeavor, impoverishment, destruction, conflict, and frustration begin because
these structures are then cut off from the rich matrix
of quality found in organic, nonintellectual reactions.

Any meaning loses depth and richness of quality
derived from this unknown depth of structured events
with quality determined by noncognitive feeling-
reactions of the organism, when it is treated as an
end instead of as a servant to creativity and all that
creativity may produce below the level of human cognition. Man can use his knowledge and the truth he seeks
to know to serve this creativity. Also he can so live
as to keep his achieved meanings closely bound to the
rich matrix of qualified events that cannot be known in
their specific detail. When he does live thus, he experiences an uncomprehended depth and richness which
give content to the abstractions of rationally compre-
hended structures. When he does not, life loses quality and value.

While we shall be concerned almost exclusively
throughout this writing with specifically definable
meanings and the creative intercommunication that generates them, because these are the fields of our intelligent endeavor, the importance of the deeper matrix of
value must not be forgotten. We live in and by and for
it. The creativity of intercommunication works to render this deeper matrix more vivid and appreciable to
conscious awareness by way of specifiable structures
known to the mind, here called "qualitative meaning."
But all this is perverted when these structures of intelligent meaning are treated as though they had value
apart from, or sovereign over, the deeper levels of
value which are too complex and rich with quality for
the human mind to comprehend. For the sake of simplicity of treatment and utility in action, we shall seem

to exclude these deeper levels; but we must not ignore them.

We shall exclude from the creative event as here treated not only all the creativity that underlies and provides substructure for communication between human persons but also every event in human experience which does not bring with it a new structure of interrelatedness connecting it with other events in such a way that the human mind and its appreciable world are transformed. Most events occurring in human existence are not appreciably creative in this sense. There may well be some minimum level of creativity going on all the time in human existence to compensate for the wastage and loss of qualitative meaning, which is also continuous. But even this continuity of creativity is one chain of events only and does not include innumerable others, some of the others being obstructive and destructive to all good, with no intrinsic good in them that can be called either "creative" or "created." Therefore, the creative event as here treated includes only those events which bring a new structure whereby the human mind distinguishes and relates events in such a way that there is more richness of quality in happenings as they occur and greater range and variety of appreciated possibility. This alone is the fourfold event described as emerging awareness of communicated meanings, the integrating of these meanings to create a new mentality in the individual, a new structure of qualitative meaning in the world, and a deeper and wider community among men.

It should be noted that the creative event, together with every one of the subevents, is an -ing. The subevents are emergings, integratings, expandings, deepenings, that is, they are not accomplished facts. After the event is accomplished, it is no longer creative. Hence the creative subevents (as well as the total creative event) are events in process. They are happenings in transit, not finished products, although they yield a finished product. The finished product of these four -ings, and hence the product of the total creative event, is always a new structure, whereby some events are more widely and richly related in meaningful connections.

This, then, is creative good. Created intrinsic good, on the other hand, is the appreciable world made richer with quality and meaning by this creative event. It is culture. Instrumental good, which is also created, is a structure pertaining to events wherein the qualities of the events are not relevant to the value of the structure. It is civilization or technology, in contrast to culture. This threefold distinction of values into creative, created intrinsic, and created instrumental has practical importance, we believe, because the three kinds of value require different kinds of action if human good is to be promoted.

. . .

The human problem is to shape human conduct and all other conditions so that the creative event can be released to produce maximum good. While this event is continuously occurring in human life, more often despite the efforts of men than because of them, it is not always equally potent and effective. The richness and scope of meaning that it creates, moment by moment, may vary from a minimum to a maximum. What it creates may be small compared to what is destroyed by the impact of uncreative existence. Nevertheless, the whole struggle of human life, the basic problem of industry and government, of education and religion, of sex and personal conduct, of family and neighborhood organization, is to provide and to maintain those conditions wherein the creative event can produce the maximum of qualitative meaning with minimum destruction of previously developed structures which enrich the world.

Much in human life hampers the full release and creative power of this event. When men deceive or fear or distrust one another, when they inflict injustice or smart beneath it, they refuse to communicate meanings that are rich, deep, and precious to them. The worldly-wise wear a poker face, hide behind a mask of bravado or indifference lest others discover the absurd and despicable pretensions they know within themselves. They hold back, lest servants disobey master, lest heroes be dragged from their pedestals. Fear, hate, and suspicion; deceit, concealment, and exploitation; misunderstanding, indifference, and sloth; vindictive cruelty, lust, and sadistic desire; complacency, arrogance, and the insatiable need to feed the ego--all these block and frustrate the creative event. The list runs on without end. Thus the great problem is how to provide conditions more favorable for this creative event so that it can bring forth structures which will endow events with more richness of quality and scope of meaning.

. . .

Serving the creative event that renews itself is the work of man--the supreme vocation of human history. Innumerable things can be done by men to remove obstacles and provide sustaining conditions which release the power of creative good to produce value. Every serious practical and theoretical problem finds its solution in clearing the path for creative transformation, and there is nothing else to be done that is worthy of man. Meeting the demands of this source of human good calls for all the moral rigor, all the labor and sacrifice, all the religious commitment of faith which human capacity can afford. There is, therefore, plenty for man to do in helping to create a better world.

The emphasis just made is important because of a persistent misunderstanding that arises when it is said that man cannot do what the creative event does. All we mean to say is that the creative event produces a structure which could not be intended by the human mind before it emerges, either in imagination or in the order of actual events.

Human effort cannot accomplish anything which the human mind cannot imagine. If something results from human effort which was not intended and which the human mind could not imagine prior to its occurrence, it is an accident relative to human effort. It is not, of course, an accident in the absolute sense of being without cause. But, even though the existence and the labors of men are part of the many causes issuing in this consequence, the consequence is not the work of man if the human intent sought a result different from this consequence.

The structure of value produced by the creative event cannot be caused by human intention and effort, because it can be produced only by a transformation of human intention and effort. We saw how the creative event transforms the human mind, the reactions of the human organism, the community of associated individuals, and the very structure of events as they occur in the appreciable world. Obviously, this cannot be the work of man in the sense that he can foresee the structure yet to be created. He cannot strive to achieve it before he has sufficient imagination to conceive it and the required hunger to seek it.

Many protest when we claim that man cannot be creative. Of course, man in many senses of the term is

creative: he exercises his imagination to envision
something that never was in existence and then proceeds
to construct it. But man cannot exercise his imagination to envision what is inaccessible to imagination
prior to the transformation which gives his mind the
added reach. Man can do only what lies within the
scope of the imagination that he has; he can seek only
the good that he, to date, is able to appreciate. To
do what lies beyond the reach of his imagination, a
greater imagination must be created in him. To seek a
good beyond what he can appreciate, a greater appreciation must be developed in him. The creative event, not
man himself, creates this greater imagination and this
more profound and discriminating appreciation.

What we have said demonstrates that man cannot be
creative in the sense in which this term applies to the
creative event we have been describing. Man's creative
ability is something produced in him as a consequence
of the prior working of the creative event. To fall
into controversy over whether or not man is creative is
to use the same word for different things. Such an argument is as futile as a merry-go-round.

The creative event is supra-human, not in the
sense that it works outside of human life, but in the
sense that it creates the good of the world in a way
that man cannot do. Man cannot even approximate the
work of the creative event. He would not come any
closer to it if his powers were magnified to infinity,
because the infinite increase of his ability would have
to be the consequence of the prior working of the creative event.

The work of the creative event is different in
kind from the work of man. Any attempt to measure the
power of man against the power of the creative event is
defeated at the start because one cannot compare the
two. It is true that man can set up conditions that
obstruct the work of the creative event so that the
good it produces will be much less than it would have
been if men had met its demands. Also, he can serve it
by removing obstacles. Men can do this in their personal conduct, in the organization of society, in the
physical and biological regime which they maintain.
When men do meet its demands, the creative event faithfully produces a far greater abundance of human good.
But the actual creative event is never the work of man
and cannot be. In that sense it is supra-human and
transcendent, but the transcendence pertains to its

character as creative of the appreciable world created to date. This appreciable world contains the meanings and the things, the goods and the goals, which are subject to human control. It is the world in which man lives his conscious life for the most part. Since creativity is not readily accessible to awareness, we can speak of creativity as "transcendent." But it is not transcendent in the sense of being nontemporal, nonspatial, and immaterial. It can be discovered in this world by proper analysis.[2]

Since this creativity has the character just stated, it was almost inevitable that man should think it supernatural. Nature, for the ordinary man, is his appreciable world. Therefore, what is not accessible to his appreciation must be supernatural, especially when it is creative of this world which he appreciates. Creativity is not beyond all human appreciation. It can be appreciated, and, when proper social conditions and required knowledge have been achieved, it can be known as a part of the temporal, spatial, material world. But, generally speaking, it has been mythically represented as supernatural; and, if the creative event be of the sort we have described, the human mind could hardly have approached it otherwise until certain cultural conditions and scientific knowledge had been achieved, especially knowledge in the fields of biology, psychology, and social psychology. Expert specialists in these several fields might not find it, but one who can draw from all of them and from other cultural conditions might well do so. Many have done so in recent years.

Like the ancient supernaturalism, and in opposition to almost all religions and philosophies that stand over against supernaturalism, the naturalism here defended repudiates the supremacy in value of all the goods and goals of the created appreciable world and turns to what creates them for the sovereign good of life.

. . .

"Instrumental" refers to what man can use and control as a means to an end. As we have seen, man cannot use and control the creative event because the structure of value it produces can never in its specific character be intended, desired, or sought by man. Man can, of course, know that the creative event will produce good and can welcome the need of his and the world's transformation; but he cannot know the kind and form of good it will produce, and if he could foresee, per impossible, with his untransformed perception, what the creative event would produce, it would at times seem hateful and fearful and the opposite of good. The kind and form of good actually produced by creativity inevitably transcends, and in some ways runs counter to, the present order of human desire; for one of the necessary subevents of the creative event is precisely this transformation of the previously existing order of human desire. The primary demand which the creative event makes upon man is that he give himself over to it to be transformed in any way that it may require. Obviously, man cannot use as a means or instrument the generative process which transforms him so as to create values which he cannot in their specific nature anticipate or see or desire.

. . .

The claim that creative good is the only absolute good can be defended only after we are clear on what is meant by "absolute" in this context. When we speak of "absolute good" we shall mean, first of all, what is good under all conditions and circumstances. It is a good that is not relative to time or place or person or race or class or need or hope or desire or belief. It is a good that remains changelessly and identically the same in character so far as concerns its goodness. It is a good that would continue to be so even if all human beings should cease to exist. It is a good that retains its character even when it runs counter to all human desire. It is a good that continues to be identically the same good even when it works with microscopic cells prior to the emergence of any higher organism.

Creative good meets all these requirements pertaining to absolute good. Its goodness is not relative to human desire, or even to human existence, although it is also good when desired and when working in the medium of human existence.

On the other hand, created good--the structure of meaning connecting past and future that we feel and appreciate--is relative value in all the senses that stand in contrast to the absolute as just described. The particular chains of qualitative meaning having value for man do not necessarily have value for microbes. The structure of interrelatedness pertaining to events which increases quality and meaning relative to one organism or race or class or culture will not ordinarily be equally good for another. Thus created good does not retain the same character of goodness under all circumstances and conditions and in relation to every different sort of organism, human person, or social culture. The creative good which does retain its character of goodness under all these changing conditions is, then, the only absolute good.[3]

A second mark of absolute good is that its demands are unlimited. A good is absolute if it is always good to give myself, all that I am and all that I desire, all that I possess and all that is dear to me, into its control to be transformed in any way that it may require. If there is some point beyond which the cost is too great to justify the claim that a good makes upon me, then it is relative in that respect. Creative good is absolute in this sense for there is no amount of created good opposed to it which can diminish the claim that it makes upon me. The value of the creative source of all good is immeasurable compared to any particular instance of good derived from this source.

Thus in a third way, inseparable from the second, creative good is absolute. It is unlimited in its demands because it is infinite in value. Its worth is incommensurable by any finite quantity of created good. No additive sum of good produced in the past can be any compensation for the blockage of that creativity which is our only hope for the future. And the created good of the past sinks into oblivion when not continuously revitalized by the recurrent working of the creative event.

Fourth, absolute good is unqualified good. There must be no perspective from which its goodness can be modified in any way. Always, from every standpoint, its good must remain unchanged and self-identical, whether from the worm's view or the man's view, whether under the aspect of eternity or under the aspect of time, whether viewed from the standpoint of the beginning or the ending, whether judged by its origin or by its final outcome, whether viewed as means or as end. In respect to created good one can always find some standpoint from which its value disappears or changes; it must be qualified. But in this sense, too, creative good is absolute.

Finally, creative good is absolute in that it is entirely trustworthy. We can be sure that the outcome of its working will always be the best possible under the conditions, even when it may seem to us to be otherwise. Even when it so transforms us and our world that we come to love what now we hate, to serve what now we fight, to seek what now we shun, still we can be sure that what it does is good. Even when its working re-creates our minds and personalities, we can trust it.

We can also be sure that creative good will always be with us. When all other good is destroyed, it springs anew; it will keep going when all else fails. In this dual sense creative good is absolutely trustworthy: it always produces good; it never fails.

A further claim might be made for an absolute good, but this claim cannot apply to the creative event. Neither can it be applied coherently to any other interpretation of the nature of absolute good. This claim is that absolute good means all-powerful good. It means a good that overrules all evil so that in the end everything will come out all right, no matter how long and how great the intervening evils may be. According to neo-orthodoxy, this blissful outcome is postponed to "the end of history," whatever that may mean. There is a transcendent realm, so it is asserted, where perfect and almighty good reigns supreme; but in our world of time and space and matter and history this almighty power of good is only partially regnant. Life may be a valley of frustration, but nothing can prevent ultimate, absolute, and complete regnancy of supreme value, somehow, sometime, somewhere, although the human mind cannot know how this may be.

. . .

Creative good will be our standard and guiding principle in dealing with all problems concerning good and evil and better and worse. Anything is good if it sustains and promotes the release of that kind of intercommunication among men termed the "creative event." It is evil if it does the opposite. One act or course of conduct is better than another if it provides more amply the conditions enabling the creative event to produce qualitative meaning; it is worse if some alternative would be more favorable. Kinds of legislation, types of economic order, methods and goals of education, habits and moral practices, forms of religion-- these and any other proposals for changing or maintaining

387

the established state of affairs are evil if some practicable alternative should enable men to communicate more fully and freely in a manner fostering creative transformation. They are good if they facilitate this event more fully than anything else under the circumstances.

According to this standard, one good is not better than another because it contains a greater quantity of good in itself. One might be much greater in value so far as concerns its content of created good. But if the lesser served to release more fully the potency of the creative event, it is the one to choose. The Roman Empire, with all its culture, may have contained far more qualitative meaning than the little Christian sect. Nevertheless, if the latter could release more widely and deeply among men the kind of intercommunication creative of all good, the latter should be chosen and the Empire rejected. Thus the quantitative standard by which one created good is measured against another is not the standard directive of wise choice.

The problem of choice involves not only good but also evil. Neither can we fully understand the nature of good until we see it in silhouette against the fact of evil. So we turn to a study of evil as one kind of value no less important than good.

FOOTNOTES

[1]How suffering is related to positive value will be considered in the next chapter.

[2]See Chap. X for the difference between functional transcendence and metaphysical transcendence. Creative good is functionally transcendent but not metaphysically so.

[3]"Absolute" in any intelligible sense cannot mean "out of relation." It is relative to conditions, circumstances, organisms, and the like; but its character of goodness does not change when these relations change. Instead of being out of all relations, it is rather the one kind of goodness that, without losing its identity, can enter into all relations. It is good always and everywhere, therefore relative to everything.

SUGGESTED READINGS

Henry Nelson Wieman

Wieman, Henry N. Religious Experience and Scientific Method (New York: Macmillan, 1926; Greenwood Press, 1968).

_____. The Wrestle of Religion with Truth (New York: Macmillan, 1927).

_____. The Source of Human Good (Chicago: University of Chicago Press, 1946; Carbondale: Southern Illinois University Press, 1964).

_____. Man's Ultimate Commitment (Carbondale: Southern Illinois University Press, 1958).

_____. "Personal and Impersonal Groups," Ethics, XXXI (July 1921), 381-393.

_____. "Objectives versus Ideals," Ethics, XXXV (April 1925), 296-307.

_____. "Value and the Individual," Journal of Philosophy, XXV (April 1928), 233-239.

_____. "Values: Primary Data for Religious Inquiry," Journal of Religion, XVI, 4 (October 1936), 379-405.

_____. "Intrinsic, Instrumental and Creative Value," Journal of Philosophy, XLII (March 1945), 180-185.

_____. "Fact and Value," Zygon: Journal of Religion and Science, IV, 4 (September 1969), 286-290.

_____. "Co-operative Functions of Science and Religion," Zygon: Journal of Religion and Science, III, I (March 1968), 32-58.

* * *

Wieman, Henry N. "Value," Review of John Laird,
    The Idea of Value, Journal of Religion, X, 2
    (April 1930), 290-291.

16. BEYOND ENLIGHTENED SELF-INTEREST:

A METAPHYSICS OF ETHICS

Charles Hartshorne

Charles Hartshorne did most of his academic
study at Harvard University (B.A. 1921; M.A.
1922; Ph.D. 1923), where his teachers were
J. H. Woods, W. E. Hocking, C. I. Lewis,
H. M. Sheffer and R. B. Perry. The years
1923-1925 were spent at the Universities of
Freiburg and Marburg where he was a student
of Edmund Husserl, Martin Heidegger, Julius
Ebbinghaus, and Richard Kroner.

In this essay* Professor Hartshorne explores the
basis for ethics within process philosophy. The most
central premise of such an ethics is the denial of psychological egoism; that is, the denial that human concerns are purely self-centered. Egoism, Hartshorne
teaches, rests on a misconceived theory of the self as
possessing an absolute identity. Personal identity is
relative and not absolute. (Though it is no less real
for being relative.) We change through time, and are
never numerically identical from minute to minute. We
are influenced by what we have been in the past and we
influence our own futures; but while we are influenced
equally by what others have been in the past we also
influence the future thoughts and behavior of others.
There is thus no clear dividing line between ourselves
and other people; no clearly distinct ego for the egoist to claim. It is no wonder then that the concerns

---

*Reprinted from Ethics, an International Journal
of Social, Political, and Legal Philosophy, LXXXIV, 3
(April 1974), 201-216. Used by the permission of the
University of Chicago Press and Dr. Hartshorne. Another selection in reference to Dr. Hartshorne's ethical perspective is "The Unity of Man and the Unity of
Nature" which is the final chapter of The Logic of Perfection and Other Essays in Neoclassical Metaphysics
(LaSalle, Ill.: Open Court, 1962), pp. 298-323.

of rational creatures naturally extend far beyond the fortunes of the isolated self.

In a very insightful way, Professor Hartshorne points out the aesthetic basis of process ethics. This does not mean that according to process philosophers we need only enjoy what is beautiful and pleasant. Rather, it means we are obligated "to seek aesthetic optimization of experience for the community." The aesthetic experience combines a maximum of intensity and harmony. (Intensity, in turn, is based on the experience of contrast, of diversity.) We must attempt to create a world for everyone, or at least for as many people as possible, in which such balanced intensity is a fundamental feature of life. The disturbing implications of such an ethic for our present social, political, and economic life are drawn in Professor Hartshorne's concluding paragraphs.

Beyond Enlightened Self-Interest:

THE ILLUSIONS OF EGOISM

The world, according to common sense, consists of a great many individual things and persons, each individual remaining identical through change but losing some qualities from time to time and acquiring others. This view has obvious truth, but it easily misleads in serious ways. Consider the human species. At a given time it consists of a number of persons, each the same person from birth to death. At every moment I am Charles Hartshorne, and John Smith is John Smith. Never have I been anyone other than Charles Hartshorne, and never has John Smith been anyone other than John Smith. That each of us is always the same human individual is true; but that each of us is always simply the same thing, the same reality, is false. We are identical through life as human individuals, but we are not identical as concrete actualities. The identity is abstract, the nonidentity is concrete. Without this distinction the language of self-identity is a conceptual trap. Into this trap have fallen most philosophers. Of all the great traditions, only Buddhism has entirely escaped the error. However, Buddhists have tended to be intuitionistic or anti-intellectual and so have failed to develop conceptual devices altogether adequate to their insight.

Personal identity is a partial, not complete identity; it is an abstract aspect of life, not life in its concreteness. Concretely each of us is a numerically new reality every fraction of a second. Think of the difference between a newborn infant and an adult person; also, of that between an adult and a senile octogenarian. These differences are not slight. The infant is only potentially a "rational animal"; actually it has no rational thoughts. A senile person may also have scarcely any.

Another difference is that between a person in dreamless sleep and the person dreaming; also between the dreamer and the person awake. In addition there may be aphasia, loss of any clear sense of one's past history, delirium, insanity, intoxication, weird drugged states, multiple personality. Personal "identity" must span all these differences. We say that at some moments a person is "not himself." The New Testament speaks of being "born anew." Personal identity as many philosophers construe it leaves out all that these expressions report. To abstract from such vast contrasts and say that from birth to death the person is one and the same entity is to emphasize the abstract or the potential at the expense of the concreteness or actuality of life. This one-sided emphasis has momentous consequences.

Let us be clear on one point. I am not disputing that there is a definite sense in which each human individual is distinguishable from any other. A person's bodily career is continuous in space-time. People could have been observing me from birth on and would have seen no gap in my physical development and persistence from infant to adult, from middle age to elderliness. Also there have been scarcely any abrupt changes in my habits, my personal style. But this physical continuity is an extremely abstract feature of one's existence. It allows very radical changes in quality from a nearly mindless infant with incomplete brain cells to full maturity, from dreamless and apparently mindless sleep to being wide awake, from irritated or furiously angry states to happy or benevolent ones, and so on.

Consider, too, that many minute portions of one's body were once parts of the environment, and vice versa. So far as these portions are concerned, spatiotemporal continuity connects one not with oneself in the past or future so much as with the environment, that is, other individual beings, in the past or future.

Forget about the bodily continuity, and think instead about the mental one. Of my thoughts or bits of knowledge, many go back to thought or knowledge not my own, and some will in the future become part of the thought or knowledge of others. If I am influenced now by what I have been in the past, I am as genuinely influenced by what others have been in the past. If I can plan now to bring about results in my future bodily and spiritual career, so can I plan to bring them about in the future bodily and spiritual careers of others. Where, in all this, is there any absolute distinction between relation to self through time and relation to others--apart from the abstract physical distinction already granted?

If we forget how relative, partial, or abstract, as well as primarily bodily, personal identity is, we

pay serious penalties in our interpretation of fundamental issues. For instance, it then seems natural to
adopt a self-interest theory of motivation. I am I,
you are you, neither of us is the other. If I care
about my future, it is because it is mine; so runs the
thought: but if I care about your future this must be
because that future, or what I do for it, will benefit
my own. My future advantage is then the end, while contributing to your advantage is but a means. For over
fifty years I have rejected this view, and my original
reasons still seem valid, though they have become enlarged and fortified. I think the view is bad psychology, even bad biology, and bad ethics and metaphysics.
It also contradicts the imperative of all the higher
religions that one should love the other as oneself. If
loving the self is a sheer identity relation and loving
the other a sheer nonidentity relation, then one can
never do anything like loving the other "as oneself";
for on the hypothesis this is a metaphysical or logical
impossibility.

My position, since 1918, but rendered much clearer
by exposure, first to Hume, James, Peirce, and Whitehead, and then to the Buddhists, has been that self-
love and love of others are alike, both being relations
of partial, not complete, identity or nonidentity. This
view is to some extent recognized in common speech but
usually denied in philosophical and theological doctrines in the West, with of course some notable exceptions. The exceptions include post-Kantian idealism,
Marxism, and the doctrine of Saint Paul in his saying,
"We are members one of another"--an epigram closer to
the truth of this matter, in my opinion, than anything
to be found in Aquinas or Kant, not to speak of Hobbes
or Bishop Paley. But none of the writers mentioned does
full justice to the degree of nonidentity abstracted
from by the common-sense notion of the "same" individual. Only in Whitehead (most nearly anticipated by
Peirce) does the West, after more than two millennia,
come to meet the Buddhists on the question of selfhood
and motivation.[1]

In common speech occur such remarks as that we
"identify ourselves with" a friend, or with offspring,
or fellow advocates of a common cause. We have the expression "alter ego" for such cases, or "better half"
for a spouse. But where are the absolute limits of
these qualifications of self-interest? I take the qualifications to show that the really basic principle of
motivation is not regard for the future of one's own

bodily and mental career. This regard is merely a principal derivative of the truly basic principle, of which regard for the future of other organisms or careers is another derivative.

The basic principle is the appeal of life for life, of feeling for feeling, experience for experience, consciousness for consciousness--and potential enjoyment for actual enjoyment. One's own future is interesting, appealing, motivating. Why? Because it is the future of a sentient and conscious career--and present experience more or less vividly and sympathetically anticipates this future. If we find means to be as aware of the prospects of others as of our own, then we may take a similar interest in their prospects. The interest may or may not be very sympathetic, it may even be more or less sadistic. But this is because of some lack of harmony between the career of the other, as we envisage it, and our own present currents of thought or feeling. It is not because the abstract thread of individual identity leads only to one's own past or future rather than to the others' past or future. The grounds of antipathy, as of sympathy, are much more concrete. And parallel to sadism is masochism. The difference is relative.

1. The first illusion of egoism, then, is the notion that motivation depends basically upon the mere spatiotemporal continuity of organic careers. True enough, it is normally the case that we are more vividly and steadily aware of and sympathetic to our own future prospects than to those of others. But this difference of degree provides no reason to make an absolute of self-interest as compared with interest in others.

To value oneself _rationally_ is to value oneself for the same reasons, and by the same criteria, as are used in valuing others. In short, "love others as oneself" is a command of reason, not just a requirement or gift of grace. We should not give the prestige of reason to the fact that every animal tends to feel its own weal and woe more vividly and steadily than the weal or woe of any other animal. To use reason (and it requires reason) to extend self-interest to include one's own entire future, but not to use it to extend interest in others so as to include in principle their entire futures, seems misuse of the power to generalize, to seek truth and value wherever they may be and as being "there" for any impartial spectator. Reason should universalize our ends as well as our means.

The value of one's own life is more in one's power than is that of other lives; one can understand it more easily, and so it is one's greatest single responsibility. But there are times, as when one is close to death, when one may be able to do much more for another than for oneself.

Mortimer Adler eloquently urges that we should have as our concern the goodness of our own lives as entire careers and, only as derivative from this concern, care about the future of others. But why should I now care infinitely for my life or career as a whole? Adler admits that this whole will never be experienced, possessed, or enjoyed by me. I have glimpses of it, and so do my acquaintances. But none of us will ever really possess it.[2] Why then is it so important? I agree that it is important, but for the same reason that makes anyones else's life important, not just to him but to any rational spectator. It is not my entire life's goodness that I have to have right now, but only the satisfaction of having a rational aim right now. The reward of virtue, which, as Spinoza said, is in virtuous action itself, is not the whole of happiness, but it is the only reward that one needs to take as absolutely essential. For a rational being it is the pearl of great price. The rest is additional good fortune to be utilized by practical wisdom.

Like Adler, though in an interestingly different way, Michael Scriven derives the motive for good conduct from rational concern for one's own career. Both writers show some realization of the limitations of the project, but neither seems to see clearly that ethics has a deeper and more rational ground elsewhere.[3]

There is of course partial agreement between the aim at future well-being for oneself and the aim at the good of others. But the value of knowing this is to weaken the force of man's natural though relative self-centeredness, not to enthrone this animal limitation as the voice of reason. A great deal of self-interested action is self-defeating, and there are often great rewards for bringing genuine good to others. I do not envy anyone the benefits he gets from selfishness. On the other hand, I cannot see any need to make the future rewards to self for now acting upon a rational aim the reason for having this aim or acting upon it. Nor can I see that giving self-interest an absolute priority is in any good sense rational.

The lower animals, which I have been studying most of my life in one way or another, are not merely self-ish, but selfish and altruistic, both of course in the same largely instinctive or genetically determined fashion. (What they cannot do is to generalize either self-interest or altruism; for they cannot symbolize abstract ideas, they cannot deal with the absent or potential as definitely as with the given situation.) The basic instincts are to keep the species going; the individual's preservation is subordinate. A male spider may risk his life in courting the female, but in running this risk he serves the species.

2. The primary egoistic illusion about motivation tends to associate itself with another. This illusion is the unexpressed but felt anticipation of living virtually forever. That one is mortal is known, but not genuinely realized and acted upon. What matters is thought to be one's own future. But which future? One's life prior to death? Or one's future altogether? Our ultimate destiny, so far as we know it, is to be heaps of dust. What then will it matter to us that we have, perhaps, been happy--or unhappy? For us there will then be no such truth. But we put this out of our minds almost completely, and face things as though we would always be there to reap any harvest we may sow. This, I hold, is an illusion, and one of the commonest. St. Exupéry wrote that, of the many persons he had seen facing their own imminent death, not one thought primarily of himself. If we lived in the full light of the truth, this would be our attitude all along.

The future that matters is not our own future as such, but rather any future we can influence, sympathize with, and in some degree understand as good or bad for someone. To serve this future can be our present aim, whether or not the good we do to the other will also be our own future good. It is our good, right now, to promote what we care about for the future, whether it be a child's welfare, even a pet animal's, or our country's, or mankind's--and one could go further still. Other things being equal, one prefers that persons, even animals, should be happy, not only while one can share in their happiness but afterward as well. Anyone of whom this is not true is insofar a subnormal or irrational human being, and may be a sick one as well.

So, far from our valuing others only for their usefulness to ourselves it is in no small part for our

400

usefulness to others that we value ourselves. Convince yourself that you are no good to anyone, and how much will you love, rather than hate and despise, yourself?

There is a great Buddhist passage that goes something like this. "You say, 'He injured me, he insulted me, how terrible!'" "But," the writer goes on, "this is writhing in delusion." Why so? It is writhing because it is unhappy. It is delusion, first, because the self that insulted you has been partly superseded by a new concrete actuality, the other person-now, which may be indefinitely different from the insulting self. It is delusion, second, because the insulted self has also been superseded. There is incomplete identity on both sides. But third, there is only incomplete nonidentity between the two persons. The other's past has entered into your present being, your past into his, and both share a partly overlapping causal future. Each helps to create a new self in the other and will influence some of the same future selves. Finally, fourth, both you and the other, as individual animals, are passing phenomena, whose careers may cease at any time.

The angry man is reacting like an injured animal, using his reason only to articulate the animal's lack of perspective rather than to overcome it. This is a misuse of reason. The human power of abstraction and generalization is ill-employed if it merely generalizes the means and leaves the end the same, or if it merely generalizes the self-protective aspect of instinct and not the species-serving aspect. The rational aim is the future good that we can help to bring about and take an interest in now, whether or not it will do us good in the future and whether or not we shall be there to share in the good. We share in it now, and that is all that present motivation requires. It is a luxury, not a necessity, if we can hope to have a future share in the good we make possible for others. Moses did not need to enter into the promised land.

3. A third illusion generated by overemphasis upon self-identity is the misconception of the meaning of death and the real problem of immortality. Thinking in terms of self-identity we seem to face the stark alternative; eventually "I" become nothing at all, or--what seems virtually the same in value terms--a heap of dust, or I survive death in some heaven or hell, or in some new animal body in which I have further experiences of a scarcely imaginable kind and for even the

401

bare possibility of which I have no clear understanding or evidence. Thinking in terms of concrete momentary states of experience, the alternative is quite different. Concretely I am not a mere self, the same through change, but a "society" or sequence of experiences, each inheriting its predecessors, so far as memory obtains. But our human memory is very selective and for the most part highly indistinct or faint. Thus, shortly before death, even though we are fully conscious, the wealth of experiences we have already enjoyed is almost entirely lost to us. Death is merely the definitive form of a lack of permanence which pervades our entire lives.

The basic question of "transience," as Whitehead profoundly and perspicaciously insists, is not what happens to our identity at death but what happens at every moment to what we were the previous moment. As Santayana put it, every moment "celebrates the obsequies of its predecessors." Santayana saw also, though not so clearly as the Buddhists or Whitehead, that the concept of substance, at least in the form of individual identity, is not the illuminating one at this point.[4] The concrete permanence, if there be one, must be something very different from self-identity as we human beings have it. For that is, at best, an extremely partial preservation of the actual quality of life.

If death means that the careers we have had become nothing, or a heap of dust, what is history about, or biography? And what is autobiography, if the past experiences and actions are now reduced to mere faint and partial recollections and a few records, photographs, and the like? On this hypothesis, the very idea of truth grows problematic. Truth about the past, it seems, must be one thing, and truth about nothing, or about humanly accessible traces of the past, quite another. Thus the great doctrine of the "immortality of the past," found in Bergson, Peirce, Montague, Whitehead, and some others, is an answer not simply to the frustration we tend to feel in thinking about death and the mutability of all individuals, but to the puzzle of historical truth, the most concrete and inclusive form of truth.

My personal view is that the complete rational aim is the service of God, whose future alone is endless and who alone fully appropriates and adequately appreciates our ephemeral good. What some term "social immortality" is literal immortality only so far as God is the social being who is neighbor to us all. For he alone is exempt from death and able to love all equally adequately. He is the definitive "posterity."

The egoist, I have been arguing, subordinates the concrete to the abstract, the whole to the part, the really inclusive future to a limited stretch of the future, and is in a poor position to see the meaning of life and death. This meaning is that the passing moment is, first, self-enjoyed, valuable in itself, and beyond that, so far as it is rational, an intended contribution to the future of sentient life, or whatever part of that life it can best hope to enrich with itself or its consequences. The future career of the same individual is normally a prominent part of future life as proximate receptacle for the present contribution. But the ultimate receptacle of values must lie beyond any one human career, and even, I hold, beyond human life as such. Of course the self, and its future, is interesting. But how much else is interesting?

Long ago I made my decision: No one will ever compel me to shut myself up in a prison of self-interest; compel me to admit that others are for me mere means and myself the final and absolute end. In that case how ghastly an affair my death should appear! And how seriously I should have to take every misfortune to myself, and unseriously every misfortune to others. "Writhing in delusion"--what else is it? But many a philosopher and many a theologian, tragic though this be, has in effect told us that such is the rational way. How grateful we may be to the Buddhists, and to Whitehead, and to the Judeo-Christian insight (indeed the insight of every great religion), when taken at its best and not explained away, for showing us another possibility!

True enough, saying that one rejects the primacy of self-interest does not prove that one is living unselfishly. But it might help at least a little to strengthen our generosity, and weaken our self-serving, self-pitying tendencies, if we gave up the theoretical adherence to self which disfigures so much of our philosophical tradition and opened our minds to the really inclusive cause we can all serve, the future of life in all its forms, human, subhuman, and (if we can conceive this) superhuman.

4. The radical abstractness of mere self-identity is obscured if one takes the view that by a certain

individual, say John Smith, one means the John Smith
career, a certain sequence of bodily and mental states
from birth to death (or perhaps beyond), as forming in
some fashion a unitary whole. Actual bodily or mental
states are concrete; but until an individual is dead
his career is, to common sense--and, process philosophers hold; in truth--only partly concrete or actual.
What has occurred in a person's life constitutes an actual or definite career; but the future is a matter of
more or less abstract or indefinite potentialities and
probabilities. Only a doctrine of the absolute predetermination of the future can equate what makes a man
himself with what actually happens to him. Shall I not
be myself tomorrow whether I do just this or that, and
whether just this or that is done to me? To deny this
(and Leibniz for one denied it) is to burden one's
thought with a radical paradox. For then, the moment
John Smith exists at all his entire future history is
already real fact. A man's notion that he, and not
someone else, could have done otherwise than he has
done and that he faces real options for the future, not
foreclosed by his character as already formed plus circumstances, must then be taken as illusion. Process
philosophers think it more sensible to take the Leibnizian view as the illusion. But then self-identity is
indeed incurably abstract; for (like every abstraction)
it is neutral as between concrete alternatives.

5. Another illusory basis of egoism is found in a
certain view about the relations of God to the temporal
process. One of the commonest ways of conceptualizing
the difference between deity and other forms of being
is to say that, while nondivine beings undergo change
and are affected by what has happened around them, God
is immutable and immune to influence of any kind. It
then follows that the good we can hope to contribute to
the future cannot be a value we would thereby confer
upon God. For, on the hypothesis, deity can receive
nothing, being timelessly complete or self-sufficient
simply in itself. And so the harvest we sow must be
reaped, its benefits collected, either by ourselves or
by others than deity or the supreme reality. But what
reason is there to think that these others will in the
end escape final destruction? Also, what reason to
think that posterity, so far as there is one, will always continue to benefit from our lives in their concrete actuality? Finally, what does it mean to say
that our achievement will have contributed something
to the happiness of many lives benefiting from our having lived as we have if these many happinesses are

scattered about in innumerable consciousnesses? The
sum of many pleasures, many happinesses, each in a different state of consciousness, is not itself a greater
pleasure or happiness, for it is not a happiness at all.
Many apples are not one very large apple--though they
are a large quantum of apple flesh and much more useful
than just one apple for several people wanting to eat
apples. But of what use is happiness, after it has occurred, except to contribute to further happiness? Our
achievements "add up" to something only if there is an
inclusive consciousness which enjoys them, which values
their having taken place. A merely timeless and wholly
self-sufficient deity cannot meet this requirement. In
many writings I, and other authors, have defended a
different conception of deity.

Orthodox Hinduism (if there is such a thing) meets
the problem of motivation by denying that it exists. It
holds that, finally, there are no human selves or careers, but only the one infinitely blissful immutable
Brahman. The rest is, to the seer, in some sense mere
appearance, or like a forgotten dream. This solves the
problem by dynamite, as it were. And why is the problem worth solving if there never was such a problem?
What does it really matter whether we accept or reject
Hinduism, since in either case nothing has really happened? Verbally one can talk in this way, but the mere
fact of continuing to talk contradicts what is said, or
at least fails to express it. I hold, with James and
Peirce, that a doctrine is merely verbal unless our
living can show that we believe it. But how can there
be a way to show by living that we believe we are not
living, that is, not changing, not reacting to influences from the past in partly determining the future?

Buddhism has never quite committed itself to the
doctrine of Maya; or, at least, Buddhism in what I regard as its best forms has not done so. We are to find
the permanent and the all-inclusive in the midst of
change. Reality is not merely impermanent and local-
ized; but still it is really so. There are these two
aspects in a mysterious unity. But the distinction
real-unreal is not the key to this unity. The key is
rather this: that the actual, concrete self is much
less permanent and self-sufficient than Hinduism took
it to be, so that all regard for the future transcends
self as concrete actuality. The Bodhisattva works for
the salvation "of all beings."

Charles Peirce spoke of the "buddhisto-Christian religion." I believe that the "meeting of East and West" must be chiefly on the Buddhist side of the heritage of India, together with those forms of Hinduism which are not orthodox, taking Sankara as the classic of Orthodoxy. The Gita, fortunately, is somewhat ambiguous and can be taken either way.

Egoism is an illusory doctrine, although the real plurality of careers is an ultimate truth. It is, however, an incomplete truth, the other side of which is that, as the identity of a career is abstract, so is the nonidentity of the diverse careers. Concretely, the momentary states or selves are the realities; but, to have a rational aim beyond the present, they must regard themselves as contributory to future selves generally, no matter to what careers these may belong, in the faith that all lives whatever are embraced in or contribute to a mysterious but real and abiding unity. This unity some Buddhists perhaps, and more easily Christians, Jews, or Mohammedans, may wish to characterize as the life of God. Others prefer a vaguer description. The essential is that the aim of the individual should in principle transcend its own future advantage and take the whole of life into account.

ETHICS AND FREEDOM

Many writers have argued that the only freedom needed for ethics is lack of constraint in making and executing choices. If an act is fully voluntary, not done under duress or threat and not while the agent is hopelessly intoxicated or impassioned, it can in the ethical sense be considered free, even though the choice was entirely determined by and in principle predictable from antecedent conditions. Nay, more, it is held that such determination is required for ethical responsibility, since acts not determined by character and conditions would be irrelevant to the judgment of persons as good or bad. It is said, too, that since all events must be caused, and since also we have to consider man as ethically obligated, we must believe that moral freedom and determinism are compatible.

With James and many others I reject the foregoing reasoning as it stands. But the issues are somewhat subtle. I agree heartily that voluntary action demonstrates freedom and that any determinism which could possibly hold of a being making conscious choices is compatible with that freedom. But I deny that unqualified determinism could possibly hold of conscious beings. Indeed, with Peirce and others, I deny that it could hold even of inanimate nature. The proper meaning of "all events are caused" is not "all events are fully determined by causes." The proper meaning of cause is necessary condition, a sine qua non of a phenomenon. But, granted that all necessary conditions for an event have been fulfilled, it follows, not that the event will, but only that may, take place--unless by "event" one means not what actually happens in all its concreteness but only some more or less abstract kind of event to which the happening belongs. "Effects" as strictly implied by the sum of necessary conditions are less concrete than actual happenings. Conditions set limits within which the abstractness, that is, the indeterminacy, of the implied effect is resolved into the concreteness of what in fact happens. With this understanding I agree that there are no "uncaused" happenings; yet I reject the notion that there are any antecedently determined yet concrete happenings. The statistical character of most natural laws as now known is relevant here. But I hold, with Wigner and some other physicists, that the quantum uncertainty in inorganic systems is not the only limitation upon determinacy; rather, in organisms, especially the highest ones, there are further limitations to causal predictability or orderliness, though even there the limitations are presumably sufficiently slight to give science plenty of scope in searching for order in phenomena.

Of course character is expressed in acts; but each new act creates a partly new character, and character as already formed implies only a certain range of probabilities and possibilities for action. Each moment we shift, for good or ill, this range. This view does all the real work of the deterministic absolutization of the relation of settled character and other conditions to conduct. Absolutes are needless and worse than needless in most problems, including this one. Often the very people who profess to be skeptical of absolutes also defend absolute determinism.

Freedom in the full sense means more than just voluntariness, and no voluntary animal is free in that sense only. Freedom in the full sense means creativity, resolving antecedent, though mostly slight, indeterminacies. Creativity is not, taken generically, unique to man, or indeed to animals. As Peirce, the mature Bergson, and Whitehead believed, it applies even to atoms and particles. But the animals have higher degrees and vastly more significant forms of creativity. Yet even in them the causal limitations are always real and important. We can, apart perhaps from rare climactic moments, shift the probabilities of future action only a little each fraction of a second. That is why life is "real and earnest." We are forever influencing our probable futures. But we are never simply determining them. The future will determine itself.

The reasons for accepting the qualified determinism just outlined far transcend ethics. They also transcend the specific questions arising from the present state of microphysics. It is not possible to do justice to them here. I am deeply confident that unqualified determinism is false, but my reasons for this confidence must be sought, if anyone is interested, in the many writings, including my recent book Creative Synthesis and Philosophic Method, in which I have set them forth.

One consequence of the doctrine of universal creativity is that no conditioning, whatever Skinner may believe, will put an end to conflict and frustration. Where free beings interact, there must always be real risks of more or less painful disagreement and opposition. Apart from God, every free agent is fallible, both in understanding and in ethical goodness. Hence neither destructive folly nor destructive wickedness can be ruled out by any institutional arrangements. True, the degree of freedom can be diminished and hence the scope of risks reduced. But the limit in this direction is to make human beings almost as lacking in intensity of consciousness as the lower animals. Intense consciousness means, as Bergson rightly saw, a higher than usual degree of freedom, a greater scope of options for action. To trivialize risks by reducing freedom means trivializing opportunities also.

Obviously Skinner would think of the foregoing paragraph as a good illustration of the bad effects of the belief in creativity. I see his point. But I think he is missing the very meaning of concrete existence. Here the existentialists are indeed right.

However, while the search for a risk-free utopia seems vain, I heartily support the search for a better system of risk-opportunity, more appropriate to our

technology than we have now. For instance, the freedom
to own handguns is not all all necessary to intensity
of consciousness. More important, the freedom for each
national group to be judge in its own cause, with no
group really judging for mankind, is clearly obsoles-
cent and needs to be combated with every educational
and political device we can find or invent for this
purpose. The 100 percent American, or Russian, or what-
have-you, is an enemy to all of us. We need an element
of world citizenship in each person. There is no other
way effectively to counterbalance the major evils and
dangers of our day, whether atomic war, pollution, un-
just extremes of rich and poor, or the coercion of one
group by another. Moreover, I think Skinner has helpful suggestions as to how needed social changes can be
made. Positive reinforcement is indeed far better than
negative. My chief quarrel with Skinner is that it
seems obvious that reinforcement is not an unqualified-
ly deterministic concept, since it implies causal probabilities, not necessities. What Skinner is really
asking us to do, and we need to try to do it, is to
shift the probabilities for the future. Conditioning
is a fundamental reality. We all agree on that, even
though it is very true that some underestimate its importance. Skinner is merely overstating a good case.
In this he has a virtual infinity of precedents.

MAN, THE OBLIGATED ANIMAL

Man is a thinking, speaking animal. "Thinking animal" is scarcely sufficient, because it is arguable
that some other animals can also think, in their humble
fashion. But a speaking animal, in a normal use of the
word "speaking," can think to a degree not closely approached by the other terrestrial creatures. Man may
not, in any very high degree, be a rational animal, but
think he does, throughout his waking and dreaming life
after infancy. We have now to show that a thinking animal is either ethical or unethical--it cannot be neutral, or simply nonethical.

All higher animals, indeed, it is arguable, all
animals, are in some sense and degree social. An animal is more or less interested in other animals. No
one who has kept pets can be in doubt about this. Moreover, the instinctive patterns of behavior divide into
those that tend to preserve the health and safety of

the individual and those that, though they may somewhat
endanger the individual, tend to secure the persistence
of the species after the individual is dead. Under
special circumstances instinct may even produce actions
directed to the benefit of individuals of other species.
But the extent of such extraspecific service is narrowly limited. And of course the instinctive provision
for future results beneficial to the species is largely
outside the animal's awareness. Birds building nests,
at least for the first time, presumably do not know the
reason for this activity. In sum, though subhuman animals act not simply for their own benefit but also for
that of other animals, yet, so far at least as their
own awareness is concerned, they do this only within
very narrow limits of space, time, and kinds of animals
benefited.

Thinking on the scale that goes with language produces a change so drastic that it is only quibbling to
argue whether it is a difference of kind or of degree.
For some purposes at least it is a difference of kind,
or if you prefer, a difference that makes all the difference. If thinking does not extend the scope of
other-regarding actions infinitely, it does extend them
indefinitely. The moment we decide on a limit, we shall
have come in sight of passing beyond that limit. We
can, in some sense and degree, care about other human
beings, wherever and whenever they may be; we can sympathize with the trodden insect, with characters in
fiction, with "all sentient beings." We can also in-
hibit or not strongly feel sympathy for anything but
ourselves and perhaps a few others. Indeed, we can
largely confine our sympathy to our present self and
its immediate or near future, neglecting the months and
years to come. Thus we stand before the option: shall
we or shall we not generalize self-regard to take the
entire personal future into account, and generalize regard for others to include the futures of the entire
circle of creatures whose welfare depends upon our actions? To use thinking to effect only a little extension beyond instinctive limitations of interest in the
future of self and others is an arbitrary restriction
of the thinking process. To speak is to be at home
with universals. Not just tomorrow concerns me but my
life as a whole, and not just that one human being which
I am, or my little circle, but human beings generally,
so far as I have dealings with them or can influence
them. Indeed, not human life only but life as such is
the final referent of thought. Here the Asiatics were

right against the Western tendency to limit value to
humanity.

In the foregoing, apart from the last remark, I
am agreeing with Kant: The ethical will is the rational
will, the only form of will appropriate to a thinking
animal. Conscience is practical reason.

It is sometimes held that ethical obligations are
only to other individuals, not to oneself. With Kant I
hold this to be a mistake--except in the sense that,
taking God into account, there can be no such thing as
a strictly solitary individual. But, however that may
be, one's present self has duties to one's future self
as truly as it has duties to other human beings. To be
enlightened, thoughtful, in one's self-interest is truly
an ethical requirement. Mere impulse will repeatedly
pull one in directions contrary to this requirement,
just as impulse will pull one in directions contrary to
the requirement to give heed to the needs of others. To
be deliberately careless of one's own needs is unethi-
cal for the same reason as carelessness about the needs
of others; for such behavior springs from failure to
generalize the instinctive sympathy of present experience for potential future experience, whether of self
or other.

Ethics is the generalization of instinctive concern, which in principle transcends the immediate state
of the self and even the long-run career of the self,
and embraces the ongoing communal process of life as
such. The privilege of thought carries with it the
sense of a goal that is universal and everlasting, not
merely individual and temporary. It makes the individual trustee for nature at large, in the sense in which
nature includes humanity. Anything short of this is
not quite ethics in the clearheaded sense but mere ex-
pediency, or failure to think the ethical business
through.

Of course we cannot design the lives of others in
the sense and to the degree possible in determining our
own actions and careers. This is especially true when
we are young, with the largest portion of our careers
still to be decided. It is much less true in the prime
of life and thereafter, for then our own destinies are
more fully determined, and our power over others is increased. But at all times it is irrational to set a
higher value upon oneself than upon others collectively,
for the others are many and we are but one. Adler may

411

possibly be right in saying the "do gooders" do less good than harm to others. Even so this is relevant only to questions of strategy or tactics, of how to promote the cause we serve, not of what cause nor why we should serve it. The ultimate principle remains: we care about life, above all life on the conscious personal level, and especially, for the reasons and to the extent just indicated, our own lives. There is also truth in Maeterlinck's saying, "It is necessary to live naïvely." Too pedantic an insistence upon altruistic considerations may, by destroying spontaneity and zest, make one a less valuable person, both to oneself and to others. Nevertheless the aim is one's total contribution, taking what one is and what one does into account.

THE AESTHETIC BASIS OF ETHICS

Granted that the ethical or rational motivation is toward the inclusive good, the question remains, how, by what rules of action, can the inclusive good be promoted? What indeed is "good," whether mine or someone else's? Here ethics must lean upon aesthetics. For the only good that is intrinsically good, good in itself, is good experience, and the criteria for this are aesthetic. Harmony and intensity come close to summing it up. Being bored, finding life insipid, lacking in zest or intensity, is not good; however, discord, conflict between intense but mutually frustrating elements in experience, also is not good. Intensity and beauty of experience, arising not only from visual or auditory stimuli as in painting or music, but in experience of whatever sort, are what give life its value. To be ethical is to seek aesthetic optimization of experience for the community.

Emerson was wont to speak of "moral beauty," or the majesty of goodness, and he could follow eloquent praise of the beauty of nature by saying that it paled before the beauty of a right act. An ethically good act is good in two senses: it contributes to harmony and intensity of experience both in agent and in spectators. A good will enjoys a sense of harmony between self and others (insofar, virtue is indeed its own reward); and its consequences, if it is wise and fortunate as well as good, will be to enhance the possibilities in the community for intense and harmonious experiences.

412

Obviously cruelty produces ugliness in the experiences
of many; genuine kindness produces beauty, directly in
itself, and indirectly in many ways. Parents who fail
to inspire in children a sense of the direct and indirect contributions of good actions to beautiful, satis-
bying experiences fail indeed. Moral exhortations and
disciplines which make life seem ugly or boring for
self and others are counterproductive.

The insane are those who unwittingly invent an unreal world that gives them more intense and harmonious--
or less inharmonious--experiences than the real one as
they are able to see it. All basic problems are aesthetic. The "beauty of holiness" is one of the finest
of biblical phrases. And one has only to read Emerson's
Journals to see that moral beauty was for him a reality.
His attitude toward slavery, toward the emancipation of
women, and in many other matters earned him the right
to emphasize the phrase. He saw the ugliness of male
chauvinism when not so many did, and no one saw more
vividly the ugliness of slavery. He saw, too, the ugliness of war and aggressive nationalism, though perhaps not the necessity of world government as the only
feasible alternative. He saw, though inadequately, the
beauty of the scientific vision of nature.

It is an aesthetic principle that intensity of experience depends upon contrast. Since memory is central
in high-level experiences, an important mode of contrast
is between the new elements and the remembered old ones
in experience. Put otherwise, for experience to have
much aesthetic value there must be significant aspects
of creativity. Now that science and technology have so
greatly increased the pace of change in the conditions
of living there is bound to be a good deal of novelty
in life. But the problem is to achieve intense harmony,
beauty, in this novelty, rather than intense ugliness.
This requires a new measure of creativity, especially
social creativity, and the reform of institutions. Here
the young are more or less in the right. We cannot simply go on as we are politically and socially. Somehow
we have to make ourselves, our whole citizenry, more
courageously aware of the possibilities of altering the
really hideous disproportion between rich and poor,
both within our nation and between nations. We cannot
much longer effectively pretend to practice democracy
while elections can be bought by oligarchically controlled wealth, and while millions, especially blacks
and Latin Americans, are given little chance of participating in social and political life in a self-respecting

413

way. We cannot much longer effectively work for peace
while failing to take any steps toward the world government without which there cannot be anything but cold
or hot war. We have to inculcate the sense of world
citizenship and of membership in all humanity, not just
in some part of humanity. Pollution problems have similar implications.

ETHICS AND REFORM

Berdyaev's ethical imperative was, "Be creative
and foster creativity in others." Today, social and
political creativity have a new degree of importance.
I agree, too, with Marxists and some contemporary theologians that the driving force for needed reforms must
come in substantial measure from the less fortunate. As
has been said, the ones to change the system are "those
who dislike it." But the fortunate, those who are
lucky and successful in providing for themselves and
their families, need to learn to dislike the present
arrangements vicariously, because of their injustice.
History shows that this is difficult and uncommon. Nevertheless, it is an ethical imperative. For those with
bitter personal grievances are dangerous reformers if
given no help or guidance by those who are more disinterested. This is a central ethical problem. The successful middle class needs to consider carefully how
far, if at all, it ought to side with the rich rather
than the poor. And the rich, including the richer nations, need to realize their ethically perilous position. The New Testament judgment on wealth has, I believe, more validity than we Americans have ever been
willing to grant. Emerson observed that the wealthy
systematically voted for the wrong things and against
every needed reform. We have to resist the natural
tendency of those who have "succeeded" to attribute
their success to ethical superiority alone or essentially (as though anyone ever achieved anything without
a liberal portion of good luck) or to view those who,
by the crude standard of wealth, have succeeded as most
worthy, and the economic failures as least worthy, of
respect or trust. Complex as these matters are, and
granted various qualifications, the basic principle
holds that the fortunate tend to overrate the rules of
the game (including the tolerated violations) and resist their revision to meet new conditions, while the
unfortunate are more willing to attempt this.

Technology has finally destroyed the possibility
of an easy conservatism such as worked well enough
among primitive tribes and fairly well even in early
modern times. Now we must change our ways, and it
seems foolish to expect those (including myself) whose
personal position pleases them to furnish the chief impetus for change. Yet even they are under obligation,
I suggest, to try to understand that their own needs
are not the measure of the common good and that some
discontent of a vicarious sort would become them. So
long as no real end to cold warfare--always threatening
hot warfare and to some extent already involving it--
and no end to race conflict or to bitter poverty, even
in this nation, is in sight (and no end is in sight),
we have no right to be content with our procedures. We
have to look for better ways.

One further point. I agree both with some of the
young and with many Asiatics that we Americans need to
revise our shamefully materialistic concept of the
"standard of living" so that it is no longer so nearly
neutral or worse than neutral ethically (and indeed
aesthetically), consisting in large part of preferring
conspicuous waste and minor comforts to essential values of health (of which the automobile has in some ways
been the enemy), natural beauty, friendship, good feeling among citizens, creative activity, and intellectual
and spiritual progress--all of which beyond reasonable
argument are more important to achieving that beauty in
life which is genuine success.

A Frenchman has coined the phrase "voluntary aus-
terity" to express the idea that there is now a new
ethical value upon not demanding for oneself and family
all the luxuries at once, a demand which intensifies
all our dangers and evils, including the evils of in-
flation and pollution and the danger of war. The old
ascetic and monastic ideals are not necessarily irrelevant, nor is the notion that the really good person is
modest in his or her claims to share in the products of
human labor and the creativity of nature. In this regard Americans in general are far indeed from the model
the world needs to copy. It is in some ways our very
selves that we need to recreate.

FOOTNOTES

[1]A. N. Whitehead, Adventures of Ideas (New York: Macmillan Co., 1929), chap. 20, secs. 1-8; Process and Reality (New York: Macmillan Co., 1929), chap. 2, sec. 2; also Charles Hartshorne, Paul Weiss, and Arthur W. Burks, eds., The Collected Papers of Charles Sanders Peirce (Cambridge, Mass.: Harvard University Press, 1931, 1958), 1:673, 8:82.

[2]M. J. Adler, The Time of Our Lives: The Ethics of Common Sense (New York: Holt, Rinehart and Winston, 1970).

[3]Michael Scriven, Primary Philosophy (New York: McGraw-Hill Book Co., 1966), pp. 229-301, esp. 250-72. For Adler's qualifications to the self-interest thesis see The Time of Our Lives, pp. 4, 6, 13, 15, 173-74.

[4]George Santayana, The Life of Reason, one-volume edition (New York: Charles Scribner's Sons, 1953), 5, chap. 8, pp. 462-63.

SUGGESTED READINGS

Charles Hartshorne

Hartshorne, Charles. Reality as Social Process
(Glencoe, Illinois: The Free Press, 1953).

_____. The Divine Relativity: A
Social Conception of God (New Haven: Yale
University Press, 1948). The Terry Lectures
of 1947.

_____. Creative Synthesis and Phil-
osophic Method (London: S. C. M. Press,
1970).

* * *

_____. "The Social Theory of Feel-
ings," Southern Journal of Philosophy, III,
2 (Summer 1965), 87-93.

_____. "Some Thoughts on 'Souls'
and Neighborly Love," Anglican Theological
Review, LV, 2 (April 1973), 144-147.

_____. "The Environmental Results
of Technology," in Philosophy and Environmental Crisis (Athens: University of Georgia
Press, 1974), pp. 69-78. William T. Black-
stone (Ed.).

* * *

Whitehead, A. N. "Requisites for Social Process,"
in Science and the Modern World (New York:
Free Press, 1969), pp. 193-208.

Jones, M. M. "Sociality in Harold Lee's Thought,"
Southern Journal of Philosophy, X, 3 (Fall
1972), 325-336.

Hoffert, R. W. "A Political Vision for the Organic Model," Process Studies, V, 3 (Fall 1975),
175-186.

417

* * *

Hall, D. L. The Civilization of Experience: A
Whiteheadian Theory of Culture (Bronx, New
Jersey: Fordham University Press, 1974).

A E S T H E T I C S

"All order is aesthetic order."

Alfred North Whitehead

Bernard E. Meland
John B. Cobb
John Dewey
Alfred North Whitehead

17. TWO PATHS TO THE GOOD LIFE

Bernard Eugene Meland

Bernard E. Meland was educated at the University of Chicago and in Europe. He first
taught at Central College, Fayette, Missouri,
and at Pomona College, Claremont, California,
before returning to teach at the University
of Chicago Divinity School where he served
as Professor of Constructive Theology from
1946 until his retirement in 1964. He was
a member of the "Chicago School" of empirical thinkers, and has made a significant
contribution to liberal and inter-cultural
thought.

Bernard E. Meland is one who has given a lifetime
to the study and expression of process thought. Being
cognizant of "the revolution in fundamental notions"
which has so altered the view of modern man and made
problematic the very meaning of human reason, he has
consistently witnessed for the need of a new imagery of
depth that would provide a better means of expressing
both the sense of "ultimacy" which faces man in the
surplusage of meaning and being which operates within
the world process and the "immediacy" of man's possession of his limitations--for he believes that only by
understanding his limitations can man understand his
possibilities. Perception he holds to be a richer
event than cognition which means that we begin with
complexity and wrestle from it some portion of clarity
for living. The common denominator within the new
stage of modern consciousness is considered to be "the
dimension of depth" which serves Meland as a continual
reminder that "reality overrides reason" and thus man
can attain only "a margin of intelligibility." In order to do the most justice to conscious experience at
its depth you must avail yourself of every sort of general structure of meaning which is available within the
empirical stance--thus not denying ontology, but still
resisting any definite ordered analysis--but at the
same time being faithful to the report of experience.

As is clear from this article,* Meland agrees with
Whitehead that "all order is aesthetic order and the
moral order is merely certain aspects of the aesthetic
order," but it should be kept in mind that he is even
more emergent in that he considers no aspect of naturalism to be unambiguous. The concrete emergent quality at work within the universe is a thrust or movement
not only beyond the natural, but also beyond the aesthetic. As a perceptive way of understanding which is
simultaneously "a bodily event" and "a valuating event"
coterminous with the act of individuation, then, the
aesthetic dimension of intelligibility may be regarded
as the nearest to the reality of experience as this relates to either the natural world or the good life.#

---

*From The Personalist, XXIII, 1 (Winter 1942), 53-
61. Used by permission of The Personalist and Bernard
E. Meland. For an appreciation of Meland's interpretation of Whitehead cf. the Dialogues of Alfred North
Whitehead (Boston: Little, Brown and Company, 1954),
pp. 217, 218, where Whitehead indicates how most com-
mentators misinterpret his thought. Along with the notion of "causal efficacy" in Whitehead's thought, Meland
considers the "More" of William James and the "Numi-
nous" of Rudolf Otto to be especially expressive of the
depth dimension of thought--but with certain limitations.

#Meland's mature ethic is expressed in the Spencer
essay, but this article is important in showing the
close relationship between aesthetics and ethics in
process thought.

Two Paths to the Good Life

Oliver Goldsmith has a statement in one of his essays to the effect that one acquires lasting esteem, not for the fewness of faults, but by the greatness of beauties.[1] This, I think, suggests a contrast between two paths to the good life: the one moving in the direction of moral perfection; the other leading to an aesthetic greatness of character. The Pharasee was a moral man; but Jesus possessed a greater goodness. Meletus was a moral person; but Socrates embodies what was more significant. In every generation, morality has been the morning star of majorities; but to discerning minorities who caught the vision of Plato, Da Vinci, Dante, Goethe, Shakespeare, Keats, or Emerson, the high sun of human effort has been the good life in a creative sense.

This contrast may be stated as the difference between the creative and the controlled way of life; between the good life sought through the ideal of art, and the goodness of life achieved through moral effort. Art is concerned with creating life; morality with controlling it. Art impels men to seek new orders of value and to synthesize them in an expression of unity; morality tends to preserve established orders of value and to resist possible new syntheses that threaten to impair existent values. Morality strives to make the world safe to live in. Art seeks to make it worth living in. Art is experimental. Morality is conservative. Art leads toward a creative and venturesome way of living; morality toward a controlled mode of existence.

I

Matthew Arnold long ago pointed out that western culture is in some sense a synthesis of these two modes of living.[2] From the Hebrews we have acquired a moral bent. From the Greeks, we have inherited an aesthetic tradition. The Hebrews were lacking in the imaginative quality that leads to adventurous living, but they were richly endowed with the capacity to be loyal to experienced realities that appeared to determine destiny. Consequently, they made morals, rather than art, their chief end in life. No race of people has been more industrious, nor more meticulous than they in the fashioning of moral codes. To the Hebrew, life's imperative

425

consisted in <u>doing the will of God</u> in terms of moral
action. The Greeks, in contrast, were imaginative and
creative, and seemingly indifferent to any supernatural
control of life. Consequently they conceived the good
life as a work of art, rather than the end of moral
duty.

The moral earnestness of the Hebraic tradition has
given it a certain advantage over the Greek spirit in
western life. It has made it more aggressive in fashioning the institutional life of the west and in estab-
lishing the <u>set</u> of the <u>mores</u>. When we speak of the
Catholic West of medieval times as a Hellenized form
of Christianity, we must remember that it was a Roman-
ized Hellenism that took root. And the Roman spirit,
in its ordering of the common life, was temperamentally
more akin to the Hebraic than the Greek tradition. Calvinism, the most aggressive of the Protestant movements,
was clearly a renewal of Hebraism with a vengeance. On
its negative side, it was an energetic drive to rid
Christianity of the denaturing influences of Hellenism.
As a positive movement, it was an ardent effort to re-
gain the moral purism of Jewish Christianity. Since
Calvinistic forces became the religious counterpart of
the rising society of capitalism, the moral emphasis,
naturally assumed increasing social importance and came
to dominate the tradition of the west wherever indus-
trialization gained ascendence; which was about everywhere. Yet America and England were influenced the
most. One does not need to reflect long to note that
the aesthetic tradition until recent years, has thrived
more effectively upon the continent, and has entered
more intimately into the shaping of its outlook and
conduct, than in either England or America.

The chief champion of the Greek spirit in the west
has been philosophy. The classics, to be sure, have
been loyal devotees; but their influence has been limited to the small groups which have been touched by
their teaching. Philosophy, through its ethical teaching and philosophy-of-life literature has kept alive
the spark of Plato's genius and of Aristotle's systematic stress upon the golden mean. Yet even its influence has varied. For where Kantian thought has dominated, the ethics of moral earnestness has prevailed.
And where utilitarian theories in ethics and the empirical emphasis in metaphysics have been given priority,
as in certain periods of British philosophy and more
continuously in American thought, the moral emphasis,
in the form of a practical interest, has carried the

426

day. Thus even philosophy has seemed to be weighted on the side of the controlled, rather than the creative way of life.

There have been ample reasons for this neglect of the aesthetic tradition as a guide to human living. Apart from the prevailing sober outlook of the west, bent upon achievement and respectability, there have been metaphysical factors contributing to the strenuous moral mood. Except for a few exponents of quiescent reflection, western thinkers of the modern era have been impelled by the theme of struggle in the shaping of their philosophic systems. Kant and Hegel were clearly activists in the moral sense. Even Royce, committed to metaphysical monism, by his very conception of evil and suffering was led to exalt the moral over the aesthetic. The empiricists from John Locke down, have for the most part, probably by the very nature of their interest, been concerned with the translation of ideas into action.

II

Struggle and action may imply effort or they may suggest creative art. Where struggle arises from a dualism of thought and experience that creates tension between two opposites such as the good and the evil, we have moral effort; where struggle issues from a creative urge to bring possible world into actual existence, we are in the presence of art.

Thus while there are activists that are impelled by moral zeal, there are also activists who simply answer the call of the creative urge. Kantian thought illustrates the former. The philosophy of John Dewey depicts the latter.

The prosaic character of Dewey's philosophizing doubtless blinds many to the aesthetic motivation of his thought. Yet Dewey is an artist in the field of reflective thought. His concern is to bring to actuality the yet unactualized possibilities.

When one turns to the writings of John Dewey dealing with man and his conduct, what strikes one immediately is the complete transformation of morals, as a code for controlling human nature, into moral theory looking to the creative release and direction of the potential powers of human nature.[3] This restatement of the moral concept, amounting to a reversal of its original meaning, might better accomplish its aim by clearly recognizing that it is not the moral path to which one points, but the creative venture known as the art of living. Dewey's ethical theory is concerned with the fashioning of present possibilities into creative events which yield satisfaction and enjoyment. It is a positive philosophy, unperturbed by dismal contrasts between good and bad, better or worse; for the bad and the worse are always lesser goods. It is not judgment, but choice that is desired--selection of those materials and acts which will bring the event in experience to consequences that may be acknowledged with satisfaction. I say this is the artist's way not the moralist's. It is the experimental procedure of creative craftmanship applied to the fashioning of life.

Santayana doubtless would readily be acknowledged the artist par excellence in modern philosophic thought. This, I think, is because his thought forms are clearly in the tradition of recognized art. His theory of the good life, like his philosophy of religion, issues from a metaphysics that distinguishes between the realm of action and the realm of the ideal.[4] And because the ideal is always vision supervening upon the world of experience, the path to the good life must be imaginative projection through contemplation. For Santayana, therefore, art, whatever form it takes, be it poetry, music, or religious contemplation, can never be creative in the sense implied in Dewey's thought. This divergence between Santayana and Dewey focuses the distinction between art and philosophy conceived in the aristocratic form of the genteel tradition and that which finds expression in the democratic medium. Thus while Dewey and Santayana both turn imaginatively to the future good, Dewey chooses the course of vision followed by the scientist, while Santayana goes the way of the lyrical poet. One needs to use discrimination, however, in interpreting Santayana lest he make of his view sheer fantasy. Santayana is not simply a dreamer who loves dreams. He is not indifferent to the transforming growth of character which contemplation of the ideal may bring about. If he stresses the contemplative life, it is because he believes that through such imaginative projection something of significance takes place. The soul "accomodates itself to destiny and grows like the ideal which it conceives."

The crucial difference between Santayana's view and that of Dewey lies in their conception of the ideal.

428

Santayana makes of it a goal outside and beyond the world of action. This is the very thing which Dewey repudiates, insisting that ideals become nullifying to the creative venture unless they are aims discovered and pursued within the world of action.

Whitehead seems to arrive at a further formulation of the aesthetic measure of life by bringing Santayana's realm of ideals and Dewey's world of action into living relationship.[5] Proceeding from the nature of the cosmos to the nature of man, he comes to a metaphysical conception of the qualitative destiny of man's life on the basis of the aesthetic order of the world. God is represented, not as the source of moral judgment, defining good and evil, but rather as the aesthetic order of the world, creating the good. This is the same emphasis, metaphysically stated, which has always issued from the view of those who saw life in terms of creative realization, rather than as moral tension. Again, he says,

Life is an internal fact for its own sake before it is an external fact relating itself to others. . . . The conduct of external life . . . receives its final quality, on which its worth depends, from the internal life which is the self-realization of existence.[6]

The fact that Whitehead's thought proceeds from organismic premises however, takes him out of the company of aesthetes in the purely contemplative sense. Or perhaps we should say his organismic premise, rising from a scientific background, makes clear that his aesthetic approach to the conduct of life is no mere substitution of contemplation for action. This is a correction that is important to note. As a matter of fact, no proponent of the aesthetic way of life has ever intended this substitution. Only by comparison with the activistic moralist has the aesthetic philosopher seemed to replace action with contemplation. Many interpretations of Santayana's philosophy strikingly illustrate this point.

Whitehead's confidence in the aesthetic way of life goes beyond the subjectivism of Santayana, positing the creative fashioning of being, a process in which formative elements, objective to man, including the non-temporal entity "men call God," participate.[7] Man not only grows like what he contemplates, but becomes creatively fashioned into higher order of being through awareness of and commitment to the aesthetic order of the world.

This suggests another aspect of Whitehead's view. In so far as man may be considered an epochal occasion he is "a microcosm inclusive of the whole universe." But the qualitative value of his life as a concretion is subject to increase within limits. One may remain a stolid beast-man; another may approach the Christ. This progression in degree of prehension defines the nature of growth in the aesthetic measure of man's life. One achieves this growth not through conformity to moral code, but through solitary identification with the aesthetic order of the world which effects its own creative fashioning of being.

III

The aesthetic route to the good life has assumed another turn in contemporary ethical thought. In its common form, it may seem to have no affinity to the aesthetic tradition. Yet, if one considers the ends sought, defining the conception of the good life, he will detect a common ground and emphasis. The Greek spirit stressed form and being. The good life was one that achieved perfection of function. In that sense it became a work of art. Since the influx of biological thought, man as an earth creature, capable of fulfilment has become an ethical end in himself.

Man, the unknown, has become increasingly better known through the inquiries and research of the biological and psychological sciences. His possibilities of growth and achievement have become more apparent and his potentialities anticipated. Man is one of the growing things of earth. Like the trees of the forest and all the verdure of life through which the sap is climbing, man is in growth. He has his own distinctive end and creature function. To explore their full possibilities is his chief end as creature. Through knowledge of the organic elements that condition him, and intelligent commitment to the environing forces that shape him, he may come to the fulfilment of his being and into the heritage of his kind.[8]

This view of man, although scientifically determined, nevertheless defines the good life as a creative venture, aiming toward the fulfilment of function and possibility. Life, like poetry, music or sculpture in

430

process, is unformed mass taking form. Yet life is more of a creative art than either the writing of poems, composing, or the fashioning of stone. The conditions of growth make it so. And the organic factors, shaping that growth, add a dimension which lifts the phenomenon beyond the human venture which is art and makes it a divine functioning, to use the only language we seem capable of to express this transcendent truth. Michelangelo's Creation of Man is the pictorial parable that expresses this truth for us.

The aesthetic measures of life, looking to the fulfilment of creature ends, is as demanding in its laws for life as any moral code; but its criteria for the good life are better adapted to assure the individual's growth in society. The history of moral codes clearly reveals that morality's chief concern has been the control of the individual in the interest of social ends. The aesthetic measure of life does not overlook this important concern, but its restraints are directed toward the creative control of life. That is, to say, its chief concern is the fulfilment of individuals in terms of the corporate life. Hence the disciplines that are brought to bear upon conduct are consonant with that creative end. Where conditions are made ripe for the operation of the growth process in society, both individuals and social institutions are brought into a mutually sustaining and enhancing relationship that assures both creativity and social control.

"All order," writes Whitehead in Religion in the Making, "is aesthetic order and the moral order is merely certain aspects of aesthetic order."[9] The very character of the world, that is to say, makes the aesthetic measure of things primary and more final. And this is as true when applied to the conduct of life as when made the basis for understanding the nature of the world.

FOOTNOTES

[1]"The Characteristics of Greatness" in The Bee and Other Essays, p. 39.

[2]Culture and Anarchy.

[3]See Human Nature and Conduct.

[4]Reason and Common Sense, Cr. VIII, ff; Reason in Society, Ch. VIII; Reason in Religion, Ch. I-III and Ch. IX. ff.

[5]Cf. Science and the Modern World. Also Religion in the Making.

[6]Religion in the Making, pp. 15-16.

[7]See Religion in the Making, Part III. A fuller statement of this view is given in Process and Reality especially Chapter X and Part V.

[8]I have tried to give formulation to this view in my Modern Man's Worship, Parts II-III, and Write Your Own Ten Commandments. A summary statement of it is given in "The Faith of a Mystical Naturalist" in The Review of Religion, March, 1937.

[9]Religion in the Making, p. 105.

SUGGESTED READINGS

Bernard Eugene Meland

Meland, Bernard. Faith and Culture (New York: Oxford University Press 1953; London: George Allen and Unwin, 1955; Paperback, Carbondale, Ill.: Southern Illinois University Press, 1970).

_____. Higher Education and the Human Spirit (Chicago: University of Chicago Press, 1953; Paperback, Chicago: Seminary Cooperative Bookstore, 1965).

_____. The Realities of Faith: The Revolution in Cultural Forms (New York: Oxford University Press, 1962; Paperback, Chicago: Seminary Cooperative Bookstore, 1970).

_____. The Secularization of Modern Cultures (New York: Oxford University Press, 1966).

* * *

_____. "Some Philosophic Aspects of Poetic Perception," The Personalist, XXII (1941), 384-392.

_____. "The Culture of the Human Spirit," Journal of Bible and Religion, XII (1944), 217-226.

_____. "The Ascetic Temper of Modern Humanism," The Personalist, XXVI (1945), 153-165.

_____. "Education for A Spiritual Culture," The Journal of Religion, XXVI (1946), 87-100.

_____. "A Good Not Our Own," Current Religious Thought, X (1950), 3-6.

433

Meland, Bernard. "The Perception of Goodness," Journal of Religion, XXXII (1952), 47-55.

_____. "From Darwin to Whitehead: A Study in the Shift in Ethos and Perspective Underlying Religious Thought," Journal of Religion, XL (1960), 229-245.

_____. "Alternatives to Absolutes," Religion in Life, XXXIII (1964), 19-27.

_____. "A New Morality--But To What End?" Religion in Life, XXXV (1966), 191-199.

* * *

Loomer, B. M. "Bernard Eugene Meland," Quest, VIII (1964), 1f.

Pittenger, W. N. "Process Thought: A Contemporary Trend in Theology," Expository Times, LXXVI (1965), 269-280.

* * *

Brown, D., James, R. E., and Reeves, G., (Eds.). Process Philosophy and Christian Thought (Indianapolis: Bobbs-Merrill, 1971), pp. 24, 34f, 49f, 116-27, 133, 138f, 411-30, 445, 483f.

Cousins, E. H., (Ed.). Process Theology (New York: Newman Press, 1971), pp. 1f, 9f, 16, 24, 35, 37-45, 67, 82, 191, 201, 203-06, 357-60.

Schilling, H. D. The New Consciousness in Science and Religion (Philadelphia: Pilgrim Press, 1973), pp. 183, 185f, 189f, 278, 283, 288.

Miller, R. C. The American Spirit in Theology (New York: United Church Press, 1974), pp. 19n, 20n, 22n, 24, 54f, 62n, 64, 65n, 67n, 68n, 72, 75, 78n, 79n, 84, 95n, 97, 103, 111, 116f, 165, 177n, 178n, 179n, 180, 193, 196, 200n, 207n, 213, 215, 221-23, 227n, 232, 234n, 235, 237, 242f, 289f.

18. TOWARDS CLARITY IN AESTHETICS

John B. Cobb, Jr.

John Boswell Cobb received his formal education from Emory University, the University
of Michigan, and the University of Chicago
(M.A., 1949; Ph.D., 1952). At Chicago he
studied under Henry Nelson Wieman, Charles
Hartshorne, Bernard Loomer, Bernard Meland,
and Daniel Day Williams. He is presently
Ingraham Professor of Theology at the School
of Theology in Claremont, California.

In this essay* Professor John Cobb sets out to explain what is meant by the word "aesthetic" and, second,
what important "nonaesthetic" functions are served by
aesthetic objects. In pursuing his enquiry Professor
Cobb utilizes the basic concepts of Whitehead's metaphysics. (His presentation of these concepts is unusu-
ally clear and concise, and should prove most useful
for students who are beginning the study of Whitehead.)
An object is aesthetic to the extent that the "subjective form" (the manner in which it enters into the
quality of our subjective experience) of its "prehension" (in a special sense, perception) in the "mode of
causal efficacy" (as raw, instinctive experience)[#] is

---

*The essay is from Philosophy and Phenomenological
Research, XVIII, 2 (1957), 169-189. Used by permission
of Dr. John Cobb and Philosophy and Phenomenological
Research.

[#]Perhaps the best way of understanding causal efficacy is in reference to "sense reception." "Sense
perception" is presentational immediacy. Thus causal
efficacy is the heavy, coercive, and determining formulation of the past. The express outcome of this for
Whitehead is that he will not identify God and creativity (or causal efficacy), even where this notion connotes creativity and novelty. He tends (with Plato) to
relate God to forms or order and not to causal efficacy.
Causal efficacy is efficient in contrast to final or

aesthetic. This definition attempts to avoid two pit-
falls, that of reducing the aesthetic to some physical
basis (like muscular response) and that of elevating it
to some purely abstract domain (purely formal concepts).
The aesthetic qualities of objects must be sought instead in the ways in which they impinge subjectively on
our perceptual fields, especially in the less clear-cut,
readily describable aspects of our experience. Concepts like unity, diversity, harmony and balance, which
are often employed to define the aesthetic, may be very
helpful; but they can not be substituted for "the fundamental subjective sense of what is aesthetically satisfactory." The author concludes by examining five
functions which aesthetic objects may perform: (1) the
providing of additional dimensions of form; (2) the
widening of capacity for experience; (3) the communication of ideas; (4) the influencing of emotions; and
(5) the affording of pleasure.

---

formal cause. Cf. Process and Reality, pp. 31ff. One
will also gain by a study of Peirce's and Bergson's
recognition and explication of this notion.

Towards Clarity in Aesthetics

I

The purpose of this essay is two-fold: first to determine what 'the aesthetic' is as the defining and delimiting characteristic of objects felt to be aesthetic; second to determine the relationship between 'the aesthetic' in this sense and some important functions served by aesthetic objects. Successful achievement of these ends should resolve most of the contradictions between aestheticians.

Two assumptions underlie the effort to find the defining characteristics of objects regarded as aesthetic. One is that there is a range of objects generally recognized as being of special aesthetic interest. The other is that these objects have in common some distinguishing trait.

The term aesthetic may not in fact always be used with fundamental reference to the distinguishing trait of those objects most widely acknowledged to be aesthetic. However, such use will prove clarifying and fruitful, and the search for a definition in this paper will be a search for this distinguishing characteristic. This characteristic must be present maximally in objects of those types most clearly and unquestioningly regarded as aesthetic, minimally, if at all, in those most surely regarded as not of aesthetic interest. Objects or types of objects about which there is uncertainty or disagreement may be expected either to possess this characteristic only to a moderate degree or to possess some qualities or functions commonly associated with 'the aesthetic' but in this case largely separate from it.

To guide the inquiry certain types of objects normally recognized as being aesthetic must be listed: poetry, music, painting, and sculpture. There is virtual agreement that these are among the more important clearly aesthetic fields and that the variety found among such fields is sufficiently reflected in this list. There is also virtual agreement that the quality in question is not found, at least not to a comparable degree, in such fields as work, sports, planning or study.

A further distinction must be made prior to initiating the search for 'the aesthetic.' The term is used in two senses, one of which is the genus of which the other is the species. The distinction is best explained by illustration. An aesthetically sensitive person is much more disturbed by a harsh, grating sound or by a room decorated in bad taste than is one who is relatively insensitive aesthetically. In an important sense of aesthetic we may speak of 'the aesthetic' as including both the aesthetically objectionable and the aesthetically satisfactory.[1]

* * *

The first object of search, then, is the characteristic by virtue of which the aesthetically relevant (whether positive or negative) can be separated from the aesthetically irrelevant. Since an object cannot be conceived as aesthetic except as in someone's experience of it, and certainly cannot be studied except as it is found in the experience of those who study, it must be regarded as aesthetic in virtue of the effect which it has upon the experience of auditors or spectators.

II

Since familiarity with Whitehead's terminology and concepts cannot be presupposed, an effort is made to explain them briefly as they become relevant to the analysis. Whitehead holds that to be actual is to be involved in experience (of which by far the greater part is lacking in consciousness), and that experience is not an undifferentiated flow but rather involves transition from one occasion to another. These occasions (actual entities, or actual occasions of experience) are the least units or atomic elements of which the realm of the actual is composed. The movement by which each novel occasion takes up into itself selectively its past and then passes into objective immortality as the past of new occasions is the creative process.

An actual occasion is internally related to its past because its past is causally efficacious for it, that is, constitutes the initial phase of the new occasion's self-realization. This relationship of causal efficacy, which is the only actual relationship among

438

actual entities as such, is, from the side of the new occasion, conceived as prehension.

A prehension of another actual occasion, which is from the side of the prehending subject the way in which its past becomes efficacious for it, is analyzed into the initial datum, which is the datum as it exists independently of the subject; the objective datum, which is the datum as it becomes causally efficacious for the subject, i.e., actually enters into the subject; and the subjective form which is "how that subject prehends that datum."[2] This "how" may be desire, disgust, interest, purpose, or any other "way" in which we may be related to objects of experience.

In addition to prehensions of actual occasions there are also prehensions of eternal objects. Eternal objects are abstract potentialities for actualization. Any quality or relationship which can characterize an indefinite number of actual occasions is an eternal object. As such it has reality (not actuality) in the sense of power to affect the actual independently of whether it is at that time or has at any time qualified an actual occasion. Prehension of eternal objects also involves subjective forms.

Finally, that which governs the process of selection which distinguishes the objective datum in the prehension of an actual occasion from the initial datum of the prehension is the subjective aim. This is the prehension of an eternal object with the subjective form of purpose.

Actual occasions are grouped together in societies. Societies may or may not be personally ordered. A personally ordered society is one which has a serial order, each occasion inheriting from all of its antecedent series and itself objectifying this past for its successors. The flow of occasions which constitutes a human experience is a personally ordered society of actual occasions of experience.

Whitehead's analysis reveals the ambiguity of many of the terms which are used in discussions of aesthetics such as feeling, emotion, and attitude. Feeling may be equated with prehension as a whole, or with the subjective form of a prehension, or with certain types of subjective forms. Emotion may be used broadly so as to be coextensive with subjective form; or narrowly as the subjective form of a limited range of prehensions such as those of visceral-motor activity; or as identical with certain prehensions as a whole. Attitude may refer either to certain kinds of subjective forms such as interest, appreciation, and approval; to the prehension (or some phase of the prehension) of the motor act or tendency of the organism; or to the subjective aim. Although greater precision in the use of terms such as these will not put an end to all disagreements, it will at least so clarify the areas of disagreement as to make fruitful discussion possible.

If whatever is actual has its being in actual occasions, "the aesthetic" must be sought there. It may be sought (1) in a distinctive form or pattern displayed by individual actual occasions; (2) in a form or pattern displayed by societies of actual occasions; (3) in the relationship of occasions, societies of occasions, or elements within occasions; or (4) in some element within an occasion considered in itself.

The first of these alternatives may be dismissed because actual occasions can be distinguished from each other not by formal differences but rather by what they feel (initial and objective datum), by how they feel it (subjective form), and by what they purpose (subjective aim).

The society referred to in the second alternative must be either a personally ordered one or not personally ordered. If it is lacking in personal order, "the aesthetic" must be perceived by some occasion within or without it, not by the society as such. Its differentia would be sought, then, in the percipient, not in the society. If it is a personally ordered society, "the aesthetic" may be perceived by it. It seems that it might then be the prehension by actual occasions of a pattern displayed by the personally ordered society which they make up. Dewey's understanding of "the aesthetic" seems to be of this sort.[3] However, this approach cannot yield the clue to the discovery of "the aesthetic" in the sense originally proposed in this paper, that is, as the common property of poetry, music, painting, and sculpture virtually absent in sports, planning, work, and study.

The third alternative is to find the locus of "the aesthetic" in the relationship which actual occasions have to each other. A certain kind of relation of actual occasions in a personally ordered society, or some of the elements within them, would be aesthetic. The

440

former of these possibilities reduces to the second alternative, but the latter in its interaction with the fourth poses a number of interesting possibilities.

Perhaps the kind of element which is the locus of "the aesthetic" may also be nonaesthetic when it does not have a specifiable external relationship. Perhaps some quality in experience such as pleasure, emotion, interest, or attention is aesthetic, but only when in some specifiable relationship to the object which gives rise to it, to future occasions, or to other elements in the occasion.

III

Now that the first three alternatives have been dismissed the search for "the aesthetic" may be directed toward the elements themselves of the actual occasion. This means ultimately that "the aesthetic" is to be found either in the subjective aim or in some phase of prehensions.

The former is what is generally thought of as decisive when a certain attitude of attention is regarded as determinative of "the aesthetic." The suggestion is that a certain attitude voluntarily taken is aesthetic, that any object toward which this attitude is taken is thereby constituted an aesthetic object, and that the entire experience of the object is indiscriminably an aesthetic experience.[4] Without questioning the importance of the subjective aim for aesthetic experience, we must still raise the question as to whether this is what is meant by "the aesthetic." Does the attitude determine "the aesthetic" or does "the aesthetic" determine the attitude? If we take the same attitude toward an acrobat which we take toward a drama, does the experience become thereby equally aesthetic? Does an attitude of intransitive attention toward the sounds of the night in a jungle, which arises out of the fascination of novelty, determine the object to be aesthetic in the same degree as attention evoked by the beauty of a great symphony? This difficulty cannot be surmounted by asserting that the more aesthetic object is the one which most facilitates the continuation of the aesthetic attitude of intransitive attention, for we may remain spellbound by athletic prowess, by a magician's tricks, or by novel sights and sounds just as readily as by music or painting.

441

If it is asserted by the proponents of the attention theory that they mean intransitive attention evoked by certain qualities in the object or arising out of certain kinds of interest in it, then the question becomes that of distinguishing aesthetic and non-aesthetic attention in terms of some factor other than attention.

Since the locus of "the aesthetic" is not in the subjective aim, it must be in the prehension itself. Prehensions of actual occasions are analyzed into three phases: the initial datum, the objective datum, and the subjective form. Since the initial datum would be the painting or musical composition as it is for itself independently of being experienced by spectator or auditor, this cannot be the locus of the differentiation here sought. The distinction between the objective datum and the subjective form is that between how the object enters into experience in terms of content and how it enters into experience in terms of the concomitant quality of subjective experience. Presumably the same content can have even simultaneously both aesthetic and non-aesthetic meaning for the auditor or spectator, as a representational painting may move a spectator both aesthetically and sentimentally. If this is true, the distinction between "the aesthetic" and "the non-aesthetic" must be made at the level of the subjective forms of prehensions.

Prehensions may be of eternal objects or of actual occasions. These actual occasions may be either within or without the body. Some aestheticians have given attention to the role of eternal objects in art appreciation and others have concentrated on the role of muscles and viscera.[5] But aesthetic experience is in the first instance experience of an object external to the auditor or spectator through his sense organs. Hence, without disregarding the importance of the contribution of the aestheticians in question, we may proceed directly to the consideration of the subjective form of the prehension of external objects through the sense organs. This occurs whenever there is aesthetic experience, although in and of itself it cannot, of course, distinguish aesthetic experience from non-aesthetic sense experience, or satisfactory aesthetic experience from that which is not satisfactory.

Before proceeding to these further questions, however, it is necessary to make an additional distinction made possible by Whitehead's subtle analysis: that between prehensions in the mode of causal efficacy and perceptions in the mode of presentational immediacy.

Prehension in the mode of causal efficacy is the initial primary consequence of the past for the present. It is the kind of prehension characteristic of all organisms down to the very lowest and is that by which the continuity of the universe is maintained. However, high grade organisms can select certain aspects of the total impact which they receive from other entities and transmute them into sense data. These are projected upon the space-time continuum as contemporaneous with the projecting occasion although they derive from occasions in the immediate past. Projected as present sense data, they are perceived in the mode of presentational immediacy. The process of transmutation has the evolutionary function of permitting high grade organisms to select for emphasis those aspects of their environment relevant to their survival. It is this process which makes consciousness possible.

"The aesthetic" previously has been determined to be some element common to the impact made by musical compositions and poems upon the auditor and the effect of paintings and sculpture on the spectator. By examination of other alternatives it has been shown that this element must be sought in the subjective form of the prehension of objects external to the organism. The question now to be decided is whether this is the subjective form of the prehension in the mode of causal efficacy or the subjective form of the perception in the mode of presentational immediacy.

The subjective form of perception in the mode of presentational immediacy is less determined by the object than is that in the mode of causal efficacy. Insofar as it is determined by the object, this determination is mediated by the prehension in the mode of causal efficacy. In the mode of presentational immediacy the perception of the same object varies greatly from one person to another and from one time to another according to differences in past experience and present interest, and such identity as it possesses through these changes is derived from the causal efficacy of the object for all the occasions which prehend it. However, "the aesthetic" as a property of the object must be found in that part of the experience of the prehending human occasion which is determined by the object and is for that reason not dependent upon particular past experiences and present interests. Clearly,

443

therefore, "the aesthetic" as a property of objects is to be found initially in the subjective form of prehensions of them in the mode of causal efficacy.

The analysis of aesthetic experience, however, although it must begin with the prehension of objects in the mode of causal efficacy, must proceed to the explanation of the different ways in which this experience is transmuted into perception in the mode of presentational immediacy. Not every experience of a particular painting is equally an aesthetic experience. The art historian may examine it to learn something of the techniques employed by the artist, the art dealer may view it to estimate its commercial value, the worshipper may seek to be lifted by it to the contemplation of the reality which it expresses. To all of these the aesthetic character of the painting is relevant, and this aesthetic character consists in the kind of causal efficacy which it has for those who look at it. However, the role of this aesthetic quality in their total experience is limited by their respective subjective aims. Only when the painting is contemplated for its own sake or for the sake of that which it effects in the experience of the contemplator can it make its full aesthetic impact. When this occurs the process of transmutation into the mode of presentational immediacy is governed more or less completely by the datum of the prehension rather than by a practical subjective aim. In this case the subjective aim is that the entire occasion be maximally determined by the art object.

This means that whereas "the aesthetic" must be located initially in the subjective form of the prehension in the mode of causal efficacy, its importance rests to a great extent upon its potentiality for the determination of the total occasion of experience and especially of the perception in the mode of presentational immediacy. To summarize, an object is aesthetic to whatever extent the subjective form of the prehension of it in the mode of causal efficacy is aesthetic; an experience is aesthetic to whatever extent the aesthetic object is determinative of the subjective form of the entire experience.

IV

The differentiation of "the aesthetic" is to be sought then in the initial impact made upon experience by external objects through the sense organs. The

444

impact which the color of the walls of a room may make
upon experience is already aesthetic in the sense of
being material for aesthetic experience, so also are
isolated notes of music, and perhaps shapes and rhythms.
However, it does not follow that sufficient intensity
of feeling of this sort is properly aesthetic. One may
prefer one color or tone to another in complete abstraction from the question as to where it is to be seen or
heard, but for the most part, at least, the aesthetic
value resides in colors or sounds in patterned relationships, not in the isolated qualities.

The sphere of "the aesthetic" in the sense which
is inclusive of beauty but not limited to it is that of
the subjective forms of the prehensions of patterned
relationships of colors or sounds, lines or rhythms, or
other sensuous elements in the mode of causal efficacy.
"The aesthetic" in this sense is one aspect of all sensuous experience whatever, although it is important
only when the subjective aim is sufficiently divorced
from practical considerations so as to tolerate some
degree of receptivity.

* * *

The conclusion now reached is that the property
shared by aesthetic fields and absent in those which
are not thought of as aesthetic is that of yielding or
striving to yield an experience of lasting satisfaction
in the form or pattern of prehensions in the mode of
causal efficacy. This does not tell us what kind of
form or pattern is essential to aesthetic experience.
This is a factual question which can best be treated by
the art critic and not by the philosopher. Even the
art critic must be careful to maintain a strictly empirical approach--not asking what properties art works
"ought" to have, but rather what properties successful
art works do have, generalizing if he wishes, but never
concluding from the fact that some masterpieces possess
certain qualities that all art must possess those properties in order to be great. Probably some very abstract rules, such as that a good art work unifies a
complex variety, are virtually universal. But such
statements, if they are to retain universality must
sacrifice specificity, because there are many ways of
achieving what may be called unity, and unity in this
context means little more than satisfactory form. The
principle then reduces to the statement that a complex
satisfactory form is, other things being equal, of more
enduring interest than a simple one. Principles like

harmony, balance, and contrast likewise can be given no clear and distinct meaning independently of the appeal to the property of being formally satisfactory, for aesthetic harmony and balance are not (or may not be) identical with mathematical harmony or balance. This is not to say that concepts like unity of variety, harmony, balance, and contrast are not of value in the analysis of the properties of the objects which are the correlatives of the aesthetic experience. But the question as to what constitutes aesthetic unity, diversity, harmony, balance, and contrast must be answered by reference to the fundamental subjective sense of what is aesthetically satisfactory, rather than being the independent basis of determining whether or not an object or experience has aesthetic value.

V

The special functions or purposes of art objects are so varied that any brief summary will necessarily prove incomplete. These functions are so complexly interrelated that any grouping must be somewhat arbitrary. Also, a classification of ends can assist but little toward a classification of works of art since most of these serve a plurality of functions often without any clear hierarchy of importance. Despite all of these limitations some grouping of aesthetic ends or purposes is needed. This grouping is made under five headings which may be labelled for convenience (1) additional dimensions of form, (2) widening of capacity for experience, (3) communication of ideas, (4) influence upon emotion, and (5) affording of pleasure. It is not claimed that all the proper functions of art can be grouped under these five headings, but only that many of the most important can be so grouped.

The following pages are devoted to an effort to explain what is meant by these headings and to indicate their subtypes and the arts relevant to each. It is of utmost importance to recognize that these special functions are called derivative only because they do not provide the basis for the definition of "the aesthetic" or the delimitation of the aesthetic field. They may well be equally important with beauty per se or even of much greater importance in many art objects, but it remains the presence of beauty or of the effort to achieve it which delimits the aesthetic field.

446

(1) It has been shown that "the aesthetic" as a property of objects is that which causes their form to be prehended as satisfactory in the mode of causal efficacy, and that aesthetic objects may be perceived with satisfaction in the mode of presentational immediacy. It should now be further noted that there are additional dimensions of form in most aesthetic experience.

Art objects may be perceived in the mode of presentational immediacy with the subjective form of meaning. The sounds of a recited poem make an impact upon us prior to their meaning, but they rarely enter consciousness apart from their meaning, denotative and connotative. The subjective forms of these meanings must have formally satisfying relations. Between the individual sounds and meanings there must be also a formally satisfying relationship. Both directly and through their meanings, sounds may arouse visceral and motor activity as well, and insofar as these are evoked, their subjective forms too must be harmonious with, i.e., have formally satisfying relationships with, all else that is involved. These dimensions of formal relationship cannot be aesthetic in the primary sense delimiting the aesthetic fields, for they are not shared by all aesthetic objects, but in much art they are of greatest importance.

* * *

(2) The new understanding or capacity may be at the level of sensation at which art makes its initial impact. The clearest illustration of this function of art is to be found in the visual arts. Its explanation requires a brief discussion of the process of artistic creativity.

It has been affirmed above that the initial and only essential phase of aesthetic experiences as such is the prehension of external objects in the mode of causal efficacy. This does not imply that the creative artistic process necessarily begins with an aesthetic experience. However, that aesthetic sensitivity to nature is a major source of creativity in the visual arts is hardly disputable.

The successful creator of art objects has or develops unusual aesthetic sensitivity. This involves both unusual intensity of subjective forms in the mode of causal efficacy and unusual sensitivity of the

447

strictly aesthetic kind, i.e., intensity of subjective form of the prehension of the pattern as a whole. When an artist is controlled predominantly by strictly aesthetic sensitivity, his work will be characterized by the primary concern for form discussed above. When, however, an artist is controlled predominantly by the intensity of his sensitivity to subjective forms in the mode of causal efficacy, he will create a distinctive kind of art which takes as its chief guide something other than satisfactory form.

The painter (or sculptor) of this type makes his primary task the copying of nature rather than its transformation into more satisfying patterns. But his imitation of nature is not a reproduction of what others see in nature. Rather it presents to others a new vision of nature. This kind of artist prehends nature in the mode of causal efficacy so intensely that the usual transmutation into the mode of presentational immediacy guided by the practical needs of life proves wholly inadequate and unsatisfactory.

* * *

The writer may paint in words a visual scene in such a way as to have results on the reader almost identical with those on the viewer of the painting. Like the painter he may be aware of aspects of visual experience commonly ignored, and through his descriptive powers he may call these aspects of reality to the attention of his readers, thereby enriching their capacity for visual enjoyment. However, the most distinctive function of the literary artist in the general area now under discussion is to describe, not visual and auditory experience, but experience as such in its subjective immediacy--its subjective forms and its subjective aims. To clarify the function of literature in these respects some comments on the relation of language to experience may prove helpful.

Subjective experience which one cannot verbally describe is for the most part not admitted to consciousness except perhaps at its fringes. Since words in common use can describe only a small percentage of all the varieties of subjective experience, the result is the extreme impoverishment of consciousness and still more of self-understanding. The learning of words by a child is an experience not primarily of gaining ability to communicate pre-existing ideas and experience but rather of achieving and extending consciousness itself.

This process continues throughout life, and perhaps the central significance of education lies in its power of expanding and developing, not information merely, but consciousness itself.

* * *

(3) Another end which influences the production of some art is the communication of ideas. Ideas are here understood in an exceedingly wide sense to include those which are not grasped consciously. Since the method of communication differs, conscious and unconscious ideas will be treated as separate subtypes in that order.

Some literature has a message or thesis which can be formulated as such propositionally. Such a message or thesis may be an assertion about life or reality as a whole--its essential goodness or hopelessness or cruelty. It may be the proclamation of a way of salvation --through love, mutual tolerance, or mystical ecstasy. It may be the denunciation of some evil--the slave trade, the treatment of debtors, or war. It may be an argument for some religious, political, or economic doctrine or philosophy. The visual arts can also be employed in similar ways, although their capacity to convey conscious ideas is somewhat limited in comparison with that of literature.

What are here called ideas may also be communicated at a non-conscious level. Some art, both literary and visual, may be understood best as the expression of subconscious needs, desires, and understandings, and it may be that its appreciation also must be a level below or beyond consciousness. Some symbolism is merely a substitute for literal language and can be translated into it. Inability to interpret it is identical in result with inability to understand words. There is, however, another kind of symbolism which is not reducible to words, at least at the time it is employed. It expresses ideas which cannot be brought through language into clear interrelations with other ideas. Often these ideas are of supreme importance for life. Perhaps men may later learn to express literally what at first they can express only symbolically, but in the case of some symbols this process is never complete. These symbols have an extraordinarily rich content which literal statement seems never to exhaust, and much of the intensity of feeling associated with the symbols is lost in translation. The subjective

449

form of the prehension of the translations is never
identical with that of the prehension of the symbol.
Symbols of this kind play a prominent role in both the
literary and the visual arts.

(4) The basic conception to which "influence upon
emotion" refers is that of the direct impact made by
the art object at the level of its meaning rather than
at that of its form. A painting or poem may be such as
to be experienced with a simple subjective form such as
gaiety or melancholy. Or it may be such as to set in
motion complex visceral and motor activities whose composite subjective forms may have peculiar intensity.
Emotion in this sense may be aroused as commonly noted
by its expression, but Stephen Pepper has shown that it
may also be aroused by direct stimulation and by representation.[6]

Emotion plays a role of great importance in relation to the functions discussed above. It is reintroduced here to point out that it may be not only a means
to the end of formal perfection, widening of capacity
for experience, or communication of ideas, but also an
end in itself. The chief function of an art work may
be the evocation of emotion in its auditors or spectators. There seems to be some intrinsic felt value in
being moved to feel joy or sorrow, fear or pity, anger
or love, cheerfulness or despair, when at the same time
we experience a "distance" between ourselves and the
object of our emotion. Probably this value closely resembles that discussed above in connection with the
growth of consciousness through the grasping of new
meanings. Variety of emotion in itself enlarges and
enriches consciousness, at least so long as it is sufficiently objective to consciousness so as not to have
the possibly deleterious effects of the same emotion
(e.g., sorrow or anger) in real life.

One special case under the general heading here
considered is of sufficient importance to warrant separate treatment. A chief consequence of the reading of
much literature is the broadening of the reach of sympathetic interest in persons whose behavior appears
from the usual perspective of the reader to be obnox-
ious or stupid. The barriers of language, custom, belief, time, and place, which normally interfere with
the flow of sympathy, can be overcome so that the range
of its flow can be extended indefinitely.

Another special case of very wide relevance is that of aesthetic objects designed to be experienced with the subjective form of piety. Architecture, painting, sculpture, and music as well as literature may cooperate to arouse such subjective forms, and much splendid aesthetic work has been directed to this end.

Art in its role as evoker of emotion has a further function of considerably greater value to the percipient than the mere arousal of one subjective form or another. This function has been discussed most in connection with tragedy, and perhaps other forms of art do not have comparable functions at all, or at least do not have them to a comparable degree. The function referred to is specifically "purgation" or "catharsis" but the general concept of which this may be but one case would be the transformation of emotional experience and the enrichment of the capacity for emotions through a guided experience of peculiar emotional intensity.

* * *

Why this is true is not the artist's question, and neither the psychologist nor the philosopher is yet prepared to answer it. I. A. Richards suggests that its understanding can be approached physiologically in terms of neuro-muscular concomitants of feelings which after a period of tension achieve a synthesis which restores balance at a deeper level.[7] Richards does not conceive of this as an explanation but rather merely as pointing in the direction in which an explanation may fruitfully be sought, and his comments are noted here in the same spirit.

(5) There remains finally a function of art which in literature at least is of the greatest importance, namely, to give pleasure. One way in which this may be done is by simply telling an interesting story. The value of a story may, of course, reside in one or more of the areas already considered, but it may also be an end in itself, as arousing intrinsic interest through a distinctive natural capacity of man to enjoy learning of what has happened to others. Pleasure may also be afforded through the opportunity provided by the story for identification with the hero and vicarious enjoyment of his triumphs and adventures.

451

Whenever any one of these special functions is made the basis for the interpretation of all aesthetic objects or for the definition of "the aesthetic," confusion inevitably follows. Many objects normally regarded as aesthetic can be shown to possess the chosen function only by the most strained interpretation and to a lesser degree, in some cases, than other objects which are normally thought of as having but trivial aesthetic importance. On the other hand, when "the aesthetic" is defined in terms of sensuous form and when this definition is allowed to give the impression that those interested in aesthetic objects should limit their attention to this one aspect of them, confusion follows equally. Many of the creators of art objects have placed other ends far above that of beauty, and many of those today who are interested in aesthetic objects are primarily motivated by other concerns. It is only by a non-sequitur that one can twist the definition of "the aesthetic" in terms of formal considerations into the affirmation that within the field so defined these elements alone are worthy of serious interest. Even among those using a single medium such as painting, there are such wide variations in purpose and procedure that the theoretical imposition of unity must be false. The painter creates an art object whenever his purpose involves either as primary aim or as a significant means to some other primary aim the achievement of beauty.

In conclusion the aesthetic character of three special groups of objects must be considered: objects of practical usefulness, prose literature, and nature.

Objects made for practical use which neither achieve beauty nor attempt to achieve beauty are clearly not aesthetic fields. Arts such as architecture and the making of clothing, utensils for eating and cooking, and furniture are not intrinsically or necessarily aesthetic since their primary aims do not involve the achievement of beauty. However, for many artists in these fields the achievement of beauty is an aim of great importance, and insofar as this is true, the objects created do constitute an aesthetic field. In addition, in some cases where a conscious aim at beauty may have been lacking, the objects created nevertheless possess beauty. These objects too are of interest to the aesthetician.

The aesthetic status of prose literature is more complex. It can be stated succinctly in three points. (1) Most prose literature is an aesthetic field to some extent in that formal excellence of sound pattern does make some contribution to the achievement of its ends. However, some authors may sacrifice beauty of language almost completely to other ends, such as a realistic capturing of the language of the slums, and in general prose authors are far less interested in the aesthetic value of their language than in other ends. Hence, those aestheticians stressing a purist aesthetic are likely to neglect prose literature, with considerable justification. (2) The dimensions of formal excellence beyond the sensuous are as important for most prose literature as they are in other more clearly aesthetic fields. These dimensions cannot be made a part of the purest definition of "the aesthetic" because they are not necessary to pure aesthetic experience, but since for so many of those interested in art they are of far greater importance than the purely aesthetic quality, the resemblance at this point makes inevitable the refusal to separate prose literature from other aesthetic fields. (3) The other functions of art objects are shared by prose literature, so that those also who find their chief interest to be in one of these will inevitably resist any separation and regard prose literature as equally aesthetic with painting and music.

Thus prose literature stands in almost complete continuity with aesthetic fields, shading off into the non-aesthetic only by virtue of the almost total indifference of some authors to sensuous beauty. At the opposite extreme, nature stands in continuity with the indisputably aesthetic field only by virtue of its richness as a source and inspiration of sensuous beauty. Thus works like Studs Lonigan and The Hairy Ape have virtually no continuity with an ocean sunset or the Japanese Inland Sea, and those definitions of "the aesthetic" which would strive to include the former can scarcely succeed in tolerating the latter. The former have only exceedingly minimal aesthetic value in the strict sense although they overlap extensively with aesthetic fields in their derivative functions. The natural scene, on the contrary, shares with clearly aesthetic fields a very considerable amount of beauty in the primary sense, but is quite without the derivative values of art objects.

Thus nature must be declared an aesthetic field, although one quite different from all other aesthetic

453

fields. The difference consists not only in the irrelevance of the derivative aesthetic values but also in the activity of the percipient in aesthetic enjoyment of nature. Nature provides the materials for aesthetic experience with a richness which hinders rather than facilitates the prehension of satisfactory patterns. In imagination the visual stimuli must be selected, bounded, and related. In the mode of causal efficacy the pattern prehended is rarely quite satisfactory. The beauty of nature is perhaps more properly the potentiality for many beauties.

Although aesthetic satisfaction is certainly gained from nature, nature is at least equally important aesthetically as the inspiration to the creation of art objects, not alone by suggesting satisfying patterns of sensuous qualities, but also by stimulating endeavor to achieve art's secondary purposes. The relationship of nature to that aesthetic end which was called "widening of capacity for experience" has already been treated. But even for the man of limited aesthetic sensitivity who cannot transfer his vision of nature to a canvas, the escape from artificial civilized life and the reencounter with an untamed nature may restore a sense of vitality and of participation in a more inclusive reality, and thereby it may heighten the capacity for emotion and for aesthetic experience and may vivify the purpose of living.

FOOTNOTES

[1]The term "satisfactory" is not used here and
elsewhere in the sense of meeting preexisting standards
or fulfilling a definite preexisting need. It may
therefore prove confusing to those accustomed to limiting their use to this meaning. Unfortunately, no other
word appears less equivocal. The term "satisfactory"
may be justified on the ground that it is at least a
denial of unsatisfactoriness, and surely we can understand that we may call a situation unsatisfactory on
the basis of how it is immediately felt--for example,
if it is felt as creating needs which it does not meet
or as being frustrating to some universal human need or
preference. To say that an aesthetic experience is
satisfactory, then, is at least to deny that it creates
tensions which it does not resolve or frustrates any
human need. Beyond this what is intended is the common
denominator of such terms as enjoyable, interesting,
and pleasant, all of which involve a positive quality,
but each of which has further specific implications not
necessary to positive aesthetic value.

[2]Alfred North Whitehead, Process and Reality (New
York: The Social Science Book Store, 1929), p. 35.

[3]John Dewey, Art As Experience (New York: Minton,
Balch & Co., 1934), Ch. III.

[4]Expositions of this view are to be found in Eliseo
Vivas, "A Definition of the Aesthetic Experience,"
Journal of Philosophy, Vol. XXXIV (1937), pp. 628-634;
and in Curt John Ducasse, The Philosophy of Art (New
York: Lincoln Mac Veagh, The Dial Press, 1929).

Vivas states on page 630: "An aesthetic object is
an object--any object--grasped in such a way as to give
rise to an aesthetic experience." On page 631 he explains: "An aesthetic experience is an experience of
rapt attention which involves the intransitive apprehension of an object's immanent meanings in their full
presentational immediacy."

Ducasse states on page 189: "Any feeling whatever which is obtained in aesthetic contemplation, is
aesthetic feeling." On page 139 he has explained:

"Aesthetic contemplation is a 'listening' with our capacity for feeling."

The conclusions of the present article bear so many resemblances to Ducasse's position that a word of explanation as to the difference may be in order. Ducasse apparently holds that every object is intrinsically equally aesthetic and that aesthetic objects vary aesthetically only according to the pleasure or pain of their contemplation, i.e., beauty and ugliness in the broad sense corresponding to that in which I have used them. The taking of the aesthetic attitude toward objects appears to be a purely voluntary act, determined, that is, by the person rather than by any characteristic of the object. Presumably one is not affected by beauty or ugliness until he has adopted this attitude. My view is that we are constantly affected by aesthetic properties of objects although their influence is most complete and consciously experienced only when we adopt the appropriate attitude. Furthermore, our adopting of that attitude is determined just as much by the intensity of the already existing effect of the object upon us as by our decision to adopt it. Thus "the aesthetic" cannot be defined in complete dependence upon the attitude as Ducasse defines it. Not only are all objects, as Ducasse would agree, not potentially equally beautiful, but also, they are not potentially equally aesthetic in the inclusive sense.

[5]Cf. Stephen C. Pepper, Aesthetic Quality (New York: Charles Scribner's Sons, 1938), pp. 93 ff. Pepper develops a theory of aesthetic experience in terms of conflicting motor tendencies arising from the perception of the art object.

[6]Pepper, op. cit., pp. 98 ff.

[7]I. A. Richards, Principles of Literary Criticism (New York: Harcourt, Brace & Co., Ltd., 1947), pp. 107 ff.

SUGGESTED READINGS

John B. Cobb

Cobb, John. A Christian Natural Theology: Based
on the Thought of Alfred North Whitehead
(Philadelphia: Westminster Press, 1965).

_____. Is It Too Late? A Theology of Ecol-
ogy (Beverly Hills, California: Bruce,
1972).

* * *

_____. "The Possibility of a Universal Nor-
mative Ethic," Ethics, LXV (1954), 55-61.

_____. "The Philosophical Grounds of Moral
Responsibility," Journal of Philosophy, LVI
(1959), 619-621.

_____. "Nihilism, Existentialism and White-
head," Religion in Life, XXX (1961), 521-533.

_____. "Perfection Exists: A Critique of
Charles Hartshorne," Religion in Life, XXXII
(1963), 294-304.

_____. "The Possibility of Theism Today," in
The Idea of God: Philosophical Perspectives,
E. H. Madden, R. Handy, and M. Farber (Eds.).
(Springfield, Illinois: Charles C. Thomas,
1968), pp. 98-123, 134-138.

_____. "Natural Causality and Divine Action,"
Idealistic Studies, III, 3 (1973), 207-222.

_____. "Ecology, Ethics and Theology," in
Toward a Steady-State Economy, H. Daly (Ed.).
(San Francisco: W. H. Freeman, 1976), pp.
307-320.

* * *

Morgan, G. "Whitehead's Theory of Value," International Journal of Ethics, XLVII (1937),
308-316.

Morris, B. "The Art-Process and the Aesthetic
Fact in Whitehead's Philosophy," in The Phi-
losophy of Alfred North Whitehead, Paul
Schilpp (Ed.). (Evanston: Northwestern
University Press, 1941).

Scriven, M. "The Objectivity of Aesthetic Evaluation," Monist, L, 159-187 (1966).

* * *

Bahm, A. J. "Aesthetic Experience and Moral Experience," Journal of Philosophy, LV, 20
(1958), 837-854.

_____. "The Aesthetics of Organicism," The
Journal of Aesthetics and Art Criticism,
XXVI, 4 (1968), 449-459.

Martin, F. D. "Unrealized Possibility in the
Aesthetic Experience," Journal of Philosophy,
52 (1955), 393-400.

19. ART AS EXPERIENCE

John Dewey

John Dewey (1859-1952) received his education from the University of Vermont and John
Hopkins Graduate School. His long and illus-
trious teaching career was in relationship
to the Universities of Michigan and Minne-
sota, the University of Chicago from 1894 to
1904, and Columbia University from 1904 until
the time of his retirement in 1929. He was
one of America's most influential and inter-
nationally known philosophers.

John Dewey has written what may be said to be the
most valuable work on aesthetics in English so far in
this century; namely, Art as Experience (1934). That
work, from which the following selections are taken,*
represents a significant effort on his part to apply
his philosophy of experimentalism to experience per se.
He sought to deny any definite alternative between
knowledge or intelligence and action, and proposed that
experiences in their actual occurrence are emotional,
volitional and teleological as well as intellectual.
The process of experimental adjustment of the living
organism is essentially a matter of intelligent action,
and so experience is "the fulfillment of the organism
in its struggles and achievements in a world of things"
which in turn "is art." Art is never to be viewed as
an end in itself, but must be used functionally for the
"heightened vitality" of human life. It should be kept
in mind that he did not mean here technology which he
considered to be concerned specifically with things as
instrumentalities. Even though the sciences had had
their beginnings in the arts, he believed they had
overlooked the epistemological category of "immediacy."
His was an effort to come to grips with immediate experience and its emphasis upon the indeterminate and contingent character not only of experience, but of nature

*From Art as Experience (New York: Minton, Balch,
1934), pp. 3-19, 22-25, 35-38. Used by permission.

as a whole. "Aesthetic quality, immediate, final or
self-enclosed indubitably characterizes natural situations as they empirically occur."# The virtue of such
a philosophical perspective is that it keeps us continually conscious of the lure for feeling which resides
within the subliminal aspect of experience. It is precisely this which, however vague or inarticulate, is
immediate and thereby the center of human experiencing.
The influence of Dewey's thought in aesthetics is incalculable and has led to an emphasis on the notion
that art is progressive, in process, and can never be
accepted as standing still or simply related to the
past. There is not a distinction of kind between the
aesthetic and the non-aesthetic experience, but only
one of degree.

#Experience and Nature (New York: W. W. Norton,
1929), p. 96. For an appreciation of Dewey's appeal to
immediate experience and mistrust of abstractions viewed
as prime realities see his 'fallacy of selective emphasis,' p. 27 of the same work.

Art as Experience

By one of the ironic perversities that often attend the course of affairs, the existence of the works of art upon which formation of an esthetic theory depends has become an obstruction to theory about them. For one reason, these works are products that exist externally and physically. In common conception, the work of art is often identified with the building, book, painting, or statue in its existence apart from human experience. Since the actual work of art is what the product does with and in experience, the result is not favorable to understanding. In addition, the very perfection of some of these products, the prestige they possess because of a long history of unquestioned admiration, creates conventions that get in the way of fresh insight. When an art product once attains classic status, it somehow becomes isolated from the human conditions under which it was brought into being and from the human consequences it engenders in actual life-experience.

When artistic objects are separated from both conditions of origin and operation in experience, a wall is built around them that renders almost opaque their general significance, with which esthetic theory deals. Art is remitted to a separate realm, where it is cut off from that association with the materials and aims of every other form of human effort, undergoing, and achievement. A primary task is thus imposed upon one who undertakes to write upon the philosophy of the fine arts. This task is to restore continuity between the refined and intensified forms of experience that are works of art and the everyday events, doings, and sufferings that are universally recognized to constitute experience. Mountain peaks do not float unsupported; they do not even just rest upon the earth. They are the earth in one of its manifest operations. It is the business of those who are concerned with the theory of the earth, geographers and geologists, to make this fact evident in its various implications. The theorist who would deal philosophically with fine art has a like task to accomplish.

If one is willing to grant this position, even if only by way of temporary experiment, he will see that there follows a conclusion at first sight surprising. In order to understand the meaning of artistic products, we have to forget them for a time, to turn aside from

461

them and have recourse to the ordinary forces and conditions of experience that we do not usually regard as
esthetic. We must arrive at the theory of art by means
of a detour. For theory is concerned with understanding, insight, not without exclamations of admiration,
and stimulation of that emotional outburst often called
appreciation. It is quite possible to enjoy flowers in
their colored form and delicate fragrance without knowing anything about plants theoretically. But if one
sets out to understand the flowering of plants, he is
committed to finding out something about the interactions of soil, air, water and sunlight that condition
the growth of plants.

By common consent, the Parthenon is a great work
of art. Yet it has esthetic standing only as the work
becomes an experience for a human being. And, if one
is to go beyond personal enjoyment into the formation
of a theory about that large republic of art of which
the building is one member, one has to be willing at
some point in his reflections to turn from it to the
bustling, arguing, acutely sensitive Athenian citizens,
with civic sense identified with a civic religion, of
whose experience the temple was an expression, and who
built it not as a work of art but as a civic commemora-
tion. The turning to them is as human beings who had
needs that were a demand for the building and that were
carried to fulfillment in it; it is not an examination
such as might be carried on by a sociologist in search
for material relevant to his purpose. The one who sets
out to theorize about the esthetic experience embodied
in the Parthenon must realize in thought what the people into whose lives it entered had in common, as creators and as those who were satisfied with it, with
people in our own homes and on our own streets.

In order to understand the esthetic in its ultimate and approved forms, one must begin with it in the
raw; in the events and scenes that hold the attentive
eye and ear of man, arousing his interest and affording
him enjoyment as he looks and listens: the sights that
hold the crowd--the fire-engine rushing by; the machines
excavating enormous holes in the earth; the human-fly
climbing the steeple-side; the men perched high in air
on girders, throwing and catching red-hot bolts.

.   .   .

So extensive and subtly pervasive are the ideas
that set Art upon a remote pedestal, that many a person

462

would be repelled rather than pleased if told that he enjoyed his casual recreations, in part at least, because of their esthetic quality. The arts which today have most vitality for the average person are things he does not take to be arts: for instance, the movie, jazzed music, the comic strip, and, too frequently, newspaper accounts of love-nests, murders, and exploits of bandits. For, when what he knows as art is relegated to the museum and gallery, the unconquerable impulse towards experiences enjoyable in themselves finds such outlet as the daily environment provides. Many a person who protests against the museum conception of art, still shares the fallacy from which that conception springs. For the popular notion comes from a separation of art from the objects and scenes of ordinary experience that many theorists and critics pride themselves upon holding and even elaborating. The times when select and distinguished objects are closely connected with the products of usual vocations are the times when appreciation of the former is most rife and most keen. When, because of their remoteness, the objects acknowledged by the cultivated to be works of fine art seem anemic to the mass of people, esthetic hunger is likely to seek the cheap and the vulgar.

The factors that have glorified fine art by setting it upon a far-off pedestal did not arise within the realm of art nor is their influence confined to the arts. For many persons an aura of mingled awe and unreality encompasses the "spiritual" and the "ideal" while "matter" has become by contrast a term of depreciation, something to be explained away or apologized for. The forces at work are those that have removed religion as well as fine art from the scope of the common or community life. The forces have historically produced so many of the dislocations and divisions of modern life and thought that art could not escape their influence. We do not have to travel to the ends of the earth nor return many millennia in time to find peoples for whom everything that intensifies the sense of immediate living is an object of intense admiration. Bodily scarification, waving feathers, gaudy robes, shining ornaments of gold and silver, of emerald and jade, formed the contents of esthetic arts, and, presumably, without the vulgarity of class exhibitionism that attends their analogues today. Domestic utensils, furnishings of tent and house, rugs, mats, jars, pots, bows, spears, were wrought with such delighted care that today we hunt them out and give them places of honor in our art museums. Yet in their own time and

463

place, such things were enhancements of the processes of everyday life. Instead of being elevated to a niche apart, they belonged to display of prowess, the manifestation of group and clan membership, worship of gods, feasting and fasting, fighting, hunting, and all the rhythmic crises that punctuate the stream of living.

Dancing and pantomime, the sources of the art of the theater, flourished as part of religious rites and celebrations. Musical art abounded in the fingering of the stretched string, the beating of the taut skin, the blowing with reeds. Even in the caves, human habitations were adorned with colored pictures that kept alive to the senses experiences with the animals that were so closely bound with the lives of humans. Structures that housed their gods and the instrumentalities that facilitated commerce with the higher powers were wrought with especial fineness. But the arts of the drama, music, painting, and architecture thus exemplified had no peculiar connection with theaters, galleries, museums. They were part of the significant life of an organized community.

The collective life that was manifested in war, worship, the forum, knew no division between what was characteristic of these places and operations, and the arts that brought color, grace, and dignity, into them. Painting and sculpture were organically one with architecture, as that was one with the social purpose that buildings served. Music and song were intimate parts of the rites and ceremonies in which the meaning of group life was consummated. Drama was a vital reenactment of the legends and history of group life. Not even in Athens can such arts be torn loose from this setting in direct experience and yet retain their significant character. Athletic sports, as well as drama, celebrated and enforced traditions of race and group, instructing the people, commemorating glories, and strengthening their civic pride.

Under such conditions, it is not surprising that the Athenian Greeks, when they came to reflect upon art, formed the idea that it is an act of reproduction, or imitation. There are many objections to this conception. But the vogue of the theory is testimony to the close connection of the fine arts with daily life; the idea would not have occurred to any one had art been remote from the interests of life. For the doctrine did not signify that art was a literal copying of objects, but that it reflected the emotions and ideas

464

that are associated with the chief institutions of social life. Plato felt this connection so strongly that
it led him to his idea of the necessity of censorship
of poets, dramatists, and musicians. Perhaps he exag-
gerated when he said that a change from the Doric to
the Lydian mode in music would be the sure precursor
of civic degeneration. But no contemporary would have
doubted that music was an integral part of the ethos
and the institutions of the community. The idea of
"art for art's sake" would not have been even understood.

There must then be historic reasons for the rise
of the compartmental conception of fine art. Our present museums and galleries to which works of fine art
are removed and stored illustrate some of the causes
that have operated to segregate art instead of finding
it an attendant of temple, forum, and other forms of
associated life. An instructive history of modern art
could be written in terms of the formation of the distinctively modern institutions of museum and exhibition
gallery. I may point to a few outstanding facts. Most
European museums are, among other things, memorials of
the rise of nationalism and imperialism. Every capital
must have its own museum of painting, sculpture, etc.,
devoted in part to exhibiting the greatness of its artistic past, and, in other part, to exhibiting the loot
gathered by its monarchs in conquest of other nations;
for instance, the accumulations of the spoils of Napoleon that are in the Louvre. They testify to the connection between the modern segregation of art and nationalism and militarism. Doubtless this connection
has served at times a useful purpose, as in the case
of Japan, who, when she was in the process of westerni-
zation, saved much of her art treasures by nationaliz-
ing the temples that contained them.

The growth of capitalism has been a powerful influence in the development of the museum as the proper
home for works of art, and in the promotion of the idea
that they are apart from the common life. The nouveaux
riches, who are an important by-product of the capitalist system, have felt especially bound to surround themselves with works of fine art which, being rare, are
also costly. Generally speaking, the typical collector
is the typical capitalist. For evidence of good standing in the realm of higher culture, he amasses paintings, statuary, and artistic bijoux, as his stocks and
bonds certify to his standing in the economic world.

465

Not merely individuals, but communities and nations, put their cultural good taste in evidence by building opera houses, galleries, and museums. These show that a community is not wholly absorbed in material wealth, because it is willing to spend its gains in patronage of art. It erects these buildings and collects their contents as it now builds a cathedral. These things reflect and establish superior cultural status, while their segregation from the common life reflects the fact that they are not part of a native and spontaneous culture. They are a kind of counterpart of a holier-than-thou attitude, exhibited not toward persons as such but toward the interests and occupations that absorb most of the community's time and energy.

. . .

Because of changes in industrial conditions the artist has been pushed to one side from the main streams of active interest. Industry has been mechanized and an artist cannot work mechanically for mass production. He is less integrated than formerly in the normal flow of social services. A peculiar esthetic "individualism" results. Artists find it incumbent upon them to betake themselves to their work as an isolated means of "self-expression." In order not to cater to the trend of economic forces, they often feel obliged to exaggerate their separateness to the point of eccentricity. Consequently artistic products take on to a still greater degree the air of something independent and esoteric.

Put the action of all such forces together, and the conditions that create the gulf which exists generally between producer and consumer in modern society operate to create also a chasm between ordinary and esthetic experience. Finally we have, as the record of this chasm, accepted as if it were normal, the philosophies of art that locate it in a region inhabited by no other creature, and that emphasize beyond all reason the merely contemplative character of the esthetic. Confusion of values enters in to accentuate the separation. Adventitious matters, like the pleasure of collecting, of exhibiting, of ownership and display, simulate esthetic values. Criticism is affected. There is much applause for the wonders of appreciation and the glories of the transcendent beauty of art indulged in without much regard to capacity for esthetic perception in the concrete.

466

My purpose, however, is not to engage in an economic interpretation of the history of the arts, much less to argue that economic conditions are either invariably or directly relevant to perception and enjoyment, or even to interpretation of individual works of art. It is to indicate that theories which isolate art and its appreciation by placing them in a realm of their own, disconnected from other modes of experiencing, are not inherent in the subject-matter but arise because of specifiable extraneous conditions. Embedded as they are in institutions and in habits of life, these conditions operate effectively because they work so unconsciously. Then the theorist assumes they are embedded in the nature of things. Nevertheless, the influence of these conditions is not confined to theory. As I have already indicated, it deeply affects the practice of living, driving away esthetic perceptions that are necessary ingredients of happiness, or reducing them to the level of compensating transient pleasurable excitations.

Even to readers who are adversely inclined to what has been said, the implications of the statements that have been made may be useful in defining the nature of the problem: that of recovering the continuity of esthetic experience with normal processes of living. The understanding of art and of its role in civilization is not furthered by setting out with eulogies of it nor by occupying ourselves exclusively at the outset with great works of art recognized as such. The comprehension which theory essays will be arrived at by a detour; by going back to experience of the common or mill run of things to discover the esthetic quality such experience possesses. Theory can start with and from acknowledged works of art only when the esthetic is already compartmentalized, or only when works of art are set in a niche apart instead of being celebrations, recognized as such, of the things of ordinary experience. Even a crude experience, if authentically an experience, is more fit to give a clue to the intrinsic nature of esthetic experience than is an object already set apart from any other mode of experience. Following this clue we can discover how the work of art develops and accentuates what is characteristically valuable in things of everyday enjoyment. The art product will then be seen to issue from the latter, when the full meaning of ordinary experience is expressed, as dyes come out of coal tar products when they receive special treatment.

. . .

467

A conception of fine art that sets out from its
connection with discovered qualities of ordinary experience will be able to indicate the factors and forces
that favor the normal development of common human activities into matters of artistic value. It will also
be able to point out those conditions that arrest its
normal growth. Writers on esthetic theory often raise
the question of whether esthetic philosophy can aid in
cultivation of esthetic appreciation. The question is
a branch of the general theory of criticism, which, it
seems to me, fails to accomplish its full office if it
does not indicate what to look for and what to find in
concrete esthetic objects. But, in any case, it is
safe to say that a philosophy of art is sterilized unless it makes us aware of the function of art in relation to other modes of experience, and unless it indicates why this function is so inadequately realized,
and unless it suggests the conditions under which the
office would be successfully performed.

The comparison of the emergence of works of art
out of ordinary experiences to the refining of raw materials into valuable products may seem to some unworthy, if not an actual attempt to reduce works of art
to the status of articles manufactured for commercial
purposes. The point, however, is that no amount of ec-
static eulogy of finished works can of itself assist
the understanding or the generation of such works.
Flowers can be enjoyed without knowing about the interactions of soil, air, moisture, and seeds of which they
are the result. But they cannot be understood without
taking just these interactions into account--and theory
is a matter of understanding. Theory is concerned with
discovering the nature of the production of works of
art and of their enjoyment in perception. How is it
that the everyday making of things grows into that form
of making which is genuinely artistic? How is it that
our everyday enjoyment of scenes and situations develops into the peculiar satisfaction that attends the experience which is emphatically esthetic? These are the
questions theory must answer. The answers cannot be
found, unless we are willing to find the germs and
roots in matters of experience that we do not currently
regard as esthetic. Having discovered these active
seeds, we may follow the course of their growth into
the highest forms of finished and refined art.

. . .

468

We cannot answer these questions any more than we can trace the development of art out of everyday experience, unless we have a clear and coherent idea of what is meant when we say "normal experience." Fortunately, the road to arriving at such an idea is open and well marked. The nature of experience is determined by the essential conditions of life. While man is other than bird and beast, he shares basic vital functions with them and has to make the same basal adjustments if he is to continue the process of living. Having the same vital needs, man derives the means by which he breathes, moves, looks and listens, the very brain with which he coordinates his senses and his movements, from his animal forbears. The organs with which he maintains himself in being are not of himself alone, but by the grace of struggles and achievements of a long line of animal ancestry.

Fortunately a theory of the place of the esthetic in experience does not have to lose itself in minute details when it starts with experience in its elemental form. Broad outlines suffice. The first great consideration is that life goes on in an environment; not merely in it but because of it, through interaction with it. No creature lives merely under its skin; its subcutaneous organs are means of connection with what lies beyond its bodily frame, and to which, in order to live, it must adjust itself, by accommodation and defense but also by conquest. At every moment, the living creature is exposed to dangers from its surroundings, and at every moment, it must draw upon something in its surroundings to satisfy its needs. The career and destiny of a living being are bound up with its interchanges with its environment, not externally but in the most intimate way.

The growl of a dog crouching over his food, his howl in time of loss and loneliness, the wagging of his tail at the return of his human friend are expressions of the implication of a living in a natural medium which includes man along with the animal he has domesticated. Every need, say hunger for fresh air or food, is a lack that denotes at least a temporary absence of adequate adjustment with surroundings. But it is also a demand, a reaching out into the environment to make good the lack and to restore adjustment by building at least a temporary equilibrium. Life itself consists of phases in which the organism falls out of step with the march of surrounding things and then recovers unison with it--either through effort or by some happy chance.

And, in a growing life, the recovery is never mere return to a prior state, for it is enriched by the state of disparity and resistance through which it has successfully passed. If the gap between organism and environment is too wide, the creature dies. If its activity is not enhanced by the temporary alienation, it merely subsists. Life grows when a temporary falling out is a transition to a more extensive balance of the energies of the organism with those of the conditions under which it lives.

These biological commonplaces are something more than that; they reach to the roots of the esthetic in experience. The world is full of things that are indifferent and even hostile to life; the very processes by which life is maintained tend to throw it out of gear with its surroundings. Nevertheless, if life continues and if in continuing it expands, there is an overcoming of factors of opposition and conflict; there is a transformation of them into differentiated aspects of a higher powered and more significant life. The marvel of organic, of vital, adaptation through expansion (instead of by contraction and passive accommodation) actually takes place. Here in germ are balance and harmony attained through rhythm. Equilibrium comes about not mechanically and inertly but out of, and because of, tension.

There is in nature, even below the level of life, something more than mere flux and change. Form is arrived at whenever a stable, even though moving, equilibrium is reached. Changes interlock and sustain one another. Wherever there is this coherence there is endurance. Order is not imposed from without but is made out of the relations of harmonious interactions that energies bear to one another. Because it is active (not anything static because foreign to what goes on) order itself develops. It comes to include within its balanced movement a greater variety of changes.

Order cannot but be admirable in a world constantly threatened with disorder--in a world where living creatures can go on living only by taking advantage of whatever order exists about them, incorporating it into themselves. In a world like ours, every living creature that attains sensibility welcomes order with a response of harmonious feeling whenever it finds a congruous order about it.

For only when an organism shares in the ordered
relations of its environment does it secure the stability essential to living. And when the participation
comes after a phase of disruption and conflict, it
bears within itself the germs of a consummation akin
to the esthetic.

The rhythm of loss of integration with environment
and recovery of union not only persists in man but becomes conscious with him; its conditions are material
out of which he forms purposes. Emotion is the conscious sign of a break, actual or impending. The discord is the occasion that induces reflection. Desire
for restoration of the union converts mere emotion into
interest in objects as conditions of realization of
harmony. With the realization, material of reflection
is incorporated into objects as their meaning. Since
the artist cares in a peculiar way for the phase of experience in which union is achieved, he does not shun
moments of resistance and tension. He rather culti-
vates them, not for their own sake but because of their
potentialities, bringing to living consciousness an experience that is unified and total. In contrast with
the person whose purpose is esthetic, the scientific
man is interested in problems, in situations wherein
tension between the matter of observation and of thought
is marked. Of course he cares for their resolution.
But he does not rest in it; he passes on to another
problem using an attained solution only as a stepping
stone from which to set on foot further inquiries.

The difference between the esthetic and the intellectual is thus one of the places where emphasis falls
in the constant rhythm that marks the interaction of
the live creature with his surroundings. The ultimate
matter of both emphases in experience is the same, as
is also their general form. The odd notion that an
artist does not think and a scientific inquirer does
nothing else is the result of converting a difference
of tempo and emphasis into a difference in kind. The
thinker has his esthetic moment when his ideas cease
to be mere ideas and become the corporate meanings of
objects. The artist has his problems and thinks as he
works. But his thought is more immediately embodied in
the object. Because of the comparative remoteness of
his end, the scientific worker operates with symbols,
words and mathematical signs. The artist does his
thinking in the very qualitative media he works in, and
the terms lie so close to the object that he is producing that they merge directly into it.

471

The live animal does not have to project emotions into the objects experienced. Nature is kind and hateful, bland and morose, irritating and comforting, long before she is mathematically qualified or even a congeries of "secondary" qualities like colors and their shapes. Even such words as long and short, solid and hollow, still carry to all, but those who are intellectually specialized, a moral and emotional connotation. The dictionary will inform any one who consults it that the early use of words like sweet and bitter was not to denote qualities of sense as such but to discriminate things as favorable and hostile. How could it be otherwise? Direct experience comes from nature and man interacting with each other. In this interaction, human energy gathers, is released, dammed up, frustrated and victorious. There are rhythmic beats of want and fulfillment, pulses of doing and being withheld from doing.

All interactions that effect stability and order in the whirling flux of change are rhythms. There is ebb and flow, systole and diastole: ordered change. The latter moves within bounds. To overpass the limits that are set is destruction and death, out of which, however, new rhythms are built up. The proportionate interception of changes establishes an order that is spatially, not merely temporally patterned: like the waves of the sea, the ripples of sand where waves have flowed back and forth, the fleecy and the black-bottomed cloud. Contrast of lack and fullness, of struggle and achievement, of adjustment after consummated irregularity, form the drama in which action, feeling, and meaning are one. The outcome is balance and counterbalance. These are not static nor mechanical. They express power that is intense because measured through overcoming resistance. Environing objects avail and counteravail.

There are two sorts of possible worlds in which esthetic experience would not occur. In a world of mere flux, change would not be cumulative; it would not move toward a close. Stability and rest would have no being. Equally is it true, however, that a world that is finished, ended, would have no traits of suspense and crisis, and would offer no opportunity for resolution. Where everything is already complete, there is no fulfillment. We envisage with pleasure Nirvana and a uniform heavenly bliss only because they are projected upon the background of our present world of stress and conflict. Because the actual world, that in which we live, is a combination of movement and culmination, of breaks and re-unions, the experience of a living

472

creature is capable of esthetic quality. The live being recurrently loses and reëstablishes equilibrium
with his surroundings. The moment of passage from dis-
turbance into harmony is that of intensest life. In a
finished world, sleep and waking could not be distinguished. In one wholly perturbed, conditions could not
even be struggled with. In a world made after the pattern of ours, moments of fulfillment punctuate experience with rhythmically enjoyed intervals.

Inner harmony is attained only when, by some means,
terms are made with the environment. When it occurs on
any other than an "objective" basis, it is illusory--in
extreme cases to the point of insanity. Fortunately
for variety in experience, terms are made in many ways--
ways ultimately decided by selective interest. Pleasures may come about through chance contact and stimulation; such pleasures are not to be despised in a world
full of pain. But happiness and delight are a different sort of thing. They come to be through a fulfillment that reaches to the depths of our being--one that
is an adjustment of our whole being with the conditions
of existence. In the process of living, attainment of
a period of equilibrium is at the same time the initia-
tion of a new relation to the environment, one that
brings with it potency of new adjustments to be made
through struggle. The time of consummation is also one
of beginning anew. Any attempt to perpetuate beyond
its term the enjoyment attending the time of fulfillment and harmony constitutes withdrawal from the world.
Hence it marks the lowering and loss of vitality. But,
through the phases of perturbation and conflict, there
abides the deep-seated memory of an underlying harmony,
the sense of which haunts life like the sense of being
founded on a rock.

Most mortals are conscious that a split often occurs between their present living and their past and
future. Then the past hangs upon them as a burden; it
invades the present with a sense of regret, of opportunities not used, and of consequences we wish undone.
It rests upon the present as an oppression, instead of
being a storehouse of resources by which to move confidently forward. But the live creature adopts its past;
it can make friends with even its stupidities, using
them as warnings that increase present wariness. Instead of trying to live upon whatever may have been
achieved in the past, it uses past successes to inform
the present. Every living experience owes its richness
to what Santayana well calls "hushed reverberations."[1]

473

To the being fully alive, the future is not omi-
nous but a promise; it surrounds the present as a halo.
It consists of possibilities that are felt as a possession of what is now and here. In life that is truly
life, everything overlaps and merges. But all too often we exist in apprehensions of what the future may
bring, and are divided within ourselves. Even when not
overanxious, we do not enjoy the present because we
subordinate it to that which is absent. Because of the
frequency of this abandonment of the present to the
past and future, the happy periods of an experience
that is now complete because it absorbs into itself
memories of the past and anticipations of the past,
come to constitute an esthetic ideal. Only when the
past ceases to trouble and anticipations of the future
are not perturbing is a being wholly united with his
environment and therefore fully alive. Art celebrates
with peculiar intensity the moments in which the past
reënforces the present and in which the future is a
quickening of what now is.

To grasp the sources of esthetic experience it is,
therefore, necessary to have recourse to animal life
below the human scale. The activities of the fox, the
dog, and the thrush may at least stand as reminders and
symbols of that unity of experience which we so frac-
tionize when work is labor, and thought withdraws us
from the world. The live animal is fully present, all
there, in all of its actions: in its wary glances, its
sharp sniffings, its abrupt cocking of ears. All senses
are equally on the qui vive. As you watch, you see motion merging into sense and sense into motion--consti-
tuting that animal grace so hard for man to rival. What
the live creature retains from the past and what it ex-
pects from the future operate as directions in the present. The dog is never pedantic nor academic; for these
things arise only when the past is severed in consciousness from the present and is set up as a model to copy
or a storehouse upon which to draw. The past absorbed
into the present carries on; it presses forward.

There is much in the life of the savage that is
sodden. But, when the savage is most alive, he is most
observant of the world about him and most taut with energy. As he watches what stirs about him, he, too, is
stirred. His observation is both action in preparation
and foresight of the future. He is as active through
his whole being when he looks and listens as when he
stalks his quarry or stealthily retreats from a foe.
His senses are sentinels of immediate thought and

474

outposts of action, and not, as they so often are with us, mere pathways along which material is gathered to be stored away for a delayed and remote possibility.

It is mere ignorance that leads then to the supposition that connection of art and esthetic perception with experience signifies a lowering of their significance and dignity. Experience in the degree in which it is experience is heightened vitality. Instead of signifying being shut up within one's own private feelings and sensations, it signifies active and alert commerce with the world; at its height it signifies complete interpenetration of self and the world of objects and events. Instead of signifying surrender to caprice and disorder, it affords our sole demonstration of a stability that is not stagnation but is rhythmic and developing. Because experience is the fulfillment of an organism in its struggles and achievements in a world of things, it is art in germ. Even in its rudimentary forms, it contains the promise of that delightful perception which is esthetic experience.

. . .

Experience is the result, the sign, and the reward of that interaction of organism and environment which, when it is carried to the full, is a transformation of interaction into participation and communication. Since sense-organs with their connected motor apparatus are the means of this participation, any and every derogation of them, whether practical or theoretical, is at once effect and cause of a narrowed and dulled life-experience. Oppositions of mind and body, soul and matter, spirit and flesh all have their origin, fundamentally, in fear of what life may bring forth. They are marks of contraction and withdrawal. Full recognition, therefore, of the continuity of the organs, needs and basic impulses of the human creature with his animal forbears, implies no necessary reduction of man to the level of the brutes. On the contrary, it makes possible the drawing of a ground-plan of human experience upon which is erected the superstructure of man's marvelous and distinguishing experience. What is distinctive in man makes it possible for him to sink below the level of the beasts. It also makes it possible for him to carry to new and unprecedented heights that unity of sense and impulse, of brain and eye and ear, that is exemplified in animal life, saturating it with the conscious meanings derived from communication and deliberate expression.

Man excels in complexity and minuteness of differentiations. This very fact constitutes the necessity for many more comprehensive and exact relationships among the constituents of his being. Important as are the distinctions and relations thus made possible, the story does not end here. There are more opportunities for resistance and tension, more drafts upon experimentation and invention, and therefore more novelty in action, greater range and depth of insight and increase of poignancy in feeling. As an organism increases in complexity, the rhythms of struggle and consummation in its relation to its environment are varied and prolonged, and they come to include within themselves an endless variety of subrhythms. The designs of living are widened and enriched. Fullfillment is more massive and more subtly shaded.

Space thus becomes something more than a void in which to roam about, dotted here and there with dangerous things and things that satisfy the appetite. It becomes a comprehensive and enclosed scene within which are ordered the multiplicity of doings and undergoings in which man engages. Time ceases to be either the endless and uniform flow or the succession of instantaneous points which some philosophers have asserted it to be. It, too, is the organized and organizing medium of the rhythmic ebb and flow of expectant impulse, forward and retracted movement, resistance and suspense, with fulfillment and consummation. It is an ordering of growth and maturations--as James said, we learn to skate in summer after having commenced in winter. Time as organization in change is growth, and growth signifies that a varied series of change enters upon intervals of pause and rest; of completions that become the initial points of new processes of development. Like the soil, mind is fertilized while it lies fallow, until a new burst of bloom ensues.

When a flash of lightning illumines a dark landscape, there is a momentary recognition of objects. But the recognition is not itself a mere point in time. It is the focal culmination of long, slow processes of maturation. It is the manifestation of the continuity of an ordered temporal experience in a sudden discreet instant of climax. It is as meaningless in isolation as would be the drama of Hamlet were it confined to a single line or word with no context. But the phrase "the rest is silence" is infinitely pregnant as the conclusion of a drama enacted through development in time; so may be the momentary perception of a natural scene.

476

Form, as it is present in the fine arts, is the art of making clear what is involved in the organization of space and time prefigured in every course of a developing life-experience.

Moments and places, despite physical limitation and narrow localization, are charged with accumulations of long-gathering energy. A return to a scene of childhood that was left long years before floods the spot with a release of pent-up memories and hopes. To meet in a strange country one who is a casual acquaintance at home may arouse a satisfaction so acute as to bring a thrill. Mere recognitions occur only when we are occupied with something else than the object or person recognized. It marks either an interruption or else an intent to use what is recognized as a means for something else. To see, to perceive, is more than to recognize. It does not identify something present in terms of a past disconnected from it. The past is carried into the present so as to expand and deepen the content of the latter. There is illustrated the translation of bare continuity of external time into the vital order and organization of experience. Identification nods and passes on. Or it defines a passing moment in isolation, it marks a dead spot in experience that is merely filled in. The extent to which the process of living in any day or hour is reduced to labeling situations, events, and objects as "so-and-so" in mere succession marks the cessation of a life that is a conscious experience. Continuities realized in an individual, discrete form are the essence of the latter.

Art is thus prefigured in the very processes of living. A bird builds its nest and a beaver its dam when internal organic pressures cooperate with external materials so that the former are fulfilled and the latter are transformed in a satisfying culmination. We may hesitate to apply the word "art," since we doubt the presence of directive intent. But all deliberation, all conscious intent, grows out of things once performed organically through the interplay of natural energies. Were it not so, art would be built on quaking sands, nay, on unstable air. The distinguishing contribution of man is consciousness of the relations found in nature. Through consciousness, he converts the relations of cause and effect that are found in nature into relations of means and consequence. Rather, consciousness itself is the inception of such a transformation. What was mere shock becomes an invitation; resistance becomes something to be used in changing existing

477

arrangements of matter; smooth facilities become agencies for executing an idea. In these operations, an organic stimulation becomes the bearer of meanings, and motor responses are changed into instruments of expression and communication; no longer are they mere means of locomotion and direct reaction. Meanwhile, the organic substratum remains as the quickening and deep foundation. Apart from relations of cause and effect in nature, conception and invention could not be. Apart from the relation of processes of rhythmic conflict and fulfillment in animal life, experience would be without design and pattern. Apart from organs inherited from animal ancestry, idea and purpose would be without a mechanism of realization. The primeval arts of nature and animal life are so much the material, and, in gross outline, so much the model for the intentional achievements of man, that the theologically minded have imputed conscious intent to the structure of nature--as man, sharing many activities with the ape, is wont to think of the latter as imitating his own performances.

The existence of art is the concrete proof of what has just been stated abstractly. It is proof that man uses the materials and energies of nature with intent to expand his own life, and that he does so in accord with the structure of his organism--brain, sense-organs, and muscular system. Art is the living and concrete proof that man is capable of restoring consciously, and thus on the plane of meaning, the union of sense, need, impulse and action characteristic of the live creature. The intervention of consciousness adds regulation, power of selection, and redisposition. Thus it varies the arts in ways without end. But its intervention also leads in time to the idea of art as a conscious idea-- the greatest intellectual achievement in the history of humanity.

. . .

Experience occurs continuously, because the interaction of live creature and environing conditions is involved in the very process of living. Under conditions of resistance and conflict, aspects and elements of the self and the world that are implicated in this interaction qualify experience with emotions and ideas so that conscious intent emerges. Oftentimes, however, the experience had is inchoate. Things are experienced but not in such a way that they are composed into an experience. There is distraction and dispersion; what we observe and what we think, what we desire and what

478

we get, are at odds with each other. We put our hands
to the plow and turn back; we start and then we stop,
not because the experience has reached the end for the
sake of which it was initiated but because of extraneous interruptions or of inner lethargy.

In contrast with such experience, we have an experience when the material experienced runs its course to
fulfillment. Then and then only is it integrated within
and demarcated in the general stream of experience from
other experiences. A piece of work is finished in a way
that is satisfactory; a problem receives its solution;
a game is played through; a situation, whether that of
eating a meal, playing a game of chess, carrying on a
conversation, writing a book, or taking part in a political campaign, is so rounded out that its close is a
consummation and not a cessation. Such an experience
is a whole and carries with it its own individualizing
quality and self-sufficiency. It is an experience.

Philosophers, even empirical philosophers, have
spoken for the most part of experience at large. Idio-
matic speech, however, refers to experiences each of
which is singular, having its own beginning and end.
For life is no uniform uninterrupted march or flow. It
is a thing of histories, each with its own plot, its
own inception and movement toward its close, each having its own particular rhythmic movement; each with its
own unrepeated quality pervading it throughout. A
flight of stairs, mechanical as it is, proceeds by in-
dividualized steps, not by undifferentiated progression, and an inclined plane is at least marked off from
other things by abrupt discreteness.

. . .

An experience has a unity that gives it its name,
that meal, that storm, that rupture of friendship. The
existence of this unity is constituted by a single quality that pervades the entire experience in spite of the
variation of its constituent parts. This unity is neither emotional, practical, nor intellectual, for these
terms name distinctions that reflection can make within
it. In discourse about an experience, we must make use
of these adjectives of interpretation. In going over
an experience in mind after its occurrence, we may find
that one property rather than another was sufficiently
dominant so that it characterizes the experience as a
whole. There are absorbing inquiries and speculations
which a scientific man and philosopher will recall as

"experiences" in the emphatic sense. In final import they are intellectual. But in their actual occurrence they were emotional as well; they were purposive and volitional. Yet the experience was not a sum of these different characters; they were lost in it as distinctive traits. No thinker can ply his occupation save as he is lured and rewarded by total integral experiences that are intrinsically worth while. Without them he would never know what it is really to think and would be completely at a loss in distinguishing real thought from the spurious article. Thinking goes on in trains of ideas, but the ideas form a train only because they are much more than what an analytic psychology calls ideas. They are phases, emotionally and practically distinguished, of a developing underlying quality; they are its moving variations, not separate and independent like Locke's and Hume's so-called ideas and impressions, but are subtle shadings of a pervading and developing hue.

We say of an experience of thinking that we reach or draw a conclusion. Theoretical formulation of the process is often made in such terms as to conceal effectually the similarity of "conclusion" to the consummating phase of every developing integral experience. These formulations apparently take their cue from the separate propositions that are premisses and the proposition that is the conclusion as they appear on the printed page. The impression is derived that there are first two independent and ready-made entities that are then manipulated so as to give rise to a third. In fact, in an experience of thinking, premisses emerge only as a conclusion becomes manifest The experience, like that of watching a storm reach its height and gradually subside, is one of continuous movement of subject-matters. Like the ocean in the storm, there are a series of waves; suggestions reaching out and being broken in a clash, or being carried onwards by a cooperative wave. If a conclusion is reached, it is that of a movement of anticipation and cumulation, one that finally comes to completion. A "conclusion" is no separate and independent thing; it is the consummation of a movement.

Hence an experience of thinking has its own esthetic quality. It differs from those experiences that are acknowledged to be esthetic, but only in its materials. The material of the fine arts consists of qualities; that of experience having intellectual conclusion are signs or symbols having no intrinsic quality

480

of their own, but standing for things that may in another experience be qualitatively experienced. The difference is enormous. It is one reason why the strictly intellectual art will never be popular as music is popular. Nevertheless, the experience itself has a satisfying emotional quality because it possesses internal integration and fulfillment reached through ordered and organized movement. This artistic structure may be immediately felt. In so far, it is esthetic. What is even more important is that not only is this quality a significant motive in undertaking intellectual inquiry and in keeping it honest, but that no intellectual activity is an integral event (is an experience), unless it is rounded out with this quality. Without it, thinking is inconclusive. In short, esthetic cannot be sharply marked off from intellectual experience since the latter must bear an esthetic stamp to be itself complete.

FOOTNOTE

[1]"These familiar flowers, these well-remembered
bird notes, this sky with its fitful brightness, these
furrowed and grassy fields, each with a sort of personality given to it by the capricious hedge, such things
as these are the mother tongue of our imagination, the
language that is laden with all the subtle inextricable
associations the fleeting hours of our childhood left
behind them. Our delight in the sunshine on the deep-
bladed grass today might be no more than the faint perception of wearied souls, if it were not for the sunshine and grass of far-off years, which still live in
us and transform our perception into love." George
Eliot in "The Mill on the Floss."

SUGGESTED READINGS

John Dewey

Dewey, John. Experience and Nature (Chicago:
    Open Court, 1925; New York: W. W. Norton,
    1929; La Salle, Illinois: Open Court, 1958).

_____. Art as Experience (New York: Minton
    Balch, 1934, 1957).

_____. Freedom and Culture (New York: G. P.
    Putnam's Sons, 1939).

* * *

_____. "The Postulate of Immediate Experi-
    ence," Journal of Philosophy, Psychology and
    Scientific Methods, II, 15 (1905), 393-399.

_____. "Reality as Experience," Journal of
    Philosophy, Psychology and Scientific Methods,
    III, 10 (1906), 253-257.

* * *

Gotshalk, D. W. "On Dewey's Aesthetics," Journal
    of Aesthetic and Art Criticism, XXIII (1964),
    131-138.

James, William. "The Place of Affectional Facts
    in a World of Pure Experience," Journal of
    Philosophy, Psychology and Scientific Meth-
    ods, II, 11 (1905), 281-287.

Martin, J. A., Jr. "The Empirical, the Esthetic,
    and the Religious," Union Seminary Quarterly
    Review, 30 (1975), 110-120.

Morris, B. "Dewey's Theory of Art," Guide to the
    Works of John Dewey (Carbondale: Southern
    Illinois University Press, 1970), pp. 156-
    180.

483

Shearer, E. "Dewey's Aesthetic Theory I," Journal
of Philosophy, XXXII, 23 (1935), 617-627.

_____. "Dewey's Aesthetic Theory II," Jour-
nal of Philosophy, XXXII, 24 (1935), 650-664.

* * *

Geiger, George. John Dewey in Perspective (New
York: Oxford University Press, 1958).

Hook, Sidney. John Dewey: An Intellectual Por-
trait (New York: John Day, 1939).

Roth, Robert, John Dewey and Self-Realization
(Englewood Cliffs, N. J.: Prentice-Hall,
1963).

Schilpp, Paul (Ed.). The Philosophy of John Dewey
(Evanston: Northwestern University Press,
1939).

Alfred North Whitehead

Alfred North Whitehead (1861-1947) received
his education at Trinity College in Cambridge
and University College in London. He returned
to these same Universities as a teacher. He
taught at Cambridge from 1884 until 1910; at
London from 1910 until 1924; and then came to
Harvard University where he served with great
distinction until his death in 1947.

Whitehead was one of those persons of genius who
was able to combine a passionate interest in detailed
facts with a devotion to abstract generalization. For
him the elucidation of the actual world as immediate
experience was the sole justification for any thought.
Always appreciative of Plato's understanding and expression of the world as a theatre which functions for
the temporal realization of ideas, Whitehead made a
special effort to relate the actual and/or factual to
the aesthetic and/or valuational aspects of nature in
such a way that all definite facts, as contingent, are
valuational as well as possibilities. Dr. Hartshorne
has indicated in a personal communication that in one
essay on the Good the term "values" is used to refer to
eternal ideas or pure possibilities as measures of value; but generally Professor Whitehead connected value
with actualities. Indeed, he identifies them as such
in one passage. It was the fact that there had been a
basic separation of these factors in philosophy and the
sciences in general rather than a harmonious interweav-
ing (inheritance of pattern) of ideas (eternal forms)
with the concrete unity of experience (actual entities)
that moved Whitehead to turn to the Romantic poets for
an expression of balance. The significance of the now
famous chapter on The Romantic Reaction* is that it

---

*This selection is from Science and the Modern
World (New York: Macmillan Publishing Company, 1925),
pp. 75-94. Used by permission of Macmillan Press.

presents the confrontation of the philosophy of organism and mechanism. He appreciated the spirit of the Romantic poets, especially Wordsworth, because they had taught him the concept of nature cannot be divorced from aesthetic values, and that these values are for the most part immediately derived from the organic wholeness of the natural world. The "metaphysics of feeling" explicit in Whitehead, therefore, relates directly to his insistence that all order in nature is aesthetic order.

Cf. also to Whitehead's effort at a formal definition of "beauty" (Part IV, Adventures of Ideas, pp. 251-272), and indication that "categorical obligations" are (odd) formulations of an aesthetic theory of actuality or of becoming for a fuller explication of his aesthetics. The essay given here is an excellent place to begin, however, for an appreciation and understanding of Whitehead's perspective on this subject.

My last lecture described the influence upon the
eighteenth century of the narrow and efficient scheme
of scientific concepts which it had inherited from its
predecessor.[1] That scheme was the product of a mentality which found the Augustinian theology extremely con-
genial. The Protestant Calvinism and the Catholic Jansenism exhibited man as helpless to co-operate with
Irresistible Grace: the contemporary scheme of science
exhibited man as helpless to co-operate with the irresistible mechanism of nature. The mechanism of God and
the mechanism of matter were the monstrous issues of
limited metaphysics and clear logical intellect. Also
the seventeenth century had genius, and cleared the
world of muddled thought. The eighteenth century continued the work of clearance, with ruthless efficiency.
The scientific scheme has lasted longer than the theological scheme. Mankind soon lost interest in Irresistible Grace; but it quickly appreciated the competent
engineering which was due to science. Also in the
first quarter of the eighteenth century, George Berkeley launched his philosophical criticism against the
whole basis of the system. He failed to disturb the
dominant current of thought. In my last lecture I developed a parallel line of argument, which would lead
to a system of thought basing nature upon the concept
of organism, and not upon the concept of matter. In
the present lecture, I propose in the first place to
consider how the concrete educated thought of men has
viewed this opposition of mechanism and organism. It
is in literature that the concrete outlook of humanity
receives its expression. Accordingly it is to literature that we must look, particularly in its more concrete forms, namely in poetry and in drama, if we hope
to discover the inward thoughts of a generation.

We quickly find that the Western peoples exhibit
on a colossal scale a peculiarity which is popularly
supposed to be more especially characteristic of the
Chinese. Surprise is often expressed that a Chinaman
can be of two religions, a Confucian for some occasions
and a Buddhist for other occasions. Whether this is
true of China I do not know; nor do I know whether, if
true, these two attitudes are really inconsistent. But
there can be no doubt that an analogous fact is true of
the West, and that the two attitudes involved are inconsistent. A scientific realism, based on mechanism, is
conjoined with an unwavering belief in the world of men

487

and of the higher animals as being composed of self-
determining organisms. This radical inconsistency at
the basis of modern thought accounts for much that is
half-hearted and wavering in our civilization. It would
be going too far to say that it distracts thought. It
enfeebles it, by reason of the inconsistency lurking in
the background. After all, the men of the Middle Ages
were in pursuit of an excellency of which we have nearly forgotten the existence. They set before themselves
the ideal of the attainment of a harmony of the understanding. We are content with superficial orderings
from diverse arbitrary starting points. For instance,
the enterprises produced by the individualistic energy
of the European peoples presuppose physical actions directed to final causes. But the science which is employed in their development is based on a philosophy
which asserts that physical causation is supreme, and
which disjoins the physical cause from the final end.
It is not popular to dwell on the absolute contradiction here involved. It is the fact, however you gloze
it over with phrases. Of course, we find in the eighteenth century Paley's famous argument, that mechanism
presupposes a God who is the author of nature. But
even before Paley put the argument into its final form,
Hume had written the retort, that the God whom you will
find will be the sort of God who makes that mechanism.
In other words, that mechanism can, at most, presuppose
a mechanic, and not merely a mechanic but its mechanic.
The only way of mitigating mechanism is by the discovery that it is not mechanism.

When we leave apologetic theology, and come to ordinary literature, we find, as we might expect, that
the scientific outlook is in general simply ignored.
So far as the mass of literature is concerned, science
might never have been heard of. Until recently nearly
all writers have been soaked in classical and renaissance literature. For the most part, neither philosophy nor science interested them, and their minds were
trained to ignore them.

There are exceptions to this sweeping statement;
and, even if we confine ourselves to English literature,
they concern some of the greatest names; also the indirect influence of science has been considerable.

A side light on this distracting inconsistency in
modern thought is obtained by examining some of those
great serious poems in English literature, whose general scale gives them a didactic character. The relevant

poems are Milton's Paradise Lost, Pope's Essay on Man, Wordsworth's Excursion, Tennyson's In Memoriam. Milton, though he is writing after the Restoration, voices the theological aspect of the earlier portion of his century, untouched by the influence of the scientific materialism. Pope's poem represents the effect on popular thought of the intervening sixty years which includes the first period of assured triumph for the scientific movement. Wordsworth in his whole being expresses a conscious reaction against the mentality of the eighteenth century. This mentality means nothing else than the acceptance of the scientific ideas at their full face value. Wordsworth was not bothered by any intellectual antagonism. What moved him was a moral repulsion. He felt that something had been left out, and that what had been left out comprised everything that was most important. Tennyson is the mouthpiece of the attempts of the waning romantic movement in the second quarter of the nineteenth century to come to terms with science. By this time the two elements in modern thought had disclosed their fundamental divergency by their jarring interpretations of the course of nature and the life of man. Tennyson stands in this poem as the perfect example of the distraction which I have already mentioned. There are opposing visions of the world, and both of them command his assent by appeals to ultimate intuitions from which there seems no escape. Tennyson goes to the heart of the difficulty. It is the problem of mechanism which appalls him.

" 'The stars,' she whispers, 'blindly run.' " This line states starkly the whole philosophic problem implicit in the poem. Each molecule blindly runs. The human body is a collection of molecules. Therefore, the human body blindly runs, and therefore there can be no individual responsibility for the actions of the body. If you once accept that the molecule is definitely determined to be what it is, independently of any determination by reason of the total organism of the body, and if you further admit that the blind run is settled by the general mechanical laws, there can be no escape from this conclusion. But mental experiences are derivative from the actions of the body, including of course its internal behaviour. Accordingly, the sole function of the mind is to have at least some of its experiences settled for it, and to add such others as may be open to it independently of the body's motions, internal and external.

489

There are then two possible theories as to the mind. You can either deny that it can supply for itself any experiences other than those provided for it by the body, or you can admit them.

If you refuse to admit the additional experiences, then all individual moral responsibility is swept away. If you do admit them, then a human being may be responsible for the state of his mind though he has no responsibility for the actions of his body. The enfeeblement of thought in the modern world is illustrated by the way in which this plain issue is avoided in Tennyson's poem. There is something kept in the background, a skeleton in the cupboard. He touches on almost every religious and scientific problem, but carefully avoids more than a passing allusion to this one.

This very problem was in full debate at the date of the poem. John Stuart Mill was maintaining his doctrine of determinism. In this doctrine volitions are determined by motives, and motives are expressible in terms of antecedent conditions including states of mind as well as states of the body.

It is obvious that this doctrine affords no escape from the dilemma presented by a thoroughgoing mechanism. For if the volition affects the state of the body, then the molecules in the body do not blindly run. If the volition does not affect the state of the body, the mind is still left in its uncomfortable position.

Mill's doctrine is generally accepted, especially among scientists, as though in some way it allowed you to accept the extreme doctrine of materialistic mechanism, and yet mitigated its unbelievable consequences. It does nothing of the sort. Either the bodily molecules blindly run, or they do not. If they do blindly run, the mental states are irrelevant in discussing the bodily actions.

I have stated the arguments concisely, because in truth the issue is a very simple one. Prolonged discussion is merely a source of confusion. The question as to the metaphysical status of molecules does not come in. The statement that they are mere formulae has no bearing on the argument. For presumably the formulae mean something. If they mean nothing, the whole mechanical doctrine is likewise without meaning, and the question drops. But if the formulae mean anything, the argument applies to exactly what they do mean. The

490

traditional way of evading the difficulty--other than the simple way of ignoring it--is to have recourse to some form of what is now termed "vitalism." This doctrine is really a compromise. It allows a free run to mechanism throughout the whole of inanimate nature, and holds that the mechanism is partially mitigated within living bodies. I feel that this theory is an unsatisfactory compromise. The gap between living and dead matter is too vague and problematical to bear the weight of such an arbitrary assumption, which involves an essential dualism somewhere.

The doctrine which I am maintaining is that the whole concept of materialism only applies to very abstract entities, the products of logical discernment. The concrete enduring entities are organisms, so that the plan of the whole influences the very characters of the various subordinate organisms which enter into it. In the case of an animal, the mental states enter into the plan of the total organism and thus modify the plans of the successive subordinate organisms until the ultimate smallest organisms, such as electrons, are reached. Thus an electron within a living body is different from an electron outside it, by reason of the plan of the body. The electron blindly runs either within or without the body; but it runs within the body in accordance with its character within the body; that is to say, in accordance with the general plan of the body, and this plan includes the mental state. But the principle of modification is perfectly general throughout nature, and represents no property peculiar to living bodies. In subsequent lectures it will be explained that this doctrine involves the abandonment of the traditional scientific materialism, and the substitution of an alternative doctrine of organism.

I shall not discuss Mill's determinism, as it lies outside the scheme of these lectures. The foregoing discussion has been directed to secure that either determinism or free will shall have some relevance, unhampered by the difficulties introduced by materialistic mechanism, or by the compromise of vitalism. I would term the doctrine of these lectures, the theory of organic mechanism. In this theory, the molecules may blindly run in accordance with the general laws, but the molecules differ in their intrinsic characters according to the general organic plans of the situations in which they find themselves.

491

The discrepancy between the materialistic mechanism of science and the moral intuitions, which are
presupposed in the concrete affairs of life, only gradually assumed its true importance as the centuries advanced. The different tones of the successive epochs
to which the poems, already mentioned, belong are curi-
ously reflected in their opening passages. Milton ends
his introduction with the prayer,

> 'That to the height of this great argument
> I may assert eternal Providence,
> And justify the ways of God to men.'

To judge from many modern writers on Milton, we might
imagine that the Paradise Lost and the Paradise Re-
gained were written as a series of experiments in blank
verse. This was certainly not Milton's view of his
work. To 'justify the ways of God to men' was very
much his main object. He recurs to the same idea in
the Samson Agonistes,

> 'Just are the ways of God
> And justifiable to men.'

We note the assured volume of confidence, untroubled by
the coming scientific avalanche. The actual date of
the publication of the Paradise Lost lies just beyond
the epoch to which it belongs. It is the swan-song of
a passing world of untroubled certitude.

A comparison between Pope's Essay on Man and the
Paradise Lost exhibits the change of tone in English
thought in the fifty or sixty years which separate the
age of Milton from the age of Pope. Milton addresses
his poem to God, Pope's poem is addressed to Lord
Bolingbroke,

> 'Awake, my St. John! leave all meaner things
> To low ambition and the pride of kings.
> Let us (since life can little more supply
> Than just to look about us and to die)
> Expatiate free o'er all this scene of man;
> A mighty maze! but not without a plan.'

Compare the jaunty assurance of Pope,

> 'A mighty maze! but not without a plan,'

with Milton's

492

                    'Just are the ways of God
                    And justifiable to men.'

But the real point to notice is that Pope as well as
Milton was untroubled by the great perplexity which
haunts the modern world. The clue which Milton followed was to dwell on the ways of God in dealings with
man. Two generations later we find Pope equally confident that the enlightened methods of modern science
provided a plan adequate as a map of the 'mighty maze.'

    Wordsworth's Excursion is the next English poem on
the same subject. A prose preface tells us that it is
a fragment of a larger projected work, described as 'A
Philosophical poem containing views of Man, Nature, and
Society.'

    Very characteristically the poem begins with the
line,

    ' 'Twas summer, and the sun had mounted high.'

Thus the romantic reaction started neither with God nor
with Lord Bolingbroke, but with nature. We are here
witnessing a conscious reaction against the whole tone
of the eighteenth century. That century approached nature with the abstract analysis of science, whereas
Wordsworth opposes to the scientific abstractions his
full concrete experience.

    A generation of religious revival and of scientif-
ic advance lies between the Excursion and Tennyson's In
Memoriam. The earlier poets had solved the perplexity
by ignoring it. That course was not open to Tennyson.
Accordingly his poem begins thus:

              'Strong Son of God, immortal Love,
              Whom we, that have not seen Thy face,
              By faith, and faith alone, embrace,
              Believing where we cannot prove.'

The note of perplexity is struck at once. The nineteenth century has been a perplexed century, in a sense
which is not true of any of its predecessors of the
modern period. In the earlier times there were opposing camps, bitterly at variance on questions which they
deemed fundamental. But, except for a few stragglers,
either camp was whole-hearted. The importance of Tennyson's poem lies in the fact that it exactly expressed
the character of its period. Each individual was

                         493

divided against himself. In the earlier times, the deep thinkers were the clear thinkers,--Descartes, Spinoza, Locke, Leibniz. They knew exactly what they meant and said it. In the nineteenth century, some of the deeper thinkers among theologians and philosophers were muddled thinkers. Their assent was claimed by incompatible doctrines; and their efforts at reconciliation produced inevitable confusion.

Matthew Arnold, even more than Tennyson, was the poet who expressed this mood of individual distraction which was so characteristic of this century. Compare with In Memoriam the closing lines of Arnold's Dover Beach:

'And we are here as on a darkling plain
Swept with confused alarms of struggle and flight,
Where ignorant armies clash by night.'

Cardinal Newman in his Apologia pro Vita Sua mentions it as a peculiarity of Pusey, the great Anglican ecclesiastic, 'He was haunted by no intellectual perplexities.' In this respect Pusey recalls Milton, Pope, Wordsworth, as in contrast with Tennyson, Clough, Matthew Arnold, and Newman himself.

So far as concerns English literature we find, as might be anticipated, the most interesting criticism of the thoughts of science among the leaders of the romantic reaction which accompanied and succeeded the epoch of the French Revolution. In English literature, the deepest thinkers of this school were Coleridge, Wordsworth, and Shelley. Keats is an example of literature untouched by science. We may neglect Coleridge's attempt at an explicit philosophical formulation. It was influential in his own generation; but in these lectures it is my object only to mention those elements of the thought of the past which stand for all time. Even with this limitation, only a selection is possible. For our purposes Coleridge is only important by his influence on Wordsworth. Thus Wordsworth and Shelley remain.

Wordsworth was passionately absorbed in nature. It has been said of Spinoza, that he was drunk with God. It is equally true that Wordsworth was drunk with nature. But he was a thoughtful, well-read man, with philosophical interests, and sane even to the point of prosiness. In addition, he was a genius. He weakens his evidence by his dislike of science. We all

remember his scorn of the poor man whom he somewhat
hastily accuses of peeping and botanising on his mother's grave. Passage after passage could be quoted from
him, expressing this repulsion. In this respect, his
characteristic thought can be summed up in his phrase,
'We murder to dissect.'

In this latter passage, he discloses the intellectual basis of his criticism of science. He alleges
against science its absorption in abstractions. His
consistent theme is that the important facts of nature
elude the scientific method. It is important therefore
to ask, what Wordsworth found in nature that failed to
receive expression in science. I ask this question in
the interest of science itself; for one main position
in these lectures is a protest against the idea that
the abstractions of science are irreformable and unalterable. Now it is emphatically not the case that
Wordsworth hands over inorganic matter to the mercy of
science, and concentrates on the faith that in the living organism there is some element that science cannot
analyse. Of course he recognises, what no one doubts,
that in some sense living things are different from
lifeless things. But that is not his main point. It
is the brooding presence of the hills which haunts him.
His theme is nature in solido, that is to say, he dwells
on that mysterious presence of surrounding things,
which imposes itself on any separate element that we
set up as an individual for its own sake. He always
grasps the whole of nature as involved in the tonality
of the particular instance. That is why he laughs with
the daffodils, and finds in the primrose thoughts 'too
deep for tears.'

Wordsworth's greatest poem is, by far the first
book of The Prelude. It is pervaded by this sense of
the haunting presences of nature. A series of magnificent passages, too long for quotation, express this
idea. Of course, Wordsworth is a poet writing a poem,
and is not concerned with dry philosophical statements.
But it would hardly be possible to express more clearly
a feeling for nature, as exhibiting entwined prehensive
unities, each suffused with modal presences of others:

> 'Ye Presences of Nature in the sky
> And on the earth! Ye Visions of the hills!
> And Souls of lonely places! can I think
> A vulgar hope was yours when ye employed
> Such ministry, when ye through many a year
> Haunting me thus among my boyish sports,

On caves and trees, upon the woods and hills,
Impressed upon all forms the characters
Of danger or desire; and thus did make
The surface of the universal earth,
With triumph and delight, with hope and fear,
Work like a sea? . . .'

In thus citing Wordsworth, the point which I wish
to make is that we forget how strained and paradoxical
is the view of nature which modern science imposes on
our thoughts. Wordsworth, to the height of genius, expresses the concrete facts of our apprehension, facts
which are distorted in the scientific analysis. Is it
not possible that the standardized concepts of science
are only valid within narrow limitations, perhaps too
narrow for science itself?

Shelley's attitude to science was at the opposite
pole to that of Wordsworth. He loved it, and is never
tired of expressing in poetry the thoughts which it
suggests. It symbolizes to him joy, and peace, and illumination. What the hills were to the youth of Wordsworth, a chemical laboratory was to Shelley. It is unfortunate that Shelley's literary critics have, in this
respect, so little of Shelley in their own mentality.
They tend to treat as a casual oddity of Shelley's nature what was, in fact, part of the main structure of
his mind, permeating his poetry through and through.
If Shelley had been born a hundred years later, the
twentieth century would have seen a Newton among chem-
ists.

For the sake of estimating the value of Shelley's
evidence it is important to realize this absorption of
his mind in scientific ideas. It can be illustrated by
lyric after lyric. I will choose one poem only, the
fourth act of his Prometheus Unbound. The Earth and
the Moon converse together in the language of accurate
science. Physical experiments guide his imagery. For
example, the Earth's exclamation,

'The vaporous exultation not to be confined!'

is the poetic transcript of 'the expansive force of
gases,' as it is termed in books on science. Again,
take the Earth's stanza,

'I spin beneath my pyramid of night,
Which points into the heavens,--dreaming delight,
Murmuring victorious joy in my enchanted sleep;

As a youth lulled in love-dreams faintly sighing,
Under the shadow of his beauty lying,
Which round his rest a watch of light and warmth doth
    keep.'

This stanza could only have been written by someone with a definite geometrical diagram before his inward eye--a diagram which it has often been my business
to demonstrate to mathematical classes. As evidence,
note especially the last line which gives poetical imagery to the light surrounding night's pyramid. This
idea could not occur to anyone without the diagram.
But the whole poem and other poems are permeated with
touches of this kind.

Now the poet, so sympathetic with science, so absorbed in its ideas, can simply make nothing of the
doctrine of secondary qualities which is fundamental to
its concepts. For Shelley nature retains its beauty
and its colour. Shelley's nature is in its essence a
nature of organisms, functioning with the full content
of our perceptual experience. We are so used to ignoring the implication of orthodox scientific doctrine,
that it is difficult to make evident the criticism upon
it which is thereby implied. If anybody could have
treated it seriously, Shelley would have done so.

Furthermore Shelley is entirely at one with Words-
worth as to the interfusing of the Presence in nature.
Here is the opening stanza of his poem entitled Mont
Blanc:

'The everlasting universe of Things
Flows through the Mind, and rolls its rapid waves,
Now dark--now glittering--now reflecting gloom--
Now lending splendour, where from secret springs
The source of human thought its tribute brings
Of waters,--with a sound but half its own,
Such as a feeble brook will oft assume
In the wild woods, among the Mountains lone,
Where waterfalls around it leap for ever,
Where woods and winds content, and a vast river
Over its rocks ceaselessly bursts and raves.'

Shelley has written these lines with explicit reference to some form of idealism, Kantian or Berkeleyan
or Platonic. But however you construe him, he is here
an emphatic witness to a prehensive unification as constituting the very being of nature.

Berkeley, Wordsworth, Shelley are representative of the intuitive refusal seriously to accept the abstract materialism of science.

There is an interesting difference in the treatment of nature by Wordsworth and by Shelley, which brings forward the exact questions we have got to think about. Shelley thinks of nature as changing, dissolving, transforming as it were at a fairy's touch. The leaves fly before the West Wind

'Like ghosts from an enchanter fleeing.'

In his poem The Cloud it is the transformations of water which excite his imagination. The subject of the poem is the endless, eternal, elusive change of things:

'I change but I cannot die.

This is one aspect of nature, its elusive change: a change not merely to be expressed by locomotion, but a change of inward character. This is where Shelley places his emphasis, on the change of what cannot die.

Wordsworth was born among hills; hills mostly barren of trees, and thus showing the minimum of change with the seasons. He was haunted by the enormous permanences of nature. For him change is an incident which shoots across a background of endurance,

'Breaking the silence of the seas
Among the farthest Hebrides.'

Every scheme for the analysis of nature has to face these two facts, change and endurance. There is yet a third fact to be placed by it, eternality, I will call it. The mountain endures. But when after ages it has been worn away, it has gone. If a replica arises, it is yet a new mountain. A colour is eternal. It haunts time like a spirit. It comes and it goes. But where it comes, it is the same colour. It neither survives nor does it live. It appears when it is wanted. The mountain has to time and space a different relation from that which colour has. In the previous lecture, I was chiefly considering the relation to space-time of things which, in my sense of the term, are eternal. It was necessary to do so before we can pass to the consideration of the things which endure.

Also we must recollect the basis of our procedure. I hold that philosophy is the critic of abstractions. Its function is the double one, first of harmonising them by assigning to them their right relative status as abstractions, and secondly of completing them by direct comparison with more concrete intuitions of the universe, and thereby promoting the formation of more complete schemes of thought. It is in respect to this comparison that the testimony of great poets is of such importance. Their survival is evidence that they express deep intuitions of mankind penetrating into what is universal in concrete fact. Philosophy is not one among the sciences with its own little scheme of abstractions which it works away at perfecting and improving. It is the survey of sciences, with the special objects of their harmony, and of their completion. It brings to this task, not only the evidence of the separate sciences, but also its own appeal to concrete experience. It confronts the sciences with concrete fact.

The literature of the nineteenth century, especially its English poetic literature, is a witness to the discord between the aesthetic intuitions of mankind and the mechanism of science. Shelley brings vividly before us the elusiveness of the eternal objects of sense as they haunt the change which infects underlying organisms. Wordsworth is the poet of nature as being the field of enduring permanences carrying within themselves a message of tremendous significance. The eternal objects are also there for him,

'The light that never was, on sea or land.'

Both Shelley and Wordsworth emphatically bear witness that nature cannot be divorced from its aesthetic values; and that these values arise from the cumulation, in some sense, of the brooding presence of the whole on to its various parts. Thus we gain from the poets the doctrine that a philosophy of nature must concern itself at least with these six notions: change, value, eternal objects, endurance, organism, interfusion.

We see that the literary romantic movement at the beginning of the nineteenth century, just as much as Berkeley's philosophical idealistic movement a hundred years earlier, refused to be confined within the materialistic concepts of the orthodox scientific theory. We know also that when in these lectures we come to the twentieth century, we shall find a movement in science

499

itself to reorganise its concepts, driven thereto by
its own intrinsic development.

It is, however, impossible to proceed until we
have settled whether this refashioning of ideas is to
be carried out on an objectivist basis or on a subjectivist basis. By a subjectivist basis I mean the belief that the nature of our immediate experience is the
outcome of the perceptive peculiarities of the subject
enjoying the experience. In other words, I mean that
for this theory what is perceived is not a partial vision of a complex of things generally independent of
that act of cognition; but that it merely is the expression of the individual peculiarities of the cognitive act. Accordingly what is common to the multiplicity of cognitive acts is the ratiocination connected
with them. Thus, though there is a common world of
thought associated with our sense-perceptions, there
is no common world to think about. What we do think
about is a common conceptual world applying indiffer-
ently to our individual experiences which are strictly
personal to ourselves. Such a conceptual world will
ultimately find its complete expression in the equations of applied mathematics. This is the extreme subjectivist position. There is of course the half-way
house of those who believe that our perceptual experience does tell us of a common objective world; but that
the things perceived are merely the outcome for us of
this world, and are not in themselves elements in the
common world itself.

Also there is the objectivist position. This
creed is that the actual elements perceived by our
senses are in themselves the elements of a common
world; and that this world is a complex of things, including indeed our acts of cognition, but transcending
them. According to this point of view the things experienced are to be distinguished from our knowledge of
them. So far as there is dependence, the things pave
the way for the cognition, rather than vice versa. But
the point is that the actual things experienced enter
into a common world which transcends knowledge, though
it includes knowledge. The intermediate subjectivists
would hold that the things experienced only indirectly
enter into the common world by reason of their dependence on the subject who is cognizing. The objectivist
holds that the things experienced and the cognizant
subject enter into the common world on equal terms. In
these lectures I am giving the outline of what I consider to be the essentials of an objectivist philosophy

500

adapted to the requirement of science and to the concrete experience of mankind. Apart from the detailed
criticism of the difficulties raised by subjectivism in
any form, my broad reasons for distrusting it are three
in number. One reason arises from the direct interrogation of our perceptive experience. It appears from
this interrogation that we are <u>within</u> a world of colours, sounds, and other sense-objects, related in
space and time to enduring objects such as stones,
trees, and human bodies. We seem to be ourselves elements of this world in the same sense as are the other
things which we perceive. But the subjectivist, even
the moderate intermediate subjectivist, makes this
world, as thus described, depend on us, in a way which
directly traverses our naïve experience. I hold that
the ultimate appeal is to naïve experience and that is
why I lay such stress on the evidence of poetry. My
point is, that in our sense-experience we know away
from and beyond our own personality; whereas the subjectivist holds that in such experience we merely know
about our own personality. Even the intermediate subjectivist places our personality between the world we
know of and the common world which he admits. The
world we know of is for him the internal strain of our
personality under the stress of the common world which
lies behind.

My second reason for distrusting subjectivism is
based on the particular content of experience. Our
historical knowledge tells us of ages in the past when,
so far as we can see, no living being existed on earth.
Again it also tells us of countless star-systems, whose
detailed history remains beyond our ken. Consider even
the moon and the earth. What is going on within the
interior of the earth, and on the far side of the moon!
Our perceptions lead us to infer that there is something
happening in the stars, something happening within the
earth, and something happening on the far side of the
moon. Also they tell that in remote ages there were
things happening. But all these things which it appears certainly happened, are either unknown in detail,
or else are reconstructed by inferential evidence. In
the face of this content of our personal experience, it
is difficult to believe that the experienced world is
an attribute of our own personality. My third reason
is based upon the instinct for action. Just as sense-
perception seems to give knowledge of what lies beyond
individuality, so action seems to issue in an instinct
for self-transcendence. The activity passes beyond
self into the known transcendent world. It is here

501

that final ends are of importance. For it is not activity urged from behind, which passes out into the veiled world of the intermediate subjectivist. It is activity directed to determinate ends in the known world; and yet it is activity transcending self and it is activity within the known world. It follows therefore that the world, as known, transcends the subject which is cognizant of it.

The subjectivist position has been popular among those who have been engaged in giving a philosophical interpretation to the recent theories of relativity in physical science. The dependence of the world of sense on the individual percipient seems an easy mode of expressing the meanings involved. Of course, with the exception of those who are content with themselves as forming the entire universe, solitary amid nothing, everyone wants to struggle back to some sort of objectivist position. I do not understand how a common world of thought can be established in the absence of a common world of sense. I will not argue this point in detail; but in the absence of a transcendence of thought, or a transcendence of the world of sense, it is difficult to see how the subjectivist is to divest himself of his solitariness. Nor does the intermediate subjectivist appear to get any help from his unknown world in the background.

The distinction between realism and idealism does not coincide with that between objectivism and subjectivism. Both realists and idealists can start from an objective standpoint. They may both agree that the world disclosed in sense-perception is a common world, transcending the individual recipient. But the objective idealist, when he comes to analyse what the reality of this world involves, finds that cognitive mentality is in some way inextricably concerned in every detail. This position the realist denies. Accordingly these two classes of objectivists do not part company till they have arrived at the ultimate problem of metaphysics. There is a great deal which they share in common. This is why, in my last lecture, I said that I adopted a position of provisional realism.

In the past, the objectivist position has been distorted by the supposed necessity of accepting the classical scientific materialism, with its doctrine of simple location. This has necessitated the doctrine of secondary and primary qualities. Thus the secondary qualities, such as the sense-objects, are dealt with

on subjectivist principles. This is a half-hearted
position which falls an easy prey to subjectivist criticism.

If we are to include the secondary qualities in
the common world, a very drastic reorganization of our
fundamental concept is necessary. It is an evident
fact of experience that our apprehensions of the external world depend absolutely on the occurrences within
the human body. By playing appropriate tricks on the
body a man can be got to perceive, or not to perceive,
almost anything. Some people express themselves as
though bodies, brains, and nerves were the only real
things in an entirely imaginary world. In other words,
they treat bodies on objectivist principles, and the
rest of the world on subjectivist principles. This
will not do; especially, when we remember that it is
the experimenter's perception of another person's body
which is in question as evidence.

But we have to admit that the body is the organism
whose states regulate our cognizance of the world. The
unity of the perceptual field therefore must be a unity
of bodily experience. In being aware of the bodily experience, we must thereby be aware of aspects of the
whole spatio-temporal world as mirrored within the bodily life. This is the solution of the problem which I
gave in my last lecture. I will not repeat myself now,
except to remind you that my theory involves the entire
abandonment of the notion that simple location is the
primary way in which things are involved in space-time.
In a certain sense, everything is everywhere at all
times. For every location involves an aspect of itself
in every other location. Thus every spatio-temporal
standpoint mirrors the world.

If you try to imagine this doctrine in terms of
our conventional views of space and time, which presuppose simple location, it is a great paradox. But if
you think of it in terms of our naive experience, it is
a mere transcript of the obvious facts. You are in a
certain place perceiving things. Your perception takes
place where you are, and is entirely dependent on how
your body is functioning. But this functioning of the
body in one place, exhibits for your cognizance an aspect of the distant environment, fading away into the
general knowledge that there are things beyond. If
this cognizance conveys knowledge of a transcendent
world, it must be because the event which is the bodily
life unifies in itself aspects of the universe.

503

This is a doctrine extremely consonant with the vivid expression of personal experience which we find in the nature-poetry of imaginative writers such as Wordsworth or Shelley. The brooding, immediate presences of things are an obsession to Wordsworth. What the theory does do is to edge cognitive mentality away from being the necessary substratum of the unity of experience. That unity is now placed in the unity of an event. Accompanying this unity, there may or there may not be cognition.

At this point we come back to the great question which was posed before us by our examination of the evidence afforded by the poetic insight of Wordsworth and Shelley. This single question has expanded into a group of questions. What are enduring things, as distinguished from the eternal objects, such as colour and shape? How are they possible? What is their status and meaning in the universe? It comes to this: What is the status of the enduring stability of the order of nature? There is the summary answer, which refers nature to some greater reality standing behind it. This reality occurs in the history of thought under many names, The Absolute, Brahma, The Order of Heaven, God. The delineation of final metaphysical truth is no part of this lecture. My point is that any summary conclusion jumping from our conviction of the existence of such an order of nature to the easy assumption that there is an ultimate reality which, in some unexplained way, is to be appealed to for the removal of perplexity, constitutes the great refusal of rationality to assert its rights. We have to search whether nature does not in its very being show itself as self-explanatory. By this I mean, that the sheer statement, of what things are, may contain elements explanatory of why things are. Such elements may be expected to refer to depths beyond anything which we can grasp with a clear apprehension. In a sense, all explanation must end in an ultimate arbitrariness. My demand is, that the ultimate arbitrariness of matter of fact from which our formulation starts should disclose the same general principles of reality, which we dimly discern as stretching away into regions beyond our explicit powers of discernment. Nature exhibits itself as exemplifying a philosophy of the evolution of organisms subject to determinate conditions. Examples of such conditions are the dimensions of space, the laws of nature, the determinate enduring entities, such as atoms and electrons, which exemplify these laws. But the very nature of these entities, the very nature of their spatiality and temporality, should exhibit the arbitrariness of these conditions as the outcome of a wider evolution beyond nature itself, and within which nature is but a limited mode.

One all-pervasive fact, inherent in the very character of what is real is the transition of things, the passage one to another. This passage is not a mere linear procession of discrete entities. However we fix a determinate entity, there is always a narrower determination of something which is presupposed in our first choice. Also there is always a wider determination into which our first choice fades by transition beyond itself. The general aspect of nature is that of evolutionary expansiveness. These unities, which I call events, are the emergence into actuality of something. How are we to characterize the something which thus emerges? The name 'event' given to such a unity, draws attention to the inherent transitoriness, combined with the actual unity. But this abstract word cannot be sufficient to characterize what the fact of the reality of an event is in itself. A moment's thought shows us that no one idea can in itself be sufficient. For every idea which finds its significance in each event must represent something which contributes to what realisation is in itself. Thus no one word can be adequate. But conversely, nothing must be left out. Remembering the poetic rendering of our concrete experience, we see at once that the element of value, of being valuable, of having value, of being an end in itself, of being something which is for its own sake, must not be omitted in any account of an event as the most concrete actual something. 'Value' is the word I use for the intrinsic reality of an event. Value is an element which permeates through and through the poetic view of nature. We have only to transfer to the very texture of realization in itself that value which we recognize so readily in terms of human life. This is the secret of Wordsworth's worship of nature. Realization therefore is in itself the attainment of value. But there is no such thing as mere value. Value is the outcome of limitation. The definite finite entity is the selected mode which is the shaping of attainment; apart from such shaping into individual matter of fact there is no attainment. The mere fusion of all that there is would be the nonentity of indefiniteness. The salvation of reality is its obstinate, irreducible, matter-of-fact entities, which are limited to be no other than themselves. Neither science, nor art, nor creation action can tear itself away from obstinate, irreducible, limited facts. The endurance of things has its significance in the self-retention of that which imposes itself as a definite attainment for its own sake. That which endures is limited, obstructive, intolerant, infecting its environment with its own aspects. But it is not self-sufficient. The aspects of all things enter into its very nature. It is only itself as drawing together into its own limitation the larger whole in which it finds itself. Conversely it is only itself by lending its aspects to this same environment in which it finds itself. The problem of evolution is the development of enduring harmonies of enduring shapes of value, which merge into higher attainments of things beyond themselves. Aesthetic attainment is interwoven in the texture of realization. The endurance of an entity represents the attainment of a limited aesthetic success, though if we look beyond it to its external effects, it may represent an aesthetic failure. Even within itself, it may represent the conflict between a lower success and a higher failure. The conflict is the presage of disruption.

The further discussion of the nature of enduring objects and of the conditions they require will be relevant to the consideration of the doctrine of evolution which dominated the latter half of the nineteenth century. The point which in this lecture I have endeavoured to make clear is that the nature-poetry of the romantic revival was a protest on behalf of the organic view of nature, and also a protest against the exclusion of value from the essence of matter of fact. In this aspect of it, the romantic movement may be conceived as a revival of Berkeley's protest which had been launched a hundred years earlier. The romantic reaction was a protest on behalf of value.

FOOTNOTE

[1]Cf. Science and the Modern World (New York: Macmillan, 1925), pp. 57-74. Chapter entitled "The Eighteenth Century."

SUGGESTED READINGS

Alfred North Whitehead

Whitehead, A. N. Science and the Modern World
(New York: Macmillan, 1925).

_____. Religion in the Making (New
York: Macmillan, 1926).

_____. The Aims of Education and Other
Essays (New York: Macmillan, 1929).

_____. The Adventures of Ideas (New
York: Macmillan, 1933).

_____. Modes of Thought (New York:
Macmillan, 1938).

* * *

Millard, R. "Whitehead's Aesthetic Perspective,"
Educational Theory, 11 (1961), 225-268.

Morris, B. "The Art-process and the Aesthetic
Fact in Whitehead's Philosophy," The Philosophy of Alfred North Whitehead (Evanston:
Northwestern University Press, 1941), pp.
461-486. Paul Schilpp (Ed.).

Schaper, E. "Aesthetic Perception," The Relevance
of Whitehead (London: Allen and Unwin, 1961),
pp. 263-285. Ivor Leclerc (Ed.).

Simmons, J. R. "Whitehead's Aesthetic of Nature,"
Southern Journal of Philosophy, 6 (1968), 14-
23.

* * *

Langer, S. K. Feeling and Form (New York: Charles
Scribner's Sons, 1953).

Shahan, E. P. Whitehead's Theory of Experience
(New York: King's Crown Press, 1950).

Sherburne, D. W. A Whiteheadian Aesthetic
    (Princeton: Princeton University Press,
    1961).

Wyman, M. A. The Lure of Feeling in the Creative
    Process (New York: Philosophical Library,
    1960).

C O N C L U S I O N

"Fluxes and changes
perpetually renew the world,
just as the unbroken march of
time
makes ever new the infinity
of ages."

Marcus Aurelius

Bernard M. Loomer

21. THE FUTURE OF PROCESS PHILOSOPHY

Bernard M. Loomer

Bernard M. Loomer did his undergraduate study
at Bates College, Lewiston, Maine, and his
graduate study at the University of Chicago.
Remaining at the University of Chicago, he
served as professor of philosophy of religion
(1942-1965), Dean of the Divinity School and
Federated Theological Faculty (1945-1955).
From 1965 until his retirement in 1977 he
served as professor of philosophical theology
at the American Baptist Seminary of the West
and the Graduate Theological Union at Berkeley.

What could be more fitting than that the post-
script to this work be written by the man Charles Hartshorne believes may be the first to use the term 'process philosophy,' and at the same time to have him indicate that he feels the movement might possess the name
'process-relational philosophy.' This new title is
needed, Dr. Loomer suggests, in order to more adequately indicate the distinctiveness of process philosophy's
view of reality as the organic joining of the two notions of process and constituitive relations. In the
essay which follows, Dr. Loomer endeavors to show how
the ultimacy of becoming is only half of the story; why
the relational mode of thought should receive equal notice; and what valuable contributions might arise from
such a courageous adventure in the pursuit of larger
meanings--practically, theoretically, physically, cul-
turally, conceptually, ethically, and socially.

In the opening remarks of the essay Dr. Loomer
raises questions as to his adequacy as a theologian to
speak on the subject of process philosophy. But we believe there are probably few others on the scene today
as adequate to the task. Since his student days at the
University of Chicago, he has involved himself in the
imagery and thought of rationalism, naturalism, and empiricism, and has sought to operate as a philosophical
theologian within the framework of process philosophy.
Process philosophy means for him, of course, the

philosophy of Alfred North Whitehead. His doctoral dissertation, "The Theological Significance of the Method of Empirical Analysis in the Philosophy of Alfred North Whitehead" (Divinity School, the University of Chicago, 1942), was not only a clear perceptive examination of the empirical analysis of Whitehead. It became one of the foundations for the discussion and assimilation of process philosophy among the students and teachers of the University of Chicago Divinity School. Dr. Bernard Meland says that although the dissertation has not been published, it has wielded an influence comparable to that of a published work and remains one of the basic documents of process philosophy.*

Dr. Loomer begins the following essay with two prefatory remarks. In the first he points out that process philosophy bears some of the limits of the epoch in which it was originally formulated. It is in some respects "dated," and must be superseded. In the second prefatory remark he argues that the relational element in process philosophy is as essential to understanding its true meaning as is the process element. Process-relational philosophy demands that we rethink old, non-relational concepts of power and of the individual. Having completed these very suggestive remarks, Dr. Loomer then examines his mode of thought from several different points of view: metaphysical, methodological, epistemological, intellectual, individual, valuational, and relational. Two great tasks remain to be accomplished by process (or process-relational) philosophy. It must develop a more complete psychology, especially a theory of the unconscious, and of the darker side of human character. And it must endeavor to become not only a mode of thought but a way of life, exemplifying man's attachment to the creative web of our interdependence.

---

*Meland, Bernard E. (Ed.). The Future of Empirical Theology (Chicago: University of Chicago Press, 1969), p. 42. Notation should be made of the fact that pages 369 through 387 of Dr. Loomer's doctoral dissertation have now been printed in Cousins, E. H. (Ed.), Process Theology (New York: Newman Press, 1971), pp. 67-82.

The Future of Process Philosophy

It is perhaps inappropriate or even presumptuous for a theologian to evaluate a variegated and complex mode of thought that is primarily philosophic in character. Hopefully the fact that theology and philosophy share a concern with the value dimensions of existence may lessen the inappropriateness and attenuate the presumption. The following discussion will reflect inevitably my own interests, biases, and above all my limitations. The assigned topic, the future of process philosophy, will be depicted not in terms of the historical destiny of this intellectual adventure, but with reference to its unfinished tasks.

Two preliminary remarks are in order. First, while I am not concerned to attempt to envision the historical destiny of process philosophy, it should be noted that this philosophic outlook does possess an historical self-understanding. Its awareness that there is no universal form of the human mind includes the recognition that the principle of historical relativity applies to its own appearance and character.

If by "mind" we have reference to a manner of understanding and communicating our experience of the world; if by "mind" we mean to indicate a way of apprehending, interpreting, symbolizing, creating, and organizing meanings; if by "mind" we mean to characterize those sensibilities, appreciations, and evaluations by which we discern and respond to the qualities and relationships experienced in our encounter with the world and its creatures; then there are only various historical forms of the human mind. Each mode of human understanding is an historical achievement. It has emerged and evolved within a particular set of historical circumstances, where "history" includes the totality of natural and cultural conditions. Its career from inception to maturity is at least theoretically encompassable. Its role as a formative element in the lives of people, even those of diverse cultures, is, again at least in theory, historically traceable. As a perspective in the world it has the virtues and limitations of its historical context and its own creative genius.

Systems of philosophy tend to be generalizations of basic insights and forms of knowledge operative in their historical times and places. Each is an extended formulation of the "mind" of its culture. A philosophy

515

tells us as much (or more) about the mind of an historical period as it does about the world it purports to
describe. These philosophies in turn help to give a
shape and style to their originating cultures. In the
history of western philosophy, systems have often been
extensions of principles derived from the current state
of one or more of the existing sciences. So it is with
respect to our present topic.

Process philosophy in its several expressions
could have emerged only in the relatively recent past.
Many of its guiding and distinctive principles are
rooted in modern developments which have arisen out of
a variety of intellectual disciplines, especially the
natural and social sciences. Its major work has been
the reconstruction of philosophy in terms of a direct
and positive relation to post-Newtonian scientific discoveries and methods. This work has included criticism
of those philosophies which presupposed a Newtonian
model of understanding the world of nature. In this
reconstructive effort its character as a philosophy has
been especially shaped by its critical responses to the
several idealisms and reductionist empiricisms of modern philosophy. In this sense, but perhaps only in
this sense, it is post-modern in its outlook.

In contrast to idealistic modes of thought, it has
defined man's place in the scheme of things in terms of
a picture of the world fashioned from the integration
of modern science and philosophy. In contrast to older
empirical modes, it has endeavored to restore man's
sensorial, affectional, and volitional qualities to an
objective status. In contrast to both, its concern
throughout the construction phases of its career has
been to define the natural world in such a full-orbed
valuational manner that it could be understood and perceived as an adequate home for the human spirit. Its
categories and epistomological principles reflect the
centrality of this value orientation.

Its period of creative growth extends (roughly)
from the last decade of the nineteenth century to the
first third of the present century. (The life and work
of Charles Hartshorne is an exception to this generalization.) In contrast to the European context of many
modern existentialists, most of the outstanding representatives of process philosophy were Anglo-Saxon and
even American in background. The basic convictions of
some of these figures were established prior to the
outbreak of World War I. In almost all instances this

516

formation occurred before, and sometimes long before, World War II. Their work reflects the liberal and democratic ethos that dominated their cultures during that historical period. Consequently, the spirit of process philosophy is essentially democratic, liberal, forward-looking yet appreciative of the past, dynamically synthetic, melioristic, and anti-finalistic. The ethnic background of these thinkers is also at least a partial explanation for the prominent strand of common-sensism in its style of thought.

In this respect process philosophy, like all modes of philosophic thought, is "dated." This intellectual vision of the world has the strength and limitations of its liberal democratic cultures, the sciences from which it drew so heavily, and its own constructive and possibly enduring insights. We may be too close in time to this mode of thought and its historical context to assess it properly. Other people at later times and in other historical contexts will have to make this evaluation. But in terms of what our history has disclosed, we should entertain some expectancy that this mode of thought will eventually pass, to be superseded and hopefully transcended by other attempts to discern and articulate the nature of things.

In the interim, some of the perimeters of process philosophy can be indicated. By and large it has had no serious engagements with either modern or contemporary forms of existentialism. This statement should be qualified by noting that contemporary existentialism made its appearance near the end of process philosophy's creative period. Analytic philosophy has emerged and developed into a ground swell within philosophy departments during the last quarter of a century. More significantly, perhaps, process philosophy has not been decisively influenced by either Marxist or psychoanalytic modes of thought. In this respect it differs markedly from contemporary existentialism which has been more closely attuned to humanistic disciplines and the social sciences. In some contrast to process philosophers, the central focus of existential thinkers has been on the distinctive humanness of the person. They have analyzed the structures of human society in relation to their import on the human individual, and they have probed the psychic and spiritual dimensions of the human spirit in ways and at depths that process philosophers by and large have not equalled.

517

The second prefatory remark begins with a semantic observation, but the point involved is more than terminological. In some place or other Charles Hartshorne generously credits me with possibly having baptized this mode of thought with the name "process philosophy." I am not concerned with the historical accuracy of Hartshorne's judgment in attributing this priestly function to me. Regardless of who devised the label, the name will probably stick. As a shorthand form of designation it is popular and convenient--and misleading. It suggests that the defining characteristic of this outlook consists in the ultimacy of becoming in contrast to the classical primacy of being. But the ultimacy of becoming is only half of the story. With equal appropriateness this metaphysical viewpoint may be characterized as a "relational" mode of thought. Except for the cumbersome quality of the phrase, the more adequate name should be "process-relational philosophy."

The full distinctiveness and unique flavor of this perspective on reality consists in the organic conjoining of the two notions of process (or becoming) and constitutive relations. "Becoming" is the most inclusive category in that all other notions refer either to dimensions or to specific concretizations of process. Empirically there are only instances of process, and concretely (to use Whitehead's expression) "process is the becoming of experience." Experience is the subjective unifying of diverse objectified data which are relationally (or vectorally) received from the environing world of the immediate past. These relational data are the very "stuff" of the process of becoming. They are the carriers of the transmission of energy. They constitute the elemental basis for the concept of causal efficacy, which is so fundamental for this mode of thought. Concrete individuals are emergents from dynamic relations. The emphasis on the ultimacy of process must be balanced by an insistence on the primacy of relations. They are equi-primordial.

The primacy and the role of constitutive relations is the key to understanding one of the dominant features of this mode of thought, namely, its capacity to synthesize contrasting elements or points of view, its ability to transform incompatibilities or even contradictions into compatible contrasts that enrich the unity of experience. This principle has practical as well as theoretical applications. Not only does it constitute the pivotal aim of the several theories of value

518

exemplified within this way of looking at the world. It underlies significant and dominant conceptions which are characteristic of this general way of looking at the world. A few illustrations may be cited.

In traditional thought the objective and the relative were thought to be incompatible if not contradictory. That which was experienced as being relative to one's social, psychological, or bodily state was understood to be subjective in nature. That which was objective was in no wise relative or subjective. Its objective status transcended the relativity of alternative standpoints. In process-relational modes of thought this incompatibility was transformed in such a way that objectivity has its determination and meaning only within some relative or relational context.

The concept of the communal individual, at least as a fully matured notion, belongs to the twentieth century. It also belongs preeminently to process-relational modes of thought. Formerly an individual was conceived as a self-centered and self-sustained reality. The individual had relations with his society, but the individual was not constituted by his relations. The self lived in a community, but the community did not live within the self in any concrete or literal sense. The self needed a community in order to be fulfilled. But the community was not understood to be of the essence of the individual. In the notion of the communal individual the self is largely composed of its relations with the world. The uniqueness of the self consists of the individual's self-creative subjective response to what it has relationally received from others.

Power has been defined traditionally as the unilateral capacity to exercise an influence on others; its accompanying characteristic was independence. The opposite of power was the situation of being influenced; this was characterized as passivity and dependence. Power was indicative of strength, and dependence symbolized weakness. In another essay I attempted to show that this conception of unilateral power is inadequate for today's problems.[1] What is required is a conception of relational power which involves the capacity both to influence and to be influenced. Power in this sense is characterized by both the qualities of independence and dependence. Here, as well as elsewhere in this general mode of thought, the role of constitutive relations is decisive.

One of the corollaries of Parkinson's law runs
something like this: A business enterprise can be
judged to have achieved its basic growth when its office appointments, including the secretaries, become
plush. In a somewhat different vein Whitehead suggested
that a system or mode of thought is finished as a creative movement when its disciples become preoccupied
with its details. On the whole this seems to be the
case with process-relational modes of thought. The major philosophical doctrines and themes have been explored and developed from diverse standpoints. The alternatives presented may be considered to be variations
within a general stance. There are no detailed agree-
ments among these alternatives on specific issues, but
there is a broad consensus of insights on important
topics. Emphases vary within these several perspectives, and yet there is a sharing of a fundamental
spirit and set of attitudes.

The general picture of the world as seen from this
vantage point might be outlined in the following fashion.

1.

The metaphysical stance is naturalistic, where
"nature" is understood in the most inclusive and qualitatively fullest sense. The term embraces the experienced and experienceable world in all its dimensions.
It refers to a world that is interpreted as self-
sufficient and self-explanatory. In this modern form
of naturalism there is an omission or rejection of
transcendental causes and unanchored self-sufficient
explanatory principles. There is an unwavering empirical insistence that the "reasons" for things are to be
found within the behavior and relationships of the
things themselves. Explanatory principles or reasons
are understood to be abstract accounts or generalized
conceptual renderings of what is concretely experienced.
Explanations are descriptive in nature. They function
as analyses of whatever coordinated behavior reality
exemplifies.

The "nature" that is experienceable is a processive world of energy, of creative activity, an evolving

unfinished universe where the principles of evolution and relativity have general (or for some, universal) scope and applicability. In this non-reductionistic outlook there is an emphasis on a continuity of analysis developed from some combination and enlargement of the foundational categories of events, qualities, structures, and relations. Within this continuum the higher and more complex levels are viewed as emergents from the simple forms of existence. This evolution is exemplified in the realm of ideas as well as in actuality itself.

This basic activity is expressed and experienced in the form of events. These events may be divided into units of varying spatial and temporal dimensions. For Whitehead, there are irreducible organismic units which are the ultimate building blocks of the universe. These miniscule atomic organizations of energy are the final or basic individuals. The visible objects of everyday life are highly complex societies of those organisms. For other thinkers within this mode of thought, the manner of dividing the processive and relational flow of things is more flexible. For them the determination of the extensiveness that may be included within the unity of an event is a function of special projects, purposes, or habits of attention. But whatever the division, these extensive units of energy, demarcated with the aid of their component qualities and structures within a relational context, compose the life of individuals and societies at all levels of existence.

Within this outlook there is general agreement about an ultimate plurality of existing things. This stress on plurality is often counterbalanced by some conception of the unity of things. The unity may be understood as restricted, general, cosmic or metaphysical in scope. It may be seen as structural or organic in character. If the type of unity is conceived of as structural or as consisting of some order of nature, the order is interpreted by some as an emergent; by others it is viewed as uncreated or primordial. If the unity is conceived of as organic or concrete (perhaps in addition to being structural) it is a wholeness that evolves with the creative advance of the universe (or of that segment of the world that is germaine to the topic being discussed).

Its methodological stance is essentially rationally empirical or (for some) even speculatively empirical, with procedures ranging from the experiential to the experimental and scientific, depending on the weight given to the factor of control. (Charles Hartshorne's concern with the ontological argument and metaphysically necessary truths is an exception to this generalization also.) Its genius includes a sensitivity to both the genetic and processive aspects as well as the structural or abstract components of concrete realities and experience.

Its adherence to the general empirical doctrine concerning the origin and confirmation of immediate experience illustrates its emphasis on the primacy of the physical and the derivative and yet "leading" character of the conceptual elements of experience. This emphasis is underlined and deepened by its insistence on the importance of the distinction between what is clearly and distinctly given and what is obscurely given, or between what is abstractly presented and what is concretely experienced. What is concretely experienced are the processive, genetic, causal, relational, and fully qualitied data. These are the earthy, messy, ambiguous, heavy, unmanageable, value-ladened and obscurely given factors of existence. What is abstractly presented are the formal, structural and spatialized data which have been abstracted from their embeddedness in concrete actualities. These are the clear, distinct, manageable, orderly, and relatively superficial data which are readily available for the purposes of sense perception and conceptual registration.

In the construction of an empirical metaphysics, the data from which categoreal generalizations are derived have their origins in the deliverances of human experience. This methodological principle may be axiomatic or truistic. What may not be so generally apparent is the directive corollary that, in contrast to certain forms of idealism and existentialism, the insights to be generalized are elicited from those factors which are necessary for our existence as organisms rather than from those elements which define us as distinctly human.

The distinction between the concrete and the abstract is basic to this whole mode of thought. The concrete consists of the processive actualities of the world, the substantial instances of activity, within which the specifiable objects of science and ordinary perceptual experience have their being. The concrete has reference to the becoming or the occurrence of these instances of formed energy. The occurrence involves the presence of its qualities, forms, and relational context. The abstract refers to any of the components of these activities, especially when these factors are considered apart from their processive and relational contexts. When they are treated as isolated or isolatible elements, forms and qualities are viewed as abstract. For some purposes, even an event when considered apart from its relevant context may be treated as an abstraction.

The realm of the possible, whether or not it includes uncreated or non-emergent forms, is abstract. Since actuality involves becomingness, the actual is more than a collection of abstractions. The actual, because of its processive nature, is more than the realization of the possible. There is no such thing as a possible individual.

3.

The overall epistemological stance of this philosophy is of a piece with its methodological principles. In contrast to many sorts of critical realism, which contend that what is directly given in perception are the abstract forms of sense data by means of which we infer the existence of concrete actualities, process-relational modes of thought hold that by means of causal bodily feelings we directly perceive particular existents, or at least perspectives of them. This position may be referred to as a kind of direct perspectival realism, perhaps similar to what A. E. Murphy had in mind years ago when he used the term "objective relativism." It is "radical" in the Jamesian sense of maintaining that particular existents, along with their relations and qualities, are the concrete data of bodily experience.

Thought is the ambassador-at-large in this mode of philosophizing. Its functions include: the solving of practical and theoretical problems in which it operates as a logic of inquiry; the creating of "useless" knowledge which adds to the capital fund of ideas whose due season of possible fertility may lie in the distant future; the constructing of a metaphysical system (including its variant renderings) whose vision may guide and shape the energies of a culture and strengthen the nerve of courageous adventure in the pursuit of larger meanings; the revitalizing of physical energy by offering new alternatives to counteract the degenerative aspects of inertial forces; and the civilizing of the human spirit through the interaction of the physical and conceptual dimensions of the human organism.

In these ways thought operates as an instrument in the ascertainment of general fact, and as an agency for the enhancement of practical and theoretical freedom. It should be added that reason also functions as a tool of uncreative and destructive forces. But this role of reason is not detailed and emphasized to a comparable or adequate degree in this philosophy.

To restate the matter, the creative functions of thought are the elucidation and the enhancement of experience. Thought is both an agent for the transformation of individual, social, and environmental life, and the indispensable means for the attainment of understanding for its own sake. It may be used to acquire specialized knowledge which may lead to the achievement of greater technical power and control in the Baconian sense. Or it may be used to gain a wholistic grasp of the general scheme of things and thereby deepen our sense of wonder.

With respect to our ability to grasp, by means of our reason, the general scheme of things, representatives of this point of view illustrate a diversity of judgments. This variety ranges from Hartshorne's convictions about necessary truths and the ontological argument to a much more tentative stance which holds that we live within "margins of intelligibility," to use Bernard Meland's pithy phrase.

On the more practical side, thought disengages forms or structures from their processive and relational contexts. This operation of thought provides us with conceptual abstractions which free us from having to deal with the unmanageable concreteness of events. Thought thereby enables us to simplify or oversimplify the entangled complexity that surrounds us. In this fashion we contrive to make life and its problems a bit more manageable. We are empowered to order our practical and theoretical activities by means of some abstract yet workable pattern or system, even if in so doing we may distort our perception and understanding of the natures and behaviors of concrete realities.

The capacity of thought to help us organize our lives needs a corrective, since organization can lapse into deadening routine. Thought has the capacity to be its own counter-irritant. It furnishes us with novel suggestions, and keeps alive a sense of alternatives which may intrigue our interest and excite our energies. In this and other ways thought becomes an agent if not the sole source of practical and theoretical freedom.

Theories which describe the relations between the physical and conceptual aspects of our experience tend to be somewhat truncated in their accounts of the transactions between these two components. To be sure, psychosomatic phenomena are generally accorded an assured status in the realm of fact. The role of thought in the coloration and interpretation of perception is part of an ancient awareness. Empirical philosophies, while stressing the derivation of ideas from physical experience, do allow that ideas in the form of hypotheses may play a decisive role by indicating possible connections between observable physical realities. Marxism, a radically reductionistic form of empiricism, in holding that ideas are reflections of physical realities (in this case, modes of economic production and divisions among classes) concludes that reason is an instrument of self-justifying ideology. One need not disavow any of these assigned roles in suggesting that many theories tend to depict the relationships between the physical and the conceptual as asymmetrical. That is, on the whole the connection between the two seems to be external from the standpoint of the physical and internal from the side of the conceptual.

In process-relational thought there is more than a passing and tremulous hint that the relationship is or may become mutually internal--granted differences in degrees of intensity. Physical experience grounds and shapes our ideas. (In some forms of empiricism thought seems to be imprisoned in physical experience.) But in turn, one of the most civilizing functions of thought is to transform the quality and character of our physical feelings. If this were not an actual or possible role of thought, then human integrity would be inherently impossible, and our lives would perforce remain compartmentalized and intrinsically incoherent. Physical realities and feelings operate as efficient causes by which we are determined and to which we conform. Thought on the other hand functions in terms of formed and final causes which are less coercive in their influence. Yet their effects on our physical feelings and emotions, though subtle, and often realized only after a prolonged struggle, are or may become decisive. What we think about and how we think has or may have some formative role in the shaping of the way we physically feel about people and events.

Sometimes these effects are insidious. Some people, whose integrity does in fact exemplify a coherence between their ideas and their emotions, are not exactly princes in the court of the human spirit. And there are Hamlets whose capacity for needed resolution gets "sicklied o'er with the pale cast of thought."

But thought need not (or always) have the effect of strengthening our baser instincts or attenuating our finer emotions. Intellectual adventure can ennoble the human spirit by sensitizing our bodily feelings to the deeper, more far-reaching, and more complex forms of human interaction. One of the aims of our conceptual entertainment of ideas of large and fertile generality is to purify and enlarge our physical feelings, so that they are released from the restrictive narrowness of parochial loyalties and small concerns. Surely this is or should be one of the major functions of a liberal arts program, especially in today's vocationally-oriented educational world.

The generality of thought, which is concerned to broaden our conceptual grasp of the interrelatedness of our world, can deepen and extend our physical sensitivity to the interconnectedness of things. This amalgam of intellectual range and physical depth and extensiveness concerning the interconnectedness of things, interfused to such a degree that they are almost indistinguishable, is apparently present in those who have

526

experienced and given voice to great religious intuitions.

The ethical advance from a sense of obligation to the restricted "some," which entails justice and compassion for the few and indifference or antagonism for all others, to a concern to see justice and humane treatment extended to the unrestricted "any," is an affair of the body and not of the intellect alone.

This conception of the contribution of thought to the formation of physical feelings can be entertained without either denying the psychoanalytic contention that thought is often the easily manipulated slave of the unconscious, or upholding the classical or liberal doctrine that reason is the actual or potential master of our passions. Like every other dimension of the human spirit, thought functions ambiguously, for both good and ill. It operates within limits and against awesome resistance. But the good that it might do and does do at this basic level of our experience should be acknowledged.

5.

The concept of identity is treated in a manner consistent with the basic categories of this philosophy. From this point of view, with reference to a concrete individual identity does not connote sameness. Identity cannot signify an underlying substantial self that maintains its selfsame unity through its changing situations. Rather, and in keeping with the canons of historical understanding, identity in the concrete sense connotes change. Identity is an affair of difference along a continuous historic route of events or occasions of experience. The identity of an enduring person consists in a transitional process of change through the successive occasions of the person's life history. This process involves the causal presence of the cumulative past in the succession of these experiential occasions. This accumulation is a way of speaking of physical as well as conscious memory. Identity is not a given. It is an historical achievement. It is an emergent from the sequence of efficient causality and self-creation whereby the present preserves and enlarges upon its past.

Concretely, identity is remembered continuity. I am, today, the person who remembers what I did yesterday.

Abstractly viewed, identity refers to a continuity of form or character that an enduring object exemplifies in the successive moments of its life-history. This character is a pattern of its unity, or a manner of behaving, or a way of responding to what it encounters. But even here identity does not, or need not, mean sameness. It may connote similarity. Identity in the precise sense of sameness of character can be approximated only at a very high level of abstraction from the concrete life of an enduring individual.

This account is incomplete. A description of the full orbit of the concept of identity would have to take into account the relational aspects of experience since an individual is also a social reality. Identity is not something the individual possesses by and in himself alone. We have our identity, we know who we are, only in the context of various relationships. This means that our identity is not only ascertained but also determined in and through our relationships. The social factor adds its complexity to the process wherein an individual's concrete identity is established.

6.

The heart of this or any other philosophy is its value orientation. In this and in every system of philosophy value is intrinsic to and coterminous with the units of reality specified by the system. Since in this philosophy the units of reality are societal individuals, value considerations must do justice to both the individual and social dimensions of reality. The individual actuality is a value for itself and then for society. Society is at once the necessary context and the recipient of whatever value the individual achieves. In this unending interplay, the individual and society are both ends and means relative to each other.

The teleological aim of this orientation looks in the direction of qualitatively richer and more complex individuals and societies. In this sometimes-realized advance, the role of contrasts in the actualization of greater value is decisive. The greater the contrasts that can be synthetically unified in an individual or a society, the greater the value that is realized. In this philosophic outlook ethical values are of course important, but for some representatives of this mode of thought they are included within the more inclusive value of beauty. Aesthetic order is that structure of

528

events and pattern of relations which is more adaptive and adequate to the dynamic manifestations of the plurality, contrasts, and entangled complexity of things.

The effort to achieve greater value occurs in an unfinished, evolving, relativistic, and deeply problematic universe. The God of this philosophy is a finite, struggling, and suffering divinity. The exponents of this outlook are not unaware of the powerful forces which are resistant to any creative advance. These obstructive and destructive elements are both internal and external to the valuing organisms. They acknowledge that neatness, clarity, and a sharply-etched unambiguous order are to be found only in a world of abstractions. Concretely, life is confused, disorderly, ambiguous, contradictory, and tragic.

This is a philosophy of freedom, cooperation, and creative advance. It believes that the ends employed to promote "the art of life" must be of a piece with the ends chosen. It finds its resources in the civilized and civilizing virtues and practices. It relies on the persuasiveness of ideals, the appeal to fact, the reasonableness of the cooperative disciplines by which confirmable truth is arrived at, the shaping influences of creative educational experiences, and the stability and flexibility of democratic institutions.

It believes deeply in the freedom of the individual and the virtues of an open society with its diversity, contrasts, and mobility. It knows at first hand, as well as through its reading of history, the destructive consequences that emanate from those whose yearning reaches for the certain and the unsurpassable. It is persuaded that tentativity and openness are not only compatible with deep commitment, but they are essential qualities of it. They are attitudes of faith by which commitment is protected from the tendency to become idolatrous. For the most part, and perhaps with some qualifications, it has relinquished a passion for perfection and devotes itself to the realization of the better.

It is an evolutionary and not a revolutionary stance. The ascent is slow and uncertain. We must live in terms of the long view with patience and hope.

To my mind, the single most comprehensive and far-reaching statement issuing from this mode of thought is the proposition that the world consists of an indefinitely extended plenum of interconnected events. This statement constitutes the widest generalization of the meaning of the conjoining of the elemental notions of process and constitutive relations. This plenum of interrelated events is the world understood as both many and in some sense one. It is the world conceived of as a web of relatedness, a community of sorts, although the community may be interpreted as restricted and partial or as unrestricted and inclusive. In either case this community is viewed as organic, ever unfinished, and evolving as the world advances. For some thinkers this weblike community has the unity of a concrete but indefinite totality. For others it has the structural and concrete unity of an unbelievably complex experiencing subject.

This bold assertion, which has at least some basis in fact, is not shared by all representatives of this philosophical persuasion. It is not held by those who are uneasy with imaginative generalizations, or who instinctively resist any expression that smacks of philosophical idealism, or who feel that religion is either a heightened form of ethics or an activity wherein man basically and experimentally shapes the course of history. For these thinkers there is no given web of interrelated events. There is only an aggregation of events, some of which are interconnected, but many or most of which are not.

The principle of relativity, like the theory of evolution, has been interpreted and utilized by several disciplines. In these contexts reaching beyond the realm of mathematical physics, the meaning of the principle has been broadened, as can be seen in the notion of historical relativity. Philosophers have contributed their own inevitable enlargements to the original scientific meaning of the principle. Whitehead has offered perhaps the widest descriptive generalization of the principle. It is in fact one of the categoreal features of his system. The spatially and temporally extended web of relatedness between events may be conceived as a far-flung generalization of the relational dimension of the principle of relativity, philosophically

understood. In a relativized world there is a plurality of perspectival standpoints. But these standpoints
are not isolated regions or occurrences. They are connected, directly or indirectly, by their mutual involve-
ment in the relational web of events.

The relational web is an image of the world existing as a communal togetherness, in spite of the ways in
which the brokenness and chaos of our individual and
social forms of existence give the lie to this claim.
But the implicit and explicit denials of this proposition, which are inherent in our behavior as well as in
many political theories and conceptions of the self,
are not necessarily decisive with respect to its possible truth. We are now a community of nations. We are
all now members of a human family of races. The fact
that we do not now treat each other as members of one
family does not dispose of the point that our lives are
enmeshed in this relational web. The actual occasions
of experience that constitute our lives are relational
and interconnected occurrences. The relational factor
is not an external condition that is added to an event.
It is intrinsic to the constitution and becoming of an
event. A concrete event derives its life-energy from
the web of interconnected events, it has its duration
as an actuality within this context, and in turn it
makes its contribution for good or ill to this web.

If the basic elements of our lives are not given
or experienced as related, there is no way of uniting
them in any important sense. At the human level we can
create important relationships and establish significant communities because we are relational creatures
and because we participate in this web of interconnectedness.[2]

Whatever order there is in our world, be it rational, ethical or aesthetic, derives from the interconnectedness of things, not the other way round.
Things are not connected or unified because they exemplify an order, whether the order is understood as
immanent or imposed. They are perceived as ordered
because they are interrelated. The order is an abstraction from the connectedness of concrete events in
their qualitative richness. (They have their qualitative fullness because of their connectedness.) The de-
lineated order is an abstract rendering of the structures exemplified in their interrelationships. The
different types of order vary in the degree of their
abstractness in relation to the concreteness of events,

531

with mathematical and aesthetic orders being the two
extremes. A conception of a "primordial order" is an
abstract way of speaking of the primacy of relationships.

We cannot order our intellectual world by trying
to synthesize the abstract principles involved in the
several autonomous disciplines of thought. We cannot
create or experience a conceptual wholeness by combining
isolated abstractions. We can more hopefully integrate
the sciences if we recognize that they are abstractions
of concrete events bound together in a relational web.
Disciplines may be regarded as autonomous only when
they neglect the presupposed background or relational
totality from which they are derived. "The explanatory
purpose of philosophy is often misunderstood. Its
business is to explain the emergence of the more abstract things from the more concrete things. . . . In
other words, philosophy is explanatory of abstraction,
and not of concreteness" (Whitehead).

What now of the future of this mode of thought?
The following opinions, judgments, and suggestions constitute only one (incomplete) version of the unfinished
business of this philosophic stance. No attempt has
been made to offer a complete catalogue. My concerns
are selective and they have a focus. In the background
of these remarks lies the conviction of the centrality
of the relational web just mentioned. These judgments
and suggestions for the most part deal with conditions
and understandings that enhance or attenuate the life
of this web, although at some points the connections
may not be obvious.

The discussion has two parts. The first is cen-
tered on certain understandings, both for the sake of
understanding itself and for their impact on the topic
of the web. The second deals with some practical and
social applications of this general point of view.

III

The openness to the persuasiveness of ideals, the
reasonable appeal to fact, the trust in the cooperative
disciplines by which confirmable truth is established,
and the eschewing of violence--these are qualities of
civilized people. The roles of reason in enlarging our
freedom and strengthening creative activity are functions which are important for the uplifting of the

532

human spirit. We may place great hope in the social consequences of applied intelligence. We may accept with courage and commitment our part in trying to fulfill the vision of some moderns, namely to shape the course of history in a constructive manner.

These are the attitudes of "the children of light" (in the Niebuhrian sense). But we are not only free. We are also driven by irrational impulses and destructive compulsions. We are sometimes held fast in the vise of emotional and intellectual fixations. We are subject to the inertial power of unresponsiveness. In our insecurity and anxiety we often cling to the good that we have rather than risk it all for something greater. If we are cornered in one of life's dark alleys we may see with our own horrified eyes the rise of the furies within us. In our felt entrapment we may have the depressing feeling that our civilized attitudes are a veneer that camouflage the hidden demons that mock at our pretensions. The good habits that surround our reasonable virtues may lack the strength to withstand the pressures of the hatreds we have repressed. The good and creative life has its passionate side. But the passions of the soul do not exist in separate compartments. They all live within the one cauldron of the individual's spirit. They partake of one another. They rise to the surface unbidden. This is the dark side, the place of shadows. Yet without this darker side, there is no light, no creative goodness. This is the ambiguity that infects the unity of all human forms of integrity.

The concept of the social self appears to be an advance in human self-understanding. But one of the consequences of this gain is that the demons who swell within each of us may not be solely of our own creation. They may also have a communal origin. There are socialized demons or communal shadows. Repression is also a social phenomenon, just as our rationality is a social creation as well as an individual possession. Repressed hatred is socialized or institutionalized.

The process-relational theory of the self holds that as individuals we originate from vectoral causal relations, and that these energies are not manageable or within our control. If this is roughly the case, then our inability to control the demons that plague us as individuals is not just a personal predicament. The unmanageability is itself socialized. The good that I would do but can't do is not simply my personal failure. It is that, to be sure. But it is also a collective incapacity.

In short, this philosophy needs a more complete psychology, especially a theory of the unconscious. But this would not be a theory simply of the unconscious as it operates within the individual. It would also be a theory of the relational unconscious. The relational unconscious would not be, or need not be, similar to a version of the collective unconscious with its primordial archetypes. Our interdependence is a primordial condition. But any specific order of interdependence may be a social emergent. Creativity and demonic activity may be inherent features of our primordial interrelatedness. But the specific forms of creativity and the specific structures of the demonic may be historical emergents.

A deeper awareness of the darker side of life would include a more penetrating account of the power of evil in human life. This would involve a recognition of the ambiguity of freedom and something akin to the classical doctrine of the bondage of the will.

In this philosophy, freedom is closely tied to the operations of reason and creativity. At times it appears that reason is the cause of freedom, and that freedom exists to serve the aims of reason and creative growth. This is an overstatement, as it stands. But I am referring to an emphasis or a tendency in this mode of thought. It can be granted that our degree of freedom is related to our capacity to think. But freedom, and reason, are dimensions of the total self, and freedom, like reason, can exist to serve the egocentric concerns of the self. The expansive quality of freedom is an impulse toward the "more." This expansive impulse can express itself in diverse ways, including the enlargement of the self's creativity. But this drive can also be manifested in the increase of the individual's self-preoccupation. Its creativity may take the form of self-enhancement and a denial of the interrelatedness of the self and other selves. The self may be free to make its limited choices without being equally motivated or empowered to relinquish its self-centeredness.

The relational self has his being in contexts. He is an emergent from them. His larger fulfillment consists in being able to participate more widely and deeply in creative and constitutive relations. Yet there

is something about the fact of being an individual that
moves him to deny the fundamental character of his being. This passion to make himself the center of his
world may be characterized as a misuse of his freedom.
It may be understood as a condition that arises from
his anxiety, or as a state that testifies to a basic
death wish which he cannot conquer. These theories do
not "explain" this bondage which the self in its freedom often exemplifies. They uncover it.

In Niebuhr's analysis the children of darkness
consist of those who acknowledge no law that transcends
their own self-interest. His analysis continues with
the contention that the children of light not only underestimate the power of self-interest in general: they
do not recognize the strength of its presence within
themselves. As a consequence, children of light entertain expectations that are not warranted, and they are
perpetually confounded by their experience.

But evil is not just a phenomenon of individuals.
Evil is socialized. There are structures of evil, historically created and institutional embodiments of obstruction and destruction. These powers exist within
the social self as part of its inner constitution.

These and similar considerations indicate the ambiguous character of life, even and especially the
structure of the relational life. There is a tendency
within the children of light, of which representatives
of this philosophy tend to be embodiments, to live life
as "cleanly" as they can. Even when they recognize the
depth of the forces of evil, they tend to isolate good
and evil. Whitehead's ontological separation between
God and creativity is a classic example. He acknowledges the factor of ambiguity, and yet he seems to
yearn for an unambiguous good.

Yet ambiguity is an ever-present quality of our
experience. It should be regarded as a fundamental
category of human experience. Perhaps it is even a
metaphysical principle. The wheat and tares co-exist
in each other's presence. Good and evil do not live
apart from each other. They intermingle. The one can
lead to or be transformed into the other. Evil cannot
be cut out of an individual without attenuating his
power to create a greater good. Our weaknesses are not
to be located in aspects of the self which are unrelat-
ed to our strengths. Our weaknesses are the obverse
sides of our strengths. The energy that led to the

535

development of our strengths and virtues is the same energy that leads us to overplay our strengths and magnify our virtues beyond their proper limitations. As I have repeatedly acknowledged, it was Niebuhr who stated one of the basic principles of the dialectical logic of the relation of interdependence: every creative advance brings with it the possibility of greater evil.

It was also Niebuhr who took the position that the Christian faith was not compatible with any naturalistic philosophy. He held this viewpoint on the grounds that God could not be identified with any natural or historical process because all such processes are ambiguous. If Niebuhr's judgment concerning the ambiguity of all natural and historical processes is correct, as I think it is, then the naturalists have no choice but to opt for a God who is enmeshed in ambiguity. An unambiguous God could be discovered only by a process of prolonged abstraction. And this God would be equally abstract and emasculated.

But a God embroiled in ambiguity is a larger God than one who lives in the separateness of his unambiguous essence.

IV

The future of this philosophy will be shaped most profoundly as it becomes a mode of life and not only a mode of thought. This challenge constitutes its greatest remaining mission.

Years ago Herman Randall, Jr., said it was apparent to the discerning observer that for centuries the naturalists had the correct methodology but the idealists had all the wisdom. What is the wisdom that is available to and appropriate for the naturalist? I believe it is of a different kind from that of the idealist or the transcendentalist.

There is the wisdom of the pilgrim. The pilgrim conceives himself as one for whom the earth is not his home. He is passing through this life on his way to another home and another life and therefore travels lightly. He is concerned about earthly life, but he has no deep attachment to it. He feels that the resources of earth and this life are not adequate for the living of it. The final resources must be derived from outside and beyond. When life comes to one of its many

536

abysses, and meaning seems to have dissolved into nothingness, the pilgrim is not in complete despair because he has his way out, his escape hatch of transcendent meaning. He lives as one who at heart is detached from the processes of this world. His anchorage is elsewhere.

There is also the wisdom of the earth. This is the stance of one who is deeply attached to this life, this earth, this world. He believes that this is his home. Like the Jew, he trusts that the kingdom will come and that it will come here and not some place else. Or, rather, he may believe that it is always happening here, although its more complete exemplification lies in the future. He does not travel lightly. He brings all his traditions and relationships and hopes and meanings with him.

The life of attachment means most profoundly that one believes that this life, including its possibilities, contains the resources that are adequate to the meaningful living of it. He knows that this faith cannot be sustained apart from the life of attachment. He has learned that one must live through all the suffering, tragedy, emptiness, brokenness, destruction, and evil; that one must not run from defeat, however deep the hurt; that like the ancient Jew, he must pour the ashes of his emptiness over his whole being and acknowledge what has happened, and wait creatively, openly, and hopefully for a new and deeper vision and understanding to emerge from the ashes.

The life of attachment means that one must be wholly present to the specific processes of life; that one is deeply attuned to the concreteness of life; that one does not commit himself to the abstractions that lure us from a discerning immersion in what is most deeply present at hand and concretely at work in our midst.

Without this sense of attachment, a naturalistic philosophy cannot provide an adequate life style. In fact, without it a naturalist becomes a living witness against himself.

This sense of attachment is of special significance for the process-relational naturalist. He is committed to the relational life in all of its depths and dimensions. He is involved in learning how to give himself to mutually internal relations with all the courage, stamina and openness that this kind of life requires. His attachment to the web of life commits him to undergo a continued evolution in his understanding of covenantal relationships, especially that primordial covenant which proclaims the elemental condition of our interdependence.

Within this attachment he becomes more appreciative of the qualities of tentativity and relativity which are the ingredients of a mature commitment.

This attachment to life is a life style of creativity lived in the midst of inescapable ambiguity. The eyes, the ears, the heart, the mind, and the spirit are to be sensitized to discern the strange and wondrous workings of the dynamic web of our interrelated lives.

The life style of an attachment to the creative web of our interdependence is not just a general commitment from which nothing specific follows. At present the most general order that seems to be exemplified in the relational life is aesthetic in nature. I have previously indicated that this type of order is more adequate to the complexities of life. The most inclusive category of value therefore is beauty. And the greatest exemplification of instrumental beauty would consist in the creation of those conditions, both natural and human, in which there might emerge human beings of ever greater stature, whose appearance would constitute some of the finest exemplifications of intrinsic beauty.

To this end I suggest, without elaboration, that philosophers of this persuasion become engaged in the monumental task of constructing conceptions of our educational, political, and economic institutions which would be grounded on the aesthetic order of beauty. Perhaps out of these sustained efforts this philosophy could become a mode of life as well as a mode of thought.

FOOTNOTES

[1]Bernard M. Loomer, "Two Conceptions of Power," *Process Studies*, VI, 1 (1976), 5-32.

[2]It could be said that within the Whiteheadian system the factor of connectedness is not established by the world of events. Rather there is a connectedness between events because there is a connectedness between possibilities.

SUGGESTED READINGS

Bernard M. Loomer

Loomer, Bernard. "The Theological Significance of
the Method of Empirical Analysis in the Philosophy of Alfred North Whitehead," (Ph.D.
Dissertation, the Divinity School, University
of Chicago, 1942).

_____. "Ely on Whitehead's God," Jour-
nal of Religion, XXIV, 3 (1944), 162-179.
Reprinted in Process Philosophy and Christian
Thought, D. Brown, R. E. James, Jr., and G.
Reeves (Eds.), (Indianapolis: Bobbs-Merrill,
1971), pp. 264-286.

_____. "Neo-Naturalism and Neo-
Orthodoxy," Journal of Religion, XXVIII, 2
(1948), 79-91.

_____. "Christian Faith and Process
Philosophy," Journal of Religion, XXIX, 3
(1949), 181-203. Also Process Philosophy and
Christian Thought, D. Brown, R. E. James, Jr.,
and G. Reeves (Eds.), (Indianapolis: Bobbs-
Merrill, 1971), pp. 70-98.

_____. "Religion and the Mind of the
University," Liberal Learning and Religion,
Amos N. Wilder (Ed.), (New York: Harper,
1951).

_____. "Reflections on Theological Ed-
ucation," Criterion, IV, 3 (1965), 3-8.

_____. "Whitehead's Method of Empirical
Analysis," Process Theology: Basic Writings,
E. H. Cousins (Ed.), (New York: Newman Press,
1971), pp. 67-82. From "The Theological Significance of the Method of Empirical Analysis
in the Philosophy of Alfred North Whitehead,"
(Ph.D. Dissertation, Divinity School, University of Chicago, 1942), pp. 369-387.

Loomer, Bernard. "Theology in the American Grain,"
The Universalist Christian, XXX, 4 (1975-76),
23-34.

_____. "Response to David R. Griffin,"
Encounter, XXXVI, 4 (1975), 361-369.

_____. "Two Conceptions of Power,"
Process Studies, VI, 1 (1976), 5-32.

* * *

Arnold, C. H. _Near the Edge of Battle_ (Divinity
School Association: University of Chicago,
1966), pp. 107-113.

Brown, D., James, R. E., Jr., and Reeves, G.
(Eds.). _Process Theology and Christian
Thought_ (Indianapolis: Bobbs-Merrill, 1971),
pp. 26f., 34.

Cousins, E. H. (Ed.). _Process Theology: Basic
Writings_ (New York: Newman Press 1971),
pp. 8-10, 24, 33, 47, 67, 204.

Meland, B. E. (Ed.). _The Future of Empirical The-
ology_ (Chicago: University of Chicago Press,
1969), pp. 5, 42-44, 50, 375n.

* * *

Boodin, J. E. "From Protagoras to William James,"
Monist, 21 (1911), 73-91.

_____. "The Field of Philosophy," in
Studies in Philosophy (Los Angeles: University of California Press, 1957), pp. 3-29.

Chappell, V. C. "Whitehead's Metaphysics," _The
Review of Metaphysics_, 13 (1959), 278-304.

Dye, J. W. "Heraclitus and the Future of Process
Philosophy," _Tulane Studies in Philosophy_, 23
(1974), 13-31.

Garnett, A. C. "Scientific Method and the Concept
of Emergence," _Journal of Philosophy_, XXXIX,
18 (1942), 477-486.

Hartshorne, C. "Twelve Elements of My Philosophy," Southwestern Journal of Philosophy, 5 (1974), 7-15.

_____. "Ideas and Theses of Process Philosophers," American Academy of Religion Studies in Religion, 5 (1973), 100-103.

_____. "Whitehead's Philosophy of Reality as Socially-Structured Process," Chicago Review, VIII, 2 (1954), 60-77.

_____. "The Philosophy of Creative Synthesis," Journal of Philosophy, LV, 22 (1958), 944-953.

_____. "From Colonial Beginnings to Philosophical Greatness," Monist, XLVIII, 3 (1964), 317-331.

Murphy, A. E. "The Anti-Copernican Revolution," Journal of Philosophy, XXVI (1929), 281-299.

Reck, A. J. "Substance, Process, and Nature," Journal of Philosophy, 18 (1958), 762-777.

_____. "Process Philosophy, a Categorical Analysis," Tulane Studies in Philosophy, XXIV (1975), 58-91.

Stokes, W. E. "Whitehead's Prolegomena to Any Future Metaphysics," Heythrop Journal, 3 (1962), 42-50.

_____. "Recent Interpretations of Whitehead's Creativity," Modern Schoolman, 39 (1962), 309-333.

Williams, D. D. "Changing Concepts of Nature," in Earth Might Be Fair, I. G. Barbour (Ed.). (Englewood Cliffs: Prentice-Hall, 1972).

* * *

Bertocci, P. A. (Ed.). Mid-Twentieth Century American Philosophy (New York: Humanities, 1974).

Browning, D. (Ed.). Philosophers of Process (New York: Random House, 1965).

542

Emmet, D. M. Whitehead's Philosophy of Organism
(London: Macmillan, 1932; New York: St.
Martins, 1966).

Gotshalk, D. W. Structure and Reality: A Study
of First Principles (New York: Greenwood,
1968).

Le Clerc, I. Whitehead's Metaphysics: An Introductory Exposition (New York: Macmillan,
1958).

_____. (Ed.). The Relevance of Whitehead
(New York: Macmillan, 1961).

Lintz, E. J. The Unity of the Universe According
to Alfred North Whitehead (Baltimore: J. H.
Furst, 1939).

Lowe, V. Understanding Whitehead (Baltimore:
John Hopkins Press, 1962).

Montague, W. P. The Way of Things (New York:
Prentice-Hall, 1940).

Novak, M. (Ed.). American Philosophy and the Future (New York: Charles Scribner's Sons,
1968).

Pols, E. Whitehead's Metaphysics (Carbondale,
Illinois: Southern Illinois University
Press, 1967).

Sherburne, D. W. A Key to Whitehead's Process and
Reality (New York: Macmillan, 1966).

Stapledon, W. O. Philosophy and Living (Harmond-
worth, Middlesex, England: Penguin, 1939).

Wyman, M. A. The Lure of Feeling (New York:
Philosophical Library, 1962).

SUPPLEMENTARY STUDIES

"The final problem
  is
  to conceive a complete fact."

Alfred North Whitehead

SUGGESTED READINGS

Samuel Alexander

Alexander, Samuel. Moral Order and Progress: An Analysis of Ethical Conceptions (London: Trubner, 1889).

_____. The Basis of Realism (London: Oxford University Press, 1914).

_____. Space, Time, and Deity (London: Macmillan, 1920), Vols. I and II.

_____. Art and Material (Manchester: The University Press, 1925).

_____. Art and Instinct (Oxford: Clarendon Press, 1927).

_____. Artistic Creation and Cosmic Creation (London: Milford, 1928).

_____. Beauty and Other Forms of Value (London: Macmillan, 1933).

* * *

_____. "Art and Science," Journal of Philosophical Studies, I, 1 (January 1926), 5-19.

_____. "The Creative Process in the Artist's Mind," British Journal of Psychology, XVII, 4 (April 1927), 305-321.

_____. "Art and Nature," John Rylands Library Bulletin, XI (1927), 256-272.

_____. "Truth, Goodness, and Beauty," Hibbert Journal, XXVIII (July 1930), 616-628

* * *

Laird, John (Ed.). Philosophical and Literary
     Pieces (London: Macmillan, 1939). Contains
     lengthy memoir.

McCarthy, J. W. The Naturalism of Samuel Alexan-
     der (New York: King's Crown Press, 1948).

John Elof Boodin

Boodin, John. Cosmic Evolution (New York: Mac-
     millan, 1925).

_____ . God and Creation (New York: Mac-
     millan, 1934).

_____ . Group Participation as the Socio-
     logical Principle Par Excellence (Berkeley:
     University of California Press, 1933).

_____ . Man in His World (Berkeley: Uni-
     versity of California Press, 1939).

_____ . A Realistic Universe; An Introduc-
     tion to Metaphysics (New York: Macmillan,
     1916, 1931).

_____ . Religion of Tomorrow (New York:
     Philosophical Library, 1943).

_____ . The Social Mind; Foundations of So-
     cial Philosophy (New York: Macmillan, 1939).

_____ . Truth and Reality; An Introduction
     to the Theory of Knowledge (New York: Mac-
     millan, 1911).

* * *

_____ . "Law of Social Participation,"
     American Journal of Sociology, 27 (1921),
     22-53.

_____ . "Value and Social Interpretation,"
     American Journal of Sociology, 21 (1915),
     65-103.

Boodin, John. "Identity of the Ideals," _International Journal of Ethics_, 23 (1912), 29-50.

_____. "Ought and Reality," _International Journal of Ethics_, 17 (1907), 454-474.

_____. "Cosmology in Plato's Thought," _Mind_, 38 (1929), 489-505.

_____. "Cosmology in Plato's Thought," _Mind_, 39 (1930), 61-78.

_____. "The Universe a Living Whole," _Hibbert Journal_, 28 (1930), 583-600.

_____. "Functional Realism," _Philosophy of Religion_, 43 (1934), 147-178.

_____. "Divine Laughter," _Hibbert Journal_, 32 (1934), 572-584.

_____. "Cosmic Attributes," _Philosophy of Science_, 10 (1943), 1-12.

_____. "Social Mind: Foundations of Social Philosophy," _Mind_, 50 (1941), 393-401.

_____. "Analysis and Wholism," _Philosophy of Science_, 10 (1943), 213-229.

_____. "Fictions in Science and Philosophy," _Journal of Philosophy_, 40 (1943), 673-682, 701-716.

_____. "Nature and Reason," _Contemporary American Philosophy_, 1 (1930), 135-166.

William James

James, William. _The Principles of Psychology_ (New York: Henry Holt, 1890), Vols. I and II.

_____. _The Will to Believe and Other Essays in Popular Philosophy_ (New York: Longmans, Green, 1897).

549

James, William. Pragmatism: A New Name for Some Old Ways of Thinking (New York: Longmans, Green, 1907).

_____. The Meaning of Truth: A Sequel to "Pragmatism" (New York: Longmans, Green, 1909).

_____. Some Problems of Philosophy: A Beginning of an Introduction to Philosophy (New York: Longmans, Green, 1911).

* * *

_____. "A World of Pure Experience, I," Journal of Philosophy, Psychology, and Scientific Methods, I, 20 (September 1904), 533-543.

_____. "A World of Pure Experience, II," Journal of Philosophy, Psychology, and Scientific Methods, I, 20 (October 1904), 561-570.

_____. "The Pragmatic Method," Journal of Philosophy, Psychology, and Scientific Methods, I, 25 (December 1904), 673-687.

_____. "The Thing and Its Relations," Journal of Philosophy, Psychology, and Scientific Methods, II, 2 (January 1905), 29-41.

_____. "How Two Minds Can Know One Thing," Journal of Philosophy, Psychology, and Scientific Methods, II, 7 (March 1905), 176-181.

* * *

Bode, B. H. "Realistic Conceptions of Consciousness," Philosophical Review, XX (1911), 265-279.

Cohen, M. R. "Qualities, Relations, and Things," The Journal of Philosophy, XI (1914), 617-627.

Boodin, J. E. "William James as I Knew Him," The Personalist, 23 (1942), 117-129, 279-290, 396-406.

Lewis, C. I. "Realism and Subjectivism," Journal of Philosophy, X (1913), 43-49.

Lovejoy, A. O. "Realism versus Epistemological Monism," Journal of Philosophy, X (1913), 561-572.

Montague, W. P. "The New Realism and the Old," Journal of Philosophy, IX (1912), 39-46.

Moore, G. E. "The Refutation of Idealism," Mind, XII, 48 (1903), 433-453.

Perry, R. B. "The Ego-Centric Predicament," Journal of Philosophy, VII, 1 (1910), 5-14.

_____. "Conceptions and Misconceptions of Consciousness," Psychological Review, XI (1904), 282-296.

George Herbert Mead

Mead, George Herbert. Mind, Self, and Society: From the Standpoint of a Social Behaviorist (Chicago: University of Chicago Press, 1934). Charles W. Morris (Ed.).

_____. The Philosophy of the Act (Chicago: University of Chicago Press, 1938). Charles W. Morris (Ed.) with J. W. Brewster, A. M. Dunham, and D. L. Miller.

_____. The Social Psychology of George Herbert Mead (Chicago: University of Chicago Press, 1956). Anselm Strauss (Ed.).

_____. Selected Writings (New York: Bobbs-Merrill, 1964). Andrew Reck (Ed.).

* * *

Ames, Van Meter. "Zen to Mead," Proceedings and Addresses of the American Philosophical Association, XXXIII (1959-1960), 27-42.

Baumann, Bedrich. "George Herbert Mead and Luigi Pirandello: Some Parallels Between the Theoretical Concept," Social Research, XXIV (1967), 563-607.

Lee, Harold N. "Action, Perception and Art," Southwestern Journal of Philosophy, I, 3 (Fall 1970), 85-90.

* * *

Ellin, Joseph. George Herbert Mead's Philosophy of Mind (New Haven: Yale University Press, 1962).

Miller, D. L. George Herbert Mead: Self, Language and the World (Austin and London: University of Texas Press, 1973).

Natanson, M. A. The Social Dynamics of George Herbert Mead (Washington: Public Affairs Press, 1956; The Hague: Nijhoff, 1973).

Pfuetze, P. E. The Social Self (New York: Bookman Associates, 1954).

INDEX OF NAMES

Hamlet, 72.
Hartshorne, Charles, 1-7, 12, 20, 83, 100n, 197f, 212n, 248n, 273f, 295n, 353, 393f, 485, 516, 518, 524.
    Collected Papers of Charles Sanders Peirce, 295n.
    Creative Synthesis and Philosophic Method, 408.
    ethics, 393f.
    Man's Vision of God, 295n.
Hegel, G. W. F., 2, 12, 95, 121, 199, 203, 427.
Heidegger, Martin, 7.
Heisenberg, Werner, 207, 301, 313.
Helmholtz, Hermann, 315.
Haraclites, 306.
Hinton, C. H., 121.
Hobbes, Thomas, 16, 397.
Hocking, W. E., 105.
Hodgson, S. H., 121, 123.
Homer, 31f.
Hoyle, Fred, 294.
Hume, David, 1, 6, 54, 63, 64, 66f, 119, 249, 253, 266, 397, 488.
    philosophy of, 1, 69.
    polemic concerning causation, 56f.
    Treatise, 63.
Huxley, Julian, 291.

J

James, Ralph E., Jr., 367n.
James, William, 5f, 21, 22, 90f, 105, 397, 405, 406, 424n, 476.
    A Pluralistic Universe, 100n.
    "Dilemma of Determinism, The," 1, 100n, 119f.
    Some Problems of Philosophy, 100n.
    stream of consciousness, 94.
    Varieties of Religious Experience, 21.
Japp, Francis Robert, 181, 183, 184, 188, 189.
Jesus, 374.
Jordan, Pascual, 317, 319n.

K

Kant, Immanuel, 13, 17, 66, 87, 201, 239, 356, 397, 411, 427.
    Critique of Pure Reason, 67.

Minkowski, Hermann, 98, 311.
Mitchell, Arthur, 151.
Morgan, C. Lloyd, 13, 22, 175f, 243n.
    Emergent Evolution, 175.
Morris, Charles, 105.
Moses, 401.
Murphey, A. E., 523.

N

Napoleon, 465.
Newton, Sir Isaac, 15, 54, 83, 299, 300, 301,
    306f, 312f.
    Optics, 306.
Newmann, Cardinal, 494.
    Apologia pro Vita Sua, 494.
Niebuhr, H. R., 327, 536.
    The Responsible Self, 327, 347n, 348n.
Niebuhr, Richard, 342.

O

Ockham, William of, 1, 310.
Oppenheimer, Robert, 312, 319n.
Otto, Rudolf, 424n.

P

Paley, Bishop, 397, 488.
Parmenides, 1, 83f, 93, 98, 314.
Pasteur, Louis, 181, 182.
Pearson, Karl, 194n.
Peirce, Charles Sanders, 1, 4, 6, 20, 21, 90,
    119, 199, 200, 204, 287, 290, 397, 402, 405f.
Perrier, Edmond, 171n.
Perry, R. B., 6, 97, 105.
    Present Philosophical Tendencies, 100n.
Pepper, Stephen, 106, 450.
    Aesthetic Quality, 113n, 456n.
Philolaus, 306.
Pierre Simon, Marquis de Laplace, 100n.
Planck, Max, 301.
Plato, 84, 201, 249, 266, 425, 426, 465.
    Phaedo, 303.
    Sophist, 252.
    Timaeus, 280.

Plotinus, 84, 199.
Pollard, William, 296.
Pope, Alexander, 489, 492f.
    Essay on Man, 489, 492.
Popper, Karl, 318.
    The Poverty of Historicism, 318.
Price, H. H., 113n, 269n.
Prior, A. N., 212n.
Proust, Marcel, 18.
Pusey, Edward, 494.
Purtill, Richard L., 210.

R

Randall, Herman, Jr., 536.
Reeves, Gene, 367n.
Reichenbach, Hans, 313, 317.
Renan, J. E., 138, 139.
Renouvier, Charles, 90, 94, 119.
Richards, I. A., 451, 456n.
Ritter, W. E., 295n.
Rousseau, Jean Jacques, 138.
Royce, Josiah, 199, 427.
Russell, Bertand, 1, 4, 6, 202, 203.
Rust, E. R., 176.
Ryle, Gilbert, 5, 283, 284.

S

Sankara, 406.
Santayana, George, 309, 402, 416n, 428f, 473.
Saint Paul, 122, 374, 397.
Sanderson, Burdon, 178, 179.
Sartre, Jean-Paul, 314.
Schlick, Moritz, 317.
Schelling, F. W. J. von, 2.
Schopenhauer, Arthur, 131, 136, 199.
Scriven, Michael, 389, 416n.
Sedgwick, W. T., 171n.
Serkovski, S., 171n.
Shakespeare, William, 425.
Sheffer, H. M., 4.
Shelley, Percy B., 494f.
        Cloud, The, 498.
        Mont Blanc, 497.
        Prometheus Unbound, 496.
Sibley, J. R., 9, 351.

Skinner, B. F., 16, 408, 409.
Smuts, Jan Christian, 1, 219f.
    Holism and Evolution, 220.
Socrates, 303, 354, 425.
Spencer, Herbert, 86, 90, 94, 135, 175, 190f, 219,
    304, 318.
    Data of Ethics, 135.
    Principles of Biology, 191.
Spencer, John B., 325f, 424n.
Spinoza, Benedict, 1, 54, 79, 84, 85, 87, 95, 197,
    203, 233f, 309, 399, 494.

T

Taine, Hippolyte, 94.
Teilhard de Chardin, Pierre, 21, 291.
Tennyson, Alfred Lord, 489, 493.
    In Memoriam, 489, 493.
Tillich, Paul, 105, 314.
Tyndall, John, 186.

V

Valerie, Paul, 5.
Vivas, Eliseo, 455n.
Voltaire, Francois-Marie, 132.
    Candide, 132.

W

Ward, James, 233, 234.
Wartofsky, Marx W., 102.
Watt, James, 185.
Weiss, Paul, 295n.
Weizsacker, Carl F. von, 97.
Whitehead, Alfred North, 1-4, 6, 9, 12, 14, 21, 22,
    95, 105, 175, 200, 204, 247f, 305, 328, 336, 353,
    361, 367, 368, 374, 397, 402, 403, 408, 424, 424n,
    429, 435, 485f, 514, 521, 530, 532.
    Adventures of Ideas, 3, 247, 295n, 347n, 416n.
    Principles of Natural Knowledge, 76n.
    Process and Reality, 3, 100n, 262, 269n, 361,
    455n.
    Religion in the Making, 431, 432n.
    Science and the Modern World, 432n, 485n, 507n.
    Symbolism, Its Meaning and Importance, 76n.

Wieman, Henry Nelson, 7, 105f, 358f, 367f.
    "Creative Good," 105, 367, 369f.
    "Perception and Cognition," 105, 107f.
    Source of Human Good, The, 358, 368n.
Wigner, Eugene, 407.
Wilcox, John T., 212n.
Williams, Daniel Day, 7, 353f.
    Spirit and the Forms of Love, The, 7.
Windelband, Wilhelm, 84, 105.
Wordsworth, William, 493.
    Excursion, 493.
Wright, Sewall, 291.

Z

Zilsel, Edgar, 317.
Zola, Emile, 138, 139.

INDEX OF SUBJECTS

A

Absolute, the, 504.
absolutism,
    intellectual, 129.
    native, 142.
    pluralistic, 6.
actual entity, 54f, 64f, 438f.
actual occasion, 56, 59f, 61, 267f, 442f.
aesthetic, 327f, 435f, 467f.
    and experience, 467f.
    definition, 435.
    Dewey's understanding of, 440.
    objects, 436f.
    obligation, 327.
    tradition, 427, 430.
    whole, 331.
aesthetics, 7, 15, 18f, 412f, 435f.
    and ethics, 424f.
    influence on Dewey's thought, 460.
    process, 18.
Age of Analysis, the, 11.
agnosticism, 1, 304.
anthropology, 5.
anthropomorphism, 234.
anti-relativistic bias, the, 201.
appreciative awareness, 341f.
Aristotelianism, 199, 307.
art, 18f, 425f, 459f.
    as experience, 459f.
    creative, 427.
    process view of, 18.
    production of, 449.
    theory of, 462.
atomism, 81f, 314.
    Greek, 81f, 206, 306.
    ancient, 306, 308.
Atomists, 304f.
atoms, 276, 287, 307, 408.
    event-like entities, 312.
    physical, 151.
    rigid and permanent, 312.
    solid, 310.

B

beauty, 7, 325f, 413, 538.
    conscious aim at, 452.
    devotion to, 330.
    inclusive value of, 528.
    love of, 330.
    most inclusive category of value, 538.
    sensuous, 453.
becoming, 1, 3-5, 55f, 86, 94, 360, 518.
    actual, 4.
    creative, 4.
    no mere appearance of being, 1.
    of a single actual entity, 4.
    single concrete act of self-creation, 4.
    successive phases of, 96.
    unison of immediate, 58.
behaviorists, 309.
being, 1, 55f.
    density and fullness of, 105.
    state of conscious, 163.
    static and immutable, 86.
    traditional concept of, 314.
    treated as an abstraction, 1.
Bodhisattva, 405.
brain, 164f.
Brahma, 405.
Brahman, 504.
Buddhists, 396f.
buddhisto-Christian religion, 406.

C

Calvinism, 426, 487.
capitalism, 465.
Cartesian dualism, 258.
Cartesianism, 199.
causal efficacy, 14, 53f, 62f, 68, 310f, 335f,
   438f.
    in nature, 95.
    pure mode of, 56f.
causal inefficacy, 317.
causality, 53f, 81f.
    classical concept of, 81f.
    Laplacian, 93f.
    meaning of concept, 81f.
    rigorous, 96.
    speed limit of, 98.

creative,
    integration, 374.
    interchange, 368f.
    passage, 329.
    transformation, 358.
creativity, 1, 3, 13, 17, 369f.
    as transcendent, 384.
    category of categories, 354.
    new meaning of, 413.
    root source of, 111.
    social, 413.
    ultimate, 336.
    universal, 408.
culture(s), 327f, 343, 380.

D

Darwinism, 13, 287, 291.
death, 401f.
deity, 7, 20f.
    properties of process, 19.
depth,
    dimension of, 423f.
determinism, 1, 119f, 129f, 207, 491f.
    absolute, 94.
    and indeterminism, 317.
    classical form of, 1, 81f, 95.
    Greek, 81.
    hard, 123, 134.
    historical, 318.
    idealistic, 93.
    La Placean, 1.
    mechanical, 134.
    mechanistic, 317.
    microphysical, 316.
    Mill's doctrine of, 489, 491.
    modern form of, 81f, 93.
    naturalistic, 83.
    necessitarian, 96.
    Newtonian, 300.
    old-fashioned, 123.
    physical, 93.
    psychological, 317.
    qualified, 408.
    scientific, 16.
    soft, 123, 134.
    strict, 80f, 316.
    theological, 79, 83f.

determinism,
      unqualified, 208, 407.
dualism,
      Aristotelian, 306.
      limited or relative, 276.
      non-theistic, 1.
      of thought and experience, 427.
      psycho-physical, 1.
      problem of, 6.
      unintellectual, 207.
duration, 33f, 58f, 151f.
      as a multiplicity, 37.
      concrete, 49.
      defined, 58.
      in the making, 34.
      intuition of, 35.
      pure, 33, 46.

E

Ecology, 238, 239, 241.
efficient causation, 256f.
egoism, 393f.
      illusions of, 398.
élan vital, 13f, 151f.
emergence, 13, 175.
      vitalistic view of, 175.
empirical methodology, 176.
empiricism, 39f, 513.
      method of, 105.
      modern, 63.
      true, 39.
empiricists, 67, 427.
energy, 2, 157f.
epistemology, 14, 105.
      process, 105f, 523f.
error, 60f.
      mark of higher organisms, 60.
esthetic theory, 468f.
eternal objects, 54f.
events, 380, 505, 521.
evil, 18, 358f, 387.
evolution, 13f, 61, 151f, 225f.
      biological, 13.
      considered to be static, 175.
      contingency in, 158.
      creative, 152, 219f, 228, 233.
      emergent, 219f.

evolution,
    inorganic, 224.
    organic, 221, 223.
    question of, 133.
    social, 152.
existentialism, 11, 517.
extension, 55f.
existence, 341f, 408.

F

feeling, 326f.
    equated with prehension, 439.
    metaphysics of, 485.
flux, 33, 94, 155, 472.
freedom, 17, 123f, 143f.
    creative, 19.
    human, 83f.
free-will, 121f, 144f.

G

Genesis, 357.
Germany, 302.
Gita, the, 406.
God, 5, 19f, 35, 147n, 279, 285f, 294, 306, 333,
    354f, 504.
    as aesthetic order of the world, 429.
    as finite, struggling, and suffering, 529.
    as unceasing life, action, freedom, 154.
    author of nature, 488.
    being of, 356.
    can have knowledge of contingent being, 197.
    conception of, 21.
    concrete working of, 357.
    enmeshed in ambiguity, 536.
    freedom of, 343.
    grace of, 342.
    identification with absolute, 200.
    involved in promoting human good, 359.
    may change, 20.
    medieval idea of, 85.
    not separate from World, 20.
    process of creative synthesis, 273.
    relation to temporal process, 404.
    source of moral obligation, 356.

idealist(s), 2, 79, 502, 536.
ideas, 35, 449.
immortality,
    of the past, 402.
    social, 402.
individual, 162f.
individuality, 163.
individuation, 341.
individualism, 466.
indetermination, 80f, 156.
indeterminism, 123f.
India, 334, 406.
intuition, 4, 14, 27f, 151, 167f.
    a simple act, 31.
    direct, 6, 60.
    intellectual sympathy, 31.
    metaphysical, 48.
    theological, 20.
Irresistible Grace, 487.

J

Jansenism, 487.
Japan, 465.
Jews, 406, 425.
Judeo-Christian,
    insight, 403.
    tradition, 19f.

K

knowing, 27f, 105f, 523f.
knowledge, 29f.

L

language, 66.
    Babylonian, 74.
    Egyptian, 74.
    example of symbolism, 72f.
    ordinary, 304.
League of Nations, 242.
life, 157f.
    nature of, 163.
    origin of, 163.

linguistic analysis, 11.
linguistic analysts, 303f.
logical positivism, 304.

M

Man, 168f, 430f.
    an ethical being, 16.
materialism, 206, 291, 491.
marxism, 11, 397, 525.
Marxists, 414.
mathematics, 4, 27, 45.
matter, 2, 82f, 309f.
    atomic structure, 82.
    quantitative unity of, 82.
Maya, 405.
mechanics,
    celestial, 15.
    quantum, 305f.
    terrestrial, 15.
mechanism, 299f, 486f.
    dilemma of, 490.
    problem of, 489.
metaphysics, 3f, 7, 13, 15, 29, 37f, 58, 177f.
    aesthetic, 326f, 334.
    classical, 200f.
    difficulties of, 203.
    empirical, 522f.
    essence of, 43, 202.
    explanations of, 177.
    Greek, 19.
    inherent difficulties of, 43.
    most important function of, 210.
    neoclassical, 197f.
    never be a popular science, 200.
    object of, 45.
    of becoming, 201f.
    of love, 211.
    of internal relations, 326.
    older, 203.
    partial eclipse of, 48.
    true, 39.
    ultimate problem of, 507.
mind, 111f, 515f.
    main function of, 43.
    two theories of, 490.
Mohammedans, 406.

Monism, 3, 131f.
    metaphysical, 427.
    radical, 1.
    static, 84, 87.
    unqualified, 1.
moral obligation, 331, 355f.
morality, 325f, 425f.

N

nature, 2f, 229f.
    classical model of, 310.
    contingency in, 82f.
    creative advance of, 14.
    discordances of, 167.
    diversity of, 831
    emotional appeal of, 235f.
    impersonal nature of, 86.
    in God, 20.
necessity, 82f.
nexus, 56f, 73, 255f.
    as a unity, 261.
    causal, 71.
    of occasions, 59.
    social, 260.
    special types, 255f.
new creation, the, 345, 378.

O

order, 470f.
Order of Heaven, 504.
organism, 54f, 273f.
    concept of, 487.
    complexity of, 154f.
    cosmic, 273, 294.
    doctrine of, 491.
organic monism, 273f.

P

panentheism, 20.
panpsychism, 6, 233.
pantheism, 20, 85.
Parthenon, the, 462.
particles, 312f.

Revolution,
    Copernican, 301.
    First Scientific, 299f.
    present, 303f.
    Second Scientific, 299f.
Roman Empire, 388.
romanticism, 137f.
Romantic poets, 485f.
Romantic Reaction, 485f.
    protest on behalf of value, 506.
Russia, 302.

S

Saint Paul, 122, 374, 397.
Scholastics, 85.
Scholasticism, 201.
science,
    abstract materialism of, 498.
    Aristotelianism, 306.
    classical, 304.
    contemporary, 303f.
    explanations of, 177.
    Greek, 207, 306.
    modern, 13, 47, 84, 197, 304.
    negation of, 169.
    Newtonian, 207.
sciences,
    natural, 15, 31.
    physical, 301f.
scientific theory, 62f.
societies,
    Whiteheadian, 3.
solipsism, 309.
sophists, the, 303.
space,
    classical Newtonian-Euclidian, 311.
    concept of, 310.
    Euclidian, 307f.
    non-Euclidian curvature of, 311f.
    of modern physics, 310f.
    of Newtonian physics, 310f.
space-time,
    Euclidian, 311.
    structure of, 311f.
Spain, 302.
species, 2, 158f.
spirit, 168f.

substance, 90.
succession,
    denial of, 80f.
supranaturalism, 179, 317, 384.
symbolic reference, 54f, 71f.

T

teleology, 275f.
    mistake of, 293.
theism, 1, 2, 85, 287.
theologians, 7, 19, 83f, 133, 281.
theology, 119, 137.
    apologetic, 488.
    Christian, 84f.
    liberal, 21.
    medieval, 85.
    process, 2, 19f.

U

unison of becoming, 57f.
universe, 229f.
    as organic, 277.
    as teleological, 239.

V

Vedantism,
    Advaita, 1.
Vienna Circle, the, 304, 317.
vitalism, 13, 151f, 175f, 491.
Vitalists, 292.

W

world, 54f, 130f, 154f.
    as undivided flux, 154.
world-view(s), 15, 307.

Z

Zeno argument, the, 4.